WEYERHAEUSER ENVIRONMENTAL BOOKS

WILLIAM CRONON, EDITOR

Weyerhaeuser Environmental Books explore human relationships with natural environments in all their variety and complexity. They seek to cast new light on the ways that natural systems affect human communities, the ways that people affect the environments of which they are a part, and the ways that different cultural conceptions of nature profoundly shape our sense of the world around us. A complete listing of the books in the series appears at the end of this book.

Shaping *the* Shoreline

FISHERIES AND TOURISM ON THE MONTEREY COAST

Connie Y. Chiang   FOREWORD BY WILLIAM CRONON

UNIVERSITY OF WASHINGTON PRESS · SEATTLE AND LONDON

SHAPING THE SHORELINE HAS BEEN PUBLISHED WITH THE ASSISTANCE OF
A GRANT FROM THE WEYERHAEUSER ENVIRONMENTAL BOOKS ENDOWMENT,
ESTABLISHED BY THE WEYERHAEUSER COMPANY FOUNDATION, MEMBERS
OF THE WEYERHAEUSER FAMILY, AND JANET AND JACK CREIGHTON.

University of Washington Press, PO Box 50096, Seattle, WA 98145
www.washington.edu/uwpress

Library of Congress Cataloging-in-Publication Data
Chiang, Connie Y.
Shaping the shoreline : fisheries and tourism on the Monterey coast /
Connie Y. Chiang : foreword by William Cronon. —1st ed.
p.   cm. — (Weyerhauser environmental books)
Includes bibliographical references and index.
ISBN 978-0-295-99139-9 (pbk. : alk. paper)
1. Fisheries—California—Monterey Peninsula—History. 2. Tourism—California—
Monterey Peninsula—History. 3. Monterey Peninsula (Calif.)—History. I. Title.
SH222C3C45 2008   338.4'79179476—dc22   2008002935

Jacket illustration: "The Old Witch Tree." E. Alexander Powell, "Autobirds of
Passage," *Sunset Magazine*, February 1949.

for Matthew and Benjamin

CONTENTS

FOREWORD: ON THE SHORE BETWEEN WORK
AND PLAY BY WILLIAM CRONON ix

ACKNOWLEDGMENTS xv

Introduction: The Voice of the Pacific 3

1   Contested Shores 12

2   The Divided Coastline 38

3   Reduce and Prosper 60

4   Life, Labor, and Odors on Cannery Row 79

5   Boom and Bust in Wartime Monterey 102

6   Remaking Cannery Row 132

7   The Fish Are Back! 155

Conclusion 182

NOTES 193
SELECTED BIBLIOGRAPHY 251
INDEX 269

FOREWORD *On the Shore between Work and Play*

WILLIAM CRONON

Monterey is nowhere near the top of California's long list of world-class tourist destinations. As measured by annual visitation rates in the early twenty-first century, it doesn't come close to Anaheim's Disneyland, San Francisco's Fisherman's Wharf, Los Angeles's Universal Studios, San Diego's Sea World, Hollywood's Grauman's Chinese Theater, or Yosemite National Park.[1] But the Monterey Bay Aquarium is still popular, attracting more than a million and a half visitors each year to its extraordinary displays of the marine life that lives offshore of this community 120 miles south of the Golden Gate. Founded in 1978 with a gift from the David and Lucile Packard Foundation and shaped from the beginning by the visionary leadership of Julie Packard, the aquarium is regarded as among the most innovative in the world, helping visitors understand the ecological habitats of Monterey Bay while also taking special care to showcase the beauty of the underwater world. Visitors from all around the globe seek out its wonders.

The aquarium stands on the site of the Hovden Cannery, which was built in 1916 and operated until it went out of business—the last Monterey cannery to do so—in 1973. Behind the ticket counter where visitors now enter the building, a few of the Hovden boilers stand as a reminder of an earlier industrial era. For the first half of the twentieth century, this was the heart of Cannery Row, the neighborhood of docks, packing plants, saloons, and brothels made famous by the novelist John Steinbeck. "Cannery Row," wrote Steinbeck in 1945, "is a poem, a stink, a grating noise, a quality of light, a tone, a habit, a nostalgia, a dream." In *Cannery Row*, he describes an industrial scene far different from what aquarium visitors see today, with the purse-seiners of a now-vanished sardine fleet pulling into the harbor to the sound of cannery whistles calling the "Wops and Chinamen and Polaks, men and women in trousers and rubber coats and oilcloth aprons" who came "running to clean and cut and pack and cook and can the fish."[2] Steinbeck haunted the Monterey docks for years, drawn there by the presence of one of his closest friends, the marine biologist Ed Ricketts, whose Pacific Biological Laboratories did a nationwide business in the sale of marine specimens gathered along the coast. (Aquarium visitors today can see a display of artifacts gathered from Ricketts's office next door to the cannery.) As the nostalgia of Steinbeck's prose suggests, the world of Cannery Row was already in steep decline by the end of the Second World War. The collapse of the sardine fisheries was the coup de grace. One by one the packing plants would close, until what Steinbeck called "the silver rivers of fish" no longer poured out from the boats to the docks and the old industrial wharves fell into disrepair and decrepitude.

It is thus easy for visitors today to experience the Monterey Bay Aquarium as reflecting a familiar story that has long been favored by environmentalists and, for that matter, by environmental historians. Here at Cannery Row, it looks as if a former era that saw the natural world chiefly as commodities and raw materials is giving way to a more enlightened age—our own—that recognizes the importance of ecosystems and the critical challenge of relating to nature in a more respectful and sustainable way. From the abandoned wharves of the packing plants where marine resources were exploited almost to the point of extinction has arisen a new institution whose mission is to educate the public about the need to protect and celebrate the beauty of the sea's creatures. We have moved from an industrial economy for which nature was just a source of raw materials for human production to a more service-oriented economy in which environmentally responsible human consumption has become a new moral imperative. Cannery Row has been both resurrected and transformed: fishermen and industrial workers have been replaced by ecotourists and those who seek to help such tourists better understand the world.

But the real story is not quite so simple and the choice between production and consumption, exploitation and enlightenment, not nearly so stark. The working-class communities and ethnic neighborhoods that

Steinbeck so lovingly evoked in 1945 have not entirely disappeared from Monterey, for the service economy here still needs workers to feed and house the tourists and to support the lifestyles of the well-to-do seasonal residents who call Monterey home for portions of the year. For that matter, the beauties and attractions of the Monterey Peninsula were hardly new to travelers when the aquarium first opened its doors in 1984. Tourists had been seeking the place out for more than a century. Far from unenlightened industry giving way to enlightened tourism, then, the two have existed side by side in Monterey, however uneasily, for a very long time indeed. In truth, they cannot be understood in isolation from each other.

This simple but profound insight lies near the heart of Connie Y. Chiang's path-breaking *Shaping the Shoreline: Fisheries and Tourism on the Monterey Coast*. The book's importance extends far beyond this small California community. Probably because the line we typically draw in our own lives between labor and leisure is so stark and because we so frequently perform these activities in different geographical locations, histories of work and play are all too typically written in isolation from each other. We have a large, rich literature on the history of tourism and an even larger, richer body of scholarship on the history of industry and labor. Environmental history in particular has attended much more frequently to places associated with leisure than with labor, no doubt because of the longstanding association in Western thought of nature with recreation. Although this has begun to change in recent years, we still have many more environmental histories of national parks, wilderness areas, gardens, and urban green spaces than we do of cities, farms, factories, offices, and stores. (An inverted claim could just as accurately be made about labor and business history, which have been far more likely to look at "workplaces" than at recreational sites.) But just because people often work and play in different places doesn't mean that the two aren't intimately tied together as integral expressions of the same lives and the same cultural values.

As Connie Chiang demonstrates, coastlines are especially revealing places to think about the arbitrary boundaries of labor and leisure that people impose on the natural world, to say nothing of the divisions within human communities that express themselves along those same boundaries. Because any harvest of underwater ecosystems must eventually bring the catch ashore for processing and sale, waterfronts are inevitably places where the fishing fleet must intersect with the working world of the shore. Little wonder, then, that Steinbeck's Cannery Row is a place like any other factory town where the packing plants "rumble and rattle and squeak until the last fish is cleaned and cut and cooked and canned and then the whistles scream again."[3] This hardly seems a scene of natural beauty. And yet this same shoreline is no less a destination for those drawn to the haunting beauty of the rolling surf, the salt wind, the rising and falling tides, and the creatures who inhabit those places on the edge where land and water meet.

It is for just this reason that the history of tourism in Monterey is nearly as old as the history of commercial fishing. Visitors to the Monterey Bay Aquarium follow in the footsteps of travelers who have been making the same kind of pilgrimage for many decades. Richard Henry Dana wrote of his visit here in the 1830s in *Two Years Before the Mast*, and Robert Louis Stevenson devoted an entire chapter of *Across the Plains* to the months he spent in Monterey during the autumn of 1879. In 1880, the railroad magnate Charles Crocker constructed the luxurious Hotel Del Monte on the headland above the town, and his Pacific Improvement Company soon gained control of most of the coastal lands of the Monterey Peninsula. In 1881, the company laid out the scenic Seventeen Mile Drive as a way for visitors to experience the stunning forests and seashores of the peninsula . . . and to tempt would-be purchasers of the luxurious vacation properties Crocker was beginning to develop along the route. The first of several golf courses was laid out in 1897, with the most famous and spectacular—Pebble Beach—opening in 1919. From the 1880s forward, Monterey's promoters could boast of it being a destination for some of the wealthiest, most powerful, and best-known travelers anywhere on the Pacific seaboard.

What such travelers found in Monterey, in addition to natural beauty, was one of the oldest Spanish settlements anywhere in California. When Sebastián Vizcaíno first sailed these waters in 1602, he identified this bay as one of the few protected anchorages anywhere along the coast of California. Partly because Vizcaíno failed to discover the far better harbor of San Francisco Bay, his enthusiastic description of Monterey helped establish the peninsula in the minds of the Spanish as a prime potential site for colonial settlement. It was not until 1770 that Gaspar de Portolà would establish the Presidio of Monterey, which with Junípero Serra's

Mission San Carlos Borromeo de Carmelo would subject the local Rumsen and Esselen Indians to Spanish rule. For the next eighty years, Monterey would be the most important colonial center anywhere in Spanish and Mexican California, with its Customs House overseeing trade for the entire province. It was here that Commodore John D. Sloat raised the American flag in 1846 to claim California for the United States during the Mexican-American War, and it was here that the first constitutional convention was held in 1849 to establish the new state of California.

As far as the local economy was concerned, though, it was the bay and its resident creatures—the marine mammals, the abalones, the mussels, and especially the seemingly inexhaustible schools of fish—that provided livelihoods for the largest number of year-round residents. During the second half of the nineteenth century, waves of immigrants settled in the vicinity of Monterey harbor, with different ethnic groups—Italians, Portuguese, and Chinese—employing quite different techniques as they fished the waters of the bay. Class and racial tensions ran high at times, and in this book Connie Chiang offers a richly textured account of the ways social conflicts can have quite profound effects not just on natural resources but also on human communities. In much the same way, she demonstrates the recurring tensions between working-class fishing communities and the elite tourists who were not especially happy to experience the bloody, smelly, polluting activities of the canneries—even as they welcomed the tasty seafood they found in the dining room of the Hotel Del Monte and other resorts.

The links between tourism and fisheries changed across the decades, of course, as the conversion of Hovden Cannery into a world-class aquarium attests. One of Chiang's greatest achievements is to show just how dynamic Monterey's economy and relationships to the natural world proved to be over time. Few books have done a better or more sophisticated job of analyzing the intersections of industry with recreation, labor with leisure, class with race, humanity with nature. By refusing ever to see these seemingly divided categories as separate, arguing instead that they make sense only when understood in relationship to each other, Chiang points the way toward a new generation of historical writing about human beings and the natural world. It is an exciting prospect. *Shaping the Shoreline* should be required reading not just for the thousands of people who visit Monterey and its famed aquarium today, but for anyone who wants to see how the things that often seem most to divide us—our work and play, our different identities of class and race and gender, our feelings toward a nature we wish both to harvest and to protect—also bind us together if only we try hard enough to glimpse their underlying connections.

NOTES

1. Sandra Larriva, "Forbes Traveler 50 Most Visited Tourist Attractions List," *Forbes Traveler* (March 31, 2007), accessed at http://www.forbestraveler.com/best-lists/most-visited-tourist-attractions-printslide.html.

2. John Steinbeck, *Cannery Row*, in Steinbeck, *Novels 1942–1952* (New York: Library of America, 2001), 101.

3. Ibid., 101.

ACKNOWLEDGMENTS

Writing this book has been an incredible journey, one that moved up and down the Pacific Coast and ended on the Atlantic. Along the way, I have incurred many debts. My thanks here are only a small token of my gratitude.

I started this book during my graduate studies at the University of Washington, where many wonderful scholars taught me how to be a historian. I was especially lucky to have an amazing dissertation committee. Jim Gregory helped me to think about the larger context of my project and was always encouraging and supportive. I am also grateful to John Findlay, whose rigor and high standards have made me a better scholar. I owe my greatest debt to Richard White, a brilliant historian and model adviser. Richard guided this project from the beginning and always pushed my thinking with his invaluable insights and incisive questions. His kindness, generosity, and dedication to his students are also legendary, and I knew that I could always call on him for support and advice with this book and my career in general. I consider it a great privilege to have had the opportunity to work with him, and I continue to benefit from his wisdom and counsel.

Several institutions and organizations provided funding for research. Thanks to the University of Washington's History Department, Stanford University's History Department, the Western History Association, the Book Club of California, the Huntington Library, and the National Science Foundation's Science and Technology Studies Program.

I conducted research at libraries, archives, and other institutions all along the Pacific Coast, and I encountered many helpful people who bent over backward to help. Thanks to the staffs of the University of Washington's Special Collections, Manuscripts, and University Archives, Interlibrary Borrowing Services, and Fisheries–Oceanography Library; the National Archives and Records Administration–Pacific Region; Stanford University's Special Collections; the California State Archives; and the Huntington Library. At the Bancroft Library, I am grateful to Theresa Salazar for tracking down a crucial collection for me. In the Monterey area, I thank Jim Conway at the Colton Hall Museum, Tim Thomas at the Maritime Museum of Monterey, John Hooper at the National Steinbeck Center, and the staffs of the Pacific Grove Public Library, the Monterey City Clerk's Office, and the Monterey County Courthouse for their kindness and for making room for me to do research. At the Monterey Bay Aquarium, I thank Steve Webster and Steve Yalowitz for taking the time to meet with me and Gail Skidmore, who opened the library to me. During my stay in Monterey, David Yamada and Michael Hemp were also generous with their local contacts and their own research. I owe my greatest debt to the staff of the Monterey Public Library, especially Dennis Copeland, archivist of the California History Room. From my long days at the library while I was in graduate school to my recent photo requests, Dennis has always responded to my inquiries with enthusiasm and expediency.

I have had the great fortune to land my first job at Bowdoin College, an institution that provides incredible support for faculty research. A fellowship from the Coastal Studies Center gave me time, funding, and a farmhouse on the Maine coast to continue the tough work of writing this book. I thank Anne Henshaw, former director of the center, for helping to make that year so productive. A Fletcher Family Grant and research start-up funds paid for photographs and trips back to Monterey. The college support staff also proved to be indispensable. Ginny Hopcroft and Guy Saldanha saved me more cross-country trips and helped me get my hands on Monterey sources. Nancy Grant assisted with illustrations, while Josie Johnson took care of many details. The Bowdoin faculty is also stellar; they welcomed me into their community of scholars and gave me many forums in which to share my work. In particular, I thank my colleagues in the History Department and Environmental Studies Program, who have created a collegial and stimulating intellectual environment. Special thanks to DeWitt John, Susan Tananbaum, and Allen Wells for being great mentors and for being so supportive of my career.

At the University of Washington Press, Julidta Tarver demystified the publishing world and steered my book through the process with great efficiency. Her patience and good humor made this experience a true pleasure. I was also fortunate to work with Bill Cronon. I first read his seminal *Changes in the Land* as an undergraduate student; I never imagined that I would have the privilege of working with him on my first book. In just a handful of phone conversations and meetings, Bill teased out the bigger questions in my manuscript and pushed my analysis in unexpected and fruitful directions. His enthusiasm for my work also gave me a much-needed push to get this book out the door.

Portions of this book have appeared as articles in scholarly journals, and I am grateful to those publications for granting permission to reprint them here. Sections of chapters 1 and 4 were published in the *Pacific Historical Review*. An earlier version of chapter 6 appeared in the *Western Historical Quarterly*. I thank the editors and staffs at those fine journals, especially Carl Abbott, David Johnson, and Susan Wladaver-Morgan at the *Pacific Historical Review* and David Rich Lewis at the *Western Historical Quarterly* for their perceptive critiques of my work.

Other colleagues and friends also deserve my thanks for their support over the years. During graduate school, Jen Seltz, Coll Thrush, Matthew Booker, and Rachel St. John provided encouragement. Jay Taylor and Ari Kelman called my attention to some key points early in my project's development. Since I have moved to New England, Kathy Morse has cheered me up on numerous occasions. I also treasured the time spent with Margaret Paton-Walsh and Nelly Blacker-Hanson while they were living in the area. Carol McKibben gave my manuscript a close read and saved me from some embarrassing errors; her warmth and enthusiasm came at an important point in this process. Karl Jacoby also provided excellent comments on the entire manuscript and helped sharpen some important ideas. Last but not least, Liz Escobedo remains my most cherished friend and colleague from graduate school. I can always count on Liz for encouraging words and a good laugh, and I thank her for her sage advice and unwavering support with all things work- and nonwork-related.

I was lucky to grow up surrounded by a large extended family of grandparents, aunts, uncles, and cousins who placed great value on education and never questioned the many years I spent in school. Our family gatherings always remind me of my good fortune. Special thanks to my cousin and fellow historian Stephanie Young for her last-minute research help. My brother, Scott Chiang, has always been an exemplary model for me to follow, and I am grateful for his support and for bringing Shannon, Christopher, and Cassidy Chiang into our family. Thanks also to my in-laws, Linda, David, Megan, and Jack Bowman and Larry Frost, for welcoming me into their family. My parents, John and Jollin Chiang, deserve my deepest thanks for all the sacrifices they made to help me achieve my goals. They opened the world to me and allowed me to follow my own path; for that and much more, I am forever grateful. My mom's perseverance and strength of character also remain a constant source of inspiration.

Lastly, I dedicate this book to my husband, best friend, and colleague, Matthew Klingle, and our son, Benjamin. Matt has been my biggest supporter since we met in graduate school, and I don't know what I would do without his constant encouragement and unfailing faith in all that I do. His boundless energy, zest for life, and incredible generosity also inspire me to be a better person. I can't imagine a more wonderful person with whom to share my life and my career. Benjamin was born as my book revisions were well under way, and he has been the most amazing gift. I am thankful he took many long naps that gave me time to work, but it was his waking hours that sustained me. His smiles, coos, and laughter reminded me to take a deep breath, enjoy the precious moment, and appreciate the really important things in my life.

Two historians and an infant under one roof may not seem like a recipe for domestic bliss. But together we have built a home that is full of warmth, love, and laughter. Thank you, Matt and Ben, for nurturing me and giving me so much more than I can ever repay.

Shaping the Shoreline

MAP 1. Monterey Bay region

INTRODUCTION *The Voice of the Pacific*

The one common note of all this country is the haunting presence of the ocean. A great faint sound of breakers follows you high up into the inland cañons; the roar of water dwells in the clean, empty rooms of Monterey as in a shell upon the chimney; go where you will, you have but to pause and listen to hear the voice of the Pacific. —ROBERT LOUIS STEVENSON

At the end of August 1879, Robert Louis Stevenson traveled to Monterey and heard the "voice of the Pacific." While he came to this town on the Central California coast to join his love, Fanny Osbourne, and stayed only a few months, his strolls along the shore left a lasting impression. He carefully observed his surroundings, writing in great detail of Monterey's beaches, wildlife, climate, and weather. The coast was "a spectacle of Ocean's greatness," and its constant changes kept his interest "perpetually fresh." Stevenson was attuned to the natural world, and the ever-changing coastline directed his movements in and around Monterey.[1]

Situated at the southern end of crescent-shaped Monterey Bay, the dramatic coastline of Monterey enchanted Stevenson and countless others before and after. Clear Pacific waters punctuated granite headlands and white sand dunes and beaches. Thick fog and offshore breezes in the morning often gave way to blue skies and onshore winds in the afternoon. Fluctuating tides, generated by the gravitational pull of the sun and moon, shifted the boundary between land and ocean daily, submerging and drying out coastal lagoons, estuaries, and mudflats. During the winter, the pounding surf stripped the shore and eroded seaside cliffs; summer waves brought the sand ashore again to create pleasant beaches. Amid these striking changes, a diverse array of marine life clung to the shore and struggled to survive and prosper. These ebbs and flows were what made the coastline so mesmerizing and memorable to Stevenson.[2]

Stevenson waxed poetic about the coastline, but he was no simple tourist. The noted writer also paid close attention to Monterey's complex social dynamics. While the town was "essentially and wholly Mexican" and Spanish was the dominant language, Americans possessed political power and had obtained vast amounts of land through "Yankee craft." Nonetheless, the Mexicans were not "morally conquered," as their customs remained supreme. Indeed, many Americans had become "Mexicanised" in Monterey. The social diversity of the "old Pacific capital" also struck Stevenson as he dined alongside French, Portuguese, Italians, Mexicans, Scots, Swiss, Germans, Chinese, and "a nearly pure blood Indian" at a local restaurant. "No wonder that the Pacific coast is a foreign land to visitors from the Eastern States," he explained, "for each race contributes something of its own." To the south in Carmel, Stevenson observed the decline of the Indians and the deterioration of the mission. He concluded, "Their lands, I was told, are being yearly encroached upon by the neighbouring American proprietor, and with that exception no man troubles his head for the Indians of Carmel."[3]

Stevenson painted a detailed portrait of Monterey in 1879, but his descriptions of the town's social relations and coastal environment appeared distinct and unrelated. The stunning beauty of the coastline was a scenic stage for the human drama that unfolded on shore. In lived experiences, however, the coastline and its inhabitants were inseparable. From the earliest human settlements, residents learned to take advantage of and move across the fluid border of earth and ocean. Prior to European-American contact, the Ohlone Indians, who were organized by tribelets, groups of two to four hundred people that united several extended family groups, lived in networks of small villages from San Francisco Bay to Monterey Bay. The Rumsen tribelet inhabited five villages in the Carmel Valley, where they hunted game and gathered acorns, seeds, roots, nuts, and berries. As the seasons changed, they moved to an encampment on the Monterey shore, filling nets and wicker baskets with shellfish and venturing offshore to collect seabird eggs and to hunt sea lions and sea otters.[4] When the Spanish established a settlement at Monterey in 1770 and made it the capital of Alta California in 1777, the Pacific became their imperial conduit for replenishing supplies and bringing new settlers.[5] And during the Mexican reign, beginning in 1821, seafaring commerce flourished, as local ranches supplied cattle hides and tallow that became part of a lucrative global trade network between Mexico, South America, New England, and western Europe.[6]

After the United States conquered Alta California in 1848 and moved the state capital from Monterey, the town's prospects seemed uncertain to some observers. Over thirty years following the end of the Mexican War, Stevenson described Monterey as "a mere bankrupt village . . . where people sat [in saloons] almost all day long playing cards." His account seemed to blame Mexicans for Monterey's languishing state, feeding off popular stereotypes that portrayed them as penniless, landless, and shiftless.[7] While many Mexicans and Californios, descendents of the original Spanish settlers, did see a decline in status with American rule, Monterey was not devoid of economic activity. Commercial enterprises extended up and down the coast and spread inland. Steamers arrived regularly on the waterfront, importing a variety of goods, from alcohol and tobacco to leather and tools, and exporting Monterey products, such as lumber and beef. They also brought passengers, many of whom loaded up on supplies and continued their travels to the Sierra Nevada goldfields.[8]

As California's economy began to move beyond mining and diversify in the 1860s and 1870s, Monterey residents and investors looked increasingly to the shore and the sea beyond as the direct source of prosperity. Whereas colonial Monterey had depended on a vibrant Pacific trade, modern Monterey saw the coastline proper as ripe for economic development. Stevenson strolled along the beach and cavorted with locals at the same time that many newcomers were arriving on the waterfront to take advantage of abundant fisheries and beautiful scenery. While Montereyans also pursued other enterprises, the fisheries and tourism were the most celebrated, putting Monterey back on the map and sustaining the city well into the twentieth century. Far from an isolated development, the growth of these industries was part of larger trends that reshaped labor and leisure in the industrial United States. In the years after the Civil War, tourism blossomed, particularly in the West, as newly constructed railroads enticed Americans and foreigners alike to travel beyond the eastern seaboard. The final decades of the nineteenth century also ushered in a period of rapid industrialization in western Europe and the United States, of which the Monterey fisheries were part.

While the emergence of Monterey's fishing and tourism industries was not unusual at this time, the fact that both converged on a single place—the coastline—certainly created a tricky and potentially volatile situation along the city's shores. Because these enterprises sought to transform the same stretch of sand and sea, they often struggled for dominance. Even when they were not at odds, they were routinely defined in relation to one another. In fact, it is difficult to study one of these coastal industries without studying the other.[9] This book thus traces the complex and often contentious interplay between Monterey's fishing and tourism industries from the late nineteenth century until the end of the twentieth century.

The development of the fisheries and the tourist trade illuminates the deeply entangled social and environmental histories that together transformed Monterey through time.[10] Historians have long recognized the need to bring these two fields together. In 1990 William Cronon identified environmental history's "failure to probe below the level of the group to explore the implications of social divisions for environmental change" as its "greatest weakness."[11] Alan Taylor later argued that bringing social and environmental history together was still overdue. While social historians often treated nature as "a constant . . . an assumed but unexplored backdrop," environmental historians slighted the heterogeneity of their human actors and overlooked social conflicts and divisions. By integrating environmental and social history, historians could illuminate the "pervasive social inequality" within the American landscape.[12] Many environmental historians have heeded these calls, casting nature as a social construction to explore how different groups evaluated and altered the natural world, but few social historians have reciprocated, despite calls, most recently from Stephen Mosley, urging these scholars to pay closer attention to nature's influence over human affairs.[13]

Although it has received limited attention from historians, the American coastline offers an ideal physical location to make these links between social and environmental history. Not only was the coastline a place of varied human activities, including extractive and service industries, it was also a major site of settlement and a zone of contact, conquest, and resistance between diverse and highly mobile groups of people. These complex social interactions intersected with an environment that was inherently unpredictable. Nature and society forged intimate connections at the meeting point of land and sea.[14]

These ties become concrete when examining the fishing and tourism industries on the Monterey coastline. Numerous social and environmental factors shaped both enterprises and complicated participants' efforts to assert control over the coastline. Because they established their operations in the unstable zone between land and sea and, in the case of the fisheries, ventured into the volatile ocean, they often found it challenging to harness natural resources consistently and shape them for specific purposes. A dynamic physical world did not always match human needs. By the late nineteenth century, moreover, an influx of immigrants from East Asia and southern Europe, many of whom were attracted to the fisheries, joined the existing population of Anglos, Indians, Mexicans, and Californios. These groups held widely different ideas of what in nature held material and cultural value and how it should be developed. As a result, coastal development rarely proceeded without conflict or disagreement—whether within each industry or between the two.

In time, both industries—and the associated categories of labor and leisure, work and play—developed in reference to shifting notions of race, ethnicity, and class. Because certain activities in nature became linked to certain groups of people, the physical changes associated with the fisheries and tourism became markers of social difference and reinforced racial, ethnic, and class divisions. Those with power and influence used these social distinctions as tools to limit access to nature and assert their dominance over the coastline *and* other groups of people. The consequences were often dramatic. Some people were expelled from their homes; others found themselves out of work. As they competed for resources and transformed nature along the coastline, then, participants in both industries also remade Monterey society.

The struggles over the coastline became so divisive because the fisheries and tourism reflected markedly different visions for nature and society.[15] As each industry jockeyed for control over the coastline, they were also positing very distinct identities for Monterey and its residents. Those who pursued both industries came to see the coastline as a commodity that could be altered and marketed to consumers, but their motives and methods were distinct, as were the groups and individuals who participated and stood to benefit. On the one hand, fishing was a productive enterprise that relied on immigrant labor and technological innovations to harvest marine resources and process them into various products— tins of food, sacks of fertilizer, barrels of oil—that could be bought and sold on national and global markets. It was part of a larger extractive economy central to the development of the American West.[16] Tourism, on the other hand, harnessed and promoted the scenic beauty of the coastline to attract elite and middle-class visitors and their disposable incomes. It was a service industry, catering to predominantly white pleasure-seekers, as important to the modern West as any extractive enterprise.[17]

Monterey was not alone in supporting industries that seemed diametrically opposed to one another. In particular, historians of the American West have told similar stories of places originally coveted for natural riches—timber, coal, minerals, agricultural land—only to face the wrenching shift to a service-based economy after resources were exhausted or investors moved elsewhere. The glittering ski-resort towns of Aspen, Colorado, and Park City, Utah, were once bustling mining and ranching communities before they sold altitude, steep terrain, and posh amenities to affluent sports enthusiasts. Real estate developers and vacation homeowners reaped profits and pleasure by displacing, sometimes intentionally, the long-time ranchers and miners who had once wielded considerable power in their communities.[18]

While the history of the Monterey coastline resonates with and parallels these places, its experience was distinct because the fisheries and tourism *both* enjoyed extensive operations up until World War II.[19] Not unlike the national forests or other waterfronts on the western and eastern seaboards, the Monterey coastline served extractive operations and tourist activities simultaneously. Fisheries did not completely displace tourism, nor did tourism entirely displace the fisheries. The two developed, side by side, sometimes uncomfortably, sometimes in open conflict. Monterey's past, therefore, suggests that the natural world inspired multiple and seemingly contradictory visions and that many places did not focus solely on one type of natural resource-based industry at any given time.

Ultimately, the fisheries and tourism industries were far more entangled and interconnected than they first appeared. These links in Monterey's past were indicative of a larger American story. All too often, Americans have viewed human interactions with the environment in competing terms, ignoring the similarities between different activities. In this simple analysis, nature was a site for work *or* play, for labor *or* leisure. The fishing industry was rapacious in its impact on nature, whereas tourism was benign. By extension, ethnic and racial minorities and other workers degraded nature, and wealthy white tourists revered it. But as the transformation of the Monterey coastline demonstrates, the natural world was the site of work *and* play, labor *and* leisure. Both fisheries *and* tourism could have a detrimental impact on the environment; white tourists could harm nature just as much as Sicilian, Chinese, and Japanese fishermen. In short, the public images associated with certain groups and their interactions with nature were neither fully accurate nor descriptive.

Exploding these oversimplified dualities suggests that many Americans need to recognize and accommodate multiple ways of valuing and interacting with the natural world and acknowledge their own connections to people and activities they deem destructive or undesirable. It has been too easy for them to designate one place in nature for their leisure and consumption and another more distant or hidden place for someone else's productive labor. In the process, they have often denigrated workers as harmful and working landscapes as degraded. But in Monterey and elsewhere, there has been no clear divide between apparently rival uses of nature. Working landscapes were often tourist attractions; tourist attractions were also working landscapes.[20] Those who played in nature were not separate from the world of labor; work, in fact, made their leisure possible. Moreover, some individuals may have actually worked *and* played in the same places, but perhaps at different times of the week and year. People's ties to the natural world were in constant flux and could not be easily pigeonholed into neat, opposing categories.

The evolution of Monterey's fishing and tourism industries and their tangled relationship demonstrate the shortcomings of the simple dichotomies used to describe human relations with the environment. Beginning in the late nineteenth century, both industries staked claims to the coastline and began to put forward numerous visions for the natural world. Initially, Chinese, Italian, and Portuguese fishermen and executives at the Pacific Improvement Company's Hotel Del Monte vied for control of the shore, but the sardine industry eclipsed tourism after World War I. Although the expansion of the fisheries generated numerous social and environmental problems, from labor disputes to pungent odors that disturbed hotel owners and tourists, most Montereyans saw the city's identity and economic future as tied to the sardine.

But the interwar years did not spell the end of Monterey's leisure economy. After a dramatic expansion of the sardine industry during World War II, the fishery crashed, due to natural phenomena and unchecked human consumption. Because the sardine's collapse made Monterey's fishing-town identity untenable, residents, city officials, and outside investors began to convert the coastline from fish factory to tourist destination. At first they took advantage of the popularity of John Steinbeck's 1945 novel, *Cannery Row*, romanticizing the fading industrial ambience along the waterfront. But the real source of the street's renewal would be the Monterey Bay Aquarium. Built in the shell of a former sardine plant, the aquarium fabricated and manipulated marine life for public entertainment, then mediated visitors' experiences with nature through thick acrylic windows. In displaying the beauty and ecological complexity of the coastline and ocean, the aquarium capitalized on the burgeoning national environmental movement, which resonated with many affluent, well-educated visitors, and sustained the city's new reputation as a place that valued and preserved its natural surroundings. But in the process, it slighted the human history that once shaped the shoreline.

The Monterey Bay Aquarium was the culmination of a century of conflict and tension between the fisheries and tourism. While it was entirely unlike the former cannery that housed it, in both its clientele and its relationship to the natural world, it became a place where extractive and service industries converged. The very fact that a once-thriving sardine plant could become transformed into a world-renowned aquarium demonstrated the malleability of Montereyans' visions for nature and how they shifted in response to changing social and environmental conditions. Monterey's coastal environs could no longer support a large fishing industry, but they could support tourism and the social movement for environmental awareness. Even as some Montereyans continued to identify themselves as fishermen, the aquarium illuminated to tourists and local residents alike how dramatically Monterey's relationship to the coastline had changed since the sardine's heyday.

In the one hundred–plus years after Robert Louis Stevenson's visit, the "voice of the Pacific" continued to lure people to Monterey's shores. It was here that the tourism and fishing industries emerged, exposing the connections between Monterey's natural environment and its complex social dynamics. In their drive to establish these enterprises along the coastline, Montereyans also discovered that their interactions with nature could not be divorced from other activities and people who worked, lived, and played on the city's shores. Despite periods when they proceeded on separate paths, tourists and fishermen, labor and leisure, production and consumption often collided and intertwined in unexpected ways. Just as numerous natural forces—tides, waves, winds, lunar and seasonal cycles— constantly remade the coastline, so, too, did the people who staked claims to the Pacific's edge.

1 CONTESTED SHORES

On May 16, 1906, a fire of unknown origin engulfed the Chinese fishing village at Point Alones, a rocky headland northwest of Monterey. Once a thriving settlement, the village was left with dozens of homeless residents and only sixteen standing buildings.

The fire was devastating for the Chinese, but it was more than just an unfortunate accident. It also marked the climax of over two decades of tension between the tourism and fishing industries. Beginning in the second half of the nineteenth century, immigrant fishermen and seaside developers gravitated to the Monterey coastline because of its valuable natural resources. Abundant fisheries and stunning scenery could both be harnessed and commodified for sale. However, these newcomers had very different ideas about *what* in nature had material value, *how* it should be developed, and *who* should have the power to do so. The fecund shoreline that provided fish and shellfish for East Asians and southern Europeans was the same picturesque shoreline that delighted tourists. Thus, the coastline came to reflect contending visions for nature and society—divergent views about the types of people and activities that should occupy Monterey's shores. While these visions, on occasion, complemented one another, social conflicts grew more common as tourists, real estate developers, and competing groups of fishermen laid claim to the same or adjacent spaces and struggled to gain control and access.[1]

Ideas of how to structure the natural world, then, intersected with ideas of how to structure society. At the same time, one's social status helped to shape one's relationship to nature. This reciprocal relationship between social and environmental change first developed *within* both the tourism and the fishing industries. Later, it revolved around a tug-of-war *between* these often opposing coastal enterprises—and the people who pursued them. Both seaside developers and immigrant fishermen refused to relinquish control of the coastline to their competitors. Their heated contests over nature came to define the shores of Monterey and culminated in the smoldering ruins at Point Alones.

RACE AND THE MAKING OF MONTEREY'S FISHERIES

While Rumsen Indians long capitalized on the fecundity of Monterey Bay, their efforts were focused largely on subsistence and trade. For the southern European and East Asian immigrants who came to Monterey in the second half of the nineteenth century, fishing was a commercial endeavor. A point of convergence for many migratory species of marine life, local waters offered these immigrant fishermen a wealth of resources that they could turn into commodities for sale.[2] But as their respective populations increased, competition intensified. Italian and Portuguese fishers tried to push aside their Chinese counterparts, while many local residents and outside observers discredited the Chinese and Japanese by accusing them of being destructive fishermen. Racial difference and fishermen's divergent methods of harvesting Monterey Bay's riches intertwined to structure and reinforce the social divisions within the fisheries.[3]

The Chinese were one of the first groups of immigrant fishermen to settle on the Monterey Peninsula. After a small group set up camp near Monterey to harvest abalone in 1853, many Chinese in San Francisco followed suit. Located about one and one-half miles northwest of Monterey in the town of Pacific Grove, Point Alones emerged as the main Chinese fishing camp on the peninsula. In 1870 the village was home to forty-seven residents, including twenty women and fifteen children under the age of eighteen. Unlike other places where Chinese immigrants settled, Point Alones was a family community. The absence of a heavily skewed gender ratio also suggested that the Monterey Chinese did not see themselves as sojourners who would make their fortune and then return to China. Instead, they established an extensive fishing operation that included kelp, rockfish, cod, halibut, squid, and shark.[4] While they shipped some fresh fish to San Francisco, Gilroy, San Jose, and other inland towns, they dried the bulk of their catch on nearby fields and loaded these products on steamers or junks bound for San Francisco.[5]

The Chinese faced competition primarily from southern European fishers. Portuguese whalers settled in the area in 1855 and organized the Monterey Whaling Company. By 1880 the company employed twenty-three men, mostly Azorean Islanders, who joined other Portuguese fishermen to catch fish for local and San Francisco markets during the off-season.[6] Italians entered the Monterey fishing community in 1873, when a company of fishermen, originally from Genoa, left San Francisco and headed south. A second Italian group came to Monterey two years later, making camp close to the railroad depot east of Point Alones to focus on catching mackerel, halibut, sardines, and salmon.[7]

Even though the ocean and its resources were, in theory, common property in which many users enjoyed equal access, the ocean was not an open field in practice.[8] Hoping to dominate the waters directly off Monterey, Italian fishermen shoved the Chinese west toward Point Pinos, Point Lobos, and Carmel Bay. This arrangement worked only when groups remained within their boundaries. When they did not, conflicts flared. In 1880 Chinese fishermen sued the Monterey Whaling Company, accusing whalers of chasing them down and cutting their nets and lines. The whalers' exact motives were unclear, but they likely sabotaged the Chinese because they were invading their territory or simply getting in the way. While the court dismissed the complaint, the *Monterey Californian* defended the Chinese, lambasting the whalers for "tormenting their brother fisherman" and describing their actions as "no less than piracy."[9]

Emergent racial divisions reflected the unequal power relations typical of other western industries. While Monterey did not experience the virulent anti-Chinese activities that erupted elsewhere during the late nineteenth century, observers routinely expressed conventional anti-Chinese sentiments. They described Chinese fishermen as filthy and inferior, the same adjectives used to describe Chinese laborers who laid railroad tracks and toiled in mining camps.[10] When J. W. Collins, writing in an 1888 United States Fish Commission report, noted that the Chinese lived in "miserable squalor . . . conditions that would be unbearable to white men, particularly those of American birth," he made Chinese living conditions a corollary of their race. When he commented that a considerable percentage of Italian and Portuguese fishermen became naturalized, while the Chinese "appear[ed] to have no desire for citizenship," he implied that applying for citizenship made Italians and Portuguese superior. However, Collins did not mention that Chinese immigrants were ineligible for citizenship because the Naturalization Law of 1790 limited this privilege to "free white persons."[11]

The federal government considered all Europeans, including Italians and Portuguese, to be white in terms of their eligibility for citizenship, but there was no monolithic white race at this time. Nativist fears that certain immigrants threatened the republic led to the development of a hierarchy of multiple, scientifically distinct white races. Italians and other southern Europeans occupied the lower rungs of this social order, as northern Europeans believed that they were primitive and lacked civilization. Nonetheless, as Matthew Frye Jacobson argues, Italians and other degraded white races were still "rendered indelibly white by the presence of populations even more problematic than themselves," such as Asians. Thomas Guglielmo describes this system by distinguishing between race and color. During the late nineteenth century, Italians may have been an undesirable *race*, but they benefited from and embraced their *color* status as whites.[12] In the context of the Monterey fisheries, it was not surprising that federal officials classified Italian and Portuguese fishers as superior whites, in contrast to the nonwhite Chinese.

Individuals who reported on the fisheries also ostracized the Chinese by casting them as destructive fishers. In particular, the Chinese use of trawl lines to take bottom fish became a source of criticism. While "white fishermen" used gill nets and hooks and lines to make their catch, the Chinese rigged trawls with two hundred hooks each, uniting eight or nine sections to form one continuous line. They baited the hooks, left them at the ocean bottom, and checked them once or twice a day. According to an 1888 United States Fish Commission report, trawls were prohibited, and this infraction on the part of the Chinese created "a very bitter feeling between the two classes" of fishermen.[13] While the California Penal Code from this period did not include any explicit laws against trawls, the taking of young fish by any method was prohibited in state waters.[14] Perhaps observers believed that trawls—and the Chinese—were harmful because they took immature fish. However, most Pacific Coast fisheries experienced hard times from the mid-1870s to the mid-1890s, and it is difficult to sort out the various forces—human-induced and natural—that accounted for any species' decline.[15]

Attacks against Monterey's Chinese fishermen were not isolated events. Criticizing Chinese gear and methods reflected a statewide attempt to regulate them out of the fishing industry and reduce white fishermen's competition. In 1880 the California legislature prohibited aliens incapable of voting from fishing in the state's public waters. The United States Circuit Court, however, struck down this act because it violated the Fourteenth Amendment right to equal protection. Other legislation tried to expel the Chinese from the shrimp industry by banning their favored net, the Chinese bag net, and instituting a closed season during the summer, the only time when they could air-dry their catch and then ship it to China.[16]

In Monterey, the Chinese did find a few allies among scientists at Stanford University's Hopkins Seaside Laboratory, the first marine station on the Pacific Coast. Founded in 1892 at the behest of Stanford's first president, David Starr Jordan, a former student of noted Harvard scientist Louis Agassiz, the laboratory was located at Lover's Point in Pacific Grove, a short distance from Point Alones.[17] Here, Stanford biology professor Oliver Peebles Jenkins explained, "the forms of plants and animals are wonderfully rich in variety, in the numbers of individuals, in interest, in novelty, and in accessibility. It proves a perfect paradise for the marine biologist." To study this environment, the facility provided collecting apparatus, two boats, and several laboratories equipped with glassware, chemicals, microscopes, and aquaria that were pumped full of fresh, running seawater.[18] In its focus on laboratory-based research and specialization, Hopkins joined a larger shift in American biology from a "museum-oriented natural history" that entailed collecting, identifying, and preserving flora and fauna to a focus on research within academic and research institutions.[19]

Hopkins's scientists took advantage of their proximity to the Point Alones fishing village and enlisted the Chinese to provide specimens. As biologist Bashford Dean remarked, "The station has never found difficulty in securing an abundant supply of fish material, thanks to the Chinese fishermen of the neighbouring village." Scientists soon came to respect their skill as collectors and their knowledge of marine organisms. Unlike other descriptions of the Chinese at Point Alones, derogatory statements were coupled with praise. Dean and F. M. McFarland, a Hopkins instructor, referred to the fishermen as "the lowest type of Cantonese" and a "peculiar poor grade of Chinamen" but then lauded them as "excellent fishermen," "intelligent collectors," hardworking, honest, and "kindly." Dean also commended "the skill with which they separate the fertile or unfertile eggs of sharks . . . and recognize what they refer to as the 'hen' or 'rooster' sharks or rat-fish."[20] Through their labor in nature, the Chinese had acquired expertise valued by scientists.[21]

Collecting specimens was only part-time work for the Chinese; they continued to pursue the fisheries and soon focused their energies on squid. Squid fishing occurred at night, when the species could be attracted to the surface of the water with a lighted torch placed at the boat's bow. Two skiffs carrying the purse seine net followed. Once the squid appeared, Chinese fishermen threw the net into the water. They rowed their boats in opposite directions to encircle the squid, pulled on a rope to close or "purse" the two ends of the net together, and dragged the full net to shore. Onshore, men and women split the squid open and laid them on flakes (racks) to dry for two or three days. They then gathered and bundled the squid to be sent to San Francisco, where Chinese merchants distributed it to dealers in China and the Sandwich Islands (present-day Hawai'i). In 1892 the Chinese of Monterey County shipped 357,622 pounds of dried squid.[22] The squid fishery proved to be profitable, and it allowed the Chinese to escape their losing conflict over the fishing grounds with Europeans who worked during the day. Under the protective cover of darkness, the nocturnal harvesting of squid created physical, ecological, and temporal separation from potentially hostile fishermen.[23]

Still, observers maintained that the Chinese fisheries and their related odors reinforced the intrinsic inferiority and wastefulness of these non-white fishers. Writing in an 1888 booster publication entitled *Picturesque California*, J. R. Fitch argued that the Chinese caught squid only because they had exhausted other species, such as flounder and halibut. While federal data indicated that these fisheries were not, in fact, depleted, he maintained that the squid fishery was a sign of destructiveness, not resourcefulness. A U.S. Fish Commission report also pointed out the distasteful nature of the Chinese fishing operations, declaring that dried seafood possessed a "repulsive odor [and] their appearance [was] anything but attractive." Fitch added that the Chinese fishing village was "unspeakably dirty and redolent with the odor of decaying fish."[24] Squid and other fish odors were revolting, and the Chinese production of such an unpleasant stench became a way to characterize them as inherently repugnant. In other words, environmental activities deemed distasteful were markers of lower social status.[25]

Witnesses also objected to how the squid fishery transformed Chinese women, as working in nature imparted certain unfeminine characteristics to their bodies. According to travel writer M. H. Field, "There is truly nothing more hideous in shape than an old Chinese woman, bareheaded and scantily clad, wading into the surf to haul in a boat and unloading fish with masculine energy." Fitch added, "Swarthy women and little children who are tanned as black as negroes by sun and wind, swarm in the squalid cabins, and tumble about in the dust of the single street."[26] Hauling and unloading fish created sweat, muscles, and tan skin—attributes that marked these women as unlike their white counterparts. By working alongside men, they also contradicted Victorian gender roles in which women were segregated in the domestic sphere and did not assume public lives.[27] The physical manifestations of their labor provided further evidence of the lack of civility in the Chinese fishing village.

Japanese fishermen also became the object of white disdain and scorn. In the 1890s, they began to congregate at Whaler's Cove near Point Lobos, where marine biologist Gennosuke Kodani and local businessman Alexander M. Allan established an abalone cannery, the Point Lobos Canning Company, in 1898.[28] While Japanese and Chinese fishermen were distinct, Pacific Grove resident G. Webster lumped them together. He argued that both groups of fishermen "contribute nothing to the revenue, growth, or business of the city," yet they were depleting the abalone population by taking undersized mollusks. Other people also violated the law, he noted, "but on so small a scale as to be of less serious consequence."[29] While more Japanese than Chinese were engaged in the abalone fishery at this point, Webster saw no difference between them.[30]

Although outside observers perceived only two groups of Monterey fishermen—white and nonwhite—the fishermen themselves likely did not. The 1900 federal census recorded nine Japanese fishermen living at Point Alones, presumably alongside the Chinese, but there is no indication that the two groups worked together on the fishing grounds.[31] There is no evidence that Italian and Portuguese fishermen formed alliances during the late nineteenth century either. As Arthur McEvoy argues in his study of the California fisheries, "Each immigrant group carried on its business in near isolation from the others, each with its own economic organization, its own methods, and its own markets."[32]

Nonetheless, federal fishery officials and other observers continued to distinguish Chinese and Japanese fishermen from "white" fishermen of European origin and used differences in fishing gear and harvest to reinforce nonwhite inferiority. This racialization of the fishermen fueled efforts to spurn Asian fishers and ensure white dominance. Because Monterey fishermen operated within a common property regime, these informal arrangements based on unequal power relations and threats of force shaped the rules of access to the ocean and its resources.

DAVID JACKS AND THE ARRIVAL OF THE SOUTHERN PACIFIC RAILROAD

While no one owned Monterey Bay, private property owners did own parts of the shoreline and the land beyond the water's edge. Scotsman David Jacks became the region's land baron. While Jacks originally came to California in search of gold, he found his fortune far from the diggings. He settled in Monterey in 1850, worked as a clerk in a local store, and served as county treasurer. He also started to buy vast tracts of property on the Monterey Peninsula and in the Salinas Valley and began business with the Southern Pacific Railroad, setting the stage for the development of Monterey's tourism industry.[33]

The key to Jacks's power in Monterey lay in his acquisition of three tracts of land. The first was the Monterey pueblo lands, thirty thousand acres in and around Monterey granted by the Mexican government in 1830. When the United States acquired California from Mexico through the 1848 Treaty of Guadalupe Hidalgo, the pueblo lands became eligible for confirmation by the United States Land Commission under the Land Act of 1851. Monterey city attorney Delos Ashley secured the patent in January 1856 and charged the city $991.50 for his services. With no funds to pay Ashley, Monterey's common council authorized the sale of the pueblo lands on February 9, 1859. Ashley and Jacks submitted the successful bid of $991.50 and paid an additional $11 in fees. When Ashley left Monterey in 1869, he sold all of his interest in the pueblo lands to Jacks for $500.[34] The second parcel was the Rancho El Pescadero, which covered 4,426 acres on the southwestern peninsula. The last tract, Rancho Punta de Pinos (Point Pinos), encompassed 2,666 acres on the northwestern peninsula.[35]

Jacks's land-holdings brought him into contact with several working landscapes in and around Monterey. He rented property to the Chinese fishermen at the Pescadero and Point Alones fishing villages. In its 1868 lease, the China Man Hop Company at Pescadero paid Jacks seventy-two dollars per year, plus two dozen abalones each month.[36] At Point Alones, the Chinese Fishing Company paid two hundred dollars per year in fifty-dollar installments every three months.[37] Jacks also leased much of his land in the Salinas Valley to farmers and ranchers and pursued other endeavors that turned Monterey's resources into commodities to ship across the nation. He sold tons of Monterey sand to several San Francisco concrete and glass manufacturers and the seeds and seedlings of Monterey pine and cypress trees to nurseries and other buyers.[38]

Although Jacks could easily ship products from the Monterey Peninsula via steamer, transporting agricultural products from the Salinas Valley was quite costly. The monopolistic control of the Southern Pacific during the second half of the nineteenth century meant that farmers had to pay its exorbitant freight rates to get crops from Salinas to other markets.[39] To extricate themselves from the tentacles of "the Octopus," ranch owner Carlisle Abbott organized other local residents to build an independent narrow-gauge railroad from Salinas to Monterey. Only three feet across, narrow-gauge rails were popular during the 1870s because they were relatively cheap to finance. Recognizing that the railroad would increase the value of his land, Jacks jumped on the bandwagon and became treasurer of the Monterey and Salinas Valley Railroad Company.[40]

The eighteen-and-one-half-mile railroad made its first run in October 1874 and became an instant success. It transported an average of three hundred tons of grain to the Monterey wharf each day and undercut the Southern Pacific's rail-ship freight rate by two dollars per ton. In its first year, the narrow-gauge averaged over six hundred dollars per day in revenue. However, the steep cost of construction and equipment and disastrous crops in 1876 and 1877 compromised the railroad's financial standing. When the Southern Pacific lowered freight charges, moreover, farmers stopped using the narrow gauge. In August 1879, the Southern Pacific purchased the Monterey and Salinas Valley Railroad at a foreclosure sale, and Charles Crocker, one of the associates of the Central and Southern Pacific Railroads, then sold its locomotives, stock, and track to the Nevada Central Pacific, which he also owned. Meanwhile, the Southern Pacific began to construct a standard-gauge line from Castroville to Monterey.[41]

To capitalize on chances for profit created by the railroad and engage in other businesses, the Southern Pacific organized holding companies. In 1874 the Western Development Company replaced the first such firm, the Contract and Finance Company, to carry out construction, manufacturing, mining, mercantile, mechanical, banking, and commercial business and to construct, lease, and operate public and private improvements. Leland Stanford, Mark Hopkins, Collis P. Huntington, and Charles Crocker—the "Big Four"—each held one-quarter of the stock and later brought in a fifth partner, David Colton. When Hopkins died in 1878, Huntington, Crocker, and Stanford closed the affairs of the Western Development Company and continued their building enterprises through the Pacific Improvement Company. By the mid-1890s, the Pacific Improvement Company had assets totaling $64 million.[42]

The Pacific Improvement Company set about to remake Monterey into something altogether new. While the standard-gauge line was under construction, company executives began to buy real estate for a seaside resort. Crocker in particular was "thoroughly alive to the importance of doing something at Monterey" and negotiated with Jacks for a beachfront parcel of the pueblo lands. The deal was finalized in January 1880, with the Pacific Improvement Company paying $2,500 for this 118-acre tract. It also acquired the Toomes Tract, 106 acres southwest of the first parcel, the Ranchos Pescadero and Punta de Pinos, and another 150-acre parcel.[43] In all, the Pacific Improvement Company bought over 7,000 acres on the Monterey Peninsula in a period of five months. With an infusion of capital and the development of transportation networks, the stage was set for the construction of the Hotel Del Monte.[44]

THE HOTEL DEL MONTE, "QUEEN OF AMERICAN WATERING PLACES"

In many respects, the development of tourism paralleled the development of the fisheries. Like fishermen, Pacific Improvement Company officials commodified the coastline and altered nature in ways that reflected their objectives; to attract elite health- and pleasure-seekers, they embellished the shoreline with exotic flora and grand facilities, creating a hybrid landscape of nature and artifice.[45] And just as in the fisheries, their material changes to the environment engendered social divisions, both between hotel guests and workers and between different groups of guests. Those who encountered the Hotel Del Monte had diverse experiences with nature depending, in part, on their social standing. Ultimately, not everyone saw the hotel as the "Queen of American Watering Places," and only certain people could fully enjoy all of the amenities that resort developers had created on this stretch of the Monterey coastline.[46]

The hotel began as the project of Charles Crocker, who saw Monterey as an ideal location for a "first-class watering place." He wrote, "I think it is the prettiest place for a hotel that I know of. . . . spent the day in looking around Monterey, going all over it, and I found no place so beautiful and available as this." Crocker wasted little time in getting the Hotel Del Monte under way, setting aside the Toomes Tract and the parcel of pueblo lands purchased from David Jacks. He hired architect Arthur Brown to design the resort, and together they picked a location east of downtown Monterey in a grove of pine, oak, and cedar trees—hence the name Hotel Del Monte, Spanish for "hotel of the trees."[47] With a depot at the hotel, the new standard-gauge railroad began running in time for the hotel's grand opening on June 5, 1880. After the original hotel burned to the ground on April 1, 1887, the Pacific Improvement Company rebuilt it immediately, enlarging the building to accommodate more guests.[48]

In creating a space for leisure, the Hotel Del Monte emulated European resorts, appealing to an elite, urban East Coast and European clientele. Because these tourists delighted in classical literature, art, and culture, promoters cast the hotel and Monterey as a place of European beauty and elegance.[49] The hotel's architecture was described as "Gothic style . . . said to resemble much that of the famous Buckingham palace," and the scenery and climate were like those of the Italian Riviera.[50] Promoters cast the hotel as the lap of luxury—"a work of art suggestive of culture and refinement"—with lush gardens, tasteful furnishings, modern bathrooms, spacious parlors, ballrooms, billiard rooms, and bowling alleys. They proclaimed the Hotel Del Monte as "the handsomest watering-place hotel in America," with "no peer in America or Europe."[51]

And elite visitors came, showering the hotel with praise. National figures, including President Benjamin Harrison, steel baron Andrew Carnegie, and publisher Joseph Pulitzer, soon arrived. Harrison testified that the hotel was the "most delightful spot," while Carnegie exclaimed: "Great corporations elevate the taste of a community by introducing higher standards. In Monterey, the Pacific Improvement Company has set the standards of standards. It is doubtful if it can be equaled in any part of the world. If the traveler has only time to see one place in California, let that be Monterey, for it is the best of its kind."[52] Because it conformed to their aesthetic tastes, the Hotel Del Monte did not disappoint visitors of high social standing.

In selling the hotel, boosters also emphasized Monterey's existing features, from its rich history to its natural beauty and pleasant weather. Capitalizing on a fascination with California's "Spanish fantasy heritage," one promotional tract described Monterey as "the cradle of far Western civilization, the commonwealth of California," marked by modern architecture and the "ghost-haunted ruins" of the Spanish past.[53] Monterey's location, moreover, embraced land and sea, from the Carmel River Valley to wide vistas of Monterey Bay and vast groves of live oaks and Monterey pine.[54] This scenery was made all the more enjoyable by a mild, year-round climate. Raymond-Whitcomb's Vacation Excursions planned winter trips to the hotel so that easterners could escape the harsh weather and enjoy the Central California coast, where "there is literally neither winter nor summer."[55]

But creating the hotel also required modifying and adding artifice to the Monterey environment. This process was most evident in the hotel's gardens. According to one guidebook, "Nature endowed them [hotel developers] with prodigal liberality, and the owners are supplementing nature's efforts with an equally prodigal expenditure of art."[56] Where "art" was applied to the native flora, noted one observer, "it has been done so skillfully and adroitly that the result is an innocent fraud perpetrated upon the beholder who believes he sees only nature."[57] In other words, the gardens were deliberate creations in which human alterations were meant to appear natural; one did not know where "nature" began or ended.[58] Thus, the Hotel Del Monte illustrated Earl Pomeroy's assertion that late nineteenth-century tourists admired nature "where art had repaired the omissions of nature, or nature seemed to counterfeit art."[59]

The Hotel Del Monte gardens, like other late nineteenth-century California gardens, reflected an American desire to transform western land into a "lush Eden." As David C. Streatfield argues, this aspiration stemmed from a fondness for the Victorian gardens of England and Europe—ornate gardens that displayed "an overflowing cornucopia of plants from different ecological zones placed side by side and representing a triumph over nature." In reality, making these changes was less a "triumph over nature" than an improvement upon California's inherent fecundity. Since California afforded a long growing season for a broad range of plants, gardeners could create lavish gardens of "unmatched prodigality." Nature and human imagination made "Eden" possible.[60]

Rudolf Ulrich, a German-born gardener trained in Italy and England, was responsible for creating the Hotel Del Monte's gardens. Ulrich was known for his ability to arrange a wide assortment of shrubs, trees, and flowers into "almost outrageous horticultural extravagances."[61] Visitors raved about the rampant growth of ivy and honeysuckles and marveled at flower beds of roses, violets, azaleas, fuchsias, and lilies arranged "in ribbons of dazzling colors, in trefoils, hearts and every other conceivable form."[62] Ulrich's ornate designs depended on exotic flora from around the world. He popularized the Arizona garden, a collection of desert plants imported from the Southwest, and also planted twelve hundred English walnut trees and rare flowering plants from South America, the Cape of Good Hope, and Australia. One brochure noted, "Here flowers from all parts of the world unfold their color and fragrance every day of the year round, reveling in a climate more generous than of the country which gave them birth."[63] The gardens, however, were not devoid of Monterey's native flora. Ulrich enhanced native live oaks, pine, and cypress by placing them next to "dainty flower beds" and by balancing "ash and elm, cypress and madrona, palm and manzanita."[64]

The hotel's fifteen-acre artificial lake—Laguna Del Rey—was another example of how nature and artifice blurred in the creation of a new idyllic landscape. While the nearby ocean was a dramatic backdrop that displayed the power and energy of nature, Laguna Del Rey was a tranquil, genteel landscape made possible by technology and labor. Dug "for the pleasure of Del Monte's guests," it included water lilies and a "little fairy island" where fountains shot into the air. To enjoy the display, guests could walk across a footbridge, drive around the lake on macadamized roads, or rent rowboats.[65] Although natural processes inevitably shaped the lake—algae, for instance, began to grow on its surface—it was intended to be a peaceful space where hotel guests could enjoy a refined and controlled version of nature.[66]

In the case of the hotel's bathhouse, developers did not construct nature out of whole cloth; instead, they modified the ocean and made it pleasurable and safe for recreational use. The pavilion was perched at the edge of the bay and enclosed with a glass roof to let in the sunshine, the light and warmth giving the feeling of being outdoors. Within the structure were four swimming tanks, each successive pool heated to a slightly warmer temperature than the previous. Private suites were equipped with tubs of fresh- or salt-water piped in from the bay, either hot or cold. While promoters also encouraged guests to dive into the ocean itself, it is more likely that, given the chilly Monterey Bay waters, they frequented the bathing pavilion.[67] Here, technology transported and altered bay water, heating it and eliminating fluctuating tides, varying depths, and dangerous undertow.

Maintaining the hotel's artificial nature, however, was a financial liability. A. D. Shepard, general manager of the Pacific Improvement Company, explained, "It should be borne in mind that Del Monte is an artificial attraction." He drew a distinction between the Hotel Del Monte and resorts at the Grand Canyon, Lake Tahoe, Yosemite, Santa Barbara, and Pasadena, noting that the latter hotels had "natural attractions to draw patronage, and have no great expense other than maintenance of the Hotel proper." Del Monte, by contrast, depended "mainly upon the Hotel park, flowers, drive, etc., all of which must be kept alive and made prominent by expenditure of much money."[68] By Shepard's definition, nature was that which cost nothing; expending money created an improved nature, but, paradoxically, not always a profitable nature. While the Hotel Del Monte was arguably no more "natural" or "artificial" than any other resort he mentioned, its finances seemed to cloud his assessment.

Shepard underscored the fact that many guests did indeed come to the hotel solely to enjoy its "artificial" spaces, reveling in the well-groomed gardens, human-made lake, and heated pools. Bostonian Susie Clark visited Monterey's historical sites but concluded that tourists came "chiefly and solely to visit the Hotel del Monte, in comparison with which everything else sinks into insignificance."[69] As an 1897 article from *Overland* noted, people went to posh resorts "not to worship nature, but to see and be seen by their kind. They play tennis and golf, swim in warmed tanks, drive behind fine horses, dress for dinner, and do all these things in the conventional and polite way."[70] Visiting resorts like the Hotel Del Monte was a status symbol, and for many there was no need to leave the hotel grounds.

This beauty and refinement, as Shepard suggested, required a huge input of money, particularly for labor. The Pacific Improvement Company brought in many Chinese to work in the hotel and lay out the scenic drives. A corps of forty to fifty men, mostly Chinese, maintained the gardens alone.[71] Chinese workers also provided the muscle to build the hotel's waterworks. Construction began in the fall of 1883, with a pipeline down the Carmel Valley, around Cypress Point and Point Pinos, through Pacific Grove and to the hotel. After the April 1887 fire, the Pacific Improvement Company constructed an even larger and more elaborate water network. One hundred Chinese laborers burned brush, cleared trees, and dug the 147-million-gallon reservoir that supplied the hotel, its gardens, and the fountain in Laguna Del Rey.[72] Japanese workers also entered the company workforce; they cleared brush and trees for the Seventeen Mile Drive, a scenic road that took guests through the forest and along the coastline.[73]

Chinese workers and white tourists shared many physical spaces at the hotel, but they were socially separate. The hotel produced a social hierarchy that elevated the status of leisured bodies. Working bodies— those bodies engaged directly in altering nature—were marked as inferior, even if their labor in nature "improved" them. For instance, one visitor believed that toiling at the hotel had a positive effect on the Chinese. He noted, "Even the Chinese boys who sweep the hotel corridors have lost the yellow, gaunt-cheeked look of their compatriots and grown absolutely pink-faced in the rosy-light of life at Monterey."[74] Chinese bodies seemed to acquire the physical traits of the white tourists they served. But even if they benefited from the hotel's environment, their role remained clear: to create and maintain amenities for guests.

In other instances, immigrant labor became a tourist attraction in and of itself. Along the Seventeen Mile Drive, tourists marveled at the stunning coastal views, but promoters also naturalized the presence of humans who lived along the drive and incorporated them into the tourism adventure. The route purposely passed by Chinese fishing villages near Pebble Beach and Stillwater Cove and other immigrant fishing grounds.[75] Soon after the drive opened, the Chinese took advantage of this influx of tourists and set up a roadside stand to sell polished shells and trinkets.[76] Tourists and fishermen marked out the coastline for different purposes and attached different values to nature, but their interactions coincided and became mutually beneficial. Tourists took in the exotic sights of the Chinese villages and purchased souvenirs along the way, while the Chinese profited from the by-products of their fishing industry.

Labor and leisure further overlapped when tourists tried their hand at fishing. The Hotel Del Monte appealed to its male visitors by showcasing the region as "a sportsman's paradise," touting hunting and fishing expeditions to the Laurelles Ranch (Rancho Del Monte), located ten miles up the Carmel Valley from the Carmel River. Other fishing enthusiasts headed out on Monterey Bay. Although it is unclear if conflicts developed between the market and sport fishermen, there is at least a suggestion that the former group, similar to the Chinese villagers, capitalized on tourism; Emanual Duarte, a longtime resident and fisherman, rented out boats and tackle to hotel guests.[77] While the pairing of sportsmen with actual fishermen blurred the divisions between labor and leisure, these two groups had very different designs on the coastline. For fishermen, the coastline was where they made their living; for tourists, it was where they showcased their wealth and masculinity.[78]

The sportsmen's excursions also illustrated the gender divide within tourism. The hotel sold adventures in nature to men, but it sold more refined social activities to its female guests. When they wanted to relax or mingle, women enjoyed separate spaces, including a ladies' billiard room and a ladies' parlor. The hotel also staged numerous galas where "the queens and belles of California society" and the East Coast could show off the latest fashions.[79] A poem in the hotel's newsletter, the *Del Monte Wave*, even proclaimed that the Del Monte was proud "Of having, always, a magnificent crowd / Of mighty fine specimens" of women.[80] When women did play in nature, they typically engaged in activities deemed appropriate for their gender, such as swimming or collecting shells and mosses for home aquariums.[81]

Despite some limitations to their mobility, women could engage in heterosocial activities and assume more gregarious public personas. At the beach, they played in the surf or swam in the heated pools, despite fears that they might expose too much of their bodies. At hotel balls, they flirted and danced with men and showed off their finest clothes. As Cindy Aron argues, "fashionably dressed women were, in part, what made a resort fashionable and potentially profitable." While resorts like the Hotel Del Monte had plenty of critics who believed that "the pleasures of wasteful idleness" would tempt and potentially corrupt middle-class vacationers, many female guests dismissed these worries and challenged larger societal concerns about female promiscuity.[82]

For other guests, a stay at the Hotel Del Monte had nothing to do with social status and had everything to do with treating a long list of chronic ailments. Armed with death statistics, promoters declared that Monterey provided a more healthful atmosphere than Nice, Milan, and Naples.[83] The late nineteenth-century American medical community corroborated these claims about the health benefits of mild coastal climates. According to Dr. P. C. Remondino, "Moist marine air and equable temperature produce the most perfect specimens of physical development."[84] Dr. John H. Packard claimed that salt air relaxed and stimulated invalids, leading to sound sleep and better digestion, while Dr. Bushrod James believed that sea air benefited sufferers of pulmonary phthisis and scrofulous affections (tuberculosis), chronic nasal, pharyngeal and bronchial inflammations, asthma, hay fever, rheumatism, and malaria.[85] These physicians equated particular geographical locales with health and believed that proper climate could mitigate many illnesses, particularly tuberculosis.[86]

But nature alone could not ensure the speedy recovery of the sick. Dr. James noted that resorts also had to provide proper accommodations, such as drainage, ventilation, pure water, and nourishment, as well as "scenery, amusements, diversions and congenial surroundings."[87] The Hotel Del Monte fit the bill on all accounts. In an 1884 address to the Middlesex County Medical Society in Connecticut, Dr. A. M. Shew called the Hotel Del Monte "the *ideal* hotel" for invalids. He concluded, "I am convinced that, considering everything—climate, hotel accommodations, sea-bathing and beautiful surroundings—Monterey approaches nearer to the Ideal Sanitarium than any place I have ever visited."[88] While some visitors left unconvinced that Monterey was an "ideal sanitarium"— Boston abolitionist and feminist Caroline Dall complained about Monterey's cold mornings and evenings and the potentially harmful presence of other invalids—others, like Dr. Shew, maintained that the physical qualities of the environment combined with fine hotel amenities made Monterey a healthful place.[89]

The Hotel Del Monte and its environs, then, meant different things to different people. The Pacific Improvement Company transformed the coastline to create a world-class seaside resort, but guests did not have uniform encounters with the hotel landscape. What was a place for leisure and luxury for many was a place of confinement and recuperation for others. For Chinese workers and immigrant fishermen, moreover, the hotel and the Seventeen Mile Drive were sites of labor. And then there was Robert Louis Stevenson, who wanted nothing to do with the hotel. He

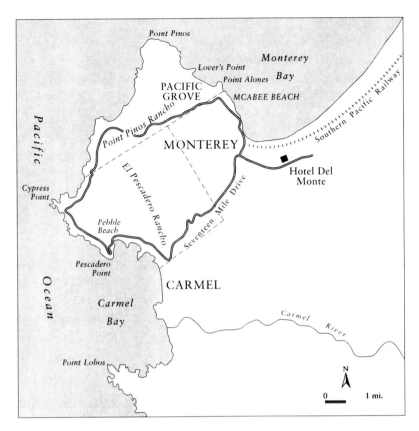

MAP 2. Monterey Peninsula, early 20th century

scorned its "flaunting caravanserai" and "millionaire vulgarians" and lamented that "the Monterey of last year exists no longer."[90] Indeed, with the tourism industry firmly established on the Monterey coastline, the sleepy town that Stevenson had first encountered in 1879 was fading away.

THE BATTLE OVER POINT ALONES

Despite occasions when fisheries and tourism developed mutually beneficial arrangements, conflict between the industries seemed inevitable. Their physical proximity on the coastline meant that it was only a matter of time before they collided. In the years leading up to the 1906 fire, competing claims to the coastline came to a head in an intense dispute over the Chinese squid fishery at Point Alones. When the embers at the village finally cooled, certain activities—and certain people—found their place on the Monterey shoreline severely compromised.

The battle began with complaints about pollution along the coastline. In 1892 Dr. W. H. Dall reported that Monterey's scientific collecting grounds would "probably be nearly ruined before long" because sewage from the Hotel Del Monte, Pacific Grove, and Monterey was dumped into the bay. "Beaches which formerly would afford several hundred species are now nearly bare, or offensive with stinking black mud," he complained.[91] Williard M. Wood corroborated Dall's observations one year later. He wrote, "Monterey is no longer the famous collecting ground it used to be. . . . The deadly sewerage flowing from the various towns into Monterey Bay is killing the marine shells."[92] Whereas some observers saw Chinese fishermen as destructive and offensive, scientists applied these same characterizations to white tourists and residents, whose waste was washing up on the beach.

An 1882 report from the California State Board of Health indicated that seaside resorts were well aware of the sewage problem and its threat to both human and marine life. As beach pollution drove away tourists and compromised human health, many seaside resorts grappled with "how to get rid of the sewage so that it will neither float about the shore or be brought back again by the tide." At the same time they acknowledged that the discharge of large quantities of sewage, if allowed to putrefy, drove away and even killed fish. This dilemma was made even more complicated by fluctuating tides and prevailing winds, which affected the efficacy of any sewage outfall system. Monterey's success as a tourist destination brought with it the same waste problems afflicting the big cities that visitors sought to escape.[93]

Nonetheless, the Hotel Del Monte bragged about the cleanliness of its facilities. When the hotel reopened after the 1887 fire, it claimed, "The sewerage system is thoroughly complete, and the pipes are so constructed that it is utterly impossible for the escape in any portion of the building, of any gases or unhealthful odors."[94] But just because guests did not see or smell their waste did not mean that it disappeared. Tourists typically gained knowledge about the ocean from afar, not from daily trips to the tide pools. They were not as cognizant of the shore's rhythms and the fluctuating abundance and diversity of marine organisms as Hopkins's scientists. While looking at the shoreline typically delighted tourists, the same vista began to disgust scientists who saw their experimental opportunities decline.

Rather than acknowledging their own role in tainting the coastline, real estate developers and residents focused their complaints on the odors emitted by Chinese squid-drying fields. In 1892 Pacific Grove residents grew so disgusted that they submitted a petition to the city trustees. The *Pacific Grove Review* reported: "As the abominable stench from the decaying fish grows daily worse, we judge there are no active measures taken. Unless we wish to court diptheria [sic], typhoid and scarlet fever, this thing must cease, and at once."[95] Odors from the Chinese fishing village had become the harbinger of illness and possibly death.

The Pacific Grove petition reflected popular understandings of disease transmission in the late nineteenth century. Despite the growing acceptance of germ theory, some medical authorities and many laypeople still associated typhoid, scarlet fever, and diphtheria with poor, densely settled urban tenements and foul-smelling vapors.[96] Concerns about odors extended from a persistent belief that miasmas, or malevolent airs, radiated from dirty places and made the surrounding atmosphere unhealthful. Whereas "good airs" were pure and fresh and imparted health, miasmas conveyed the harmful aspects of the environment into the human body. According to Conevery Bolton Valenčius, odors were a sign of miasma, "an important diagnostic aid" in determining the health of people and places. Even as late nineteenth-century medical practitioners began to reject odors as a cause of disease, many Americans could not easily dissociate bad smells from poor health.[97]

Because odors wafted from a specific place, disease was also associated with a particular neighborhood and a particular social group. The perceived unhealthfulness of the Point Alones village marked the Chinese as repulsive and harmful. This link between Chinese living quarters, disease, and social difference was not limited to Monterey. In San Francisco, for instance, health officials in the mid- to late nineteenth century saw Chinatown as an epidemic danger because the Chinese lived in "dirty, filthy dens." As Nayan Shah argues, Chinese cultural behavior indicated "innate dispositions to illness," and as a result, "Disease was conceived as organic to every Chinese racialized space." Similarly, in Monterey, smelly squid indicated Chinese fishers' lack of proper hygiene and sanitation, making their village the perfect breeding ground for infectious diseases.[98]

Despite the perceived health dangers of the squid fishery, the Chinese remained at Point Alones and continued to dry squid for another decade. There was no concerted effort to stop their operations until May 1902, when a sudden rain shower spoiled a field of squid and created an especially pungent odor. Nearby residents complained again to local law enforcement and the Pacific Improvement Company, which owned the Point Alones village. The stinking mounds of spoiled squid prompted Robert F. Johnson, president of the Monterey Board of Trustees, to order an investigation by Assistant District Attorney Jesse W. Bryan, who concluded that the Chinese were creating a nuisance. As a result, B. A. Eardley, Pacific Improvement Company superintendent, issued an order that forbade them from drying squid on company property.[99]

When the Pacific Improvement Company bought Point Alones from David Jacks, its executives probably did not anticipate these complaints. They continued to collect rent from the Chinese, who pursued the squid fishery. Yet their ownership also meant that they became accountable for their tenants' fishing practices, practices that transcended property boundaries. Squid odors could not be confined to a particular space. Winds carried them far beyond Point Alones to property that the company did not own. Since the company owned the *source* of the odors, it had to address the grumbles of other property holders, who claimed that Chinese squid drying created a nuisance and purportedly injured their property.[100]

The Pacific Improvement Company decided that a ban on squid drying would end an ongoing nuisance and bolster tourism and real estate development in the process. While the Chinese spent from five to ten thousand dollars each year in Monterey, the odors began to overshadow their economic contributions. As the *Monterey New Era* explained, previous visitors "must surely have been kept away by the smell of the squid drying in the fields and stored at the wharf awaiting shipment by steamer." The resulting demise of Chinatown would make nearby building sites "immensely more valuable" and "Chinatown itself would in time form as beautiful and desirable villa sites as can be found in America."[101] Eardley did not know of another place where the Chinese could dry squid and predicted that Chinatown "would probably cease to exist."[102]

Nonetheless, the Pacific Improvement Company dragged its feet in enforcing the squid ban. In June 1902, Johnson visited the company offices in San Francisco, where President Horace Platt "expressed himself as unwilling to injure Monterey in any manner, and said he was personally in favor of refusing to renew the lease to the Chinese."[103] Platt's promises appeared to go unfulfilled; in May 1904, the local board of health announced its intention to take the squid-drying matter up with the state board of health.[104] Finally, in 1905, the company announced that the Chinese would have to leave Point Alones at the end of their lease in February 1906. When the deadline came and went without their departure, company general manager A. D. Shepard resisted forcible ejection and began to explore how he could move the Chinese to an isolated spot where they would not create a nuisance.[105] Why Shepard took an interest in the future Chinese living situation was unclear.

The Chinese relocation never materialized because the Point Alones village went up in flames on May 16, 1906, destroying about two-thirds of the village. While there was no incontrovertible evidence, it is hard to dismiss arson as a plausible if not the probable cause. Nonetheless, the *Pacific Grove Review* also speculated that a carelessly discarded cigarette or inattentive Chinese burning garbage may have started the blaze. The Chinese may have contributed to the scale of the disaster by building a village of cramped wooden structures and drying racks that became soaked with fish oil. They tried to contain the fire and salvage their belongings, but their efforts were futile. As the blaze engulfed the village, curious spectators lined the railroad tracks, while other troublemakers looted the buildings that remained.[106]

Presumably, the near destruction of the village ended the battle over Point Alones. As the *Pacific Grove Review* concluded, "The question of the removal of Chinatown is now settled. . . . Now that the settlement is so nearly destroyed, [the Chinese] will not be allowed to rebuild."[107] However, keeping the Chinese away was not that simple. Led by village resident Tom Yuen, they refused to concede and attempted to rebuild on a portion of land above the railroad tracks.[108] They also enlisted the services of Monterey law firm Sandholt and Shaw, which presented Pacific Improvement Company general agent J. P. Pryor with a demand for the surrender of the former fishing village.[109] For its part, the company hired guards to watch the location, shut off most of the water supply, and built a fence around the site.[110] Company executives were not going to allow the Chinese to rebuild their village and threaten their efforts to attract tourists and home buyers.

Pryor explained that Chinese resettlement would degrade the company's land and cause unnecessary expenses. In a letter to Shepard, he wrote, "If they [the Chinese] should gain possession of this land for only a temporary period, they would at once erect their old shacks and accumulate considerable dirt and filth, all of which would have to be cleared up again after we had regained possession of the land."[111] Implicit in Pryor's argument was that the Chinese would make the area unfit for the company's well-heeled clientele and diminish property values. He wanted to ensure that the coastline would be a place where elite visitors would spend their leisure time on clean, valuable oceanfront property. In his mind, the Pacific Improvement Company was the best agent for improving Point Alones and developing Monterey into a premier tourist and residential destination. But the persistence of Chinese fishermen was a reminder that property ownership did not automatically yield social control.

The battle drew to a close when the Chinese agreed to resettle at McAbee Beach, a parcel of land east of Point Alones. Shepard approved of this plan because it would allow the company to donate the former village site to the University of California for a marine station.[112] Pryor, however, believed that the Chinese presence at McAbee Beach would continue to drive away "the class of citizens whom we are desirous of attracting." Other residents were similarly outraged and tried to raise money to buy the land from under the Chinese. Such protests came too late, and the Chinese settled at their new village. As the *Pacific Grove Review* concluded sarcastically, "Pungent odors from the new Chinese quarters mingled with the sea b[r]eezes ought to make a lively advance in the price of real estate."[113]

Even with this relocation, racially motivated policies still undercut Chinese fishing activities.[114] Because the Chinese continued to harvest and dry squid, white citizens continued to complain about the odors. In 1907 the city of Monterey responded by passing an ordinance prohibiting the drying of squid within city limits. Legal statutes now replaced cruder instruments of social exclusion and social control. Despite the law, police records from 1907 and 1908 indicate that several Chinese—San Moy, Ah Tai, Ah Fook, Ah Shue, Yee Sing, Yee Hoe, Ah Wong, and Ah Hoe—risked fines and imprisonment to dry squid in Monterey.[115] But such cases were rare. To avoid city authorities and possible punishment, the Chinese had to move their squid-drying fields to the outskirts of town. Since this was far from the shoreline, production declined, and the number of fishers dwindled. Out of a total of eighty-six Chinese at McAbee Beach in 1910, only eighteen were fishermen. One year later, the city directory recorded only seven Chinese fishermen at the village.[116]

Ironically, even as the Pacific Improvement Company expelled the Chinese, it supported the community's efforts to sentimentalize their culture and customs for tourism promotion. In July 1905, Pacific Grove began celebrating the Feast of Lanterns. This annual celebration featured an evening parade of fishing boats lighted with lanterns, resembling the sight of Chinese squid fishermen who worked at night. Residents also posted lanterns at their homes or carried them to the beach to search for Queen Topaz, who, according to their rendition of Chinese legend, drowned herself rather than forsake her lover and marry her father's choice for a husband.[117] In July 1906, just two months after the Point Alones fire, the Pacific Improvement Company donated twenty dollars toward the festival. J. P. Pryor, the same person who refused to let the Chinese rebuild their village, remarked that the festival "was by far the best display that has ever been given in Pacific Grove, and tended largely to advertise us to the outside world."[118]

Pryor apparently found no contradiction between expelling the Chinese at Point Alones and supporting a festival that staged a Chinese legend and romanticized the Chinese industry he had found so offensive. He recognized that *dramatizations* of Chinese fishermen working in nature could be picturesque. The sight and smell of *real* Chinese fishermen catching and drying squid were not. While Pacific Improvement Company leaders constructed the coastline as a place for white residents and tourists, the festival encouraged them to embrace an exoticized Chinese fishing community as part of the scenic coastline. Like the California boosters who promoted a Spanish fantasy heritage that exalted a mythological Spanish past while slighting the Mexican and Indian populations— including the latter group's decimation following Spanish settlement in 1769—the Pacific Improvement Company engaged in a sort of Chinese fantasy heritage. It highlighted charming, romantic Chinese folklore, but it ignored its own complicity in undermining the community's self-sufficiency.[119]

Paradoxically, the Pacific Improvement Company deemed the Chinese fishermen as both a detriment and a boon to its efforts to attract elite tourists and homebuyers to the coastline, rejecting and embracing them depending on the circumstances. This turbulent relationship developed as Monterey's landscapes of production blurred with its landscapes of leisure. While company executives tried to control the boundaries between tourism and fisheries, they found it difficult to keep the industries separate. In the case of the Chinese squid fishery, they could not prevent pungent odors from wafting to elite homesites and hotels. Intensifying competition over the coastline, in turn, heightened racial tensions and entrenched social divisions. In the end, Chinese fishermen's activities in nature proved too offensive for seaside developers and some residents. The fire added drama to the debate, but it only expedited an impending eviction. The eventual banishment of the Chinese could not be disentangled from their race *and* the olfactory changes they brought to the shoreline.

Chinese fishermen were objectionable in one context but quaint in another. Staged, sanitized, and idealized for a white audience, their labor and cultural traditions became the focus of the Feast of Lanterns. The festival recast the Chinese fishermen as an intriguing spectacle while keeping them at arm's length from easily offended white tourists and residents. In this case, fisheries and tourism overlapped in a way that solidified the Pacific Improvement Company's hold over the coastline and benefited its tourism operations, as the Chinese fishermen now decorated, rather than tainted, Monterey's spectacular shores and provided local color.

But seen another way, the soft glow illuminating the beach during the Feast of Lanterns also served as a reminder that the borders between the fisheries and tourism and their respective participants were under constant negotiation. While the flickering lanterns made the Chinese fishermen appear as peaceful accoutrements to the tourist's coastline, this act was short-lived, and they continued to ply Monterey Bay's waters, even as their numbers declined. So long as the Pacific Improvement Company and Monterey's fishermen, Asian and European alike, pursued their businesses along the same scenic and fecund coastline, the tensions between the industries were never far from the surface. No one group's dominance was ever assured along Monterey's shifting shores.

Indeed, tourism may have appeared to be ascendant, but the rise of the fishing industry was on the horizon. Just as Chinese fishermen began to face efforts to eliminate them, new groups of fishermen and entrepreneurs began to descend on the town to further capitalize on the fisheries. They brought their own visions for the Monterey coastline and produced dramatic environmental and social changes in the process. While the Pacific Improvement Company also remained a major player on the city's shores, this new competition would ultimately be much harder to control and displace than the Chinese fishermen and their smelly squid fields.

2 THE DIVIDED COASTLINE

"Times Look Bright" declared a June 1907 editorial in the *Monterey Daily Cypress*. As investors began to take advantage of promising business opportunities, "a new life has been instilled into the Peninsula and its people, and they realize they have a city that is bound to be a great commerci[a]l center."[1] Other editorials were filled with similar discussions of Monterey's swift rise to greatness. Vacant storefronts were nonexistent, commerce was booming, and property sales were brisk.[2] But these boosters were not satisfied; they implored residents to do more to promote Monterey, particularly its tourism and fishing industries. As a resort, the coastal community had "everything Nature could do for a place"—mild climate, fine beaches, and recreational activities. The fisheries also held the potential to make Monterey famous. With an "unlimited" supply of fish, "the bay is one of the richest natural resources of the state. Millions of dollars can be made from it yearly without any great risk of capital."[3]

By expanding their operations and further capitalizing on the coastline, the tourism and fishing industries were poised to contribute to Monterey's bright future. Catering to a larger vacationing public, the Pacific Improvement Company moved beyond the Hotel Del Monte and began to improve and promote its vast holdings on the Monterey Peninsula. This growth was indicative of a widespread decline in the grand hotels of the American West during the early twentieth century.[4] As tourism decentralized, the fisheries centralized. Abundant runs of salmon and sardines prompted entrepreneurs to build fish canneries along the waterfront. These facilities took control of nature and increased output by concentrating production and applying new technology. In the process, they rendered the dispersed, small-scale fishing villages obsolete and attracted new groups of immigrants to Monterey's shores.

In the years following the Point Alones fire, then, tourism did not completely dominate the Monterey economy. Instead, both tourism and the fisheries established firm roots. By and large, they grew independently of one another and coexisted without major clashes. However, both industries continued to confront internal divisions and produced new markers of social status and social difference that sharpened class, racial, and ethnic distinctions.[5] Given participants' divergent visions for and relationships with the natural world, both industries also brought widespread environmental changes that instigated disputes over the best way to develop the local coastline. Thus, transforming Monterey into "one of the leading cities on the Pacific Coast" had social and environmental ramifications that were absent from boosters' polished and emphatic rhetoric.[6]

"THE COST OF THE SOJOURN IS WELL WITHIN THEIR MEANS"

By the early twentieth century, the Pacific Improvement Company had learned how to alter and enhance nature to attract specific people—namely, white elites. Now it decided to entice visitors of wide financial means by applying its strategy to other parts of the coastline. The impetus for the company's expanded approach likely stemmed, in part, from the Hotel Del Monte's declining profits. While the hotel made over $46,000 and $41,000 in 1901 and 1902, respectively, it reported losses of almost $7,000 to $20,000 each year between 1908 and 1912.[7] Increased competition accounted for some of these financial troubles. When the hotel first opened, general manager A. D. Shepard noted, "it was the only resort in California; today there is a score of first-class places drawing upon the public demand. . . . It is this competition of new resorts that has done much to prevent the Del Monte patronage increasing proportionately with [the] wealth of the country."[8]

Just as hotel profits began to nosedive, the Pacific Improvement Company unveiled its plans for an exclusive resort, Pebble Beach, on a protected cove along the Seventeen Mile Drive. Rather than providing transient housing, the resort was to be a "city of homes" composed of private villa lots sold to individual owners. To create "a neighborhood of attractive homes in ample grounds," it prohibited the subdivision of homesites for five years after purchase, required owners to spend at least fifteen hundred dollars to build their homes, and mandated that residences be situated at least fifteen feet from adjoining property boundaries. The resort also banned town sites and businesses. As the *Monterey Daily Cypress* reported, "The aim of the company will be to make Pebble Beach one of the most fashionable as well as the prettiest resorts on the coast. . . . an effort will be made to attract wealthy people there."[9]

Although designed to supplement it, Pebble Beach mirrored the Hotel Del Monte. It resembled a larger, more decentralized hotel. Like the hotel, Pebble Beach took advantage of its natural setting to appeal to the social elite. The roads and homesites "carefully considered" the topography of the area, and the entire frontage between the Seventeen Mile Drive and the ocean was a reserve to ensure coastal access.[10] The resort also saved the surrounding acreage known as the Del Monte Forest, which according to the *Monterey American*, "has been without use. It is now being put to the right use. The division into large villa tracts will preserve the splendid forest which surrounds."[11] The development of Pebble Beach as an elite residential community seemed to improve the land without destroying its natural allure.

Pebble Beach also provided privacy, material luxuries, and modern conveniences—physical markers of social status emblazoned on the new landscape. "Nowadays one wants a home in the forest within the sight of the sea and amid rustic scenes, if possible, but withal the conveniences of life must not be lacking," claimed one promotional brochure. Pebble Beach provided such comforts with an electric omnibus transportation service and hookups for water, electricity, and sanitation. In addition, the Pacific Improvement Company built the Pebble Beach Lodge, a homey clubhouse that served as the "nucleus" of the resort and provided entertainment and fine dining. People could become part of this community by purchasing sites of at least one-half acre up to twenty acres, at a cost of five hundred to twenty-five hundred dollars per acre. Many prominent businessmen, including Louis Hill of the Great Northern Railway, came on board.[12]

As Pebble Beach became a resort for an exclusive clientele, the Hotel Del Monte began to slide down the social ladder. The Pacific Improvement Company marketed prime real estate to the wealthy, but it marketed the proximity to wealth to the less affluent. According to A. D.

Shepard, Del Monte was no longer "an exclusive place"; it enjoyed "a class of traffic that were formerly afraid of the place, and, at the same time, it has not lessened the former line of patronage." In other words, the middle and upper classes mingled at the hotel. Thus, he assured the "plain people" that "they will be welcome at Del Monte, and that [the] cost of the sojourn is well within their means." Those still unable to afford the Hotel Del Monte could book a room at the Pacific Grove Hotel, which had opened in 1886 and charged one-half of Del Monte's rates. "This arrangement duly provides for all classes," Shepard concluded.[13]

Auto camping was another affordable option for tourists who enjoyed even closer contact with nature. The company began plans for the Del Monte Forest Camp in the late 1910s, choosing a forested spot in Pacific Grove that could accommodate seventy-five vehicles. When the camp opened, it charged a nominal one dollar per day for "spacious, secluded campsites" with running water, firewood, and "sanitary arrangements." Campers had to provide their own food, utensils, and equipment, but these expenses could be "as much or as little as you please." A promotional brochure concluded, "Load your outfit onto your car, pile in with the family and run down to the coast. . . . It is unlikely you could spend as delightful vacation or week-end outings for so little expense as at Del Monte Forest Camp."[14]

By the 1920s, auto camps like Del Monte were popular among both middle-class vacationers and those of more modest means. Initially, automobile ownership was a luxury reserved for the wealthy; the Hotel Del Monte even hosted the Automobile Club of California's first tournaments in 1903 and 1904, complete with races and trophies for the fastest vehicles.[15] When the Model T began to roll off the Ford Motor Company's assembly lines in 1914, the automobile became increasingly affordable and, in the 1920s, represented "a new democratization of vacation travel." Indeed, cars opened up more travel options to a wider segment of the population and ensured that tourist destinations no longer catered solely to elite tastes.[16] For middle-class and even some affluent vacationers, auto camping offered adventure, invigorating outdoor living, and an escape from "the boredom and restraints of Victorian resorts." For those with limited financial resources, auto camping also provided an inexpensive vacation option.[17]

The Pacific Improvement Company's various accommodations reflected both the growing number of Americans who started to take vacations in the early twentieth century and the class divisions within tourism. For many middle-class men and women, taking a vacation was central to their growing participation in mass consumer culture; buying a car both reinforced their status as consumers and facilitated their leisure trips. At the same time, reformers began to advocate vacations for the working class, and people of various social backgrounds soon "came to harbor the reasonable expectation of enjoying the benefits of at least an occasional short summer vacation."[18] Thus, a journey to the Monterey Peninsula or any other destination was no longer regarded as an elite privilege. Tourists of various class backgrounds toured the coastline and likely rubbed shoulders in the process. However, their lodging distinguished them. The wealthiest tourists clearly stood out from the middling crowds. Owning a home in exclusive Pebble Beach carried a certain cachet that visiting the Del Monte Forest Camp, the Pacific Grove Hotel, or even the Hotel Del Monte simply did not possess.

The Pacific Improvement Company was not satisfied to attract new tourists for just short-term stays; selling property was a top priority. To turn upwardly mobile tourists into home buyers, the company rented out cottages in Pacific Grove near the Del Monte Forest Camp and gave guests the option to buy these cheaper, smaller parcels.[19] The company also used the Seventeen Mile Drive as a billboard to sell its more expensive land. The entire route was choreographed with scripted stops, where drivers told passengers about lots for sale.[20] H. R. Warner, Hotel Del Monte manager, insisted that drivers understand "how important it is for the best interests of our property that they explain to people as much as they can about the extent of the Company's holdings that they pass through, and of their future plans for the improvement and sale of that property."[21] Samuel Morse, who replaced A. D. Shepard as general manager in 1915, explained that "the wealthier class of people" who bought this property first learned about it during their hotel stays.[22] Ideally, a short visit to the hotel, coupled with an auto tour, would lead to a permanent investment.

Such advertising worked only for those physically present in Monterey. For those who were unfamiliar with the attractions of Monterey, the Pacific Improvement Company devised a statewide advertising campaign. It featured a stereopticon show, "Fairyland of the Pacific," which displayed colored images of the area on a curtain. D. E. Bernays traveled to twenty-seven predominantly inland California cities—including Fairfield, Napa,

Santa Rosa, Petaluma, Bakersfield, Fresno, Merced, Modesto, and Stockton—to present the images and discuss the Hotel Del Monte, the Seventeen Mile Drive, and other tourist destinations on the Monterey Peninsula. In each town, he also recruited a real estate agent who had sole authority to sell Pacific Grove lots to local residents. James King Steele, who was in charge of the company's advertising department, proclaimed Bernays's work a great success.[23]

While the rash of Pacific Improvement Company construction and advertising provided vacations and summer homes for many, it provided jobs for others. To clear wood and brush, the company often enlisted the services of Onojiro Uchida, who immigrated to San Francisco from Japan in 1905 and started a labor contracting business on the Monterey Peninsula in 1906. Many Japanese pursued this work before and after the salmon season, which usually ran from March until the end of July.[24] The Japanese, however, would not be permitted to own or live on the land they worked. Anti-Japanese sentiment in the United States culminated with the 1907 Gentlemen's Agreement, which banned the immigration of Japanese laborers. The California legislature passed an alien land law in 1913, prohibiting the Japanese from land ownership and denying them its political and economic advantages and social prestige.[25] As Dorothee Kocks argues, "It should never be forgotten that land's legerdemain has benefited certain privileged interest groups."[26]

The Pacific Improvement Company had clear ideas of how and for whom its property should be developed. Its inclinations were further evident in the redevelopment of Point Alones. After the Chinese expulsion, the company donated the entire point to the University of California. University President Benjamin Wheeler hoped to build "University Park" on the property but backed out due to a lack of funding.[27] When Stanford University expressed an interest in relocating its marine station there, Samuel Morse devised a plan in which Stanford received a less valuable portion of Point Alones in exchange for the existing site of the Hopkins facility at Lover's Point. This deal left the Pacific Improvement Company with the more valuable land fronting the railroad and a small protected bay.[28] With the board of directors' approval, Stanford opened the new Hopkins Marine Station in 1917, slightly west of the former Chinese village. The sale virtually eliminated the possibility that immigrant fishermen could resettle there.

While the Pacific Improvement Company could develop its property to include and exclude certain people, it could not so easily control nature. Natural events deprived the company of precious guests and profits and compromised its financial status. First, the San Francisco earthquake and fire of March 1906 and then unseasonably cold and wet weather in 1907 reduced patronage. Storms caused a tunnel on the Los Angeles–Del Monte railroad line to cave in, blocking traffic from Southern California for three or four weeks, just at the peak of spring business.[29] Without railroad access, Southern Californians could easily visit an oceanside resort in Santa Monica, Santa Barbara, or San Diego instead of Monterey.

The Del Monte Forest also proved to be a difficult landscape to control. The Pacific Improvement Company's desire to create scenic nature, coupled with private property rights, compromised its ability to manage the forest as scientists advised. After a devastating fire in 1901, pine mistletoe and bark-boring beetles, such as the pine-engraver and red turpentine beetles and the Monterey pine weevil, began to invade the forest; the dead, damaged, and downed trees provided a perfect breeding ground for these parasites.[30] Eliminating these pests meant treating the entire forest, which now encompassed several separate parcels of private property. However, there was no guarantee that multiple parties with diverse interests would agree to a singular management plan.

The company's first plan of attack was to call on Professor George A. Coleman of the University of California to conduct a study of the Del Monte Forest's Monterey pine. Coleman found that 10 percent of the trees over and 20 percent of the trees under six inches in diameter were injured by several species of beetles and parasitic plants. To create a healthy forest more resistant to future attacks, he experimented with applications of hydrocyanic acid gas, carbon bisulfide, and kerosene. He also cut out roughly fifteen thousand cords of diseased timber.[31] Coleman's work for the Pacific Improvement Company was not unusual. Before American foresters found their niche in the public lands and corporate forests, they worked in smaller private reserves.[32] Like other Progressive-era natural resource managers, they applied scientific principles and emphasized efficiency and large-scale, long-term conservation policies. Following in the footsteps of Gifford Pinchot, chief of the United States Forest Service under President Theodore Roosevelt and one of the leaders of the Progressive conservation movement, they adopted sustained-yield principles, which called for annual cutting and the reduction of fire and disease to maintain steady production and to provide timber for the "greatest good" in perpetuity.[33]

The Pacific Improvement Company, however, was far more interested in maintaining an aesthetically pleasing forest for Pebble Beach residents than in procuring a fixed supply of timber.[34] To assist in this endeavor, the University of California's Division of Forestry returned to the Del Monte Forest in 1915. According to Professor Donald Bruce, the company wanted to "manage the forest in a manner which is at once the most scientific and which will preserve to the utmost the scenic beauties for which the region is famous."[35] Professor David T. Mason enlisted his graduate student Duncan Dunning, who recognized that the forest's primary value derived from its "aesthetic properties." "The object of management, therefore, is, first to maintain the forest in the best possible condition, from the standpoint of appearances, especially in the immediate vicinity of drives and residence sections," he noted. He subdivided the 5,638-acre forest by site quality and twenty-year age classes and developed a separate cutting plan for each class. His logic was to leave trees along the drives, where motorists would appreciate the greenery, while cutting older trees that were hidden from public view. Dunning, moreover, discouraged planting seedlings because he assumed that open land would be used for golf links.[36]

While Dunning was mindful of the Pacific Improvement Company's aesthetic needs, private property owners precluded the implementation of this plan. As the company sold off villa sites, foresters worried that a growing number of property owners would not see the importance of comprehensive management. To address the pest problems effectively, the cooperation of all property holders was imperative. Mason explained, "It is evident that the great value and beauty of your land is due quite largely to the forests now existing. It would be very unfortunate if large tracts were sold from it and were allowed to degenerate through improper forest management." He suggested that the company employ a forester and even argued that scientific management could be yet another tourist attraction of great interest to visitors.[37]

It is unclear if the Pacific Improvement Company implemented Dunning's plan, but his strategy illustrates the difficulties of addressing the often-conflicting objectives of scientists, developers, and private property owners. The forest was not solely a natural ecosystem consisting of trees, fungi, and other flora and fauna. Divided into parcels of property, the forest was also a social system in which owning land became a marker of upper-class standing. Compromising owners' rights to change their land as they saw fit undermined the status associated with land ownership. Scientists adapted to the company's desire to create a beautiful forest, but they insisted that the forest could not be preserved if individual property owners did not comply with their plans.

Pests in the Del Monte Forest, however, were relatively small worries for the Pacific Improvement Company. Despite considerable investments in its Monterey operations, the company decided to liquidate its vast holdings and brought Samuel Morse on board in 1915 to complete the task. The job was formidable. In addition to the Monterey Peninsula property, Morse had to liquidate real estate in seventy-six town sites, fifteen ranches, industrial property in Alameda, California, plus Louisiana, and a mine in Washington State.[38] The Hotel Del Monte and Pebble Beach were small parts of a far-flung corporate network of nature and property.

Morse quickly discovered the financial liabilities of the Monterey Peninsula property. He explained that the best lots and most attractive property had already been sold or lacked commercial value and that the hotel was over thirty years old and continued to sustain losses. He appraised the property for one million dollars, well below its book value of four million dollars. Morse's low estimate may have been motivated by self-interest, as he thought the area had great potential.[39] He informed the Pacific Improvement Company board of directors of his desire to buy the property and approached Herbert Fleishhacker, a San Francisco banker, who loaned him the money and became his partner. In 1919 they formed the Del Monte Properties Company and finalized the purchase for a little over $1.3 million.[40]

Morse acquired some of the most beautiful land on the Monterey Peninsula, not to mention hotels, golf courses, home lots, scenic drives, and a clientele that included many wealthy Americans. But there was more to this property than met the eye; it was embedded with complex social arrangements and environmental problems. A class hierarchy of tourists developed along Monterey's shores, while the Del Monte Forest was plagued with pests and disease. The Pacific Improvement Company's efforts to develop the coastline for a growing number of tourists conflicted with an unpredictable natural world and the contending visions of new property owners. These predicaments all came with the price of purchase.

As tourist facilities spread throughout the peninsula, Monterey's first canneries began to pop up along the waterfront. Unlike earlier Italian and Chinese fishermen who caught and sold a diverse catch of fish and shellfish, cannery owners focused their efforts on local salmon and sardine runs. To process these species for expanding markets, they developed new technology and recruited a large pool of immigrant labor. Output increased, but mechanized fish plants also ushered in an industrial era that brought more pollution to the coastline, fundamentally altered human relations with the natural world, and reconfigured the social dynamics of the fisheries.

By granting Monterey ownership of the waterfront, the State of California stimulated this industrial development. In 1868 it conferred title to a depth of twenty feet at low tide and permitted the leasing of the waterfront for up to ten years. The state amended the act in 1903 to allow Monterey to sign leases of up to fifty years, provided that no more than three hundred feet was occupied by one person or group. Another amendment in 1919 extended the title to sixty feet at low tide.[41] Essentially, Monterey came to own a shifting combination of land and water. Because of changing tides, what was land one part of the day was submerged under water several hours later. But this space was ideal for facilities—like fish canneries—that needed both a land-based headquarters and easy access to the ocean.[42]

During the early twentieth century, city officials deemed fisheries development as advantageous to the public good and leased the waterfront accordingly. San Franciscan H. R. Robbins became the first businessman to mark out a portion of the waterfront to build a fish cannery. He chose roughly two hundred feet of waterfront next to Fisherman's Wharf, east of Point Alones and McAbee Beach, and opened his cannery in 1901 to can, smoke, and dry salmon, sardines, and other fish. Using presses and cookers, Robbins also reduced fish offal, the fish heads and entrails that were by-products of the canning process, into oil and fertilizer. He then sold the fertilizer to sugar beet farmers in the nearby Salinas and Pajaro Valleys. Despite Robbins's efforts to make full use of his fish supply, the cannery remained unprofitable and inefficient. Because he relied on hand labor and had limited technology at his disposal, he lost money when fishermen delivered more fish than his workers and equipment could process.[43]

The partial answer to these problems appeared in Frank E. Booth of the Sacramento River Packers' Association. Before his arrival, one newspaper article explained, "the fish were there, but they needed exploitation."[44] Booth addressed that problem in short order. While his first attempt to can Monterey salmon in 1896 was short-lived, he returned in 1902 to open the Monterey Packing Company, close to Fisherman's Wharf. Initially focused on salmon, the plant soon added sardines to the production line. Processing these two species allowed the cannery to operate and turn profits for most of the year, since the sardine season began in the fall, just as the salmon season ended. Salmon was processed through a mild curing method in which the fish was chilled, salted, and packed in brine. Sardines were sealed and cooked in metal cans.[45] When a fire in 1903 destroyed Booth's cannery, he bought Robbins's ailing operation, investing over ten thousand dollars and doubling the size of the plant.[46]

Robbins and Booth capitalized both on the rich supply of marine life in Monterey Bay and on the growing markets for canned sardines. Several firms in Southern California had begun to can sardines in the 1890s and found ready markets in Chicago, Boston, New York, and other East Coast cities. Still, domestic demand fluctuated because many Americans preferred the French variety of sardines.[47] But in 1902 Robert Dollar, a San Francisco merchant, traveled to Asia, where he successfully marketed California sardines. Canneries began selling their products all over Asia as well as Cuba and parts of Europe. Foreign markets eventually absorbed much of the state's sardine supply.[48]

Other canners soon joined Booth on the waterfront to take advantage of this heightened demand. In March 1902, Otosaburo Noda, one of the first Japanese immigrants to settle in the Monterey area, and Henry Malpas joined forces to open the Monterey Fishing and Canning Company. Located on Ocean View Avenue, this cannery specialized in processing both abalone and salmon. Noda and Malpas were in business for only a short time before selling their cannery to James Madison (Booth's former superintendent), Benjamin Senderman, and Joseph R. Nichols, who together formed the Pacific Fish Company in 1908. The Pacific Fish Company and Booth's Monterey Packing Company dominated the local fish canning industry until World War I.[49]

Booth believed that mass production was the only way to compete with cheaper foreign brands of canned fish, but, like Robbins, he relied entirely on hand labor during the first few years of his Monterey operation. He had over seventy-five employees who hoisted the fish from the boats to the wharf by hand and carried them in wicker baskets to the cannery. They then cut the heads and tails off the sardines and placed them in the sun to dry. After such drying, they dropped the fish into boiling oil, hand-packed them into oval cans, and hand-soldered the cans shut. With this labor-intensive process, Booth packed an average of 166 cases of sardines (48 one-pound cans per case) each day during the peak of the sardine run.[50]

Fish processing became vastly more efficient with the arrival of Knut Hovden. Born in Norway, Hovden attended the National Fisheries College in Bergen and subsequently worked in Liverpool and other seaports as a fisheries engineer and technician. He immigrated to the United States in 1904 and met Alfred Booth, Frank Booth's uncle, at the offices of the Booth Fisheries Corporation in Chicago. The elder Booth offered him a job, but Hovden continued west, where he started a salmon smokehouse on the banks of the Columbia River in Kalama, Washington. After a rough season in the Northwest, Hovden traveled to San Francisco and met with Frank Booth, who also offered him a job.[51]

After accepting Frank Booth's offer, Hovden modernized California's sardine industry. His innovations pervaded every stage of the canning process, from live fish to tin of sardines. To stabilize the fish supply, he installed holding ponds, or hoppers, to store excess sardines. He introduced the purse-bottom brailer, which helped workers hoist the catch from the boats to the cannery. Hovden also developed the mechanical dryer, eliminating the need to air-dry the sardines, and the mechanical cooker, which used a chain-driven conveyor to move the fish through the vats of frying oil for a set amount of time. And in 1910 he introduced two soldering machines to seal the lids on the cans. By 1913 Hovden also began experimenting with a sardine-cutting machine, which he "perfected" in 1918.[52] These labor-saving devices brought immediate results. The mechanical dryer boosted production to fifteen hundred cases daily, while the two soldering machines expanded output from sixty to seventy cans a minute, with only a fraction of the labor.[53]

New technology, however, could not completely eliminate the need for human labor. Monterey's cannery workers were diverse in terms of race, national origin, and gender. Out of roughly seven hundred cannery workers in 1920, 30 percent were women. Fifty percent of all workers were American-born, while the other half consisted of people from China, Japan, Spain, Italy, Mexico, Canada, and other European nations.[54] Workers did not mingle indiscriminately in the canneries, as different social groups performed distinct tasks. Chinese, Japanese, and Spanish workers were often cutters. A common job for Asian cannery workers until the advent of fish cutting machines, this skilled position entailed chopping the heads and tails off the fish. Most women were packers; they placed the fish into tins before the tins were sealed and cooked. White men filled many of the supervisory positions, such as foremen and engineers, and the year-round jobs performing general maintenance or working in the warehouse.[55] While there was no clear racial divide, particularly given southern Europeans' struggle to attain whiteness, the canneries displayed some characteristics of a dual labor system, common in the extractive industries of the West, in which native-born whites and Europeans typically occupied the upper echelon of jobs, while nonwhites were in the bottom tier and had limited occupational mobility.[56]

Even with new technology and a secure workforce, Booth was not satisfied and wanted to increase output by expanding his cannery out onto the tidelands. To double the size of his cannery, the Monterey Board of Trustees granted him a twenty-five-year lease on a 175-foot waterfront parcel in February 1910.[57] The new cannery design both increased and expedited production. Booth put up a new building to cook and dry the fish at the northern end of the building and extended the cannery floor 40 feet over the water. He also enlarged the wharf, built a new warehouse, and put the cleaning room on the same level as the rest of the cannery so that the fish could be run directly to the cooking room. The *Monterey Daily Cypress* proclaimed that the new facility was "the best equipped cannery on the Pacific Coast," capable of processing eighty to one hundred tons of sardines each day.[58]

The impact of cannery technology and cannery labor extended out to the ocean. Because the canneries could process more fish, they demanded that fishermen bring in bigger catches than their equipment was initially capable of providing. In the early twentieth century, Monterey's fishing fleet used lateen sailboats and the chinchola net, gear imported from the Mediterranean fisheries. Fishermen set the chinchola nets close to shore and then hauled them onto the beach by hand. They also placed gill nets where they thought sardines may pass, but the catch varied widely from day to day, and the entrapped fish were often too damaged to be canned.[59]

Sardine fishermen subsequently adopted the purse seine net—the same net used by Chinese squid and other Pacific Coast fishermen.[60] While this net brought in a consistent supply of undamaged sardines, it was heavy and slow to operate, often allowing fish to dive under the mesh and escape before the fishermen trapped them.[61]

Pietro Ferrante, a Sicilian fisherman who worked for Booth, believed that the lampara net, a net he had used in Sicily, could solve these problems. Booth heeded his suggestion and sent away for a lampara net from Tangiers. The new net immediately brought in impressive amounts of fish. In 1904 Booth's sardine fishermen used purse seines and gill nets to catch two hundred thousand pounds of sardines, worth $5,130. With the lampara net, fishermen landed over four million pounds of sardines in one season, worth roughly $27,000. As a result, the lampara replaced the purse seine in Monterey's sardine fishery by 1913.[62]

The key to this success lay in the lampara's ease of operation. The upper edge of the net was secured to a line of cork floats, while the lower edge was weighted down with lead strung on a rope. The bag was an area of fine webbing, with the wings off to the side tapering toward the ends of the net. When fishermen went out to sea at night in their launch and spotted a school of fish, indicated by a phosphorescent glow lit by the sardines' agitation of certain plankton, they secured the right wing to a buoy. The launch began to circle the school, letting the net out to the left and rear. After reaching the center of the net, the fishermen put the entire bag over the side. The launch continued to circle until they recovered the buoy at the other end of the net. They then hauled the net, now resembling a fence around the fish, by pulling the cork line, lead line, and webbing at the same time. This action drew the lower part of the bag down toward the boat and underneath the fish, preventing them from swimming away. As the fishermen continued to draw in the webbing and cork line, other crew members brought a separate lighter to the side of the bag and began brailing—or scooping—the fish aboard. The lampara's lightweight twine also made it faster to operate than the purse seine.[63]

Equally as important as the lampara net was the introduction of motorized fishing vessels. By the 1910s, most boats were equipped with gasoline-powered engines, replacing the sail-powered boats of the late nineteenth and early twentieth centuries. A new type of Italian boat, the "Monterey clipper," also redesigned the bulwarks and bow to withstand heavy seas. These new boats meant that fishermen were not "at the mercy of the ever-changing wind," and they could make trips to more distant fishing grounds.[64]

Southern European and East Asian immigrants put this equipment to work on Monterey Bay. Italians, primarily from Sicily, dominated sardine fishing, as Booth and Ferrante recruited many Italians from company headquarters in Black Diamond (present-day Pittsburg), California, to supply fish for the burgeoning operations in Monterey. Of Monterey's roughly 350 fishermen in 1920, about half were of Italian origin. The Japanese were the second-largest group of fishermen after the Italians, comprising nearly 25 percent of the fishing labor force in 1920; they found their niche in the salmon fishery and operated 125 of 180 salmon boats in Monterey in 1907. Immigrants from Spain accounted for another 12 percent of local fishermen. Eighty-three percent of Monterey fishermen were resident aliens, and over 85 percent of the immigrant fishermen had arrived after 1900.[65] In other words, most fishermen were noncitizens and recent arrivals to the United States.

While the immigrant fishermen may have seemed like independent laborers who took to the sea at their own discretion, they were really contract workers employed by the canneries. During the late nineteenth century, Chinese, Italian, and Portuguese fishermen preserved a great deal of autonomy when it came to catching, shipping, and marketing their fish. The canneries, however, gradually came to control all stages of output and even owned fishing gear and some boats.[66] Immigrant fishermen's labor was simply one cog in the wheel of production.

Because immigrant fishermen were in a precarious position, they began to form protective organizations to collectively negotiate the terms of their labor. The Japanese led the way, forming the Japanese Fishermen's Association in 1907. Before the start of each season, representatives met with the canneries to settle on a price for salmon.[67] In 1908 they secured a raise from 3.25 to 3.6 cents per pound, 3.5 cents of which went directly to the fishermen and 0.1 cent to the association to be used in case of illness or to replace damaged boats.[68] Three Italian fishermen subsequently established the Monterey Bay Sardine and Squid Union in 1914, while the Monterey Fishermen's Association emerged in 1915. The latter group was comprised primarily of salmon fishermen, both "American and foreign."[69] Presumably, there were few Japanese in its ranks since they had their own organization.

The growing importance of the fishing industry also prompted the Japanese and Italian communities to establish fisheries-related businesses and services. The Japanese clustered around Washington Street in downtown Monterey. There, boardinghouses, such as the Higashi Restaurant and Rooming House, provided room and board to single itinerant workers, some of whom followed the California agricultural and fish seasons in search of work. In addition to his labor contracting business, Onojiro Uchida opened a general store in Monterey, as did Rokumatsu Ono, to stock supplies for Japanese fishermen. Unosuke Higashi, in partnership with Ikutaro Takigawa, established a wholesale fish dealership on Fisherman's Wharf.[70] Italians also operated a variety of maritime businesses, including a ship chandlery and a fishing supplies and machine shop.[71]

As these businesses suggested, fishermen remained divided along racial and ethnic lines, despite occasions when they had cause to unite. For instance, an Italian-Japanese alliance in 1915 proved short-lived. While the Japanese Fishermen's Association supported the Monterey Fishermen's Association's efforts to negotiate a price of four cents per pound for salmon, Japanese fishermen replaced striking Italian fishermen two years later.[72] Social divisions even escalated into overt confrontations. In 1908 a "miscreant" cut nets hung near the pier; "fish catchers of some other nationality" were possibly to blame because only certain nets were targeted.[73] Similarly, in 1915, for unclear motives, six Italian fishermen— Guiseppe Passanessi, Giachino Ferrante, Natale Pizzimento, Salvatore Russo, Vincente Ferrante, and Salvatore Catania—allegedly towed Wallace Mathers to the wharf and warned him that he was fishing "at his own risk."[74] With the growth of the fisheries, some fishermen went to great measures to remain a step ahead of their competition.

To discredit Chinese and Japanese fishermen, local white fishermen and non-fishermen alike bombarded them with unrelenting criticism. One reporter claimed that Japanese fishermen bruised fish, whereas "white fishermen" kept fish in "better condition."[75] Chinese and Japanese fishermen also purportedly used "small hooks and nets with small mesh" to destroy large quantities of immature fish.[76] Not only were they depicted as destructive, but others claimed that they failed to contribute to the local economy. When Booth hired solely "white fishermen" in 1910, the *Monterey Daily Cypress* celebrated, as they "will spend their money freer among the merchants than the Japanese or Chinese fishermen."[77] Benjamin Senderman of the Pacific Fish Company concurred. He preferred white workers to Chinese workers because the former spent their wages "in the trade of the town and keep it all at home."[78] These critics likely faulted the Chinese and Japanese for patronizing their own businesses, rather than the stores owned by other Montereyans.

The Sicilians were not immune from criticism and also became the target of nativist attacks because of the lampara net. The controversy seemed to revolve around the net's destructiveness, but the debate actually stemmed from tensions between immigrant fishermen who worked for the canneries and other fishermen who used gill nets and defined themselves as "native" and "local." The latter group came to resent the dominance of immigrant fishermen and the success of the lampara net; in time-worn nativist rhetoric, they condemned the immigrant menace and circulated a petition in 1912, asking the California legislature to declare lampara nets illegal. They claimed that the net was destructive and that, by extension, the men who used this gear, primarily Sicilians, were destructive as well.[79] This strategy was an attempt to eliminate their immigrant competition and dominate the ocean commons. But the question of proper equipment also reflected their unease with the growth of the canneries and their fear of losing control over their labor and livelihood.

In response, a Booth employee circulated a counter-petition, which over three hundred local businessmen and residents signed, while Knut Hovden submitted an editorial to one of the local newspapers in support of immigrant labor and the lampara net. According to Hovden, the "local fishermen" were lazy and "mostly find it their pleasure and sacred duty to polish the cement seats around the custom house, talking about old times and how fish used to swim up on the beach by itself." Immigrant Japanese and Sicilian fishermen, on the other hand, performed legitimate "hard labor." He described the local fishermen as "small men" with "small ideas" and "small methods," unwilling to try new techniques. Their petition was "a plain case of having a big industry suffering and two hundred people deprived of their employment by the egotistic, partist, narrow-minded fishing interests of a handful of 'local fishermen' and a few misinformed well-meaning supporters."[80]

One of these "local fishermen" responded with an anonymous editorial dripping with racialized disdain for immigrant fishermen and their gear. When they went out to sea, he noted, "the crew of voluble Italians or Japs get ready for the slaughter." He continued: "Nothing can escape the insatiable maw of the murderous Lompara [sic]. Thousands, aye, millions of immature fish are destroyed." These juvenile fish, in turn, did not grow to become "a source of food and revenue to our population." He also speculated that the taking of fish in the lampara net reduced the food supply of Monterey Bay's migratory species, such as salmon, sea bass, and barracuda, and endangered their populations. The local fisherman concluded by dispelling the argument that the canneries would go out of business without the lampara: "Ask any native fisherman, and he will show you how manifestly ridiculous this assertion is."[81]

The ways in which Hovden and the anonymous local fisherman interpreted the sardine population reflected very different visions for the fishery and Monterey society. For Hovden, the sardines in Monterey Bay were part of a vast population stretching from "the Chilean coast to Australia, from the islands of Japan to California." He also maintained that the fish processed by the canneries represented a small percentage of the total number of sardines consumed by other marine life, such as salmon, hake, rockfish, and sea lions. With the help of technology like the lampara net, this immense sardine supply could support extensive industrial operations. And hardworking, enterprising immigrants had proved themselves most deserving of this bounty, Hovden implied. The anonymous fisherman, on the other hand, saw the sardine fishery as local and finite. In his estimation, the sardine fishery should not be overextended to support a growing number of alien Sicilian and Japanese fishermen, at the expense of native fishermen's livelihoods.[82]

The debate over the lampara continued into the following year, when the state legislature introduced a bill to ban the net in Monterey Bay. The California Fish and Game Commission decided to gather more information, sending fisheries scientist Norman Bishop (N. B.) Scofield to Monterey. Scofield was perceptive and noticed that the lampara's opponents were fishermen who were not employed by the canneries and criticized the rapacity of the new net and its users. They used gill nets and staunchly defended this gear, arguing that they caught sufficient amounts of mature sardines without bruising or crushing them. But gill netters were at a severe disadvantage because their nets did not have the capacity of the lampara. Moreover, the canneries, with some exceptions, supplied most of their fishermen with nets, saving them a major expense. Scofield concluded, "Other fishing is not so good and they have difficulty in making a living. They would like an equal chance with the others in taking sardines."[83]

Scofield was clearly aware of the social conflicts behind the lampara controversy, but he insisted that he needed more accurate information in order to regulate the matter properly. "There are no data as to the amount of fish they capture or per cent of waste," he explained. In the end, he treated the problem primarily as a technical issue that could not be addressed until he had precise statistics. Given the emphasis on scientific expertise during the Progressive era, Scofield's vacillating conclusion was not surprising. The California Fish and Game Commission heeded his advice and came out in favor of the lampara unless future investigations proved its destructiveness. The California legislature eventually defeated the bill.[84]

While the "local fishermen" had legitimate reasons to be worried about the additional pressure on the sardine stocks that followed the lampara's introduction, their ecological concerns were inseparable from their animus toward the immigrant fishermen. As they descended on Monterey and contributed to the industrialization of the fisheries, their upward mobility, it seemed, came at the expense of local fishermen's financial security. To regain control over the coastline, the local fishermen formed an alliance based on their "native" status and their use of gill nets, then marked the lampara net—and the fishermen who used it—as harmful to the marine ecosystem. They also defined the lampara fishermen as outsiders; they were noncitizen aliens, not "locals" who should reap the profits from Monterey Bay's resources.[85]

This strategy was one of the few ways the local fishermen could try to resist the power of the canneries and reassert their small-scale independent fishing operations. Given limited understanding of and data on the sardine fishery at this time, however, whatever real insight they possessed about the lampara's potential environmental repercussions appeared as conjecture, refracted through nativist resentment. This ethnically and racially charged rhetoric alone could not convince the California Fish and Game Commission to ban the net. The locals were also ineffective because the sardine industry was becoming central to the Monterey economy, and Sicilian fishermen, able to bring in large hauls of fish, garnered the support of the canneries and business leaders to successfully resist these attacks.

Other environmental problems, such as pollution, could not be blamed entirely on immigrants. Initially, canners just dumped their refuse into the bay, contaminating the beaches and angering the groups who owned or used this space. Canners then hired barges to load their waste and empty it at sea at a cost of up to three dollars per ton. But city officials feared that residual waste, swept back by the tides, would pollute the coast and endanger human health. The Pacific Improvement Company echoed the city's reservations. In 1906 general manager A. D. Shepard asked general agent J. P. Pryor to speak with the canners and public officials. He wanted the barges to travel even farther to dump the offal, "where the birds can eat it and none will drift ashore."[86]

The City of Monterey tried to regulate this complicated problem by passing an ordinance in 1907 that made it unlawful to discharge sewage, garbage, refuse, or waste material into or upon Monterey Bay or within city limits.[87] The city wanted to ensure the cleanliness of the bay, in part, because pollution at sea could become pollution on land. But its desire to keep the water and beaches clean for residents and tourists was at cross-purposes with its desire to encourage industrial development along the waterfront. Many residents implored the city to enforce its laws because visitors "surely will not have a very good impression of Monterey unless the beach is cleaned up."[88] However, boosters also wanted to develop the industrial potential of the coastline and bay. It was becoming increasingly difficult to reconcile or separate the fisheries and tourism.

The Chinese saw pollution problems as a way to reenter the fisheries. They opened a plant at McAbee Beach to reduce fish offal into oil and fertilizer. By solving the waste dilemma, they could simultaneously help the canneries, prevent pollution, and reestablish their presence in the Monterey fishing industry. In August 1909, they also began construction on a cannery and wharf so that they could also ship edible fish products to Asia and various Chinatowns in the United States. The Chinese were hopeful that the plant would attract more Chinese to McAbee Beach, revitalizing the settlement and helping it become "larger and more prosperous than before it was burned on China Point [Point Alones]."[89]

But like the canneries, the Chinese could not contain or control their industrial processes. Monterey residents complained that the odors from the fertilizer plant were offensive and harmful, just as in the squid battles a few years earlier. In December 1909, W. F. Allen and eight other residents presented a petition to the Monterey Board of Trustees, declaring that the smells of drying fertilizer were "worse than a slaughter house." The trustees referred the complaint to the board of health. Although the board expressed some doubt that odors were injurious to human health, there was consensus that "the fertilizer will have to go if it continues to be offensive."[90] Many Montereyans likely fell victim to the waste and fumes that originated from the fish processing plants, as they increasingly could not isolate themselves from the industrialization of the fisheries. Nonetheless, they did not accept the odors without question or hesitate to associate the Chinese with disease and filth to discredit them once again.

Undeterred by or unaware of these complaints, Booth also took an interest in reducing fish waste after moving to his expanded facilities. Reduction was appealing because it was profitable and required little labor. Workers collected fish offal in bins, where it moved via bucket conveyer and passed through an agitating cooker, a revolving cylinder heated by steam. Once the fish were cooked, presses removed the liquid, which was conveyed to settling tanks to separate oil from water. The solid material went to the wet meal disintegrator for pulverization. After drying, grinders sized the meal before curing and sacking. Booth got started by installing a dryer in 1912, and he operated a floating reduction unit the following year, equipping a lime-kiln barge with a cooker, dryer, and hydraulic press and anchoring it at sea.[91] As the canneries realized the profits available in reduction, they stopped giving their waste to the Chinese, who eventually went out of business.[92]

Reduction facilities would become central to the sardine industry in later years, but it was canned sardines that gave Monterey a boost in the short term. With the outbreak of World War I in 1914, France halted the export of its foodstuffs to feed its army, leaving Americans without French or other European sardines. At the same time, foreign troops demanded more food, while shortages in the United States encouraged Americans to eat canned fish rather than fresh meat. New entrepreneurs took advantage of this boom.[93] Knut Hovden left his position at Booth's cannery in 1916 to open his own plant.[94] E. B. Gross also opened a cannery, while Booth and the Pacific Fish Company added new equipment. By 1917 there were five canneries on the waterfront, with two others under construction.[95] While some residents resisted new canneries because they wanted the waterfront to become a residential district, the *Pacific Fisherman* concluded, "Monterey . . . has apparently waked up to the immense potential value of her fishing industry."[96]

Just as boosters had predicted, the early twentieth century became a time of tremendous growth in Monterey. Between 1900 and 1920, the population almost quadrupled. The 1900 census recorded 1,411 people living in Monterey, a modest increase from 1,336 residents in 1890. By 1910 the population had jumped to 4,923. This figure rose again to 5,479 in 1920.[97] While it is difficult to pinpoint the exact factors behind this growth, the tourism and fishing industries certainly played important roles. The Pacific Improvement Company made the region an appealing place to both live and visit, while the fishing business had become a principal industry and attracted new residents to the region.

The expansion of tourism and fisheries, however, came with social and environmental costs. As the Pacific Improvement Company built up its land and enticed more visitors to the peninsula, it complicated the management of the Del Monte Forest and highlighted the class and racial divisions between those who owned property, those who did not, and those who could not, in the case of the Japanese workers who cleared the land. Its efforts to improve the coastline also conflicted with the property rights of the wealthy elites whom it wanted to attract. For their part, the canneries introduced industrial processes that simultaneously accelerated the development of the salmon and sardine fisheries, produced increasing amounts of waste, and created social conflicts between workers and employers, native-born residents and immigrants.

In harnessing coastal resources to produce consumer goods, from lovely villas to tins of sardines, Pacific Improvement Company executives and canners unleashed divisive social changes. In the process, they discovered that their control over the coastline and its inhabitants was illusory. Fortunately, the problems were not large scale, and the two industries operated in separate spheres, avoiding major conflicts with one another. This relative peace, however, would not last. By strengthening Monterey's ties to the global economy, World War I turned the city into a premier fishing port, well beyond the imagination of early twentieth-century boosters. Soon the sardine industry began to overshadow tourism and attractive residential developments, and the internal conflicts over how to best develop the fishery intensified.

3 REDUCE AND PROSPER

"When the war was finished, we thought we were all through," Monterey canner E. B. Gross reflected. Renewed competition from European sardine canners and reduced military demand meant that Monterey's World War I expansion could not be sustained. While sardine landings increased in the immediate postwar years, they dropped off considerably in the early 1920s. During the 1918–19 and 1919–20 seasons, Monterey fishermen landed 36,100 and 43,090 tons of sardines, respectively. Two seasons later, they caught only 16,285 tons. But the end of World War I did not mark the end of the local sardine industry. As Gross explained, "We learned the lucrative reduction game."[1]

Although tourism remained a fixture on the coastline during the interwar years, it became secondary to the reduction of whole fish and fish waste into fertilizer, meal, and oil. With demand from agribusiness and other industries, these products sustained Monterey's sardine industry, brought about its expansion, and began to transform the city's identity. Monterey increasingly became a fishing town that revolved around the rhythms of the sardine business—not the tourist trade. During the season, which spanned from August until February, the line of canneries along Ocean View Avenue—often referred to as Cannery Row—was a place in motion. After boats crawled into harbor in the early morning hours to deliver their hauls, Cannery Row "would awake from slumber."[2] Whistles blew, machinery began to churn, and cannery workers shuffled into the plants to process the night's catch. During the off-season or the full moon, the pace of life slowed down as workers and fishermen prepared for the next flurry of activity. Even those not directly involved in the fishing industry felt these cycles; many businessmen saw their profits drop when the sardines were not running.[3]

Monterey's focus on the sardine industry during the interwar years would soon call attention to the fishery's irregularities. To maximize output, canners and fishermen embraced yet more technology that increased and stabilized the sardine supply. As catches rose, however, the state government entered the fray. Entrusted with protecting the state's fishery resources, the California Fish and Game Commission conducted extensive scientific studies of the sardine and grew alarmed by the rapid expansion of the industry. It began to push for restrictions but found incredible resistance among fish processors, fishermen, local residents, politicians, and other scientists.

Just as battles brewed *between* Monterey's tourism and fishing industries, conflicts also developed *within* the sardine fishery. Various stakeholders agreed that sardines should be harvested to produce in-demand commodities; as the Great Depression hit, any industry that turned a profit and provided jobs could not be dismissed. Yet precisely because the industry became so lucrative, competing local and outside groups fought to define the fishery—both how it functioned and what constituted its best uses. In particular, they disagreed about the goods that should be manufactured and the degree to which the fishery should and could be exploited. Whichever group managed to gain control over the fishery would help to determine whether or not Monterey's emerging identity as a fishing town was secure. The silvery fish that swam along the Pacific Coast, then, became the center of a power struggle to control natural resources and determine their material and social value.

TECHNOLOGY IN THE INTERWAR SARDINE FISHERY

The profitability of reduction ensured that the sardine industry's postwar slump was relatively brief. Whereas canning sardines for human consumption was a losing proposition—the price per case of sardines fell from $7.50 during the war years to $3.98 in 1924—the fish by-product market was solid.[4] No longer just a way to get rid of waste and fish unsuitable for canning, reduction became the key to the industry's prosperity. Agricultural buyers, particularly in the poultry industry, found sardine meal to be a cheap, protein-rich feed, while manufacturers used sardine oil for soap, linoleum, and paint. By 1919 most California sardine canneries also engaged in reduction.[5]

As reduction expanded, the California legislature stepped in to regulate the industry. The Fish Conservation Act of 1919, amended in 1921 and 1922, allowed canners in Monterey and San Pedro, California's other major sardine port, to reduce an amount of whole fish equal to 25 percent of their monthly canning capacity. This figure was in addition to the fish waste that they were already reducing. Since one ton of fish typically yielded twenty cases of one-pound ovals—flat oval cans each filled with four to seven sardines doused in tomato sauce—packers had to process fifteen cases for every ton received, the equivalent of 75 percent of the catch, before reducing the rest.[6] The Murphy-Youngman Bill in 1929 lowered the requirement to thirteen and one-half cases, which increased the reduction limit to 32.5 percent of the catch.[7]

To abide by these regulations *and* increase profits, the fish plants needed to both expand their canning operations and make them more cost-effective. The more fish they could can, the more fish they could reduce. And the more efficiently they canned that fish, the lower their production costs and the higher their overall returns. Thus, canners were quick to install new machines and adopt new canning methods. Rather than cooking sardines in oil, they began to adopt the raw-pack method by the 1920s and 1930s. With this technique, workers packed fish directly from the brine tanks and steam-cooked them. After draining oil and water, the condiments were added and the cans were sealed and pushed into the retorts for a final, sterilizing cook. Because raw packing eliminated the frying solutions and the drying step, it reduced production costs by 52 percent.[8] Canners also began to install other labor-saving equipment; the California Packing Corporation put in fish cutters and the Carmel Canning Company and the Monterey Canning Company opted for high-speed can-closing machines.[9] Although markets for canned sardines did not provide a return on these investments, Frank Booth explained that most canners were willing to take a loss in canning and make up for it with reduction.[10]

Since new cannery equipment would remain idle without a steady supply of sardines, improvements in fishing gear soon followed. During much of the 1920s, Monterey fishermen used the lampara net, a longer launch with a diesel engine, and a lighter to transport the catch back to shore.[11]

But lampara outfits failed to keep pace with the growth of the sardine industry, giving the edge to the purse seine boats that began to fish for sardines in 1925. By December 1929, twenty-eight purse seine boats operated out of Monterey.[12] The enthusiasm for the purse seine stemmed from the increasingly scattered distribution of sardines. While nearly 90 percent of the sardine catches were made within ten miles of Monterey between November 1919 and March 1924, the fleet fished closer to Santa Cruz and as far as Half Moon Bay, about seventy miles northwest, during the 1924–25 season.[13] As the fishing grounds became more distant, purse seine boats became more desirable. Their diesel engines and sleeping and cooking quarters allowed them to travel farther and for longer periods of time. Because the lampara boats were smaller and towed a lighter, they rarely ventured outside of Monterey Bay unless the weather was calm. Purse seine boats were also larger, from fifty-five to eighty-five feet in length, and could carry eighty tons in their fish holds, compared to the fifty-ton capacity of the average lampara lighter.[14]

The installation of power equipment, moreover, corrected the earlier deficiencies of the purse seine net. Before, the purse seine failed to provide a reliable supply of sardines largely because the nets were set and pulled by hand. The slow process of laying out the net allowed the sardines to dive under it and escape. But with a power boat and power winch, the purse seine net could be set and pursed with machines, negating the earlier advantages of the lampara. Purse seiners could get bigger catches over a wider area with less effort and at lower costs than the lampara net.[15]

Nonetheless, many Monterey fishermen remained loyal to the lampara, with anywhere from fifty-one to sixty-one in use during the 1929–30 season.[16] They maintained that the net delivered plenty of sardines and opposed the tremendous investment that the purse seine required. They also accused purse seiners of wasting fish and depleting stocks—the same complaints that "native" fishermen had used against them over a decade earlier. Paul Bonnot of California Fish and Game, however, discredited these claims when he compared Monterey purse seine and lampara boats, concluding that the former did not destroy young fish populations or deliver substandard fish.[17]

Lampara fishermen soon modified their outfits to compete with the purse seiners. They installed power winches and booms to pull in their nets and unload their hauls. They adopted the ring net, a lampara net with purse rings along the lower edge. The ring net was easy to han-

FIG. 3.1 This diagram demonstrates how fishermen set a purse seine net, which dominated the Monterey sardine fleet by the 1930s. John M. Dennis, *Monterey's Cannery Row: A Brief Survey, June 4, 1945.* Monterey Public Library, California History Room Archives.

dle, but purse seiners still had an advantage when they had to range widely in search of fish.[18] Purse seiners also proved unwilling to let the lampara fishermen catch up with them; they increased their boats' hold capacities and tanned their nets in bark and water, which made them lighter and faster to operate.[19] Eventually, several Monterey fishermen took the plunge, investing five to six thousand dollars for the purse seine net and up to forty thousand dollars for the boat. As skipper Sal Colletto remembered, "In order to stay in the fishing business you had to build a purse siene [*sic*]."[20] By 1931 there were seventeen Monterey-owned purse seine boats and several new vessels under construction for Monterey fishers.[21]

The canneries encouraged the use of the purse seine by modifying their unloading equipment. Because purse seine boats were larger than lampara launches, they could not navigate close enough to shore to use existing inclined cable hoists. Canneries extended their wharves to allow the purse seiners to unload alongside the conveyors, or they installed large floating hoppers in the bay into which the fishermen unloaded the catch. A pipe, roughly six to ten inches in diameter, snaked underwater from the hopper to the cannery, and an electric motor then sucked the fish onshore like a gigantic vacuum cleaner. By the end of the 1929–30 season, only four Monterey plants were without this machinery, although one plant used a vertical hoist to unload the purse seine boats instead.[22]

While Monterey purse seine deliveries during the 1929–30 season were nearly double that of the lampara, large sardine hauls were never guaranteed.[23] Nature was inherently unpredictable and unstable, and the purse seine net could not be relied upon as a sure-fire solution to the canneries' constant supply requirements. Ideally, a cannery wanted to receive a continuous amount of fish equal to its estimated daily capacity, but canners recognized that the sardine supply was subject to wide fluctuations. In response, each canner contracted several crews "so that during periods of relative scarcity he may receive as many fish as possible, and under normal conditions insure himself against an insufficient supply when one or two crews fail to make a catch," observed Fish and Game scientist W. L. Scofield, N. B. Scofield's younger brother. The flip side of this strategy was that canneries had to limit the amount of fish any one crew delivered during periods of abundance.[24] Improved technology, therefore, was not foolproof, and canners had to use an imprecise system of trial and error to provide fish for their plants without overwhelming them.

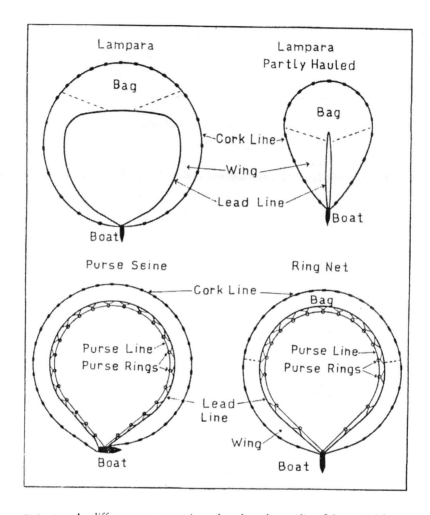

FIG. 3.2 As different nets were introduced to the sardine fishery, California Fish and Game scientists began to study their operation and their impact on the fish stocks. This diagram illustrates the distinctions between the lampara, purse seine, and ring nets. Donald H. Fry, Jr., "The Ring Net, Half Ring Net, or Purse Lampara in the Fisheries of California," California Department of Natural Resources, Division of Fish and Game, *Fish Bulletin No. 27* (1930): 39.

As the sardine industry poured more capital into the fishing fleet and the canneries, Montereyans also devised technological means to protect their collective investment in the industry. They believed that a breakwater in Monterey harbor was imperative to provide a barrier from wind and waves and prevent storm-related damage to wharves and boats. By mitigating dangerous currents and undertow, it would also allow deep-sea vessels to anchor and make direct shipments of agricultural products and other goods. Concerned residents had recommended a breakwater as early as 1909, but plans stalled due to lack of financing.[25]

The growing importance of the fishing industry made breakwater proposals more viable in the 1920s. After disastrous storms in 1915 and 1919, engineer Fred H. Tibbetts warned, "A repetition of such a disaster might easily discourage many of the fishermen from attempting to equip themselves again until proper anchorage protection is afforded to the industry."[26] A public hearing in February 1927 finally revived the project. Monterey city manager R. M. Dorton explained how undertow interrupted boat unloading and forced fishing crews to spend the entire day waiting on their boats.[27] Major John W. N. Schulz of the U. S. Army Corps of Engineers concurred, noting that the fishing industry and harbor commerce had been "handicapped and retarded in their development and have suffered large losses in property damage and in delays."[28]

In May 1934, the army corps finished a 1750-foot-long breakwater on the western edge of Monterey Harbor using rock from a nearby quarry.[29] This long branch of boulders protruding into the bay sheltered the fishing fleet and one fish processing plant, the Booth operation; the remaining eleven canneries on Cannery Row were outside the protective barrier.[30] It was the Montereyans' latest and largest effort to address the irregular patterns of nature and ensure steady output. These measures were all the more important as the reduction industry became more lucrative. By employing state-of-the-art technology, fishermen and canners hoped to keep production lines in constant motion, with fish going in one end and the most profitable proportion of canned sardines, fish meal, and fish oil coming out the other.

REGULATING THE FISHERIES

While canners and fishermen saw the sardine fishery as a source of profits and financial security, it was a source of conflict and frustration for the

California Fish and Game Commission. The State of California was responsible for managing the fisheries within three miles of the coastline, and it established the commission in 1870 to help with this task. More specifically, the commission was "to provide for the restoration and preservation of fish in [California] waters."[31] Because the explosive growth of the sardine industry came with potentially dire consequences, the commission stepped up efforts to ensure the fishery's long-term future. According to Arthur McEvoy, "It had simultaneously to devise controls for the new industrial fisheries and to amass biological information on which to base those controls."[32] However, several parties questioned its evidence of sardine depletion and ignored its pleas for restraint.

The California Fish and Game Commission's efforts to manage the sardine fishery began with reduction operations. Reduction was the most rapacious element of the industry because of the steady demand for fish meal and oil. With reliable profits available, canners and fishermen had huge incentive to increase their hauls of sardines and process as many tons as they could. The commission, however, privileged processing fresh fish for human consumption, rather than for livestock feed or industrial products. Thus, the logic of the Fish Conservation Act and the subsequent Murphy-Youngman Bill was to discourage the use of fish for inedible products and to reserve sardines for food. While it could not eliminate demand for fish by-products, it could at least try to limit production and hopefully keep the fishery in check.[33]

Rather than rely solely on technological advances to increase production, some Monterey canners devised ways to evade the law. One strategy was to underreport catch figures. When a boat delivered its haul, the cannery filled out a receipt with the date, time, boat name, type of boat, and amount of fish. One copy went to the skipper and the other was submitted to Fish and Game, which made sure that the canneries did not receive fish that exceeded their capacity. Some canneries accepted extra fish, paid for in cash, under the table, which allowed them to reduce fish beyond their limit. The skippers benefited as well, since they usually pocketed the money without splitting it with their crews.[34] This clandestine practice later helped to give impetus to Monterey fishermen's unionization efforts.

The use of substandard measuring techniques also exacerbated the commission's efforts to obtain accurate catch figures. In the early 1920s, most canneries filled boxes or buckets with fish and estimated the weight according to volume. According to B. Houssels of the Van Camp Sea Food Company in Terminal Island, Monterey canners estimated that a full bucket of sardines contained 615 pounds, even though "the least weight found in any bucket was 685 pounds." His informants claimed that some Monterey canners reported only 70 percent of the fish they received and thus produced less than ten cases of canned sardines from each ton. In his letter to Major John L. Farley, executive officer of the commission, he concluded, "Most canners are supporting you in trying to enforce the law, and it is not fair to them to let the condition complained of, continue to exist, if it does." [35]

While the Progressive principles of wise use, scientific planning, and efficiency continued to shape California's sardine regulations, securing compliance was difficult given the pro-business slant of conservation in the 1920s. U.S. Secretary of Commerce Herbert Hoover, who oversaw the Bureau of Fisheries, believed that conservation should be based on decentralization, voluntarism, local autonomy, and cooperation between industry and government. But since it was the states' responsibility to regulate the fisheries, his philosophy had little statutory impact on sardine canners. [36] For all the canners like Houssels who subscribed to Hoover's vision of industry-government partnerships, others abused the law, prompting the state to respond with more regulations. The California Division of Weights and Measures required the canneries to use more stringent weighing procedures and uniform equipment in 1929 and 1934, while the Fish and Game Commission issued General Order No. 12, which prohibited fishermen from bringing in more sardines than ordered by their canners. But some fishermen still caught in excess of their limits in the hope that the canneries would accept the extra fish at a reduced cost. If fishermen were unable to unload this excess fish, they often dumped it. [37]

Some Monterey canneries also purportedly ignored state regulations altogether, eschewing the commission's efforts to curb the fishery's growth. When the commission refused to reduce the canning requirement from fifteen to twelve cases at the start of the 1928–29 season, Monterey canners agreed among themselves to pack only twelve cases in protest. The commission asked the Monterey County Superior Court to issue a temporary restraining order against four of the offending canneries, charging that they were in "willful violation" of the law. The court ordered the plants to be closed for three months. [38] In January 1930, the commission ordered three other Monterey canneries to close for ten days, again charging that they had reduced fish above the legal limit.[39] The commission scored yet another victory in 1931, when the Monterey County Superior Court found the Hovden cannery guilty of violating the reduction law.[40]

Although the courts sided with the commission and affirmed the state's right to regulate the fisheries, the state legislature seemed to lack the political will to curb sardine production. Large agricultural companies, including General Mills, Quaker Oats, and Ralston-Purina, wanted to keep the price of fish meal low, and they were quick to pressure politicians if industry restrictions increased the cost of goods.[41] Sardine canners also gathered political clout and formed associations, such as the Sardine Canners' Association of California.[42] When Assemblyman Sanborn Young introduced legislation in 1931 that would have limited reduction to 15 percent of canning capacity and shortened the sardine season by one month, most sardine canners protested. Canning association representatives traveled to Sacramento and met with legislators to negotiate. They failed to devise a solution, and the bill died in the assembly.[43]

The proliferation of floating reduction plants added another obstacle to the commission's attempts to curb reduction and protect the fishery. Since the state had jurisdiction only within three miles of the shore, these floaters did not have to abide by state laws as long as they remained outside this limit. During the late 1920s and early 1930s, the *Peralta*, the *Lake Miraflores*, and the *Lansing* operated off the coast of California and focused solely on sardine reduction. As many as nine floating plants anchored off the coast during the 1930s. After the commission tried unsuccessfully to challenge the floaters in court, it acknowledged that "there appears to be no present way of preventing the operation of such plants which lie just outside the State's jurisdiction and make free use of what are considered the State's fish."[44]

The rise of the floaters coincided with the onset of the Great Depression, an economic crisis that relaxed reduction restrictions and undermined the ecological health of the sardine fishery in the process.[45] A drop in foreign trade for canned fish, limited domestic demand, and low prices for meal and oil halted the industry's growth, so local producers pressured the commission to allow the reduction of up to seventy-five hundred tons of sardines during the 1932–33 season. A *Monterey Peninsula Herald* editorial insisted that this measure was imperative: "This is . . . a human and capital conservation question rather than one pertaining to fish. The welfare of the Monterey fishing fleet and the hundreds of families the fishermen support must be conserved."[46] The *Herald* editorial turned the conventional use of the term "conservation" on its head and applied it to human society. Because the sardine could sustain Monterey's economy and its citizens during a time of crisis, the editorial claimed, the fishery should not be left untouched. Yet as much as the editorial tried to treat nature and society as separate, they were intertwined. Producers could not increase reduction without affecting the sardine's material abundance.

Caving in to pressure, the Fish and Game Commission agreed to increase reduction permits in order to alleviate the hardships of the Depression. For the 1932–33 season, it issued open reduction permits in which canners could reduce up to 7,500 tons of fish without also having to pack sardines for human consumption.[47] This policy, in part, accounted for a dramatic increase in the total catch of sardines in California.[48] During the 1932–33 season, the catch was 53 percent more than the previous season. The 1934–35 season was so successful that the Northern California sardine canneries had exhausted their reduction quota of 5,000 tons each by midseason. With the issuance of more permits, most plants had reduced 12,000 tons of sardines by the end of the season. Monterey fishermen caught almost 230,000 tons of sardines, roughly 80,000 tons more than the previous season.[49] As production increased and wages rose, one industry official even called Monterey "a local island of prosperity in a sea of depression."[50]

Despite the possibility of overtaxing the sardine fishery, Fish and Game also issued open reduction permits so that shore plants could compete with the floating plants. While floaters were licensed by the federal government to operate in international waters, they had a key advantage over their land-based counterparts; there were no limits placed on their catches, so they could take sardines with abandon. By the 1936–37 season, they accounted for 33 percent of the total California sardine catch. While issuing unlimited reduction permits did not eliminate the problem and, in fact, increased sardine landings, the commission also knew that strict limits on shore plants would only drive these producers to open their own floating plants. And thus, "the rapid expansion of the reduction industry is not stopped."[51]

Because the federal government had the power to regulate the high seas, it soon became embroiled in the floater controversy. The House Committee on Merchant Marine and Fisheries and the Fisheries Subcommittee of the House Committee on Commerce held a joint hearing in 1936 to discuss possible legislation, but it devolved into a debate over the amount of physical expansion the sardine fishery could withstand. Herbert Davis, executive officer of the California Fish and Game Commission, noted that the floaters made "a farce of the efforts of the State of California to conserve its resource." He concluded, "Generally when depletion has set in to a point where it is very obvious, then it is too late to do anything about it." N. B. Scofield, head of the commission's Bureau of Commercial Fisheries, added, "the very fact we have developed the sardine catch to a point that [it] is greater than that of any other fishery in North America . . . is fact enough to make us sure that we are headed for destruction."[52]

Argyle Campbell, attorney for the California Sardine Fishermen's Association, the San Francisco Sardine Fisheries, Inc., and the Monterey Sardine Industries, Inc., the local boat owners' association, testified that his clients supported efforts to regulate the floating reduction plants. He stated, "We do not contend that depletion has actually been arrived at now, but we do contend that regulatory measures should be passed in order to prevent depletion from occurring." While they did not want floaters to go out of business, they argued that the ships should not be left to decide "just when depletion has arrived and just when they are ready to be regulated." Fishermen could act out of "their own selfish interest" and catch as many fish as possible, Campbell explained, "but if depletion occurs they know that will result in their detriment," namely a huge loss on their investments in boats, gear, and nets, amounting to roughly three million dollars in Monterey alone.[53] In other words, fishermen acknowledged that they all needed to be subject to some degree of regulation in order to ensure the stability of the sardine supply. Floaters should not be left to their own devices and allowed to evade the law.

The U. S. Bureau of Fisheries agreed that depletion had not arrived, but it argued that commercial fishing should be left unrestricted until there were actual declines in catches. Reginald Fiedler, chief of the bureau's Division of Fishery Industries, explained that fishery conservation meant "wise use," which implied "making the most economic disposal of the species after harvesting." Nearly two decades after the waning of the Progressive era, he still adhered to its central tenets. Bureau scientist Elmer Higgins, who had previously worked for the California Fish and Game

Commission, also suggested that restrictions would hinder business.[54] The bureau's attitude was not surprising; scholars have argued that its primary purpose was to promote and expand the fishing industry, rather than regulate it.[55]

Judge William Denman of the U.S. Ninth Circuit Court of Appeals, a former member of a creditors' committee for a floating plant, and Lyman Henry, a representative of the Membership Corporation Association of the Federally Licensed Floating Processing Plants, came to the defense of the offshore processors. They discussed the fecundity of sardines and argued that the larger shore canners, Fish and Game scientists, and sportsmen conspired to monopolize the industry and put the floaters out of business.[56] They elaborated on their theory in a report with the incendiary title *A Review of the California Sardine Industry with Incidental Consideration of Its Racketeers, Its Politician Pseudo-Scientists, and Its Misguided Sportsmen Enemies.* Denman and Henry pointed out that the Fish and Game Commission exacted a fee from the sardine processors to fund scientific research, which caused an "abandonment of the scientific for the political." By advocating restrictions on the catch and the elimination of the floaters, they claimed, the commission's "pseudo-scientists" tried to limit production, keep fish meal supplies low and prices high, and line the pockets of large canners. "Misguided" sportsmen joined these efforts, claiming that the depleted supply of sardines, a bait fish, had caused popular game fish like tuna and albacore to disappear.[57]

Denman's and Henry's report was primarily a reaction to the Fish and Game Commission's extensive sardine investigations. Scientific research was a major component of its duties. In response to the rapid growth of California's fisheries, the commission established a separate department in 1914 to study the commercial sector. To collect the necessary data, N. B. Scofield, with the help of Will F. Thompson, set up the nation's first state-operated fisheries laboratory in San Pedro. Espousing the principles of Progressive conservation, Thompson explained in 1920 that the sardine investigations would help the state government meet its responsibility to help procure "the greatest possible use" of a resource and "to insure its continuance. . . ."[58] The scientific work on the sardine began during the last quarter of 1919, when commission scientists started to study the fishery in San Pedro and Monterey. Oscar E. Sette was in charge of the commission's office and laboratory at the Hopkins Marine Station.[59]

One of the key questions of the sardine investigation was to distinguish between depletion and natural fluctuations. While the fishery could experience natural changes in abundance, the expansion of the fishing grounds, technological improvements, and the growing quantity of gear in use could also hide signs of exhaustion by keeping the sardine harvests steady and the prices low. Thus, Thompson recommended gathering statistics on meteorological and oceanographic factors, boat catches, types of boats and apparatus, age and size composition of the catches, spawning season, age and rate of growth, life history, and location of various ages of fish at different times of the year. He hoped that this data would help scientists to ascertain the fluctuations in sardine stocks, predict future catches, and determine the possibility of overfishing.[60]

By the early 1930s, scientists had made significant discoveries about the sardine's life history. In 1929 they found sardine eggs and larvae near Santa Barbara, providing some clues about its spawning grounds.[61] One year later, Frances Clark concluded that the size of sardines in California started small in the fall, increased to a maximum in the winter, and decreased slightly in the spring. This pattern, she speculated, was a reflection of sardines' movement into and out of certain fishing areas in response to their spawning practices. In addition, through an analysis of eleven years of commercial catch samples, Clark discerned the presence of three dominant size-groups, also called size-classes, that appeared at three- or four-year intervals. As they grew, they lost their dominance with the entrance of new and more abundant size-groups. Because the fishery was dependent on the appearance of new sardines, "the final disappearance of the last abundant group unaccompanied by an entering dominant size-class might cause a gradual collapse of the fishery." Clark warned that an abundance of large fish did not necessarily indicate a healthy fishery.[62]

Scientists soon integrated their data on size-groups, spawning, and migration to make preliminary conclusions about depletion. They speculated that sardines stayed south until adolescence, moved north each summer, and headed south again during the winter so that they could spawn between February and August. Older fish went farther north at the close of each spawning season. Thus, fishermen caught small or medium fish during the fall (August to November) and large sardines in the winter (December to February) as they made their way south to spawn. Scientists believed that the intense fall fishery for young adults was causing a scarcity of smaller sizes and would eventually create a dearth of large sardines and result in depletion.[63] Clark concluded, "Unless the magnitude of the fall fishery is abated the time is not far distant when each new year-class will be practically destroyed before it has grown to sizes which support the winter fishery. Such conditions may eventually result in inadequate numbers of spawning fish and serious depletion of the sardine population."[64]

Catch per unit of effort, one of scientists' best measures of depletion, provided further evidence of diminished sardine stocks. If, in using similar boats and gear and supplying the same amount of work, a fisherman caught fewer fish, "it means that the population is being fished out faster than it is being rebuilt by nature." During the 1937–38 season, fishermen caught roughly half as many fish as they had six seasons before with the same expenditure of effort. Because they had taken roughly half their tonnage during the fall months when only younger adults were present, they had placed excessive strain on smaller sizes; the life span of a year-class had decreased from ten or more years to four or five. Since the sardine was a migratory species, moreover, fishing in one locality took its toll on the entire population. Clark recommended reducing the total sardine catch, which had averaged five hundred thousand tons per season, to at least one-half of its present total. "To build up the population with any rapidity an even more drastic cut, perhaps one-third of the present total may be necessary," she concluded.[65]

For the commission, the mounting scientific evidence of overfishing was difficult to ignore. W. L. Scofield warned that the fishery was in crisis. Current management, he argued, would determine if the sardine would "drop back into darkness after a brief burst of glory" or if it would "bring continuous wealth and satisfaction to the people of the State for years into the future." He criticized the "heroic depression treatment" that allowed for liberal reduction permits during the early 1930s, as the fishery was already overtaxed and "increasing the annual catch did not help a bit." Like Clark, Scofield believed in sustained yield management that balanced harvests and replacements "so as to maintain a full breeding stock in our waters."[66]

Given the drastic cuts that the commission scientists recommended, it is not surprising that Denman, Henry, and others dismissed their cries of depletion. Steadfast in their belief that sardines were abundant, Denman and Henry called the reports deceptive and misleading, criticized scientists' research methods, challenged their data, and rejected their gloomy predictions. They claimed that the scientists found evidence of depletion only in order to keep their jobs.[67] Monterey fisherman E. S. Lucido turned the focus away from politics and conspiracies and called on his years of experience working at sea. He explained that the sardine population always fluctuated, and "the cry of depletion had been heard before." Monterey had experienced poor catches in the past, only to bounce back soon thereafter.[68] Lucido implied that there was no need to take a few bad seasons as incontrovertible evidence of the fishery's demise. His intimate knowledge of the fishery was potentially more valuable than the scientists' data.

Despite what it believed to be credible evidence of depletion, the California Fish and Game Commission could do little to stop the fishery's growth. It could not set a seasonal catch limit, and state lawmakers rarely followed its recommendations. While it did set reduction permits, it issued them annually and readjusted them only after the fact. For instance, when the catch for the 1937–38 season was only 60 percent of the previous season—despite sixty additional boats and reduction permits of 12,500 to 22,500 tons per plant—Fish and Game cut permits by over one-half.[69] The commission finally circumvented the legislature with Proposition No. 5, which banned the operation of and delivery to floating plants inside or outside state waters unless the plants received permits, but its passage in November 1938 came after several years of heavy catches.[70] According to Arthur McEvoy, "Rather than lose its control over the fishery entirely, [the commission] yielded ground step by step."[71]

Ultimately, a combination of factors—the profitability of the reduction industry, the rise of the floating plants, and the onset of the Great Depression—intersected to create conditions that fueled production. As a result, federal officials, state lawmakers, and industry representatives slighted or ignored the call for restraint, while Monterey producers devised ways to evade regulations in overt and surreptitious ways. As long as they caught fish and sold fish by-products, there seemed little reason to practice self-control. All of these predicaments made it next to impossible for the California Fish and Game Commission to stop the industry from further expansion. While it would be easy to place the blame solely on the fishermen, as Joseph E. Taylor argues, "only rarely do [fishery problems] result from a single activity or event."[72]

While Monterey had landed only 36,000 tons of sardines in 1918, that figure had jumped to 227,231 tons by the end of the 1939–40 season.[73] The fisheries moved to the center of the local economy, pushing aside tourism in the process. Because high demand for fish meal and oil made the sardine industry profitable, reduction became canners' top priority; to focus on canned sardines alone would have spelled disaster. They only produced pound-ovals in order to comply with state regulations, and they pressured the California Fish and Game Commission to relax its canning requirements so that they could devote even more fish to by-products.

But the debates over the sardine fishery and its management were about more than just dollar signs. They also involved varied opinions about what gave nature—in this case, sardines—social value. Canners and other supporters were quick to call attention to the Great Depression and the reduction industry's ability to stave off destitution for numerous Montereyans. Surely, operating reduction plants was less objectionable than throwing hundreds of residents out of work when other jobs were scarce, they claimed. The California Fish and Game Commission, on the other hand, believed that reduction was an improper, even "repugnant" use of nature.[74] Sardines were edible fish that should be eaten by people, not livestock. That reduction drove catches sky high, prompted the development of floating plants, and put further pressure on this food fishery made it even more objectionable.

These value judgments helped to shape understandings of the sardine fishery—whether it was healthy, at risk, or on the verge of collapse—but it was never completely clear who would dismiss or embrace theories of overfishing. For instance, cannery owner Frank Booth was one of the few sardine processors who agreed wholeheartedly with the commission's sentiments and pointed to the need to curb reduction. While he had pioneered reduction early on, he found its expansion troubling and continued to churn out fish by-products only in order to stay in business. He compared the plight of the sardine to the extinct passenger pigeon and noted, "If ever wild life needed friends to save it from fiendish commercialism the sardines do."[75] While some people shared Booth's sentiments and lamented the sardine fishery's unchecked industrial growth, others opposed any effort to undermine the lifeblood of Monterey's bustling community of fishermen and cannery workers.

Even as the city's industrial identity solidified, the divisions within the fishing community grew deeper. Industrial processes—from catching sardines to packing them into tin cans—entrenched social inequalities and aggravated social conflicts. At the same time, the swift expansion of the sardine fishery also sparked clashes with the tourism industry. Given the fishing industry's firm hold over Monterey's economy, however, real estate developers and tourism boosters faced an uphill battle in carrying out their leisure-driven visions for the coastline.

Chinese fishing village, Monterey, 1875. Monterey Public Library, California History Room Archives.

Hotel Del Monte, ca. 1886. The Huntington Library.

Guests arriving at the Hotel Del Monte train depot, ca. 1885.
California Views, Pat Hathaway Collection (78-010-008).

Two girls playing in the Hotel Del Monte's Arizona garden. Monterey Public Library, California History Room Archives.

Hotel Del Monte bathhouse, ca. 1885. California Views, Pat Hathaway Collection (82-003-016).

Taking advantage of the influx of visitors who toured the Seventeen Mile Drive,
Chinese fishermen set up a stand to sell shells and trinkets, ca. 1895.
Monterey Public Library, California History Room Archives.

Guests arriving at the first Pebble Beach Lodge, ca. 1910. California Views,
Pat Hathaway Collection (82-029-011).

The odors emitted by these squid-drying fields, ca. 1888, eventually led to a campaign to banish Chinese fishermen from Point Alones. The Huntington Library.

The Chinese fishing village at Point Alones after the May 1906 fire. California Views, Pat Hathaway Collection (2003-046-001).

Before Monterey became the "sardine capital of the world," the canneries processed both sardines and salmon. Fishermen used sailboats like the ones pictured here at Fisherman's Wharf, ca. 1910. Monterey Public Library, California History Room Archives.

Along with the Booth Cannery, the Pacific Fish Company, pictured ca. 1910, was one of Monterey's major fish canneries before World War I. Monterey Public Library, California History Room Archives.

Before the introduction of fish hoppers, boats like the *Anacapa*, pictured in 1913, delivered sardines to the canneries using a bucket conveyor system. Monterey Public Library, California History Room Archives.

Fishermen unloading sardines at Booth's cannery dock, 1937. Monterey Public Library, California History Room Archives.

The fish canneries attracted diverse workers, like the Booth Cannery employees pictured here, ca. 1914. California Views, Pat Hathaway Collection (92-012-0006).

The purse seine fleet in Monterey Harbor, ca. 1940. California Views, Pat Hathaway Collection (2003-034-003).

Fishermen with a purse seine net. Monterey Public Library, California History Room Archives.

Santa Rosalia procession on Fisherman's Wharf, 1950. Monterey
Public Library, California History Room Archives.

Cannery worker "spiking," or adding sauce to, sardines, ca. 1940.
Monterey Public Library, California History Room Archives.

Cannery worker moving canned sardines to boiler, ca 1940. Monterey Public Library, California History Room Archives.

Women packing sardines on the canning lines, ca. 1949. Monterey Public Library, California History Room Archives.

This famous George J. Seideneck photograph from ca. 1945 captures the
hustle and bustle of wartime Cannery Row. California Views, Pat Hathaway
Collection (1972–012–0053).

Sardines on
cannery conveyor,
ca. 1949.
Monterey Public
Library, California
History Room
Archives.

A young boy play-
ing in abandoned
cannery equipment
on Cannery Row,
1959. Monterey
Public Library,
California History
Room Archives.

The City of Monterey officially changed the name of Ocean View Avenue to Cannery Row in 1957. Two years later, the new sign pointed to the tourism-oriented neighborhood, with the shrinking fleet of purse seine boats in the background. Monterey Public Library, California History Room Archives.

In 1959 the Monterey Canning Company building was home to stores selling antiques, office furniture, and flooring. Monterey Public Library, California History Room Archives.

The Custom House Packing Company fire of October 1953 was one of many blazes that hit Cannery Row between the 1950s and 1970s. Monterey Public Library, California History Room Archives.

Aldon's Restaurant, pictured in 1966, offered patrons views of both Monterey Bay and deteriorating fish canneries. The City of Monterey hoped that this juxtaposition of scenic nature and industrial decay would attract tourists. Monterey Public Library, California History Room Archives.

This view of Cannery Row from the late 1960s shows the crumbling fish processing plants that clung to the coastline in the decades following the sardine fishery's collapse. Monterey Public Library, California History Room Archives.

Hovden Cannery, 1960s. In 1973 the Hovden cannery became the last fish processing plant on Cannery Row to close. Monterey Public Library, California History Room Archives.

Monterey Bay Aquarium opening celebration, October 20, 1984. Eleven years after the Hovden Cannery closed, the Monterey Bay Aquarium opened on the same site, preserving the facade of the former sardine cannery. Photo by Pat Hathaway. California Views, Pat Hathaway Collection (84-107-0007).

Cannery Row's coastline continues to be dotted with industrial remains, like these from the California Packing Corporation, also the former site of the Pacific Fish Company. Author photo, 2003.

4 LIFE, LABOR, AND ODORS ON CANNERY ROW

Monterey's Sicilian community staged its first *festa* in honor of Santa Rosalia, the patron saint of Palermo, Sicily, on September 5, 1933.[1] Born in the twelfth century, Rosalia Sinibaldi left her royal family at the age of twenty-two and lived a life of prayer and penance in a mountain cave until her death. According to legend, when a devastating plague hit Palermo 450 years later, a soap maker saw a vision of Rosalia, who told him that he could end the epidemic if he took her bones, carried them through the city, and gave her a proper burial. The plague ended after he obeyed her orders, and citizens subsequently began holding an annual festival in her honor. Since Palermo was a fishing port, fishermen invoked Santa Rosalia for protection and success while at sea.

The tradition continued in Monterey. Francesca Giamona, Rosa Ferrante, Giovanna Balbo, and Domenica Enea, all wives of fishermen, planned the festival with the help of other members of the Italian Catholic Federation and funding from the Monterey Sardine Industries, Inc. The festivities kicked off with an Italian-style dinner at the San Carlos Church parish hall on Sunday night. The next morning, four fishermen carrying a life-size statue of Santa Rosalia led a procession from the church to Fisherman's Wharf as the rest of the Sicilian community followed. With the purse seine boats crowded into Monterey Harbor, Bishop Philip Scher blessed the fishing fleet, praying for safety and prosperity throughout the sardine season. Although Sicilians organized the *festa* as a way to bring together their own community through religion, more than three thousand people of diverse faiths and backgrounds poured onto the pier to watch the ceremony.[2]

The Santa Rosalia Festival provided only a brief diversion from the social conflicts that came to shape the Monterey coastline. Despite unionization efforts that united fisheries workers, racial, ethnic, gender, and class divisions persisted on the cannery work floor, aboard fishing boats, and in Monterey's residential neighborhoods.[3] For those who supported tourism and real estate development, Cannery Row incited disgust and disdain. The fish factories attracted "undesirable" workers and created foul odors, both of which the Del Monte Properties Company, visitors, and some residents found intolerable. Once again, fisheries and tourism collided. But given the extensive reach of the sardine industry, these groups simply could not isolate themselves from the social and environmental changes brought by the fisheries. Visions of the coastline as a place for white leisure and settlement became superfluous to an increasing number of residents who saw the city's fortunes tied to sardines, not hotels and resorts.

Thus, the possible depletion of the fishery was just one problem that the interwar sardine industry generated. As scientists, politicians, and canners debated the fate of the sardine population off the Pacific Coast, other conflicts unfolded onshore. Disputes over wages, labor conditions, new workers, and smells all pointed to the local consequences of industrial growth. While many Montereyans recognized that the canneries were important to the economy, the social and environmental transformations that stemmed from the fish business meant that their support was neither unconditional nor universal. As they jockeyed for position within and against the sardine industry, they struggled to determine whose interests should be served and displaced during Cannery Row's meteoric rise.

UNIONS AND DISUNITY ON CANNERY ROW

Labor became one arena of heightened social conflict on Cannery Row. As soon as the fish plants opened in the early twentieth century, cannery workers and fishermen proved unwilling to allow their employers to organize production unilaterally. Their activism picked up steam during the interwar years. One of the first major cannery strikes unfolded in July 1920. Fish cutters, who were primarily Japanese and Chinese men, demanded a piece rate of ten cents per bucket of fish, two cents higher than the existing rate.[4] They also asked that all canneries pay the same wages so as to reduce dissension among cutters who worked at different plants. While one reporter blamed the strike on the "Americanized" Japanese—educated and conversant in English—the Japanese countered that "Chinese, Italians, Mexicans and all the other cutters were as much to blame."[5] In other words, they claimed that dissent stemmed from a diverse group of workers who all found their wages to be inadequate.

Canners cared little about who started the strike; fearing a halt in production, they advertised for new workers, enticing potential employees with the possibility of earning fifty dollars per week.[6] They also warned Japanese fish cutters that they would be excluded from future cannery jobs if they did not return to work. The *Monterey Daily Cypress* supported the canners' efforts, insisting that "the prosperity of the city depends upon the fish business and it cannot afford to have the business hampered by trouble makers at a time when market conditions are anything but promising."[7]

To curb further disruption, the canneries announced a compromise and another ultimatum in September. They offered eight cents for a twenty-five-pound bucket of sardines in canneries where scales were installed.

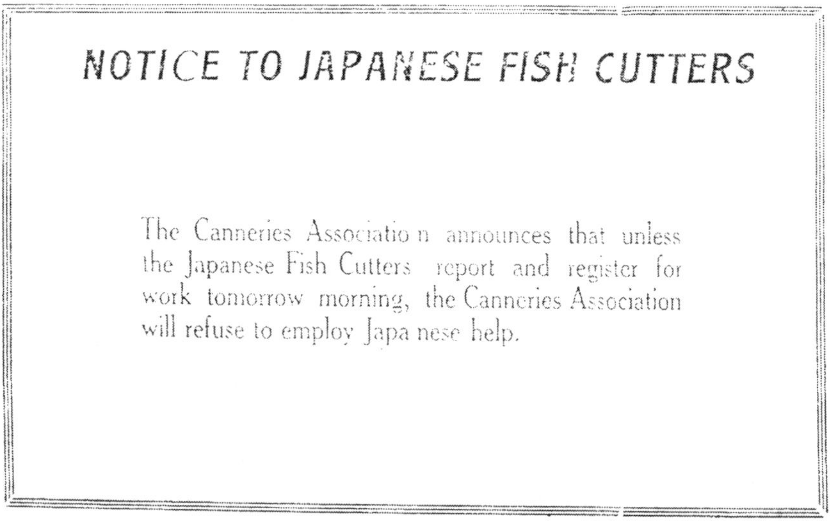

NOTICE TO JAPANESE FISH CUTTERS

The Canneries Association announces that unless the Japanese Fish Cutters report and register for work tomorrow morning, the Canneries Association will refuse to employ Japanese help.

FIG. 4.1 Cannery owners made their threats public, publishing this notice to Japanese fish cutters in a local newspaper. *Monterey Cypress and American*, July 28, 1920.

In canneries without scales, they would pay ten cents per bucket. If the Japanese fish cutters did not accept the offer by the evening, all Japanese employees would be fired. This bargain assumed that the Japanese were a united group, but they were not. Any resistance jeopardized the jobs of compliant Japanese cutters and Japanese fishermen, many of whom worked directly for the canneries and were considered cannery employees. The nonstriking Japanese tried to persuade the others, but they did not do so in time to meet the deadline.[8] True to their threats, the canneries fired and replaced all Japanese workers.[9]

The fish cutters' strike demonstrated both the divisions within the working class and the growing rift between labor and management. There was similar social unrest within the Sicilian-dominated fishing fleet.[10] This tension stemmed from the distribution of profits within a purse seine crew, which consisted of eight men and a captain who typically owned the boat and gear. Profits were divided into twelve shares, with each crew member receiving one share and the captain receiving three or four.[11] To defend their respective interests, fishermen organized the Monterey Fishermen's Protective Union (also referred to as the Monterey Sardine Fishermen's Protective Union), while the boat owners formed the Monterey Sardine Fishermen's Organization, later reorganized as the Monterey Sardine Industries, Inc. (MSI). Before the start of each season, canneries proposed a price for fish, which had to be approved by both groups.[12]

Even though workers began to unite and stand up to employers, their desire to maintain control over the terms of their labor made Monterey a difficult place to unionize. When the Deep Sea and Purse Seine Fishermen's Union, an affiliate of the American Federation of Labor (AFL), came to Monterey in 1936 to start a local branch, fishermen feared the loss of local independence. In January 1937, AFL business agent Matt Batinovich worked out a merger with the Monterey Sardine Fishermen's Protective Union by giving the local more "home rule" than any other branch. As union leaders later explained, "We are opposed to outsiders telling us what kind of a union we are to join and form and how we are to conduct our business." AFL organizers also enlisted cannery laborers in Cannery Workers Union Local No. 20305 in 1936, allowing them to retain local autonomy in bargaining situations as well.[13]

Shortly after the fishermen joined the AFL in 1937, their Deep Sea and Purse Seine Fishermen's Union called a strike against MSI, demanding union recognition and other concessions. The cannery workers initially walked out only in sympathy but later decided to present a list of their own demands.[14] The fishermen ended their walk out two days later, receiving union recognition, preferential hiring for union members, and a greater share of the catch profits. The cannery workers agreed to a contract the following week. In addition to union recognition and preferential hiring, their agreement established a minimum wage for men and women, hourly wage and piece-rate scales for fish cutters, and the eight-hour day. In return, the union agreed to settle future disputes according to AFL rules, lessening the likelihood of hastily called strikes.[15]

The contracts also contained provisions that addressed the unpredictable and dangerous nature of cannery labor. As much as the canners probably desired an industrial time clock, their employees had to follow the rhythms of nature, which meant that work hours were highly irregular. When boats delivered their fish—often in the early morning hours since sardine fishing occurred at night—each cannery blew its own distinct whistle, signaling workers to begin their shifts. Depending on the size of the catch, they could be at work for one hour to fifteen hours. Their new contract stipulated that employees would have one hour to report to work after a supervisor called a shift and that they got paid for at least two hours if called between 10 P.M. and 6 A.M.[16] In other words, cannery workers tried to manage the vagaries of sardine fishing and reduce the exploitation of their time. Fishermen's contracts focused more on the hazards of the job. In its 1940 agreement with MSI, the AFL union contract required that, in case of injury or illness, crew members were entitled to their share of the earnings and received job security until they recovered. Boat owners also had to keep fully equipped medicine chests on board at all times.[17]

Union successes, however, did not mean that the AFL united all fisheries workers. A minority of Monterey fishermen and cannery workers affiliated with the more radical Congress of Industrial Organizations (CIO).[18] The ensuing power struggle between rival unions divided along ethnic and racial lines. In the canneries, Chinese, Japanese, Mexicans, Portuguese, Spaniards, Filipinos, and some Okies, Depression-era migrants from the nation's interior, labored alongside a large number of Italian—mostly Sicilian—women.[19] Sicilian women resisted labor radicalism and were content with the AFL. For one thing, some women were related to cannery owners, so it was difficult for them to see their interests as separate. Focused on creating and sustaining a distinct Sicilian fishing com-

munity, moreover, they did not see themselves solely as industrial workers and "never seemed to believe that unions alone would allow them
the upward economic mobility they sought." The Portuguese, Mexicans,
Spanish, and Okies, on the other hand, typically supported the more militant CIO because of its promises of better working conditions for the
poorest laborers.[20]

As radical labor activity intensified, the AFL decided to step in. In July
1937, Edward Vandeleur, secretary of the California State Federation of
Labor, revoked the AFL charter for the cannery workers' Local No. 20305
because of "Communistic and CIO activity" and issued a new charter,
Local No. 20986. In response, several former members established the
CIO Fish Cannery and Reduction Workers Union Local No. 73.[21] Similarly, the AFL charter of the Deep Sea and Purse Seine Fishermen's Union
was revoked in April 1938 because of alleged CIO tendencies and failure to pay a per capita tax; the Monterey fishermen subsequently received
another AFL charter from the International Seamen's Union.[22] These tensions came to blows in June 1938, when Horace Enea, president of the
AFL fishermen's union, saw Mildred Bowen, secretary of the CIO
United Fishermen's Union, remove an AFL sign posted on the CIO's office
door. An altercation ensued, and Enea was charged with battery.[23]

In the case of the cannery workers' AFL local, the CIO charged that
it was a "company inspired union" that did not speak for the workers.
CIO representative Jack Anderson claimed that most of the charter members were superintendents or foremen who practiced coercion. For
instance, San Carlos cannery forewoman Mamie Dillon allegedly threatened to fire workers if they did not join the AFL.[24] The CIO union, on
the other hand, represented "the majority of the bona fide cannery workers in the Monterey canneries."[25] To prove its claims, Anderson petitioned
the National Labor Relations Board (NLRB) in July 1937 to hold an
election so that workers could choose their collective bargaining agency.
But the AFL local continued to gain strength. It had two thousand members by October and signed preferential hiring agreements with seven canneries.[26] When the NLRB held the election in February 1939, the AFL
won a resounding victory and became the cannery workers' sole bargaining union. The vote was timed toward the end of the sardine season,
when the most militant workers had already left Monterey for inland
agricultural work.[27]

Although the AFL successfully organized Monterey's cannery workers and fishermen and helped them secure higher wages and improved working conditions, unionizing efforts did not extend to tourism industry workers. In the 1930 census, 368 Monterey residents reported hotel employment, from a handful of white-collar jobs as managers and accountants to numerous service jobs as waitresses, chambermaids, bellhops, gardeners, and janitors.[28] The latter employees may have had grievances that paralleled those of the cannery workers and fishermen, but their industry was not an arena of labor organizing in Monterey. Because their work was rendered invisible, hidden behind the scenes of places like the Hotel Del Monte and beyond the view of the visitors they served, it lacked the appearance of work. Tourism continued its association with leisure, fisheries with labor.

Unionization gave Monterey fishermen numerous advantages. For one thing, it allowed them to secure jobs for union members, who were typically permanent local residents, while excluding nonmembers, outsiders who followed the migrating sardine to Monterey during the fall and winter. Fishermen had first become concerned with these interlopers when San Pedro purse seiners began to fish successfully in Monterey in the 1920s. When Paul Bonnot of California Fish and Game investigated the purse seine and lampara nets in 1929, he speculated that Monterey's Italian fishermen were hostile to the purse seine, in part, because of their prejudice against Austrian crews from outside ports.[29] Ethnic difference and better equipment seemed to fuel their resentment. Even though sardines were a migratory species and a common resource, Monterey fishermen seemed to believe that they should reap the profits from "their" fish—the stocks present in Monterey Bay.

Yet the Sicilian-dominated fishing fleet, like the sardines it caught, was also mobile. While the fishermen had families, owned homes, and paid taxes in Monterey, many migrated to San Pedro and San Diego to fish for albacore or Alaska to fish for salmon during the off-season. This mobility was critical to their decision to affiliate with the AFL. Both Alaska and San Pedro were AFL ports at that point; if Monterey fishermen had remained unorganized, their summer jobs might have been in danger.[30] When Alaska subsequently became a CIO port, however, AFL membership created complications. The CIO Alaska Fishermen's Union expelled about one hundred Monterey fishermen because of dual unionism, and the CIO cannery workers' union reported that it would not handle any fish brought in by Monterey men.[31] Monterey fishermen retaliated a few months later, staging a strike to force Monterey fresh fish whole-salers to sign a closed-shop contract with the local AFL union and elim-inate outside CIO boats.[32]

In September 1939, the CIO hatched its own scheme to compel the Monterey canneries to accept its fish. Two CIO boats from San Fran-cisco, the *New Madrid* and the *Cesare Augusta*, caught an excess of twenty tons of sardines and sold them to Monterey's Del Mar cannery. When the boats tried to deliver the catch, cannery workers pronounced them "hot fish," declared a strike, and refused to bring the fish into the plant. Francisco D'Agui and Joe Lopez, the boat owners, attached their vessels to the hopper, preventing any AFL boats from unloading. Del Mar filed for an injunction in Monterey County Superior Court, while the CIO filed complaints with the San Francisco Superior Court, the federal dis-trict court, and the California Fish and Game Commission, charging the Monterey canneries and boat owners with monopolistic practices.[33] The NLRB finally resolved the situation by holding an election the follow-ing year, which secured a closed shop for the AFL Seine and Line Fish-ermen's Union.[34] This victory gave Monterey's AFL fishermen exclusive claims to the local canneries. Technically, outside fishermen could deliver to Monterey canneries if they joined the local AFL union, but this opened up the possibility of dual unionism if they came from CIO ports.

Unlike the fishermen's union, the cannery workers' union did not seem concerned about the presence of outside workers. Local reporters often mentioned that the union admitted migrants who drifted "to other local-ities, following seasonal work in other lines, such as cotton picking, fruit picking, work in fruit and vegetable canneries and similar occupations."[35] The union's indifference to outsiders may have stemmed from the grow-ing number of jobs as the industry expanded throughout the 1930s; when sardines were plentiful, migrant laborers were necessary to keep the can-neries operating at full force. Cannery labor, moreover, did not involve territorial claims to fishing grounds and was inherently less competitive than fishing.

The unions' occasional hostility toward nonresidents did not erase the divisions *within* Monterey's fishing community. As the AFL-CIO power struggle suggested, Sicilians controlled the canneries. Mary Soto, a Por-tuguese cannery worker, recalled, "The Italian women really dominated. They were really tight together, always talking Italian. They thought they were better." Sicilian women secured their position by becoming floor ladies or supervisors, which gave them the power to assign more desirable, less arduous jobs to their Sicilian friends and relatives.[36] According to cannery worker Rudy Rosales, the same favoritism applied among the male workers:

> The guys were the same way too, like a lot of the Italians or Portuguese would be driving the trucks, the easy jobs. The Spanish, and Indians, and the Mexicans, and maybe Oakies, would be doing all of the dirty work. Like cleaning the fish or hauling all of the dead fish. . . . That was one job I did not want to do because it was terrible. . . . That type of job was for the people the foreman did not like."[37]

Sicilians also commanded the fishing fleet. With the exception of a few Spaniards and Portuguese and eight Japanese, most of the fifty-nine sardine boat owners in 1937 were of Italian—specifically Sicilian—descent. As skipper Sal Colletto explained, "That was rare to have a Genoa fisherman because all the fisherman [*sic*] were mostly Sicilian and Japanese crews."[38]

Residential patterns in Monterey reflected the diversity of the fishing community and the divisions within it. The area around Cannery Row evolved into a working-class neighborhood where it was not uncommon for a Japanese cannery worker to live down the street from a Sicilian fisherman. Fishermen and cannery workers with surnames such as Shibasaki, Hernandez, Yee, Garcia, Cardinale, Ferranti, Watanabe, and Pargo all lived along Foam and Wave Streets, just one and two blocks south of the canneries on Ocean View Avenue. Numerous boardinghouses and small shacks also catered to the single men who worked in the canneries. But residential integration was not city-wide. Many Chinese and Japanese residents continued to cluster near downtown Monterey, with entrepreneurs running businesses that catered to their fishing compatriots.[39]

Some Sicilian fishing families also congregated in certain parts of the city. Taking advantage of their growing earnings, they began to buy houses in the hills above Monterey. Their neighborhood preserved the "Old World's ways," from the street vendors who peddled goods door-to-door to the Mediterranean-inspired stucco homes with red-tiled roofs. Fishing equipment hung in garages, and several backyards sheltered large cauldrons to tan purse seine nets. Because of its distinct Sicilian ambience, this neighborhood became known as "Garlic Hill" and "Spaghetti Hill."[40]

But many Sicilians could not afford to live on Garlic Hill. The location reinforced its relative upper-class status in Monterey's Sicilian community. Garlic Hill was also called "Boatowner's Hill" because residents often owned purse seiners and thus enjoyed a greater share of the catch. Non–boat owners typically lived closer to downtown and often rented their homes. As Rosalie Ferrante noted, "There was Uptown versus Downtown. Everyone was part of it and you knew where you fit by where you lived. And if your family owned a boat or cannery or property." This geography of class created jealousies. When Sicilians first arrived in Monterey, they were all poor. "Then some people did better than other people. They made something of themselves. Nobody liked that," explained fisherman Mike Maiorana. To complicate matters further, Sicilian village loyalties also divided the community, with intense rivalries between people from Marettimo, San Vito Lo Capo, and Isola Della Femmine.[41]

The gendered labor of the canneries also revealed the class fissures within the Sicilian community. Wives of boat owners rarely worked in the canneries. As middle-class women, they had "good manners, did not work for wages outside the home, owned nicer houses and furniture than their working class counterparts, and participated in community and social events and good works." Most female cannery workers, on the other hand, were relatives or spouses of fishing crew members—men who worked on boats but did not own them. In working in the canneries, they subverted traditional Sicilian gender roles and often became seen as disreputable. But their labor in the canneries was a means to an end—a way to support the family and provide funds to purchase the very houses and boats that were symbols of middle-class status. Their long hours in the canneries also supported their kin members, who were often bringing in the sardines that needed to be processed.[42]

The Santa Rosalia Festival was a way for the Sicilians to patch over these regional and class divisions and present themselves as a united group, but inter-Italian tensions persisted behind the scenes. Sicilian organizers purportedly restricted the involvement of non-Sicilian Italians. Theresa Canepa, whose family was from Genoa, insisted that she was an outsider. She remembered, "I was never in the parade. . . . That was for the Sicilian girls." Her mother, moreover, was never invited to sew costumes or bake with the Sicilian women in preparation for the festival. While the greater Monterey community often made no distinction between Sicilians and other Italians, the planning for the Santa Rosalia Festival demonstrated that they were distinct groups with unequal power.[43]

Nonetheless, Sicilians and other Italians firmly established their place in Monterey society during the interwar years and became ethnic white Americans. According to Matthew Frye Jacobson, the period after the Immigration Act of 1924, which set immigration quotas for each country, witnessed an "ascent of monolithic whiteness." It was then that the assimilation of European immigrants seemed inevitable, and the previous hierarchy of white races became replaced by a culture-based idea of "ethnicity."[44] The Santa Rosalia Festival thus became an *ethnic* celebration that showcased Sicilians' cultural—not racial—difference. Sicilians' strong sense of ethnic identity also precluded the development of radical labor activism and working-class solidarity. As Carol McKibben argues, "Sicilians were busy coming together into a distinctive community bound by fishing and work in the fish canneries. They were not assimilating into a broader culture of American workers."[45]

For Frank Manaka, the Sicilians' rising status had potentially grave consequences. They tried to use their power to exclude him and others from the sardine industry. Born in San Francisco to Japanese immigrants, Manaka and his family settled in Monterey to join his uncle, who owned a fishing boat. Frank soon began plying local waters, eventually buying his own boat, the *Ohio III*. Exorbitant debts forced him to sell his vessel and charter the *Ocean Gift* from San Pedro during the 1940–41 season. When Manaka tried to deliver his catch to the Del Mar cannery, workers turned him away. The Monterey Sardine Industries, Inc., had closed Monterey to all outside boats, which included Manaka's chartered vessel. Because Del Mar was contracted to buy fish only from MSI boats, it could not accept his catch. Manaka had to fish in San Pedro for the rest of the season.[46]

Manaka decided to fight back. He was appalled that MSI, which was dominated by Sicilians, had denied him the right to fish out of his own port. He was also concerned about his twelve crew members, all Japanese residents of Monterey or San Pedro, who depended on him for their livelihood. In 1941 he filed a lawsuit against the association in U.S. District Court. He charged that there had been a conspiracy to restrain him from fishing and selling his products at Monterey. As Manaka reflected, "I had no choice. Back then, I felt if I don't fight for my rights right now, my future is dead." Even though Manaka's father did not believe that he could defeat such a powerful organization, he carried through with his case.[47]

From MSI's perspective, it excluded outside boats in order to give local boat owners priority to sell their fish to Monterey canneries and assure them all profits.[48] In other words, it wanted Monterey capital to stay in Monterey. This was the same logic used when the *New Madrid* and the *Cesare Augusta* tried to deliver fish to the Del Mar cannery the previous year. Technically, Manaka was working on an outside boat, and letting him deliver fish would have meant that a local boat may have been left idle at port. MSI also feared that making an exception for Manaka would undermine its power over the canneries. As it was, MSI assigned boats to deliver to each cannery, so the canners were beholden to the association for their fish supply. However, MSI's policy was supposed to *protect*, not *exclude*, Monterey fishermen like Manaka, who *was* a Monterey resident and just happened to be renting a boat from San Pedro. In October 1941, Judge James Alger Fee ruled that MSI had indeed prevented Manaka from fishing and ordered the group to pay damages of over twenty-eight thousand dollars.[49]

While Fee's ruling focused on MSI's monopolistic control and did not frame the dispute in terms of race, it would be foolhardy to dismiss this factor. When he reflected on the case forty years later, Manaka made a point to state that Italians dominated MSI. His brother, Royal Manaka, also noted that MSI had pressured the Del Mar cannery to reject Frank's fish, despite the fact that its lawyer explained that it was illegal to discriminate against American citizens, regardless of their parentage. Manaka also faced racial animosity when he tried to collect his damages, just after Japan's bombing of Pearl Harbor in December 1941. According to Manaka, MSI's sentiment was "we're not going to pay money so that they could send money to the shoguns in Japan." Manaka, in turn, insisted that he and half his crew were citizens and threatened to charge 6 percent interest. The group finally paid up.[50]

Frank Manaka's lawsuit illustrated the intense local competition that developed within the sardine industry. It did not welcome all comers and give them an equal chance to succeed. Cannery workers, fishermen, boat owners, and canners developed a variety of strategies to protect their interests and ensure the greatest returns on their investments and their labor. Economic prosperity, in turn, often translated into social prestige and power, as was the case with many Sicilian boat owners. But Manaka undermined their command over the local fishery and their ability to determine who could and could not share in the profits. He, like other Montereyans, found a way to retain his autonomy in what could be a cutthroat industry.

THE FILIPINO PROBLEM AND THE ODOR PROBLEM

The sardine industry became central to Monterey's interwar economy, but it did not enjoy universal support. The fish plants attracted unwanted social groups, while booming production resulted in distasteful odors. These changes interfered with the Del Monte Properties Company's enduring desire to promote Monterey as a seaside resort and white residential community. As before, fisheries and tourism continued to clash. By fighting these social and environmental problems, developers and residents hoped to assert their claims to the shore and challenge the sardine industry's dominance.

The changing social makeup of Monterey was one concern. The Filipino "problem" emerged after the 1920 fish cutters' strike, when the canneries brought in Filipino laborers, presumably male, from inland agricultural fields to replace the Japanese.[51] Many Filipino workers continued to travel to Monterey in subsequent years as part of a labor migration route that followed California's agricultural and fishing seasons. But with the onset of the Great Depression, the Monterey and Pacific Grove Chambers of Commerce in 1930 identified the influx of seasonal Filipino cannery laborers as an economic problem because they supposedly deprived local residents of work. In deference to these complaints, Luis Agudo, a Filipino representative, suggested that Filipinos be hired only after locals had been employed or "in such positions as 'white' laborers cannot or will not fill." Agudo also indicated that surplus Filipino workers in Monterey could be forced to go elsewhere.[52]

Even though Agudo was responsive to complaints, the chambers of commerce sought further assurances that Filipinos would not establish a permanent community in Monterey. A week later, they passed a resolution stating that local laborers should be given first preference at the canneries and elsewhere. Most canneries complied with the resolution and agreed to oppose Filipino employment in positions that could be filled with local hires. Meanwhile, a Filipino leader promised the canneries that they would not solicit work but would wait until they were called through an employment agency. For Knut Hovden, who claimed in a promotional brochure that his plant employed "only white help," these measures may have been quite welcome.[53]

Although Pacific Grove resident W. J. Gould insisted that the problem was purely economic and that the two cities were "not discriminating against the Filipinos as a race," the situation clearly reflected a desire to exclude nonwhites. The chambers of commerce believed that the Filipinos would create both "social and economic problems" by establishing a permanent colony in Monterey. The "colonization" of Filipinos, added Del Monte Properties Company representative Jack Beaumont, would also devalue property. He believed that Filipino migrants should be able to live only in neighborhoods with low property values, perhaps referring to the Chinese and Japanese enclaves near downtown Monterey.[54]

The chambers of commerce and the Del Monte Properties Company saw the presence of Filipino labor as inimical to their efforts to promote investment and settlement in Monterey and Pacific Grove. Even though the Filipinos hardly represented a dire threat—in September 1930, a local newspaper reported that there were 32 Filipinos out of a total of 822 cannery workers—these business leaders and developers did not want yet another nonwhite immigrant group to settle in the area.[55] They were troubled by the sardine industry's social impact on the local community and feared that new workers could translate into lost sales. By framing the Filipino "problem" as an issue of protecting local jobs, the chambers of commerce were able to prevent the workers from settling in the area and wrested some power from the canneries.

Other developers and residents were far more concerned about the sardine industry's environmental impact. Noxious odors intensified, particularly as the reduction business exploded after World War I. According to Monterey city engineer H. D. Severance, the odors became particularly acute when high-temperature fish meal dryers malfunctioned and burned the offal. Even though a 1918 ordinance prohibited canneries and fertilizer plants from emitting "any unwholesome, offensive, disagreeable, nauseous, or obnoxious smells, odors or gases," the problem did not stop. Several canneries operated in close proximity along Cannery Row, so it was difficult to trace the odors to a specific plant.[56]

Concerned that cannery pollution and odors hurt Hotel Del Monte business, the Del Monte Properties Company hired University of California sanitary and hydraulic engineer Charles Gilman Hyde to conduct a preliminary study in September 1925.[57] After his inspection, he called attention to the "foul condition" of the water caused by the canneries' discharge of sewage and waste. This pollution had rendered the Hotel Del Monte bathhouse, which pumped saltwater directly from the ocean, unsanitary. According to Hyde, these problems were readily evident. "Indeed, even the most casual inspection by any sensitive, cultured person would reveal the very undesirable conditions which prevail because of the bay pollution just referred to," he explained. Hyde concluded that the company needed to undertake a complete investigation in order to protect the "fullest enjoyable use of the Hotel property" and to prepare data for future legal action against the canneries. To build its case, he recommended collecting and analyzing water samples and hiring a "reliable observer" to record odors at the hotel and the beach at various intervals throughout the day. The company could then use these data to correlate water quality and odors with currents, winds, and industrial operations.[58]

Although it is unclear if the Del Monte Properties Company carried out Hyde's plans, his ideas suggest how empirical, scientific data about the environment could be used to recover damages for pollution. The company needed specific evidence, as "in any court procedure it will probably be necessary to show the degree of responsibility attaching to the several sources of pollution which cause damage to the Company."[59] While Hyde did not address the problem of isolating cannery pollution from other sources of contamination, he clearly recognized the importance of pinpointing blame as much as possible in order to have legal recourse.

The Del Monte Properties Company continued to drive the opposition to cannery odors in the following years. In October 1926, Monterey mayor W. G. Hudson and city manager R. M. Dorton traveled to San Francisco to hire an industrial chemical engineer to study the odors, but their trip came too late to address the arrival of the California State Real Estate Convention in Monterey that same week. Local developers hoped that this event would bring more investors to the region, but Del Monte Properties Company president Samuel Morse complained that the odors would ruin the city's reputation as a residential community because conference attendants "will be greeted by the smell of dead fish." He continued, "It is impossible to estimate in dollars and cents just how much damage we will receive as a result. What should have been estimable advertising benefit will result in serious and permanent damage." In response, the canners agreed to restrict production during the convention in order to eliminate offensive odors.[60]

The abatement of odors was only temporary, as the smells continued to drift into residential neighborhoods and hotels after the convention left town. In October 1928, several local residents called the city manager's office to complain about an especially pungent stench emanating from Cannery Row.[61] One year later, Monterey hotel owners began to grumble that the odors scared away patrons. Jean Juillard of the San Carlos Hotel in downtown Monterey noted that one of his guests cut his visit short, complaining "that he could not sleep all night and that he had been poisoned by the odor of fish." Carl Stanley of the Hotel Del Monte added that many visitors commented on the "beautiful surroundings made uninhabitable by such a terrible stench." He concluded, "There is not the slightest doubt that guests cut short their stay because of it, with resulting loss, not only to the hotel but to the community as a whole."[62]

In response to mounting complaints, the city intensified its odor abatement programs, creating the office of cannery inspector in 1929, a measure deemed "urgent and necessary for the immediate preservation of the public peace, health and safety." The inspector visited the canneries and checked that they had installed thermostatic controls on all meal-drying equipment and a thermographic instrument to record the temperature.[63] In 1931 the city passed another ordinance, administered by the Monterey County Health Department, making it mandatory for fertilizer plants to obtain operating permits. Health department inspectors could revoke permits if machinery did not function properly, and obnoxious odors could bring a fine, imprisonment, or both.[64] For their part, some plants tested new drying equipment that was supposed to mitigate odors, often without success.[65]

Stricter regulation and monitoring did not seem to improve odors, and by 1934 the Del Monte Properties Company had become so frustrated that it filed for an injunction against all twelve Monterey canneries in Monterey County Superior Court. As canners intensified their reduction operations, Del Monte Properties Company lawyers argued that they had permitted large amounts of rotting fish to remain in and about their plants and allowed offensive odors to escape into the air. The odors spread well beyond Cannery Row, creating a public nuisance and causing "great annoyance" and distress to those who encountered them.[66]

The bulk of the Del Monte Properties Company's complaints focused on how odors interfered with tourism and its long-standing efforts to attract home buyers to the region. During the sardine season, the prevailing winds blew from west to east, sending odors directly to the Hotel Del Monte and its extensive grounds. The stench was often so strong that guests and employees became "nauseated and physically distressed." As a result, the company had lost patronage, and it expected "the value of its said hotel and resort property [to] be greatly depreciated." Even though the canneries operated during only part of the peak tourist season, company lawyers argued that the odors had to cease so that tourists would continue to regard Monterey as a desirable vacation destination.[67] Maintaining this reputation was all the more important, as tourism actually experienced growth during the Depression. Even at a time of economic decline, vacation spending, in relation to national income, increased. Employers and politicians believed that expanding paid vacation benefits and increasing tourism promotion would squelch industrial rancor, encourage consumption, and revitalize the economy.[68]

In defending the canneries, attorney John Milton Thompson deployed class-based rhetoric that implicitly pointed to the economic anxieties of the Depression. He argued that any injury suffered by the Del Monte Properties Company was slight in comparison to the impact that plant closures would have on the public welfare. The sardine industry employed thousands of workers and paid out large sums of money for labor, fish, materials, merchandise, supplies, equipment, taxes, fees, and assessments. The sale of canned fish and reduction products also brought money into the region and helped support the local economy. The sardine plants, therefore, directly and indirectly benefited most of the fifteen thousand residents of the Monterey Peninsula.[69]

Thompson did not offer any concrete statistics to support his claims, but data from the 1930 census suggest that the fishing industry was an important regional employer. Out of a total population of 9,141 in Monterey, there were 397 cannery workers and 563 fishermen. The canneries also employed 180 Pacific Grove residents, which had a total population of 5,558.[70] However, the census probably underreported the number of sardine industry workers. Since the census takers canvassed Monterey and Pacific Grove in April and May, after the end of the season, many residents may not have reported their cannery employment. During the 1936–37 season, the *Monterey Peninsula Herald* estimated that the canneries employed two thousand people daily.[71] Even after subtracting migrant laborers who did not have permanent residence, the number of local cannery workers in the 1930s, in all likelihood, far exceeded the census figures.

Thompson drew clear social distinctions between these local residents, who depended on the sardine industry, and tourists, who had no vested interest in the region. He noted that the odors were a "mere matter of aesthetics affecting only the olfactory organs of super sensitive persons seeking pleasure at the pleasure resort conducted by the plaintiff." Any odors created by the defendants had caused "little, if any, financial loss to said Peninsula and little, if any, real discomfort or distress but rather a fanciful annoyance to . . . persons having no true relation to the public welfare of said community."[72] Put another way, it was absurd to force the canneries to eliminate odors and undermine the local economy for the benefit of effete interlopers. Visitors might turn up their noses at the fish plants, but the stench signified jobs and paychecks for locals.

Thompson also turned the odor problem on its head and claimed that tourists had created the very odors that their sensitive noses found so offensive. The hotel's sewer outfall was slightly west of the grounds, and the sewage flowed "for several hundred feet across the beach sands near the Del Monte Bathhouse and near said Hotel causing a very unpleasant, disagreeable and obnoxious odor and stench, greater in extent than that from any of the defendants' plants." Thus, the hotel itself was causing "much of the discomfort and distress alleged in the complaint and attributed to these defendants."[73]

Although Thompson played upon class consciousness and local identity, it is important to remember that he represented wealthy and powerful corporations with minimal community ties. Local citizens who had personal connections to the region operated several canneries, such as the San Carlos Canning Company and the Hovden Food Products Company, but outside interests ran some of the other plants. For instance, Frank E. Booth's company was based in San Francisco, and the California Packing Corporation had extensive operations in the West.[74] While Thompson adeptly emphasized the importance of fishing to the local community, this strategy was ultimately intended to protect the economic interests of more affluent canners. His clients' actual concern for Monterey's working-class citizens likely varied.

The defense concluded by pointing to the difficulties of measuring and quantifying odors and their effects. According to the Booth cannery, the Del Monte Properties Company simply did not have evidence to support its allegations. It could not prove definitively that gases and odors coming from the plants were polluting the hotel grounds. It could not ascertain if the equipment was obsolete or if it was even possible to operate without any odors escaping into the atmosphere. It could not determine how much patronage had been lost due to any odors. And it could not demonstrate that the odors constituted a public nuisance. In short, canners argued that the Del Monte Properties Company's allegations were baseless and purely subjective.[75]

Nonetheless, the canners and the Del Monte Properties Company agreed to a settlement that mandated the elimination and mitigation of odors. Beginning August 1, 1934, the plants had to meet stringent new provisions. All equipment had to be installed with temperature regulatory devices and hoods to catch vapors. These gases, in turn, had to be heated and conveyed through a system that supposedly eliminated odors before discharge into the atmosphere. Any water left over from reduction had to be free of solids before release, and the plants could not process or keep any spoiled fish or fish that had been caught more than forty-eight hours prior. In case of future complaints, the court placed the burden of proof on the canners to demonstrate that odors did not originate from their plants. All of the canneries signed the agreement, except the Hovden cannery, which signed a separate order.[76]

The plants experimented with odor abatement equipment, but the smells persisted and caused more community outrage.[77] An October 1934 editorial in the *Monterey Peninsula Herald* proclaimed that residents had been deprived "of the right to breathe clean air." The writer went on to challenge John Milton Thompson's class-based arguments in support of the canners: "What is good for the guests of Hotel Del Monte and the other hotels of Monterey and Pacific Grove IS NOT TOO GOOD FOR THE PEOPLE OF MONTEREY AND PACIFIC GROVE. Why should the people of this region be treated with contempt and be made to suffer ignominy because of conscienceless greed?" In other words, residents and tourists alike deserved to inhale fresh air, and canners had no right to foul the atmosphere simply because they supplied jobs and revenue to the city.[78] Rather than accusing the Del Monte Properties Company of attacking the economy, canners needed to be held accountable for the odors. And to some extent, they were. In November 1934, the Del Monte Properties

Company requested a contempt of court hearing for the E. B. Gross and Del Mar canneries because of their alleged violation of the settlement. Gross was found guilty and paid $250 in fines, while Del Mar dodged prosecution. Local residents also formed the Peninsula Health and Welfare League to act as a watchdog over cannery odors.[79]

Recognizing the continuing rancor over odors, Monterey mayor Walter L. Teaby tried to open the lines of communication between competing parties. In January 1935, he presided over a dinner with local officials, cannery owners, and representatives of the Del Monte Properties Company. Teaby's goal was to come up with a solution that would be acceptable to all interests. Samuel Morse noted, "I believe the canneries can be operated without harm to other interests of the community." While many canners concurred and agreed to help eliminate the odors, George Harper of the Monterey Canning Company refused to pledge his support. He declared, "Nobody has died of fish odor yet—in fact it's one of the healthiest things we have!"[80] By this point, scientists had long disputed the contention that odors caused or were a sign of disease. For Harper, they were a sign of economic well-being. He appeared unwilling to budge.

Likewise, the opposition intensified. Pacific Grove Mayor Sheldon Gilmer jumped on the anti-odor bandwagon, and much like Pacific Improvement Company executive J. P. Pryor thirty years earlier, he argued that the fish smells prevented the region from becoming a tourist mecca. He noted, "The Monterey Peninsula was intended by nature as a place of scenic beauty suitable for fine homes and vacation attractions. The [sardine] industry is an enemy to this pre-destined purpose. . . . There is no question that the shoreline from China Point to Pt. Pinos is the most attractive of any portion of the Peninsula but through the oppressive stench, for which the canneries are responsible, it has depreciated greatly in value."[81] Gilmer, like Pryor, envisioned the coastline as a place for recreation and tourism; the elimination of fish odors would allow Pacific Grove to achieve its full potential.

Facing pressure from numerous parties, the City of Monterey passed another ordinance in May 1935 to mitigate "offensive" or "obnoxious" odors. As in the previous ordinance, all plants were required to pay two hundred dollars for a license to reduce fish materials. It also set up numerous provisions, many of them identical to the superior court settlement. Floors, gutters, walls, ceilings, and doors had to be made of a material, such as concrete, that could be easily cleaned. Plants could not allow fish or vegetable matter to accumulate and decompose or discharge this material from their buildings. Gases created by drying fish meal had to pass through an incinerator, or they had to be disposed of or dissolved to prevent the escape of odors. The cannery inspector could revoke licenses for failure to comply with these provisions, and any violation would be considered a misdemeanor.[82]

The odor ordinances were well intentioned, but they did not noticeably reduce smells or eliminate the growing tensions between Pacific Grove and Monterey. While Monterey cannery inspector Major W. H. Landers insisted that the canners had made "real progress" toward odor abatement and wanted to "remedy the abuses of the past," Pacific Grove residents continued to complain.[83] At a city council meeting in February 1936, the city clerk read letters from eight people reporting noxious odors, allegedly caused by reduction activity. Residents explained that the smells had devalued their property and driven five families from Pacific Grove south to Carmel, well beyond the reach of foul offshore breezes. The city council agreed that the problem had become particularly acute and decided to consider taking legal action against the City of Monterey.[84]

Although Pacific Grove's lawsuit appeared imminent by September 1936, support for legal action dwindled the following year. The city council ordered city attorney Reginald Foster to file the lawsuit in November and allocated two thousand dollars to cover legal costs, but several Pacific Grove residents began circulating a petition in March 1937 asking the city to drop the complaint. In a curious turnabout, they claimed that the canneries were important to Pacific Grove commerce and employed roughly six hundred residents.[85] Against the backdrop of the Depression, odors probably seemed less onerous than unemployment. Canners also agreed to help purchase a machine that chlorinated cannery waste, and they participated in an antipollution campaign during the 1938–39 season.[86] Thus, Landers assured Gilmer that all fish odors, except for a slight odor at low tide, could be eliminated during the next season.[87]

Not surprisingly, Samuel Morse was not satisfied with Landers's odor abatement program. He made another complaint to the Monterey City Council in 1939, alleging that the Del Monte Properties Company continued to lose valuable real estate sales due to persisting odors. But after all of its efforts, the city council was no longer sympathetic and did not cave in to Morse's demands. City officials insisted that they had taken active measures to abate the nuisance and that it would be impossible to eliminate all smells associated with the fishing industry.[88]

While the city council stood by industrial activities on Cannery Row, it still tried to bolster tourism elsewhere along the waterfront. Cleaning up the rest of the city's shoreline was key to tourism promotion. In 1941 it decided not to renew the lease of the Booth cannery, the only cannery outside of Cannery Row and inside Monterey harbor. Because the council wanted to beautify this area for recreation- and pleasure-seekers, the cannery had to go. Compared to his reduction plant on Cannery Row, Booth was losing money in the sardine canning business anyway. As a result, company executives decided not to relocate the plant elsewhere in the city. The cannery ceased operations in May 1941 and was largely destroyed by fire in December 1941, prior to its complete demolition.[89] The city thus continued its tricky balancing act, simultaneously promoting both tourism and fisheries on the Monterey waterfront.

By and large, the sardine industry, odors and all, benefited from widespread local support during the interwar years. Indeed, many Montereyans believed that the odors bode well for the local economy. As one self-proclaimed "Proud Fish Packer" wrote in the *Monterey Peninsula Herald* in 1941, "I am proud of my job as a fish packer and only wish that it was a year-around job. . . . I don't see why you should complain about a little fish smell."[90] Canneries provided jobs to many local residents, and the odors, this worker implied, were a minor inconvenience.

But odors were a major inconvenience for the Del Monte Properties Company and other tourism-minded residents. They envisioned the coastline as a seaside resort flanked by white residential neighborhoods, not as an industrial place of nonwhite workers and foul odors. While they prevented the establishment of a "permanent Filipino colony," a favorable court settlement and several anti-odor ordinances did not stop the smells. Enforcing these regulations was simply next to impossible because, unlike other forms of pollution, odors could not be quantified or measured empirically. Odors, moreover, were subjective and did not offend everyone. Indeed, most Montereyans accepted the Cannery Row stench and welcomed full boatloads of sardines and canneries buzzing with activity. They proved more than willing to tolerate the odors.[91]

During the interwar years, most Montereyans catered to the sardine industry and concentrated less attention on tourism. A *Monterey Peninsula*

Herald editorial from 1940 illustrated this shift in favor of the fisheries. It acknowledged the region's reputation as a resort and retirement destination but then concluded that the fishing industry made the community "real":

> We are not just birds in gilded cages, thank heaven! Nor are we merely purveyors of luxuries and enticements for meandering tourists. We have been saved from that. . . . Our scattered historic landmarks are noble and worthy, attractions and assets to the community. But the fishing fleet in Monterey Bay is the grandest picture on the coast of California—and when those boats, heavily laden, come in with their catches it is a sight to be remembered.[92]

Monterey was no longer simply a tourist attraction made famous by the Hotel Del Monte and nearby Pebble Beach. Instead, the city boasted a lucrative fishing industry that had gained prominence in a few short decades. In extracting sardines from local waters and turning them into desirable commodities, the sardine business had enabled many residents to prosper during a time of national economic hardship.

Beneath this triumphant rhetoric, however, was a community that quarreled bitterly over the social and environmental transformations that had unfolded along the coastline. The benefits of the interwar sardine industry were spread unequally among Monterey's residents, and some individuals found little about which to celebrate. In particular, those involved in the tourism industry could not disentangle their operations from the fisheries and complained that their businesses were suffering. Nonetheless, these debates all but evaporated with the United States' entrance into World War II. Wartime Monterey became a sardine machine, bringing even more dramatic changes to the fishery and to Monterey society— changes that residents found themselves virtually powerless to control.

5 BOOM AND BUST

IN WARTIME MONTEREY

Much as it did throughout the American West and the nation as a whole, World War II transformed Monterey.[1] Appearing inconsequential to a country fighting a war against fascism, tourism stagnated. The Del Monte Properties Company even leased the Hotel Del Monte to the U.S. Navy for use as a preflight training school. When military personnel began to filter onto the hotel grounds, the days of genteel railroad tourists strolling through the manicured gardens or relaxing on the verandas came to a permanent end.[2] On the other hand, wartime needs translated into a tremendous boost to the sardine industry, as the protein-rich fish were required to feed Americans at home and soldiers abroad. Conservation policies were largely abandoned, and the federal government took over production, setting high quotas for canned sardines statewide. The manufacture of tins of fish now superseded that of fish meal and fish oil—reduction products that were instrumental to the growth of the interwar fishery.

Monterey's sardine industry became an asset to the war effort, but the city's coastal locale and social makeup also made it a target for government directives that undermined efforts to meet federal sardine quotas. The military draft drained the workforce, while the Pacific Coast's vulnerability to a sea-based attack limited fishermen's mobility and prevented them from ranging widely to find sardines. By virtue of race and national origin, Italian and Japanese fishermen also faced enemy alien restrictions and forced evacuation, which banished them from the sardine industry and reconfigured the social contours of Monterey in the process. Despite these challenges, Monterey answered the call to duty, landing more sardines during the war than in any period before.³ Local residents' command over the industry and its workforce fell by the way-side, but most Montereyans willingly stepped up production to meet wartime orders. Of course, they reaped higher profits in the process.

The end of the war and the phasing out of federal mandates did not mean that Monterey returned to business as usual. Montereyans, in fact, were never able to regain complete control over the fishery. Beginning in 1946, one disastrous sardine catch succeeded another. While the industry had encountered unpredictable natural cycles in the past, this time the predicament was much more ominous. Given their overwhelming dependence on the sardine industry, many fishermen and cannery workers did not know where to turn, and they could not rely solely on their own resources and tactics, as they had before. Meanwhile, scientists entered the fray again and embarked on even more ambitious studies to develop an explanation for the sardine's disappearance and a plan for its revival.

In the course of a decade, Montereyans encountered two over-powering forces—World War II and the collapse of the sardine fishery—that undermined their visions for the coastline. Those who pursued the tourist trade saw their industry swept up by patriotic fervor and a single-minded focus on fish production. Most participants in the sardine industry benefited, but federal wartime imperatives also weakened their autonomy and excluded all Japanese residents and many Italians in the most discriminatory fashion. After the war, the scarcity of fish threatened to obliterate years of hard work and prosperity. In both instances, local residents could no longer direct the sardine industry as they had in the past. Many refused to accept their complicity in the sardine's decline; ultimately, they could neither sustain the immigrant success stories of the interwar years nor save Monterey's reputation as the sardine capital of the world.

"THE FISH OF THE SEA ARE THERE TO BE TAKEN"

Federal intervention in the sardine industry came shortly after the United States entered the war. Canned sardines quickly became critical for domestic markets, Allied troops, and the Lend-Lease program, which gave President Franklin Roosevelt the power to dispose of arms or goods to any country whose defense was considered vital to national security.⁴ In order to maintain an adequate supply of seafood, Roosevelt issued Executive Order 9204, appointing the secretary of the interior as fishery coordinator and giving him the power to designate parts of the United States Fish and Wildlife Service as the Office of Fishery Coordination. The office maintained a close relationship with government agencies and fishery industries in order to obtain information about conservation, consumption of fish, and production at fishery facilities. It could also encourage "coordination of effort and maximum utilization" in order to meet the government's needs for fishery products.[5]

The federal government's power over the California sardine industry expanded further in September 1942, when the War Production Board issued Order M-206, allowing the board to allocate sardine boats between ports and the catch of sardines within ports to make "the most efficient use of sardine facilities." Initially administered by the California Fish and Game Commission, the federal Office of Fishery Coordination took over the allocation program by the 1943–44 season.[6] All boats had to report to the fisheries coordinator, who sent them to a cannery with an empty hopper so that each plant had an adequate supply of fish. During heavy catches, the coordinator even forced boats to deliver to other ports.[7] Monterey producers often balked at these new policies. When Oscar E. Sette, district pilchards coordinator, instructed one-third of Monterey boats to unload in San Francisco, AFL Seine and Line Fishermen's Union secretary John Crivello told Secretary of Interior Harold Ickes that the order was "impractical, arbitrary, and can in no way contribute to the Federal Government's goal of 'maximum production' of food for human consumption."[8]

Some federal mandates were at cross-purposes with calls for increased production. For instance, the requisitioning of Monterey fishing boats for military shore patrol duties made it difficult for fishermen to meet federal quotas. At the start of the 1941–42 season, the local purse seine fleet numbered roughly seventy boats. In November, the navy took twelve boats and the army took two. By the end of the season, the navy had confiscated an additional twenty-seven boats, forcing fishermen to charter boats from other ports.[9] For Sal Colletto and others, the program represented a huge financial loss. Colletto had paid forty-four thousand dollars to a shipyard in Tacoma, Washington, to build the *Dante Alighieri* before the navy took it to Treasure Island; he subsequently spent sixty-thousand dollars in two years to charter boats. Frustrated, he wrote a letter to Harold

Monterey's sardine industry is an essential war industry.

It produces no aircraft, guns, ships or tanks.

But it does produce a highly nutritious article of diet for the men who do the fighting.

Yes, Monterey-packed sardines have probably fed our fighting men on every front in this war.

Today on Fishermen's wharf and along the beach you'll see soldiers in helmets, with guns. And men in the blue of the navy.

Physical things have changed. Many of the ships have gone off to war. The men that sailed them, too.

There is fresh in the mind the inexorable hardness of the sea. It gives no quarter, asks none. Those familiar with the pages of Conrad need no tragic stories of wartime disaster to bring home this lesson.

But the appeal of the sea is not physical alone.

It is mostly of the soul—a primitive thing going deep down and far back.

There is still about Monterey's waterfront that same drawing power exerted by waterfronts the world over.

And the same balm.

There is no other place like it.

Yet it is all the waterfronts of the world.

FIG. 5.1 This illustration from the *Monterey Peninsula Herald*'s annual sardine edition argues that the sardine industry was an essential wartime enterprise, but it also suggests that the lure of the sea went beyond patriotism and distinguished Monterey and other coastal communities. *Monterey Peninsula Herald, Sardine Edition No. 8*, February 26, 1943, p. 7. Copyright © 2007 The Monterey County Herald. All rights reserved.

Ickes in September 1943. The Interior Department responded by issuing Colletto a priority contract to build a new boat.[10]

Even as it demanded peak production, the federal government also circumscribed fishing activities because the Pacific Coast was a sensitive military zone. Boats could depart and return to port only during daylight, a complete reversal of the nighttime excursions that were essential for sardine fishing. Before leaving, fishermen had to report to the port captain and tell him where they were planning to fish. They could not work in the "danger zone" near Fort Ord, about ten miles north of Monterey, unless they had written permission. While they were at sea, they could not use their radio phones.[11] These restrictions constrained fishermen's mobility, as they could no longer travel whenever and wherever they wanted to bring home a full load of sardines. Federal priorities snubbed fishermen's intimate knowledge of the coastline and eradicated their various strategies for locating and catching fish.

Protecting the Pacific Coast also required eliminating enemy infiltration. The United States classified all noncitizen residents from the Axis nations—Germany, Italy, and Japan—as "enemy aliens" and placed restrictions on them. Only fishing boats with all-citizen crews could work, and each crew member had to receive U.S. Coast Guard clearance and carry identification.[12] In addition, enemy aliens were forbidden from working in the canneries, had to surrender weapons, ammunition, cameras, shortwave radios and transmitters, and other papers, and needed permission to travel more than five miles from their homes. By the end of the 1941–42 season, 2,234 of 8,759 California fishermen had been prohibited from fishing because of these directives.[13] While some enemy aliens insisted on their loyalty, federal officials responded that "it is necessary to inconvenience the many loyal aliens by regulations which are required to curb the subversive activities of a few disloyal aliens."[14]

The German presence was insignificant, but Italians and Japanese, many of whom lacked or could not obtain (in the case of the Japanese) American citizenship, formed the backbone of the Monterey fishing fleet. Out of 10,084 Monterey residents in 1940, there were 1,724 foreign-born whites, including 795 Italians and 74 Germans. There were also 389 Japanese, of whom 143 were foreign-born.[15] While the enemy-alien ban did not have a major impact on the canneries, which had a more diverse workforce with a sizable migrant contingent that did not have permanent residence on the Pacific Coast, it affected roughly 25 percent of Monterey's eight hundred sardine fishermen.[16] It also affected almost 75 percent of the market fishermen, as well as abalone fishermen, who were mostly Japanese, and albacore fishermen, who were both Italian and Japanese.[17] Further, without immigrant fishermen taking to the sea, local ethnic businesses suffered. As Jim Tabata, proprietor of Sunrise Grocery, noted, "A large part of our business was connected with supplying the Japanese fishing boats with their grocery supplies. And, of course, they stopped fishing, so that part of the business stopped."[18]

The federal government took its fears one step further, establishing a policy to evacuate enemy aliens, including Italians, from the Pacific Coast beginning on February 24, 1942. In Monterey's Sicilian community, most families had at least one member without United States citizenship. Unless they were willing to split up, entire families had to move, relocating inland to Salinas or elsewhere for six months. The *Monterey Peninsula Herald* estimated that six hundred noncitizen Sicilians would have to move from Monterey; in taking their families with them, the total evacuation topped more than fourteen hundred. According to Carol McKibben, it was often the Sicilian women who had not acquired citizenship, as they often led private lives that focused on family and community. Even Sicilians who had lived in Monterey for decades were considered potentially dangerous.[19]

Most Monterey Sicilians acquiesced to the forced evacuations, but they also made it a point to distance themselves from the Japanese by emphasizing the issue of citizenship. Since it was only noncitizen Sicilians who were under attack, the Sicilian community emphasized the loyalty and patriotism of their community as a whole. Sicilian boat owners took a leadership role and sent a telegram to President Roosevelt to voice their support of the Allied forces. They also purchased war bonds and highlighted their contributions to the fishing and canning industries. As soon as alien Sicilians were allowed to return to Monterey, many began attending citizenship classes. World War II compelled the Sicilian community to adopt an American political identity.[20]

For Monterey's Japanese community, the issue was completely about race and had nothing to do with citizenship. Because of the Japanese attack on Pearl Harbor, all Japanese, regardless of citizenship, became targets. On February 19, 1942, President Roosevelt issued Executive Order 9066, which authorized the Western Defense Command to secure the West Coast for military purposes. Fearing Japanese subversion, the government sub-

sequently rounded up the coastal Japanese—both alien and citizen—
and sent them to temporary assembly centers. Exclusion Order No. 15,
issued in April 1942, forced 1,578 Japanese in Monterey County to the
Salinas rodeo grounds and then to Poston or Gila, Arizona, and other
inland relocation centers, where they stayed for much of the war.[21] The
Japanese had owned more than 50 percent of the retail fish markets and
wholesale fish processing plants on Fisherman's Wharf, but they had to
sell their belongings and businesses before they left, usually for a fraction of their value.[22]

Within the context of wartime security, the federal government reorganized the social contours of Monterey. The city's physical locale sub-
jected the community to extreme measures that targeted people from Axis
nations and those who worked at sea. Local identities based on race, ethnicity, class, village, kin group, and residence wielded less power over
the social hierarchies within the sardine industry. World politics and wartime imperatives now determined which groups were ostracized and
banned from local waters. Most Montereyans in question had little choice
but to comply with the orders. When they could, as with the Sicilians,
they tried to reassert their social position. In emphasizing their patriotism and separating themselves from the Japanese, Sicilians bridged class,
gender, and generational divisions to put forth a united front.

As they did across the United States, the armed forces also put a significant drain on the local labor force. With military enlistments, the fishing fleet faced a serious labor shortage. In an effort to teach a local
knowledge of nature that usually took fishermen several years to acquire,
Knut Hovden advised establishing a school to train young men to be crew
members.[23] Harold Ickes recognized the gravity of the situation and asked
the War Manpower Commission to give California sardine and mackerel fishermen and cannery workers a ninety-day selective services deferment in 1943.[24] Normally, deferments were available only to men in certain
age groups and to those "active in war production or in support of the
National health, safety or interest"; these "essential activities" included
commercial fishing and food processing. Men aged 18 through 25 were
exempt only if they met specific conditions, such as being the captain or
engineer of a fishing vessel of twenty tons or more. Men aged 26 through
29 and 30 through 37 remained in civilian life "for the time being" or
for "an indefinite period," respectively.[25] The goal was to keep experienced men engaged in the fisheries, "of which the sardine fishery is far

and away the most productive," according to Kenneth Mosher, area coordinator of fisheries.[26]

Finding these exemptions to be inadequate, Horace Mercurio, president of the Monterey Sardine Industries, Inc., asked that deferments be extended to other "key men" in the fishing industry. In particular, he asked that skiff men be added to the list. Each boat had two designated skiff men who took care of the net once a set was made, jumping between the purse seiner and the skiff. According to Mercurio, skippers needed "young, energetic, lively skiff men"; older fishermen simply could not replace them.[27] They knew how to navigate the unstable vessel during rough storms, and they had acquired a familiarity with sardine habits and setting nets. Their specialized understanding of nature and fishing technology, combined with their youth and strength, made them indispensable members of a fishing crew. Initially, Elmer Higgins, Mosher's superior, denied Mercurio's request, but some skiff men were eventually able to obtain deferments.[28] Skippers had to convince government officials that crew members were not easily replaced and that they could not expect higher production without experienced workers.

Even with deferments, sardine fishermen found that their jobs no longer afforded them the same freedom. Not only did they have to fish at certain times and in certain places and to deliver to designated canneries, but their off-season options became constrained. To maintain their eligibility for deferments, fishermen had to find employment in another "essential" industry during the off-season. They could stay in Monterey and fish for the fancy summer pack or the market fisheries; they could go south to San Pedro and fish for tuna and mackerel; or they could travel north and work in the shipyards in the San Francisco Bay area. However, if the government did not see these jobs as "essential," the fishermen would be drafted during the summer and would be unavailable at the start of the sardine season in August.[29] They could no longer take a break from work or pick up a few odd jobs to make ends meet.

Wartime policies also reduced the cannery workforce. The draft forced many female workers to leave their jobs when they followed their male relatives to other military posts.[30] Although cannery foremen, managers, supervisors, superintendents, and refrigerating engineers were exempt from the draft, membership in the Cannery Workers Union dropped by nearly half by the end of the 1942–43 season.[31] The labor shortage became a topic of considerable concern for many canners, including

Frank J. Leard, head of the Custom House Packing Corporation. He explained, "The government has insisted that we increase the number of fish put in cans and minimize the reduction end but we can't very well do this if they take away all our manpower." Some canneries began hiring workers from outlying communities, such as Salinas and Watsonville, and sent trucks and buses to transport them to and from Monterey. Others suggested changing school hours in order to hire local high school students.[32]

Like industrial factories throughout the nation, Monterey canneries addressed the labor shortage by recruiting local housewives, invoking their patriotism and emphasizing the importance of the fishing industry to the war effort. Many women responded to these campaigns and began the difficult work in the canneries. California Packing Corporation (Cal Pack) manager George Dollar praised the women's contributions and noted that he had employed an average of twenty-three "volunteer" women, who packed more than five hundred cases a day. The *Monterey Peninsula Herald* published the women's names and exclaimed, "We love the women! Hurrah for their side!"[33] But the female workers lacked skill and loyalty and irritated other canners, who aspired to keep production efficient and orderly. Hovden was upset with their fickle behavior, noting, "It takes three weeks to train these girls to work fast and pack fish the right way. Then what happens? They meet some sailor or soldier, they get married, they leave me flat."[34] In response to complaints that the women also damaged equipment, George Clemens, secretary of the Monterey Fish Processors Association, suggested distributing instructions and teaching classes to demonstrate canning techniques.[35]

Frustration spread to longtime cannery workers, who resented the newcomers' unwillingness to join the union. Margaret Fahrion, president of the Woman's Civic Club, insisted that they had no intention of becoming union members because "their principles will not allow them to have any part in it." Facing intimidation, some chose to leave their new jobs. Union member Neely S. Best lambasted Fahrion, explaining how hard the union had fought for better wages and working conditions. Many union members, including her two sons, were fighting the war overseas. If the women did not join the union, "then I am very sure they would rather be a little short of food than to eat the fish you people could have packed while aiding in destroying their Union." *Monterey County Labor News* editor W. M. O'Donnell also urged the workers to put aside their "principles" and join

HER PIN-UP PICTURE

Like many other Peninsula housewives . . . she took a war job helping to produce food. To help HIM.

In the heart of almost every woman, the regulars and the volunteers who did such a magnificent job during the season just closed, there's the picture of a relative in uniform.

Those willing workers will be welcomed back again next season to keep up the production of food which is so vital to the war effort.

They know their fighting men are depending upon them as they are depending upon the men on the fighting fronts.

It's a cooperative affair, this American way of life we've got to work for each other, fight for each other, pull together to defend it.

CARMEL CANNING CO.

J. R. PERRY, Supt.

MEMBER MONTEREY FISH PROCESSORS ASSN.

FIG. 5.2 The Carmel Canning Company tried to lure women back to the canning lines by invoking their patriotism and their femininity. As the headline suggests, they were "pin-up" material, like Rita Hayworth and Betty Grable, the most famous bombshells of the day. *Monterey Peninsula Herald, Sardine Edition No. 10*, April 6, 1945, p. 6. Copyright © 2007 The Monterey County Herald. All rights reserved.

the union as part of their patriotic duty. "We can no more afford to let our personal feelings interfere with our contributions to the war effort than do the men in uniform," he noted.[36]

The employment of these presumably white middle-class women in the canneries both exposed and stirred up class tensions in Monterey society. While all cannery workers felt some need to contribute to the war effort, their patriotism did not necessarily unite them. Temporary women workers did not prize union membership or embrace its benefits because they did not see their employment as long-term. They were loyal Americans, not loyal labor supporters. Permanent cannery workers seemed to interpret the rejection of unionism as a blow to their calls for labor solidarity and as a sign of disrespect to the men whose jobs these women filled.

Despite workers' emphasis on unionism, wartime demands for maximum production often suppressed labor activism. In March 1942, the AFL fishermen's union agreed to work seven nights per week, instead of taking the usual Saturday night off.[37] Monterey fishermen and cannery workers suffered another blow when federal circuit judge William Denman ended the AFL closed shop in 1943 and prohibited the AFL from forcing CIO members to join its union, collecting a fee of twelve dollars per CIO crewman delivering fish to Monterey, and refusing to process CIO fish.[38] Cannery workers also had limited power to negotiate higher wages, as the War Labor Board refused all wage hikes and requests for equal wages with workers in San Pedro and San Francisco during the 1943–44 season.[39] Canners provided other incentives instead, such as granting bonuses if cannery workers accepted all work opportunities offered during any one month.[40] They also raised the price paid to fishermen per ton of sardines from $16.50 during the 1941–42 season to $22 during the following two seasons.[41]

Although canners and federal officials adopted a variety of strategies to churn out a continuous supply of sardines, nature sometimes interfered with their efforts.[42] As Cal Pack personnel manager Jane Boone noted, "People on the outside don't understand what an irregular, peculiar industry this is. The weather and fishing conditions are irregular; every day is different. The quantity of fish is undependable."[43] This unpredictability was evident toward the end of the 1941–42 season. A combination of human and natural factors—stormy weather, submarine scares, and naval restrictions—limited the catch in Northern California, so California governor Culbert Olson allowed fishing for thirty days after the end of the season. California Attorney General Earl Warren ruled that Olson had exceeded his powers, but the season was ultimately a success, with Monterey landing 250,290 tons of sardines.[44]

The federal government demanded even more sardines the following season—an additional 20 percent of the canneries' production, bringing the total amount of sardines earmarked for the government to 80 percent. But by January 1943, California sardine output was 1.5 million cases behind the previous season. In addition to a shortage of boats, the *Pacific Fisherman* noted "that the essential difficulty in rationalizing sardine production this season has rested in the vagaries of the sardines themselves. They have not followed the pattern on which boat allocations have been based."[45] Otto Lang, pilchard administrator of the War Production Board, responded by prohibiting reduction of whole sardines and requiring canners to pack a minimum of 13.5 cases for each ton of fish received.[46] While these orders diverted more fish to canning, they did nothing to control the actual supply of sardines.

The federal government wanted nature to conform to its arbitrary demands and quotas. Harold Ickes, for one, believed that the supply of fish was unlimited. "Unlike all other foodstuffs, the fish of the sea are there to be taken, if manpower and equipment are available," he noted.[47] Ickes's statement was consistent with national wartime attitudes that put conservation policy on the "back burner." Nature was supposed to provide; its resources were needed "to stock the arsenal of democracy."[48] This stance assumed that nature could respond to shifting human desires, but sardine stocks could not always become available when the government wanted. The size of the workforce, the quantity of equipment, and the length of the season only partially determined production; the ability to harvest large amounts of sardines also depended on a nature that was unpredictable and limited. Ickes's vision of nature made endlessly abundant through labor and technology was illusory.

During the next two seasons, Monterey bounced back to lead the California sardine industry. The total tonnage for the 1943–44 season was roughly 212,000, about 30,000 tons higher than the previous season and 6 percent above the average for the previous five years. Monterey canned 1.5 million cases, 9 percent above the last season and within 1 percent of the five-year average. Meal and oil production were 18 and

20 percent higher, respectively. Monterey operators produced these impressive numbers in spite of a smaller fishing fleet and cannery workforce.[49] And they kept up the pace the following season. The catch of October 1944 was the greatest in the city's history up to that point—82,929 tons. "This was fishing such as the War Food Administration had been begging for," according to the *Pacific Fisherman*. Nature was finally fulfilling government demands. While labor shortages diverted many sardines into reduction, which required fewer workers than canning, Monterey plants still produced 464,900 cases of sardines that month.[50]

After the successful 1944–45 season, Sette declared that the government would need an even greater amount of sardines the following season. The War Food Administration set a goal of 5 million cases of sardines, with Monterey's quota at 2.15 million cases. The federal government, moreover, did not foresee a reduction in the need for sardines or any changes in regulation even after the war.[51] In anticipation of postwar demand, local entrepreneurs planned new construction. Buster Sollecito opened Enterprise Packers in 1945, while Christopher Palma, Ray Lucido, and Tom Alliotti broke ground on the Sea Beach Packing Company later that year. The Del Vista Packing Company, erected shortly thereafter, became the last plant constructed on Cannery Row. Twenty-three fish processing plants lined Ocean View Avenue by 1946.[52]

While the war had boosted production along Cannery Row, it had the opposite effect on the scientific investigations of the California Fish and Game Commission's Bureau of Marine Fisheries.[53] Many staff members were drafted into the armed forces. The bureau lacked equipment and materials, and the military requisitioned several commission patrol boats. In 1939 Governor Olson also replaced the three commission officials with his own appointees, who had, in hindsight, an overly optimistic view of the fishery. They reported that the sardine population was in "good health" in 1944, despite the commission scientists' cautionary reports in the late 1930s. The bureau continued the essential phases of the sardine work,

FIG. 5.3 *(facing page)* According to this Monterey Canning Company advertisement, fishery workers, like soldiers on the front lines, answered the call to duty and successfully met wartime demands. *Monterey Peninsula Herald, Sardine Edition, No. 10,* April 6, 1945, p. 5. Copyright © 2007 The Monterey County Herald. All rights reserved.

He's The World's Best
Fed Fighting Man

Uncle Sam's fighting forces are the best fed and healthiest in the world.

And men and women of the Monterey Peninsula are doing their part to keep them that way. It takes both kinds of fighters to win a war—those on the home front and those on the fighting front.

The cannery worker is every inch a soldier. Not shooting down Zeros, lying in a fox-hole or blasting Nazis with a machine gun ... but doing a magnificent job producing food for the men on the fighting front.

There must be hundreds of plain, garden-variety Americans that the men on the front never hear about ... Americans who are backing them up as surely as though they were fighting side by side.

Monterey Canning Co.
1918-1945

MEMBER MONTEREY FISH PROCESSORS ASSN.

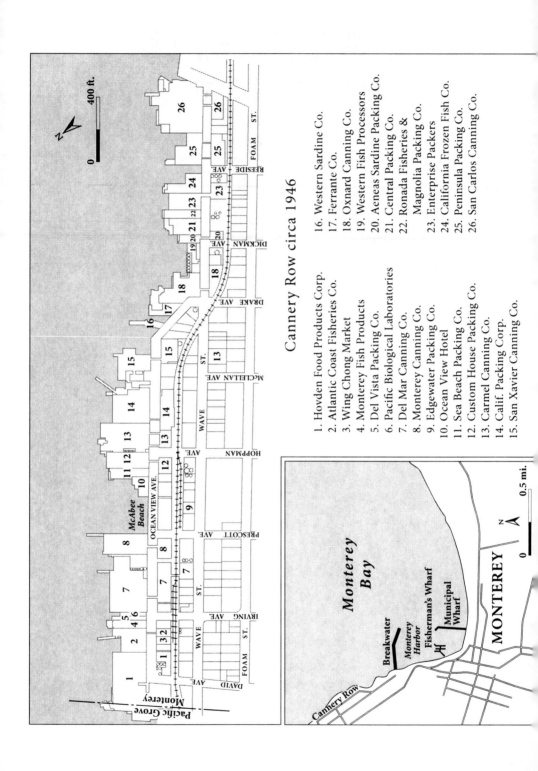

Cannery Row circa 1946

1. Hovden Food Products Corp.
2. Atlantic Coast Fisheries Co.
3. Wing Chong Market
4. Monterey Fish Products
5. Del Vista Packing Co.
6. Pacific Biological Laboratories
7. Del Mar Canning Co.
8. Monterey Canning Co.
9. Edgewater Packing Co.
10. Ocean View Hotel
11. Sea Beach Packing Co.
12. Custom House Packing Co.
13. Carmel Canning Co.
14. Calif. Packing Corp.
15. San Xavier Canning Co.

16. Western Sardine Co.
17. Ferrante Co.
18. Oxnard Canning Co.
19. Western Fish Processors
20. Aeneas Sardine Packing Co.
21. Central Packing Co.
22. Ronada Fisheries &
    Magnolia Packing Co.
23. Enterprise Packers
24. California Frozen Fish Co.
25. Peninsula Packing Co.
26. San Carlos Canning Co.

sampling the daily catch to study changes in age, size, and catch per unit of effort, but it did not pump out a steady stream of critical reports and recommendations as it had during the interwar years.[54] Like canners, workers, and fishermen, Fish and Game officials focused on supporting, not squelching, production.

Catch statistics indicated that Monterey had done its part to support the war effort. From 1940 to 1946, Monterey landed no less than 145,000 tons of sardines in a given season.[55] But transforming the sardine industry into a defense industry had costs. At the local level, federal officials reordered Montereyans' interactions with nature and altered the social structure of the fishery. Federal mandates also ignored the physical limits of nature and weakened state regulations. Wartime expansion soon proved to be more than the sardine could sustain.

"THAT'S THE FISH BUSINESS"

With unrelenting demand for sardines, Montereyans had every reason to believe the prosperity would extend into the postwar years. However, the good times came quickly to an end. First, Japanese residents began to return from their wartime internment and encountered lingering anti-Japanese sentiment. Montereyans then faced a precipitous drop in sardine catches. Fishermen, canners, and residents developed different explanations for the dearth of fish based on their years of observing and working in the fishery, but ultimately their local knowledge and past experiences could not solve the crisis. The fish were nowhere to be found.

The first source of tension in postwar Monterey was the return of Japanese residents. Similar to other communities where the Japanese resettled, the response was decidedly mixed.[56] In April 1945, the Monterey Bay Council on Japanese Relations, Inc., published an advertisement in the *Monterey Peninsula Herald* discouraging the return of the Japanese to the Pacific Coast and calling for the deportation of aliens with questionable loyalty to the United States. The group also recommended strict

MAP 3. (*facing page*) Cannery Row and Monterey Harbor, World War II

Sources: Tom Mangelsdorf, *A History of Steinbeck's Cannery Row* (Santa Cruz, CA: Western Tanager Press, 1986) and Michael Kenneth Hemp, *Cannery Row: The History of Steinbeck's Old Ocean View Avenue* (Carmel, CA: The History Company, 2002)

supervision and regulation of Japanese schools, the enforcement of alien land laws, and the elimination of dual citizenship. A few weeks later, almost 450 local residents signed a letter, also published in the *Herald*, that countered anti-Japanese sentiment and asked the community to ensure "the democratic way of life" for everyone. Mrs. Joseph Schoeninger of Carmel even asked people to provide short-term housing for the Japanese as a way of "helping these American citizens to find their rightful places in the community."[57]

In addition to housing shortages and local discrimination, the Japanese also found that state and federal restrictions persisted when they tried to resume fishing. Only in February 1945 did Captain S. B. Johnson, operations officer of the Twelfth Naval District, declare that Japanese American citizens would be allowed to fish freely. At the same time, the War Relocation Authority announced that it had no intention of helping the Japanese recover their fishing vessels or reenter the fishing business.[58] The Japanese did score a critical victory in 1948 when the United States Supreme Court overturned a state ban on alien Japanese fishermen in *Takahashi v. California Fish and Game Commission*. Kiyoshi Nobusada, president of the Monterey Japanese American Citizens League, estimated that the ruling affected seventy-five local fishermen. However, many of these men were too old to resume fishing or had already secured other jobs.[59]

The Japanese also faced resistance in the canneries. When the Del Mar cannery hired two Japanese men—both United States citizens—in September 1945, some cannery workers protested. "The fact that one of the newly employed men was an honorably discharged veteran of the U.S. Army, while the other had formerly been a member of the [cannery workers] union, failed, at first, to overcome objections on the part of those who left their jobs," reported the *Monterey Peninsula Herald*.[60] Dwight Campbell, business agent of the Cannery Workers Union, immediately declared that he would not tolerate discrimination on account of creed, color, or nationality. He wrote, "It will be my duty and policy to file charges against any member showing discrimination against a fellow worker for any of the above reasons." The Monterey Fish Processors Association, the employers' group, issued a similar statement.[61]

Tensions created by the Japanese return to Monterey, however, paled by comparison with the dire condition of the sardine fishery. Monterey fishermen faced barren seas at the start of the 1946–47 season, and by December many had left the "dead" waters in Northern California to fish in San Pedro. Likewise, some cannery workers traveled to Salinas to find other employment.[62] By the end of the season, Monterey had landed only 31,240 tons of sardines. The following season the figure dropped to 17,630 tons.[63] As skipper Sal Colletto noted, "It was evident that the once abundant sardine was disappearing from the Monterey Bay. As a result Cannery Row was on a fast down hill slide."[64]

To address the shortage, Montereyans diversified the catch, returning, ironically, to squid. Once reviled for its odors and associated with the degraded Chinese population, squid became Monterey's salvation. Led by Chinese merchant Wing Chong, the dried-squid industry had resumed briefly during the 1920s and early 1930s, but market instability and competition from Japan curbed production in 1933.[65] The postwar sardine bust brought the squid industry back for the third time. As one observer noted, "We may have lost temporarily the title of Sardine Capital of the World, but we have become the Squid Capital of the World instead."[66] Hopkins Marine Station scientist W. Gordon Fields explained that squid could make up for the sardines because "it appears in huge numbers and . . . may be captured and preserved by present methods and with existing equipment."[67] In addition to squid, the canneries also began to process mackerel, anchovies, tuna, and herring—basically anything fishermen caught in their nets.[68]

Since the sardines were not migrating to Monterey on their own, local processors also tried to bring the fish to them. Angelo Lucido of the San Carlos Canning Company initiated the shipping of sardines from San Pedro, Santa Barbara, and Port Hueneme during the 1946–47 season. By November 1947, Monterey operators shipped as many as one thousand tons per day, using modified grape trucks and chilling the fish with copious amounts of ice and rock salt. But George Clemens noted that trucking in sardines was a "poor substitute" for boats unloading at Cannery Row hoppers. Canners curtailed sardine trucking in early 1948 when San Pedro fishermen received a raise from forty-five to sixty dollars per ton of sardines, making the cost of shipping fish even higher. In the meantime, the industry actively searched for sardines by water and by air.[69]

Like wartime mandates, the scarcity of sardines forced Montereyans to alter the ways in which they had once interacted with the natural world. Monterey fishermen had guarded "their" fish during the interwar years, but now they no longer had any stocks to protect. Canners had to contract with non-Monterey fishermen and exploit Southern California stocks, disrupting the normal sardine migration. In canning squid and other fish, moreover, postwar fishermen returned to the practices of earlier immigrant fishermen: harvesting several species of marine life rather than relying on only one. For cannery workers, these activities made their already irregular work patterns even more burdensome. Because trucked sardines did not arrive until the afternoon, they worked later than usual and complained that they did not get paid more for night work.[70]

New strategies allowed the canneries to stay open, but fishermen still experienced financial hardships. Typically, most fishermen made a total of $4,000 to $5,000 during a good season. For the 1946–47 season, their earnings dropped to an average of $800. According to the *Monterey Peninsula Herald*, fishermen "maintained themselves and their families by dipping frequently into their life savings, by seeking aid from the grocer and the butcher, and by drawing on their unemployment insurance for the $80 monthly."[71] But fishermen often faced difficulties receiving unemployment benefits. The AFL Seine and Line Fishermen's Union claimed that their members were entitled to partial benefits during the season when their weekly earnings fell below the level established by the unemployment insurance act.[72] The State Unemployment Insurance Appeals Board countered that fishermen did not qualify as "partials" because it was "impossible to arrive at what constitutes a normal customary full-time work week." Because fishermen were paid in shares, the board explained, there was "no relation between the number of hours of work and their compensation." Even when a fisherman worked for no remuneration, "he nevertheless expects to be compensated for this work at a later date." The board also claimed that fishermen could not be considered totally or partially unemployed when required to stand by to fish.[73] Despite declining catches, the board held firm; in 1953 it rejected a proposed regulation to allow commercial fishermen to draw partial benefits if they had poor catches.[74]

Recognizing that the sardine industry was in a crisis, a handful of cannery owners and fishermen advocated stricter regulations. J. R. Perry, manager of the Carmel Canning Company and Monterey's mayor, attributed the sardine scarcity to shifting offshore currents and believed that the fish would come back, but he also recommended restrictions on net size and the number of reduction permits, as well as economic diversification.[75] Frank Raiter of the San Xavier cannery advocated more drastic measures. Blaming overfishing for the minuscule catches, he proposed a fifty-ton limit per boat, a restricted net size, a shorter season, a sardine size limit of 8.5 inches, and a one-year moratorium on reduction. He reminded canners of the Fish and Game Commission's grave predictions and implored restraint so that they could enjoy the sardines "for a good many years to come."[76] Similarly, at a Monterey meeting of concerned citizens, Fish and Game scientists, and legislators in 1948, Sal Colletto testified that he had seen signs of depletion in the late 1930s and proposed a two-year closure of the sardine industry on the Pacific Coast to give fish a chance to "multiply and increase their population."[77]

However, most canners and fishermen insisted there was insufficient cause for alarm. George Clemens noted, "The fact that such a small tonnage was taken can only mean that the sardine spawning period this year should be of an astronomical magnitude. . . . Maybe we should take heart in the knowledge that because we have a drought one year no one is so bold as to predict that there will not be rain the next year."[78] Many canners seemed to concur that the poor catches were only temporary, an inherent part of the "natural" fluctuations in the fishery; banner years had followed periods of scarcity in the past. The fact that they made improvements to their plants before the start of the 1947–48 season demonstrates their optimism.[79] As Sal Ferrante, managing partner of Oxnard Canners, concluded, "This has been a poor season. Last year was a good season. Next year—who knows? That's the fish business."[80]

Most Monterey canners also scoffed at the overfishing theory, with Knut Hovden leading the charge. He noted, "Experience has shown us that the abrupt total disappearance of Sardines is not a sign of overfishing with its gradually diminishing take."[81] He called overfishing and depletion simplistic explanations, "empty words that the experts and the State Fish and Game Commission have learned to repeat." He continued, "Don't let yourself be mislead [sic] by people with lots of theories and untried ideas, and who have no financial interest in the industry, but who would sacrifice one of the world's best industries . . . perhaps to attain personal prominence for themselves."[82] To Hovden, the commission ignored the thousands of fishermen and canners who depended on sardines and failed to find the root of the problem.

To explain the dwindling number of sardines, Hovden placed the blame squarely on the federal government. The navy had purportedly dumped ammunition near the northern entrance to Monterey Bay, and Hovden correlated these activities with the absence of large migrating sardine stocks entering from the north. "The northern end of the discarded fishing areas resembles a dead sea," he explained. He also believed that the government recklessly dumped arsenic and other chemicals, killing off the plankton on which the sardine fed.[83] Making matters worse, predatory animals and birds, such as sea lions, seagulls, sharks, and other large fish, also depleted the sardine stocks, Hovden explained.[84]

Monterey fishermen spun their own theories based on years of fishing in Sicily and in Monterey. John Russo, skipper of the *Star of Monterey*, also attacked the overfishing hypothesis. Because he believed that the runs stopped abruptly off Monterey rather than diminishing slowly, he speculated that the sardines had migrated farther out at sea. Although he had traveled to San Pedro to fish, he considered taking his boat over one hundred miles off the shore of Monterey. He explained, "I think the fish are out there, and I would like to go out and see." However, the necessity of delivering fish to the canneries quickly made exploring the open ocean waters an untenable option.[85]

Russo's theory was based on local knowledge of the sardine, knowledge gained by spending several seasons fishing. His daily and seasonal observations of the sardine and his labor in nature—not any scientific training—had led him to speculate about the status of the fish. While Hovden and other individuals were not actively plying the waters for sardines, they, too, based their theories on experiential knowledge. Hovden had been involved in the Monterey sardine industry for over thirty years, and he had little reason to doubt his past observations. Ebbs and flows were part of the business, and their experiences had given them the authority to declare that overfishing was not an adequate or accurate explanation.[86]

The local knowledge of Monterey fishermen and canners both conflicted with and corresponded to the conclusions of California Fish and Game scientists. While they agreed that natural fluctuations factored into the sardine's decline, they also pointed to overfishing, which peaked with the relaxation of conservation measures during the war. According to J. B. Phillips, oceanographic changes, such as shifting currents, could have relocated the sardine's usual feeding grounds. But he also argued that poor spawning, due to natural and human factors, industry expansion, and increased gear efficiency could be the root problems. Richard Croker added that heavy catches were particularly damaging because the Pacific Coast sardine population was subject to great variation in spawning success. If the catch was not low enough to allow for the growth of a "backlog" of fish, "the sardine industry will be subject to good and bad seasons in accordance with success or failure of spawn survival," he explained. The strong 1939 year-class had sustained the wartime fishery, but "nature has not adequately replaced losses due to fishing activities and natural causes."[87]

Preliminary results from sardine migration studies corroborated the gravity of the situation. From 1936 until 1944, Fish and Game and the Biological Board of Canada conducted a sardine tagging program. Scientists collected samples from fishermen's hauls, placed nickel-plated steel tags inside the fish, and released them. Electromagnets in the reduction plants recovered the tags.[88] While tag recoveries were problematic and inconsistent, data suggested that the sardine moved throughout its range from British Columbia to Mexico and gradually dispersed, with the population to the north comprising the greatest proportion of large fish.[89] In other words, Pacific Coast sardine fishermen drew from a common sardine population.[90] Thus, sparse catches in Monterey did not bode well for the sardine stocks as a whole, and shipping fish from San Pedro only delayed the downward spiral of the Pacific Coast sardine industry.

Since the size of the catch was the "only controllable factor," Croker suggested setting a statewide quota of 150,000 tons of sardines per season. While he did not want to weaken the sardine industry, he believed the state had "a responsibility to the people of the state to see that the sardine industry is a lasting one."[91] For the 1948–49 season, Fish and Game imposed a 100,000-ton quota on sardine reduction. The Sardine Advisory Committee, made up of industry and Fish and Game representatives, also recommended voluntary restrictions, including taking sardines at least eight inches long, shortening the season by one month, and fishing only five days a week.[92] The state saw severe restrictions as the best strategy and adopted additional conservation measures for the 1949–50 season, including the elimination of summer sardine packing and ending the Monterey season on January 15 instead of February 15.[93]

Local scientist Edward F. Ricketts occupied a middle ground between state scientists and local fishermen and canners. Originally from Chicago, Ricketts moved to the Monterey Peninsula in 1923 with his college roommate A. E. Galigher and opened a biological supply house, the Pacific Biological Laboratory. Ricketts eventually took over the business, working out of a small building crammed between the fish processing plants on Ocean View Avenue. There, he preserved and shipped marine and terrestrial organisms—frogs, starfish, sea urchins—to schools, universities, and other biological supply houses all over the country. When writer John

Steinbeck was living in Pacific Grove in 1930, the two men met and developed a deep friendship.[94] Ricketts is perhaps best known as the inspiration for the character "Doc" in Steinbeck's novel *Cannery Row*.[95]

Ricketts never finished a college degree, but his studies at the University of Chicago exposed him to the work of ecologist Warder Clyde Allee. From Allee, he learned about the social behavior of animals, the organization of their communities, and the importance of the environment to their activities.[96] In Monterey, he built upon this training through his interactions with Hopkins Marine Station scientists and prepared a field guide to the Pacific Coast, *Between Pacific Tides*. Published in 1939, Ricketts's work showed Allee's influence; rather than adopting a phylogenic system that organized flora and fauna by their scientific classifications, he used an ecological approach, describing species according to their habitat and explaining the effects of tides and predation on distribution and community structure.[97]

Ricketts moved south for his next project, a collaboration with Steinbeck on Mexico's Sea of Cortez. At the end of the sardine season in 1940, they chartered a Monterey purse seine boat, the *Western Flyer*, hired a crew of sardine fishermen, received clearance from the Mexican government, and embarked on their journey on March 11. Steinbeck and Ricketts collected and catalogued over six hundred specimens along the sandy beaches and rocky shoreline of the Gulf of California before returning to Monterey on April 20. The product of the journey, *Sea of Cortez: A Leisurely Journal of Travel and Research*, was published at the end of 1941. Drawing heavily from Ricketts's writings, notes, and journal, Steinbeck wrote the narrative portion, which vividly described the trip, the landscape, and the diverse marine life they encountered. Ricketts organized the scientific appendix that identified and classified the specimens.[98]

Ricketts's scientific background and his intimate view of the fishing industry thus gave him a distinct perspective on the sardine. Like Fish and Game scientists, he thought that natural conditions and overfishing had led to depletion. Like Hovden and other fishermen, he believed that the sardine could bounce back.[99] But he also issued a damning critique of industry's greed and lack of foresight. While the sardine "perhaps won't be hurt" in the long run, he wrote in 1946, "Our policy of insisting on taking everything at the moment, free enterprise at its freest, hurts only us." Despite warnings that they were taking too many fish, canners and reduction plant operators "refused to listen, selected their evidence, petitioned for more and more permits, put pressure on the Fish and Game Comm., lobbied the legislators, [and] always got their way."[100] If industry had adopted conservation earlier, "a smaller but streamlined cannery row in all liklihood [sic] this month would be winding up a fairly successful season, instead of dipping as they must be now, deeply into the red ink of failure."[101]

Ricketts also faulted scientists for being unwilling to "stick their necks out," but he acknowledged that they were in a no-win situation. If they refused requests for higher reduction permits, they would hear "cries of anguish" and accusations that they were damaging free enterprise and preventing businessmen from making "an honest dollar." If they tried to encourage the state legislature to enact stricter laws, "they will be merely running up against a powerful and skilled lobby maintained to pr[e]vent just that sort of thing." Fish and Game had done all that it had the power to do: warn the industry of depletion and recommend limits.[102] It was up to state legislators and Monterey's fishermen and canners to heed the call.

Ricketts theorized that feeding and reproduction were at the root of the sardine's decline. If plankton production was high, the sardine would put on fat and produce larger quantities of eggs. Small year-classes resulted when plankton production was low. If fishermen took the usual amounts of fish during these low years, they dug "further into the breeding stock," reducing sardines to the "danger point." Ricketts concluded, "The answer to the question 'Where are the sardines?' becomes quite obvious in this light. They're in cans. The parents of the sardines we need so badly now were being ground up then into fish meal, were extracted for oil, were being canned; too many of them, far too many." If the breeding stock were given "a decent break" and if sardine harvests were limited, "there's no reason why we shouldn't go on indefinitely profiting by this effortless production of sea and sun and fertilizer."[103]

In Ricketts's mind, a combination of politics, industrial activities, plankton production, and other natural factors had caused the sardine's precipitous decline. He integrated his scientific expertise and his local experiences to develop these theories and eventually published them in the *Monterey Peninsula Herald*. His opinions were likely unpopular with some residents, but they were not unwarranted given the bleak condition of the industry by the end of the 1940s.[104] While the 1949–50 season brought a faint glimmer of hope to Monterey with total landings of 130,990 tons, the catch fell to 19,100 tons during the 1950–51 season.[105]

UNDERSTANDING DEPLETION: THE CALIFORNIA MARINE RESEARCH COMMITTEE

Monterey was not alone in its confrontation of the environmental consequences of World War II industrialization. Other communities that supported wartime industries—shipbuilding, aircraft construction, mining—also paid ecological costs for prosperity and victory. For instance, a thermal inversion trapped industrial emissions beneath layers of fog in the Northeast and Midwest in October 1948, causing traffic jams and respiratory distress. Nonetheless, conservation continued to lack influence in the immediate postwar years, and many Americans ignored these problems, instead adhering to the era's "dominant ethos" of "growth and development."[106]

The virtual disappearance of sardines, however, had calamitous economic implications that simply could not be overlooked. With funding and support from the state and federal governments and the sardine industry, scientists and industry representatives formed a coalition to determine the causes of the sardine collapse and to develop solutions. These efforts proceeded slowly because the various parties disputed whether the decline was a temporary result of natural fluctuations in the fishery or a product of intense fishing. In other words, they maintained divergent ideas of how the fishery operated and how humans affected it.[107] In the meantime, sardine catches continued to fall, and Montereyans' hopes that the industry would bounce back turned out to be wishful thinking.

In an effort to develop a coherent response to the sardine crisis, Wilbert McLeod Chapman, curator of fishes at the California Academy of Sciences in San Francisco, and Montgomery Phister, an executive with the Van Camp Sea Food Company in San Pedro, brought together representatives from industry, the California State Fisheries Laboratory, the University of California's Scripps Institution of Oceanography (SIO), and the United States Fish and Wildlife Service (USFWS) in 1947. They asked the California legislature for three hundred thousand dollars to begin research on the California Current, a slow-moving body of ocean roughly 350 miles wide that runs along the Pacific Coast, north to south. Industry also lobbied for a fifty-cent-per-ton landing tax on sardines to support research and asked the USFWS for additional funding. The proposed California Marine Research Committee (MRC) would oversee this program, the California Cooperative Sardine Research Program. Governor Earl Warren and the state legislature approved the MRC and the sardine tax, while Congress granted funds to the USFWS.[108]

The MRC's research agenda provided comprehensive coverage of the sardine fishery, with each agency responsible for a different part of the research. The California Division of Fish and Game conducted statistical studies and young fish surveys and tested methods of locating and identifying sardine schools. The USFWS worked on spawning surveys and recruitment research, while the SIO carried out oceanographic surveys, including studies of plankton and marine vertebrates. The California Academy of Sciences investigated sardine behavior and physiology, and Hopkins Marine Station, which joined the group in 1951, examined oceanographic conditions in Monterey Bay.[109] Oceanography became the primary focus; according to Arthur McEvoy, the California Current became the "best-studied oceanic ecosystem on the planet."[110]

Many Monterey canners supported the MRC and abandoned their previous confidence in the sardine's imminent return. As the *Pacific Fisherman* noted, "No more in Monterey does one hear the complaint of a few years ago when operators were prone to say: 'The sardines are out there all right, but the fishermen won't make an honest effort to find them. They won't go out and scout for fish.' That was a common story in the early years of sardine depletion. You don't hear it anymore. It just isn't true." One canner added, "Research is beginning to point the way. There is good hope that the program soon will show how men must help nature to restore the sardines, and thus help themselves." However, only the "soundest, strongest and smartest" would still be in business when scientists came up with the "saving solution," he concluded.[111]

Industry's faith in science was not universal. Invoking Western stereotypes, Chapman called many industry representatives "rugged individualists," opposed to any restrictions on their operations. Those who acknowledged the need for scientific research were "only a dozen or two men out of thousands who compose the industry."[112] John Radovich, a California Fish and Game scientist, added that the fishing industry comprised a majority on the nine-person MRC. He speculated that it supported the MRC only as a stalling tactic to delay regulation.[113] When new regulations came to the table, industry typically balked. For instance, at a meeting called by the California Fish and Game Commission in December 1951, William O. Lunde of Monterey's Hovden cannery objected to a fixed total tonnage, also known as a seasonal bag limit, arguing that it would be too small for the industry to survive. He also opposed a shortened season and the elimination of sardine trucking and straight reduction—the reduction of all fish received, not just a percentage of the catch or the offal. Instead, he favored requiring canners to pack twenty cases of sardines for every ton landed, an increase from the previous rule of thirteen and one-half cases.[114]

Over the next few years, the MRC brought more disheartening news to the California sardine industry. In its 1952 report, it noted that the outlook for the next two seasons was "very bleak," as the 1950 and 1951 year-classes were below average in abundance.[115] By 1953 the forecast was even worse; there were too few sardines of any age group to support a fishery. During the 1953–54 season, California fishermen landed only thirty-five hundred tons of sardines, mostly from Southern California waters. Because the scarcity of sardines prompted canners to pursue Pacific mackerel, jack mackerel, and anchovies, the MRC expanded its focus to include these species. Thus, the California Cooperative Sardine Research Program became the California Cooperative Oceanic Fisheries Investigation (CalCOFI) in June 1953.[116]

Still, scientists continued to debate the cause of the sardine's demise. California Fish and Game scientist Frances Clark believed that the fishery's failure stemmed from heavy fishing and lack of spawning survival. The 1947 and 1948 year-classes were abundant enough to allow for a partial recovery in the 1949–50 and 1950–51 seasons. But since they were too young and small to reach the northern fishing grounds, they were only "a slight aid to the Monterey fishery." Fishing pressure concentrated on these two age groups, even though no one year-class could sustain the fishery indefinitely. To encourage recovery, the fishery needed to draw on larger and older fish, at least four years old. This required the catch to be low enough to increase the life expectancy of each year-class.[117]

Other scientists disagreed with Clark's interpretation of scientific data and maintained that natural factors, not overfishing, had caused the scarcity of sardines.[118] This conflict was most apparent when Clark and John C. Marr, head of the USFWS's South Pacific Fishery Investigation, coauthored a 1955 CalCOFI report in which Marr pointed to environmental changes to explain the sardine's collapse.[119] Chapman had identified this schism during the early days of the MRC. One branch of scientists took a "broad ecological approach" to fisheries problems, while the other group, which presumably included Clark, focused on "the effect of fishing mortality on the population." Chapman adhered more to the second group.[120]

Nonetheless, instead of focusing on fishing activities, subsequent Cal-COFI studies pointed to the environmental conditions affecting the sardine population. In its 1960 report, scientists noted that a strong and steady California Current characterized ocean conditions from 1948 to 1957—the same period that the population of sardines off California reached its low point. They speculated that the strong current could have swept sardine larvae into inhospitable waters, although the sardine did not rebound when the current was weak and warm in 1957 and 1958.[121] Garth Murphy of the California Academy of Sciences also emphasized the role of temperature in the sardine's decline. Cooler waters both prolonged larval stages, which heightened the sardine's vulnerability, and increased the crop of zooplankton, which preyed on the larvae.[122]

The large anchovy population was another possible explanation for the sardine's failure to return under favorable conditions. Scientists speculated that the anchovy had taken over the niche previously dominated by the sardine, perhaps because of the long period of cooler waters. These conditions favored the anchovy, as it spawned at a lower temperature than the sardine.[123] This interdependent relationship piqued scientists' interest because there was a possibility that simultaneously reducing pressure on sardines and putting pressure on anchovies could bring back sardines. A report explained, "This constitutes an exciting opportunity for marine science to assist society in meeting its complex needs." Scientists wanted to manipulate and try to control the supply of different species of fish. The California Fish and Game Commission assisted this program by authorizing a trial anchovy reduction fishery of seventy-five thousand tons in November 1965.[124]

CalCOFI's growing interest in the anchovy and other eastern North Pacific fisheries did nothing to stop the continuing decline of the sardine. Internal debates persisted, and Chapman found it difficult to get competing agencies to reach any agreement. These groups had distinct visions for the fisheries, approached the sardine crisis differently, and interpreted data in disparate ways. With no consensus, sardine stocks continued to plummet.[125] As the postwar environmental movement began to expose the ecological destruction and public health hazards brought by modern industry and technology and alerted Americans to the need to exercise restraint with natural resources and amenities, California governor Ronald Reagan declared a two-year moratorium on sardine fishing in June 1967 and allowed only a 15 percent incidental sardine catch in any load of mixed fish.[126] On January 1, 1974, the state adopted an even stricter law that prohibited the taking of Pacific sardines for any purpose until the estimated spawning biomass reached 20,000 tons. At the same time, the Fish and Game Commission continued to authorize anchovy reduction permits, using them in place of the severely compromised sardine.[127]

The California legislature dissolved the Marine Research Committee at the end of 1978. The Fishery Conservation and Management Act of 1976 made the MRC obsolete, as the federal government established a conservation zone between three and two hundred miles off the coast and held management authority over all fishery resources except tuna. This new legislation, part of the postwar era of environmental reform, reflected a dramatic shift in federal fishery policy from expanding the supply to monitoring the use of the nation's fisheries. The University of California, the National Marine Fisheries Service, and the California Department of Fish and Game agreed to continue CalCOFI as a cooperative research unit. In the end, the MRC succeeded in undertaking "large-scale, multidisciplinary research in the high seas of the eastern Pacific" and produced "much of lasting value." But as Arthur McEvoy concludes, "It did so at the cost of tolerating further depletion of the [sardine] fishery."[128] With this crisis unsolved, Monterey would have to turn to its own resources.

Fish and Game scientist Frances Clark made an ominous prediction in 1940, shortly before the United States' entrance into World War II. She claimed, "The California State Fisheries Laboratory of the California Division of Fish and Game has been crying wolf of future scarcity for several seasons until it now seems futile to repeat the cry. Nevertheless, it appears that that wolf will be at our doors in the all too near future."[129] That "near future" was closer than Clark may have anticipated. From the start of the 1941–42 season to the end of the 1944–45 season, California landed 2.1 million tons of sardines, the majority of which went toward government quotas. Monterey was the most prolific port, accounting for slightly less than 900,000 tons, or roughly 42 percent of the state catch during this period.[130] This rapid wartime expansion preceded an equally rapid postwar crash. Clark proved to be a remarkably accurate forecaster.

But even when fishermen's nets began to come up empty, many residents continued to maintain that the fisheries defined Monterey. Given the industry's wartime ascendancy and dominance over the coastline, the hum of cannery equipment—regardless of what was being canned or where the fish originated—reinforced the city's fishing identity. Some Montereyans simply knew no other kind of work. As John Steinbeck observed in 1941, "They [Monterey fishermen] frankly didn't believe in the activities of the land—road-building and manufacturing and brick-laying. This was not a matter of ignorance on their part, but of intensity. All the directionalism of thought and emotion that man was capable of went into sardine-fishing; there wasn't room for anything else."[131] Plying Monterey's coastal waters was a way of life, and to face another alternative was distressing.

As a result, many Montereyans demonstrated an unwavering faith in the sardine. If the cry of overfishing was unfounded, as Knut Hovden argued, and if the sardine was bound to come back to local waters, as it had before, Monterey needed only a temporary plan to see the community through the tough days. But residents soon learned that they underestimated the severity of the situation. Their years of labor and the vast knowledge they had attained on Monterey Bay could not explain or counteract the sardine's demise. The scarcity of sardines was not short-lived, and there were neither simple solutions nor simple explanations. Oceanic conditions and years of human pressure on the fishery, culminating with the dramatic wartime expansion, forced Montereyans to figure out another way to support the local economy. In a return to the past, many argued that the solution to the sardine crisis would come in the shape of the tourist.

6 REMAKING CANNERY ROW

John Steinbeck's 1954 novel *Sweet Thursday*, the sequel to *Cannery Row*, opens with a dismal account of the sardine industry's precipitous postwar decline. "When the war came to Monterey and to Cannery Row everybody fought it more or less, in one way or another. . . . The canneries themselves fought the war by getting the limit taken off fish and catching them all. It was done for patriotic reasons, but that didn't bring the fish back. As with the oysters in *Alice*, 'They'd eaten every one,'" he writes.[1] Once a thriving street lined with over twenty sardine processing plants, Cannery Row was no longer a place swirling with activity. As Monterey resident Ed Larsh recalled, "In 1949, most of the sardines had been netted, and the entire industry was gasping like a fish out of water."[2] The future of Cannery Row appeared altogether bleak.

When it became clear that the fishery was not going to rebound quickly, Monterey city planners and developers turned their attention back to tourism. Tourism never disappeared from the city's shores, but it did become less important during the sardine's heyday. The return to tourism, therefore, was not an entirely new development, nor was it unusual for a western community on the tail end of a boom-and-bust economy. Many other places once dependent on extractive industries also directed their energies to tourism when natural resources became scarce or investors moved elsewhere. Like developers in other towns whose past fortunes had evaporated, Monterey tourism boosters promoted the city's natural beauty and recreational amenities. They also romanticized its industrial past by turning old buildings into restaurants and shops.[3]

But Monterey's connection to John Steinbeck's novels, especially *Can-*

nery Row, also made the city's promotional efforts distinct. Although deteriorating fish plants seemed to mar a stunning stretch of oceanfront property, city planners and developers recognized that this fading industrial ambience could attract tourists who were nostalgic for Steinbeck's fiction.[4] Abandoned machinery and crumbling canneries, they argued, could also punctuate the seascape. Ironically, they saw the decayed built environment as enhancing Monterey's nature even as it stood for its overexploitation. A romantic, Steinbeck-inspired account of the sardine's past could be reconciled with and integrated into an enduring impulse to sell the natural beauty of the coastline.

Postindustrial tourism on Cannery Row, then, was deeply entangled with the fisheries and reinforced Monterey's connection to fishing even after the sardine industry had collapsed. In the process, it neglected the causes and consequences of the fishery's demise and began to erase the racial and ethnic diversity that had once defined Cannery Row.[5] Despite the contradictions of their approach, developers and city planners were not willing to renounce or analyze critically the environmental exploitation that had led to Cannery Row's decline. Nor did they see the neighborhood's rich immigrant and labor history as a selling point. Instead, they believed that nature, literature, and the physical remnants of the industrial past could be brought together in such a way to renew Cannery Row and transform it from a desolate harbor to the center of activity once again.

"ALMOST A GHOST HARBOR"

As sardine catches continued to plummet, Monterey devolved from "the greatest sardine port in the world" into "almost a ghost harbor," according to the *Pacific Fisherman*.[6] Several consecutive years of poor catches suggested that the sardine's return was not imminent, and many canneries began to shut their doors. In March 1952, the Aeneas Sardine Products Company became the first cannery put on the auction block. By 1958 there were only five canneries still in operation, and they were barely getting by. As Thomas Logan, who worked in a cannery during the summer of 1960, remembered, "We rarely got sardines and the economy was shot." Cannery Row took another major hit when the California Packing Corporation, one of the oldest and largest canneries, closed in April 1962 and sold its machinery to a Puerto Rican tuna cannery. As manager D. T. Saxby explained, "You can't run a sardine cannery indefinitely without sardines."[7]

Most of the canneries were stripped and abandoned, while some were converted to other uses. In 1952 the Westgate–Sun Harbor Cannery closed and moved most of its machinery to San Diego. In 1958 the Richmond Transfer and Storage Company took over the former cannery after securing a one-year contract with nearby Fort Ord to pack and crate household goods and military supplies. The large building was perfect for the operation, which built, loaded, weighed, and stacked boxes along conveyor belts much like the ones used on a fish cutting line. Partner and owner William F. Bottoms noted, "These buildings are wonderful. . . . There is nothing like this anywhere. Rail siding, large buildings, when space is at a premium."[8]

Selling plants and equipment became Monterey canners' best option. Some canners tried to keep their operations going, but their efforts proved to be futile. During the 1950s, they packed tuna, and during the early 1960s, they campaigned to replace sardines with anchovies in their reduction operations. Tuna never became a large part of production, and only the Hovden Food Products Corporation remained on Cannery Row once the state issued anchovy reduction permits in 1965. Even when the sardine fishery showed some signs of recovery in 1958, Monterey canners could not sell their products. Their pack was too expensive to compete with Japanese and South African canned sardines in the export market, and the domestic market could not absorb all of the catch.[9]

Although Knut Hovden had retired in 1953 and passed away in March 1961, his employees were not ready to shut down and liquidate the fish plant. Manager William O. Lunde noted, "You don't buy a coffin for a man just because he's sick." As he lobbied for anchovy permits, he also noted that the fishing industry was part of what made Monterey:

> What would Monterey be like without a fishing industry? Every day cars pass the cannery. You know what they're looking at? Cannery Row—the famous Cannery Row that's known all over the world. What kind of a cannery [row] would you have without a cannery? What kind of harbor would there be without a fishing fleet? Believe me, we're not dead yet—we've got a lot of fight left.[10]

Lunde tied Monterey's identity to a prosperous industrial waterfront, yet he also suggested that Cannery Row was becoming a place for tourism. He did not justify the continuance of the canneries because of their direct contributions to the local economy, which were minimal. Instead, he implied that the canneries needed to stay open because visitors wanted to see a working waterfront with real, functioning canneries and a harbor filled with actual fishing boats. Extractive and service economies, in other words, complemented one another.

The Hovden cannery was in the minority, as most canners cut their losses and sold their factories. The Cannery Row Properties Company, established in 1953 by Salinas Valley businessman Wesley Dodge, former cannery manager George Leutzinger, and a handful of other stockholders, bought much of this property. By 1957 it had acquired twelve former canneries and reduction plants, the Ocean View Hotel, an apartment building, and holding interest in Ed Ricketts's laboratory. The company did not have massive redevelopment designs for the area. Instead, it developed a simple scheme of buying the former plants, selling the cannery machinery to the highest bidders, and renting out the empty buildings. Fish meal driers made their way to sand and dried-apple plants. A machine that had removed fish heads now cut off carrot tops. Other equipment and personnel left the country for canneries in South America and South Africa. Sal Ferrante, former manager and operator of the Oxnard Cannery, decided to manage a cannery in Peru, where liberal regulations allowed for the nonstop, year-round reduction of anchovies.[11]

Unlike Ferrante, most residents who had worked in the fishing industry did not have the expertise, resources, or desire to relocate overseas. Some fishermen migrated to Southern California, where fishing was still active in the 1950s, or pursued the tuna industry in Mexico. Others simply tried to eke by. As one "old-timer" explained in 1959, "It's what we do. We make a living. If we don't make any more than that—well, it's still a living." Les Caveny, business agent of the cannery union, added, "Once you get into the business, you're like an old firehorse. You just can't stay away."[12] Still, many former cannery workers and fishermen found themselves out of work. In June 1955, female employees of the fish canning industry comprised the largest surplus of workers in Monterey County. Approximately five hundred fishermen were also unemployed. A local employment study concluded, "Fishermen must convert to other means of earning a living or move elsewhere."[13]

Obtaining non-fisheries employment proved easier said than done. While some former fisheries workers were flexible—Hope Gradis's father, for instance, lost his reduction plant, regrouped, opened a laundromat, and went on to make "a good living"—those who had spent much of their lives at sea or in the canneries were often ill-suited for available service jobs.[14] A California Department of Employment report explained that Monterey's first-generation Italian, Spanish, and Portuguese fisheries workers "generally find great difficulty in fitting themselves into the resort or wholesale and retail fields due to age and language problems."[15] Fishing and canning had defined many workers' identities for years, and asking them to take jobs that required an entirely different set of skills and engendered a different work culture proved unrealistic.

There were exceptions. Fisherman-turned-restauranteur Slats Lucido made a relatively smooth transition to the tourist economy. Lucido began fishing in Monterey in 1916 and worked his way up the ranks, first as a teenage crew member and eventually to a respected skipper and boat owner. During the wartime heyday, he bought a large purse seine boat and also decided to take over the Bruno Fish Market on Fisherman's Wharf. After the war, Lucido tried to scrape by, fishing out of San Pedro during the 1947–48 season. When the sardine runs failed to recover, he sold his boat and took over another vacant spot on the wharf to open Slat's Fish Grotto in 1948. With his fish market in front, Lucido's restaurant was a big success, serving up abalone, squid, and other seafood dishes. In 1957 he moved his operation to Lover's Point in Pacific Grove, leaving his son Sal to take care of the wharf business.[16] Similarly, Vito Spadaro gave up fishing in the early 1960s and along with his wife, Pat, went into the restaurant business.[17]

Lucido and Spadaro defied those who believed that fishermen knew only how to be fishermen—that there were rigid boundaries between fisheries and tourism and those who participated in both industries. These men had capitalized on the sardine boom, but now they also wanted to take advantage of the postwar growth in Monterey's tourist economy. Monterey's fortunes were changing, and they were savvy enough to give up on any chance that the sardine fishery would rebound to its prewar and wartime levels. As much as their identities continued to be connected to fishing, they also came to understand how to make a living from tourism.[18] Their fishing pasts were not incompatible with their new jobs as restauranteurs.

The success of the Lucido and Spadaro families also spoke to the enduring presence of the Sicilians in postindustrial Monterey and one of the keys to their resilience: real estate ownership. Since they often controlled their families' finances, many Sicilian women had invested in commercial and rental properties, in addition to their homes, when the sardine industry prospered and earnings were high. According to Carol McKibben, Sicilians owned one-third of Monterey's houses and small businesses in 1951. These investments helped the Sicilian community to weather the sardine's collapse and sustained their long-term settlement in Monterey.[19]

The growth of the local military establishment also began to fill the void left by the fishing industry. During World War II, the Presidio of Monterey became an enlistment center, while Fort Ord became a major site for basic training and debarkation and a permanent military installation after the war. Moreover, the former Hotel Del Monte, site for a U.S. Navy preflight training school during the war, became the campus for the Naval Postgraduate School, which began its first classes in February 1952.[20] In a study of Monterey Peninsula employment and education that same year, Harold Parker predicted that "the permanent staff of civilians needed to staff this [military] organization will provide employment indefinitely for many persons." These employees, in turn, would create a demand for "more homes, more stores, more recreational facilities and should contribute more than any other single factor to the continued prosperity of the Peninsula."[21]

The military did become a major regional employer. Some former fishermen and cannery workers even obtained military construction jobs, although the extent of this trend is unclear.[22] By the late 1960s, Fort Ord, the Defense Language Institute, the Naval Postgraduate School, the Coast Guard Naval Reserve Station, and the Naval Auxiliary Landing Field had roughly 4,500 civilians on their payrolls. Sociologist Elaine Johnson estimated that 60 percent of the Monterey Peninsula economy depended on the military.[23] However, unlike other urban areas in the American West, Monterey was small and lacked the political influence to attract more national funds and establish lucrative defense-related manufacturing or supply industries, such as munitions or aircraft plants. The military's importance to the local economy was undeniable, but one economic report estimated that roughly half of the federal outlays for military installations, including a significant portion of the military payroll, was spent outside the region. The report also doubted that military growth could be sustained.[24]

According to the California Department of Employment, it was the combination of military growth and the "steady expansion of the resort trade" that would "offset to some extent the diminishing rate of activity in fishing and fish-canning."[25] The emphasis on tourism was part of larger national and regional trends in the postwar period. As the population of California surged and the national economy prospered, more Californians had the leisure time and income to go on vacation. They also purchased automobiles and took their trips on the road, where they navigated the expanding interstate highway system. A Monterey Peninsula regional plan from 1963 explained that tourism and recreation had become the fastest-growing economic activity in the nation during the preceding decade.[26] Only a day's drive from Los Angeles and two hours from San Francisco, Monterey was poised to take advantage of California's increasing number of auto tourists. Now Montereyans needed to construct an identity that would give potential visitors the incentive to make the trip.

"SOMETHING NEW"

John Steinbeck's 1945 novel *Cannery Row* provided part of the inspiration for postwar tourism in Monterey. The book had local roots. As a child in Salinas, about fifteen miles to the east, Steinbeck and his family—much like the tourists and home buyers the Pacific Improvement Company was trying to lure at this time—spent many summers at a cottage in Pacific Grove, and the author frequently made his way back to the Monterey Peninsula in subsequent years. Between 1930 and 1936, the early years of his literary career, he spent a considerable amount of time writing in Pacific Grove and soon met Ed Ricketts. According to biographer Jay Parini, this encounter was "certainly one of the most important meetings of his life," as Ricketts helped him to "crystallize thoughts about human nature and its relationship to the natural world which for Steinbeck had been inchoate for some time." As the two men spent more time together at Ricketts's lab and the adjacent tide pools, Steinbeck began to see similarities between humans and marine life, as they responded to "the same biological drives." Ricketts also impressed upon him that the novelist's job, like the marine biologist's, was to observe and decipher relationships between organisms.[27]

Along Cannery Row, Steinbeck enjoyed a dynamic human laboratory in which he could immerse himself. As he caroused and conversed with

Ricketts, he witnessed the constant hubbub of the sardine canneries and reduction plants and was intrigued by the diversity of people who lived and worked in the neighborhood. He talked to them, listened to them, and became an "expert in sifting the various strands of their society." Ricketts encouraged Steinbeck to develop stories about these lively individuals.[28] They would eventually inspire three novels: *Tortilla Flat*, *Sweet Thursday*, and, of course, *Cannery Row*.

By the end of the 1930s, however, Steinbeck's ties to Monterey grew more tenuous, particularly as his fame surged with winning the Pulitzer Prize in 1940 for his 1939 novel *The Grapes of Wrath*. After his marriage to Carol Steinbeck ended, he moved to New York in 1941 with his new wife, Gwyndolyn Conger. Following a stint as a correspondent in Europe during World War II, he wrote the manuscript for *Cannery Row* in the New York office of Viking Press in July 1944. "I just finished a crazy kind of book about Cannery Row and the lab etc. All fiction of course but born out of homesickness. And there are some true incidents in it. And some of it is a little funny I think," he explained to his Monterey friends Tal and Ritchie Lovejoy. Longing for the coastal town that inspired his novel, Steinbeck moved back to Monterey before the book hit the shelves, but his homecoming was bittersweet. He felt awkward around his old friends and uncomfortable with his growing celebrity. As biographer Jackson Benson explains, "His mistake was that in returning to Monterey he thought he could just ignore fame when he chose, and lead his life as he had before." Disillusioned, Steinbeck, Gwyn, and their infant son, Thom, returned to New York.[29]

In the meantime, the release of *Cannery Row* put Monterey on the map. Despite mediocre national reviews—Orville Prescott of the *New York Times* claimed that the novel had "no real characters, no 'story,' no purpose"—local sales were brisk, as residents were eager to read what Steinbeck had to say about Cannery Row. Monterey bookstore owners noted that the novel gave a boost to their profits. In fact, some Montereyans began to consider poor reviews as an affront to their hometown. According to biographer Roy Simmonds, "Steinbeck found it all immensely amusing."[30]

When local residents read *Cannery Row*, they found a superb depiction of the Cannery Row ambience on the first page. Steinbeck writes, "Cannery Row is the gathered and scattered, tin and iron and rust and splintered wood, chipped pavement and weedy lots and junk heaps, sardine canneries of corrugated iron, honky tonks, restaurants and whore houses, and little crowded groceries, and laboratories and flophouses." Steinbeck goes on to describe the daily ritual of Cannery Row, a scene that was familiar to any Montereyan during the wartime boom. "In the morning when the sardine fleet has made a catch, the purse-seiners waddle heavily into the bay blowing their whistles. . . . Then cannery whistles scream and all over the town men and women scramble into their clothes and come running down to the Row to go to work." When the day is over, the last fish cleaned, cooked, and canned, workers "straggle out and droop their ways up the hill into the town and Cannery Row becomes itself again—quiet and magical. Its normal life returns."[31]

But after this evocative opening, the Cannery Row of sardines, fishermen, and cannery workers quickly fades away, and Steinbeck turns his attention to a collection of eccentric characters who live on the margins of Cannery Row society. Mack and the boys hang out under the black cypress tree and begin living in a fish meal storage warehouse, which they call the Palace Flophouse and Grill. Dora Flood, the street's madam, runs the Bear Flag Restaurant, while Lee Chong provides groceries, alcohol, and other goods from his overflowing general store. And then there is the owner of the Western Biological Laboratory, Doc, a man of generosity and erudition who is at the center of all the action. The novel's plot details the characters' intersecting lives and humorous exploits, culminating with Mack and the boys' attempts to throw Doc a well-deserved party for his many kindnesses to the local community.

Some literary scholars have argued that *Cannery Row* reflects Steinbeck's ecological thinking, as influenced by Ricketts, and expresses the tide pool metaphor. According to Robert M. Benton, Steinbeck saw man "as an organism related to a vast and complex ecosystem." In the novel, he tries to demonstrate that "Cannery Row cannot be known and understood apart from the relationships and interrelationships which exist in it. It is more than people, than real estate, than buildings. It is all these, as they react upon one another."[32] More specifically, the people of Cannery Row were part of a tide pool, exhibiting similar traits as organisms in this ecosystem. For instance, Steinbeck's characters develop commensal relationships; like those in nature, they are mutually beneficial for the parties involved.[33] Yet Steinbeck pays little attention to a huge segment of the Cannery Row population—the immigrants who labored in the fish plants and plied the local waters—and the relationships they forged. Thus, his metaphoric tide pool lacks the complexity and diversity one would find in nature. It is highly selective and missing some key components.

Nonetheless, curious literary fans were intrigued by *Cannery Row* and soon began to descend on Monterey. As local columnist Margaret Hensel noted, visitors drove down Cannery Row "looking to right and to left for Lee Chong's Grocery, for Doc's Western Biological Laboratory, for Dora Flood and the girls of the Bear Flag Restaurant. . . . They think they recognize one of the Palace Flophouse boys in a bum lounging on a street corner." Steinbeck's characters were "so warm and meaningful" that "they live on for the readers," she concluded. Even though *Cannery Row* was a work of fiction and only partially based on reality, fans hoped to find the novel's characters and landmarks exactly as Steinbeck described them. They took little, if any, interest in the real immigrant cannery workers and fishermen who once sustained Cannery Row and were displaced by the sardine fishery's collapse. According to Martha Norkunas, Steinbeck's "literary landscape" had come to replace the historical one.[34]

While it was illogical for tourists to expect the "real" Cannery Row to duplicate the novel or vice versa, Wing Chong's store, the prototype for Lee Chong's grocery, was one place that satisfied some tourists' cravings for Steinbeck's Cannery Row.[35] In the novel, Steinbeck describes Lee Chong's as "a miracle of supply." When tourists entered Wing Chong's, writer Peggy Rink explained, they could not help but feel "a pleasant thrill of recognition" because of the "incongruous variety of merchandise that delighted Steinbeck." According to Frances Yee, sister-in-law of Won Yee, the store's original proprietor, visitors came from "all over the country." But apparently they came to look rather than buy. By December 1953, Yock Yee, Won Yee's son, and his partner C. M. Sam liquidated the store, no longer able to make a profit.[36]

Otherwise, tourists did not find many remnants of Steinbeck's Cannery Row. The hustle and bustle that he described in his opening vignette had gone the way of the sardine. After several years of poor catches, Cannery Row was like a ghost town. As Rink explained, "If the tourist came during the busy years when the now-vanished sardine thronged the Bay he may have peered into the faces of booted and bandanned [sic] cannery workers. . . . Any tourist inspecting Cannery Row in the years since the mass evacuation of the sardine has had trouble finding any faces at all to look into."[37] Cannery Row of the 1950s was quiet and deserted, not charged with excitement and activity, as Steinbeck had observed.

As Montereyans mulled over Cannery Row's future, they looked to Steinbeck for guidance and advice. In 1957 the *Monterey Peninsula Herald* published his four proposals for Cannery Row, each described with his sardonic flair. The "old-old" would rebuild shacks and Chinese gambling dens with scrap wood and tin. "The purchasers could re-create this pylon of the past with the help of Hollywood set designers," Steinbeck suggested. The "new-old" would re-create the look and smell of the sardine industry. Existing canneries would be sprayed with plastic to prevent rust buildup, while rocks and beaches would be stocked with artificial fish guts and wind machines would restore the odor of rotting fish. The third possibility, the "pseudo-old," would reconstruct Monterey's Spanish past by erecting "adobe" houses made of concrete and stainless steel.

Steinbeck acknowledged the allure of Monterey's past, but he ultimately advocated that developers start over and create "something new" out of Cannery Row:

> Young and fearless and creative architects are evolving in America. . . . I suggest that these creators be allowed to look at the lovely coastline, and to design something new in the world, but something that will add to the exciting beauty rather than cancel it out. Modern materials do not limit design as mud and tile once did. Then tourists would not come to see a celebration of a history that never happened, an imitation of limitations, but rather a speculation on the future. We never had a Notre Dame or a Chartres. But who knows what future beauty we may create? The foundation is there; sea rocks and beach, deep blue water, and on some days the magic hills of Santa Cruz. It would be interesting to see what could be added to this background. I don't think any such thing will be done, but so far dreams are not illegal—or are they?[38]

Steinbeck was undoubtedly aware of his impact on Cannery Row, but he implored the city to embrace the beauty of the coastline and start with a clean slate. In his mind, this approach offered the best chance of revitalizing Monterey's former industrial center.

Creating "something new" did not take hold, as city officials seemed eager to capitalize on Steinbeck's novel and romantic visions of the industrial heyday. This process began with changing the name of the street from Ocean View Avenue to Cannery Row in 1957. While Montereyans had referred informally to the street as "Cannery Row" for years, the formal name change meant that visitors could now look on a map and find their destination. Even though the name change was, in part, a tribute to Steinbeck and a testament to his popularity, he was entirely amused by the city's action. When his sister Beth, who was living in Monterey, passed along the news, he remarked, "This strikes me as a triumph of city planning logic. Ocean View Avenue was named at a time when you coul[d]n't see the ocean from it and now they change it to Cannery Row when there are no canneries there."[39] Steinbeck's sarcasm aside, the renaming was significant. As geographer Paul Carter has argued, names gave space "a character, something that could be referred to." In this case, the name "Cannery Row" evoked Steinbeck and signified a public identity inspired by his fictional account of Monterey's past.[40]

Through the late 1950s and early 1960s, Cannery Row remained a combination of "both the new and the old," shifting slowly from a fish processing center to an arts, shopping, and entertainment hub. Parts of the street, according to Ray March's 1962 guide, seemed frozen in a previous era. He noted, "You'll see nothing but boarded up canneries and piles of scrap iron. This is Cannery Row as it was left when the sardine left." Elsewhere, Cannery Row's low rent and ample space attracted a furniture dealer, several art galleries and studios, a handful of bars and restaurants, a dance studio, and a butterfly dealer. "If the sardines come back there will be no canneries to take them, and no workers to pack them into large oval or small flat cans," March explained.[41] Monterey's 1959 General Plan affirmed these developments, particularly as tourism became "one of the most important elements in the economy of Monterey." Although the plan recommended that the remaining canneries stay open, it also wanted cannery buildings to be used for "more active land uses, such as restaurants, art galleries, and craft studios suitable to this location in Monterey."[42]

When Steinbeck visited Monterey in 1960 after a cross-country road trip, described in his book *Travels with Charley*, he noticed the changes in Monterey and particularly along Cannery Row. The beaches were clean, no longer "festered with fish guts and flies." And, "the canneries which once put up a sickening stench are gone, their places filled with restaurants, antique shops, and the like. They fish for tourists now, not pilchards, and that species they are not likely to wipe out." But Steinbeck also seemed troubled by Monterey's transformation. "You can't go home again because home has ceased to exist except in the mothballs of memory," he concluded.[43] Curiously, the same person who had advocated "something new" lamented that Monterey was no longer the place he had remembered.

And the changes were just beginning. To develop a coherent plan for Cannery Row, the Cannery Row Properties Company, the City of Monterey, and other property owners hired planner Sydney Williams in 1961. Williams wanted to capitalize on a predicted surge in tourism as California's population grew. He projected a 31 percent increase (2,160 rooms) in lodging demand by 1970 and an 86 percent increase (3,070 rooms) by 1980; at the time of the report, the Cannery Row area had only one hotel. To entice tourists, Williams's "Cannery Row Plan" focused on retaining a flavor of the "Old Cannery Row," while providing new retail, commercial, professional, residential, and recreational uses. He wanted to both recapture the natural beauty of the shore "long hidden from public view by the Cannery structures" and preserve Cannery Row's former plants.[44] In short, Williams tried to reconcile contradictory ideals—historic preservation and development, scenic nature and industrial remains.

To achieve his objectives, Williams divided the Cannery Row area into two parts at McClellan Avenue. The northern half would be designated the "old" Cannery Row. It would provide for a mixture of land uses while retaining existing structures and making new structures conform to the architectural style. At the center, a broad plaza would surround a former cannery on both sides of the street. The southern portion would be earmarked for visitor and commercial purposes, using onshore building sites for motels and related uses. The balance of the area between Wave and Foam Streets was set aside for multifamily uses, while other areas were designated for public recreation and parking. He estimated that it would take ten to twenty years to develop the sixty-six-acre Cannery Row planning area.[45]

Williams tried to incorporate a variety of land uses, but his plan generated considerable controversy. One vocal opponent was Donald Dubrasich, a planning commissioner, who believed that the plan would fail precisely because it offered "something for everybody." In particular, he objected to high-rise buildings, as the plan allowed hotels and apartment buildings of up to ten stories. He concluded, "I don't think Mr. Steinbeck would much approve of the attitude we have to preserving old Cannery Row." Yet Dubrasich seemed to have little interest in historic preservation. As an alternative, he proposed an urban renewal program. With funding from the federal government and property donations from the City of Monterey, he recommended moving the railroad tracks eighty feet to the east and eliminating all buildings on the seaward side of the street, clearing the beach and returning it to a state of "natural beauty, highlighting a winding, rocky shoreline." Along this stretch of shore, the city could build a coastal drive with terraced bay-view buildings on the landward side of the road.[46]

In favoring ocean vistas and coastal access, Dubrasich adopted Steinbeck's "something new" approach, but his plan to eliminate some of the former canneries made it unpopular among people who relished Cannery Row's built environment. Dave McCafferty, one of the last canners, insisted that the railroad would have to be left in its existing location for the sake of the remaining fish plants. Planning commissioner Jack Doughery noted that Monterey did not want a "Riviera," while Harlan Watkins, who now owned Ed Ricketts's lab, added that tourists came "to see the beat-up canneries." The Cannery Row Committee, comprised of Cannery Row property owners and members of the Monterey Planning Commission, eventually endorsed Williams's plan. The planning commission later adopted it as an amendment to the general plan on July 10, 1962, and the Monterey City Council followed suit on September 4, 1962. In May 1964, the city approved a new zoning ordinance to develop the "Cannery Row Zone" into a "distinct visitor-commercial and multi-family residential area."[47]

The plan's passage was not the final word on Cannery Row, as merchants continued to hold conflicting visions for the neighborhood. While most agreed that the street should retain its "old character" and keep away "any gaudy motel-convention center things," bookstore owner James Campbell dissented. He noted, "Tradition is hard to come by, and 25 years doesn't compound tradition." In other words, Cannery Row was not "old" enough to warrant preservation. Instead, he advocated opening up the bay to create "an Atlantic City without the steel pier."[48] However, such radical new proposals, as Steinbeck had suggested, did not prevail. Preserving the remnants of the sardine industry—a response that suggested *Cannery Row*'s enduring influence—proved to be the more widespread and dominant vision.[49] Williams's plan tried to satisfy both camps, but putting his ideas into practice proved to be more difficult than local planners and developers anticipated.

Transforming Cannery Row into a tourist attraction was a formidable task. Montereyans could not eliminate the natural processes that came into contact with Cannery Row or the ne'er-do-wells that Steinbeck celebrated. Exposed to the harsh conditions of the coast, canneries rotted and fell apart. Vandals, vagrants, and arsonists destroyed them. Believing that Cannery Row's decay could enhance, rather than detract from, its aesthetic beauty, the city decided to restore some factories, incorporate the ruins of others, and blend these remains with the rocky shoreline. It sought to naturalize the built environment, making it an inherent and desirable feature of the Monterey coastline. But the city's plan did not fully acknowledge the underlying cause of Cannery Row's much-needed redevelopment: the sardine collapse. Instead, it romanticized a past ambition to exploit natural resources and combined this impulse with a persistent desire, dating back to the days of the Hotel Del Monte, to market the splendor of the Monterey coast. In the process, the social dynamics of Cannery Row were transformed, as new groups were encouraged to make their way to this coastal neighborhood.

Cannery Row's rapid deterioration, accelerated by fire, prompted this refashioned strategy. While several fires marked the industrial period, conflagrations proliferated as the canneries shut down. Few plants escaped unscathed. A huge blaze in November 1956 leveled the former San Carlos cannery, which had become a manufacturing warehouse, while the defunct San Xavier and Carmel Canning Company buildings burned in 1967. The rash of fires persisted into the 1970s. An arsonist set three fires in 1972 and 1973, confessing that he had chosen Cannery Row because he knew the buildings would burn well. After a few quiet years, fire hit the Hovden warehouse in July 1977, and another blaze followed in February 1978, damaging several new businesses and destroying the Monterey Canning Company building, one of the oldest canneries. Between 1952 and 1978, the fire department fought at least twenty-one fires on Cannery Row and classified seventeen of these blazes as arson or of unknown origin. Given their age, ease of access, and drafty interiors, the abandoned canneries provided ideal settings for large fires.[50] As Monterey Fire Chief Herb Scales explained, "Any fire on the Row is pretty much the same. They [the warehouses] are so wide open, the fire spreads fire. . . . Once it starts, it's so wide open there is a heckuva draft."[51]

Cannery Row's collapsing, burnt buildings were a depressing sight for most, but a sublime, even poetic sight for others. As journalist Mark Hazard Osmun put it, the canneries were "in spectacular ruin." When he visited Cannery Row in the mid-1970s, the few standing canneries "leaned over the water on shaky wooden braces, like dry, crippled skeletons. The corrugated tin walls and iron girders were rusted, and the rust had run and given even the timbers and concrete pilings a red-brown patina." Where the canneries had burned to the ground, leaving only foundations, "the steel was melting into the water and the concrete was becoming rock on sand." He concluded that the canneries possessed "an unquestioned goodness."[52] Even Ag Shea, who owned Ag Shea's Driftwood Bar, salvaged the charred timber from the San Carlos cannery to make cocktail tables.[53] The remnants of Cannery Row became his interior decoration.

However, John De Groot, Monterey's chief building inspector, did not regard Cannery Row's physical blight as virtuous and inspiring. Beginning in February 1970, he conducted a study of Cannery Row's built environment and found the area to be an unsightly safety liability. While some fires leveled the buildings, "the typical site has much of the building still in place, offering all kinds of protrusions, holes and hazards to fall upon and into. Not only do these sites offer every kind and degree of hazard but they leave a beautiful shoreline looking like a series of dumps." Age, neglect, and severe natural conditions had caused many canneries to crumble. Tattered rooftops allowed rain to enter. Doors, windows, stairs, railings, and gutters were in disrepair. For buildings that faced the ocean, waves and sea air rusted steel, split reinforced concrete beams and floor slabs, and rotted wood. Many of these buildings simply could not be salvaged, in De Groot's estimation. "All the money the City ever received for the leasing of this shoreline will not pay a fraction of the cost of restoring it to its original condition and one wonders if the earnings of the canneries were really worth the despoliation and the problems that they have now left us with," he noted.[54]

Empty, dilapidated canneries, in turn, attracted vandalism. De Groot and his crew were able to enter every vacant cannery building with relative ease. He wrote, "It is almost impossible to find an intact window pane. Everything droppable has been dropped, bundles of paper have been spread far and wide, machinery dismantled, plaster kicked in, plywood torn down; there is no limit to the energy and ingenuity of the vandal and there is no better example of his work than Cannery Row." While De Groot found little evidence of vagrancy, likely because of the cold, damp winter weather, he believed that it could become a problem with milder conditions.[55] Ironically, the deterioration of Cannery Row attracted the kind of misfits that Steinbeck celebrated in his novels. Real vagabonds and troublemakers, however, did not help Cannery Row tourism. Planners wanted to reproduce the physical ambience of *Cannery Row*, but they did not necessarily want to duplicate all aspects of its social ambience.[56]

De Groot also concluded that the former fish processing center had not witnessed any substantial or coherent tourism development. For one thing, roughly 70 percent of the square footage (410,063 square feet) along Cannery Row was unfit for occupation, while nearly 52 percent (367,200 square feet) was unused. Retail uses accounted for only 21 percent of the land, with warehousing and light manufacturing making up the largest use at almost 26 percent. While some people believed that Cannery Row was "full of glittering theaters, shops and restaurants," De Groot countered that there had been little commercial growth and that most occupancies were below minimum standards.[57]

In other words, Cannery Row was far from revitalized. Local developers could not repel the natural processes that ate away at the canneries, nor the vandals and arsonists who preyed on empty buildings. When Sydney Williams introduced his plan in 1961, most buildings were in good or fair condition. A decade later, many structures were on the verge of collapse. According to Tom Mangelsdorf, the Cannery Row Properties Company made no effort to reverse this deterioration; the partners "seemed content to 'sit' on their investments while waiting to see what would become of the area." Even when San Francisco hotelman Ben Swig bought the company's holdings to form the Cannery Row Development Company in 1967, Cannery Row remained, according to writer Anne Poindexter, "in a state of suspended animation, not yet dead and gone, but not exactly growing in leaps and bounds either." While art galleries and stores selling furniture, antiques, imports, clothing, and books cropped up in the area during the late 1960s, they did not bring substantial economic growth.[58]

Even though the local tourism economy was gaining steam—tourist dollars spent on the Monterey Peninsula more than doubled from thirty-two to sixty-seven million dollars between 1959 and 1969—Cannery Row made only a minor contribution. A 1970 employment survey indicated that the Cannery Row area provided just 3 percent of the city's jobs; six hundred people worked in the neighborhood, out of a total of eighteen thousand people employed citywide. While the taxable sales for Cannery Row grew 23 percent from the third quarter of 1970 through the second quarter of 1971—far exceeding the 14 percent average citywide—this only comprised roughly 3 percent of the city's total taxable sales. Moreover, Cannery Row property accounted for a paltry 1 percent of the city's property and building improvements.[59]

It is difficult to pinpoint the exact reasons why redevelopment did not take off. Recovering from the sardine collapse and shifting to a tourism economy was not going to happen overnight, yet time did not work in Cannery Row's favor. The neighborhood continued to deteriorate, potentially deterring the many tourists who, according to a 1963 survey, came to the Monterey area "simply to look at the natural beauty of the Peninsula." But there were other factors. The high percentage of multifamily dwellings proposed in the 1961 plan became unfeasible. Attempts to revitalize Cannery Row, moreover, coincided with a large urban renewal project that targeted downtown Monterey. Cannery Row eventually benefited from and became incorporated into these efforts, but construction was not completed until the 1970s, well after many of the former canneries were in decline.[60]

The City of Monterey modified its strategy in the Cannery Row Plan of 1973. The revised plan had similar goals as the original 1961 plan, such as preserving the area's "unique character," recapturing the beauty of the coast, and guiding tourism development. But it also took a distinct approach by highlighting the juxtaposition of the natural and built environments. The foundations, pilings, and contours of the old sardine plants punctuated rocky points, sandy beaches, and crashing surf; this blending provided "one of the important attractions on the Row." As city planners explained, "One does not expect to find an industrial area nestled on a stretch of magnificent coastline in a residential and tourist oriented community." Capitalizing on this "unique heritage and special environment" would turn Cannery Row into "one of those outstanding tourist attractions that also enjoys great economic success."[61]

Pointing out the positive physical and historical attributes of the fish factories and their remnants was key to the plan's refashioned approach. "The visual forms created by the old canneries are a source of delight, and certainly are a major contributor to the unique physical environment of Cannery Row," it explained. Discarded cannery equipment that littered vacant lots was really "landscape furniture," while cannery foundations that survived fire and decay appeared "as sculptural elements on the beach and in the surf." As a whole, the canneries comprised "abstract visual composition" that inspired some "to have a brief romance with the past" and others "to become nostalgic about American know-how and ingenuity." For instance, the crumbling Hovden cannery was significant because "most of the technological advances in the fish canning process took place in this building." The plan explained, "Items which would be regarded as junk anywhere else arouse feelings of nostalgia for days gone by."[62]

Rather than seeing Cannery Row's built environment as a liability and eliminating the collapsing structures, city planners adapted their proposals to the material conditions they found. Even as they called for the preservation of Steinbeck-related landmarks, including Wing Chong's store and Ed Ricketts's lab, they also cast the seemingly unattractive elements of Cannery Row as assets, items of curiosity for tourists to seek out and enjoy. They also recognized that industrial relics could provide evidence of past feats. As David Lowenthal explains, decay heightened "temporal awareness, inducing nostalgic and other reflections on time's changes."[63] Thus, Cannery Row did not have to be the run-down, seedy part of town. Combined with the natural features of the coast, the residue of industry could be a fascinating tourist attraction and a source of the street's renewal.

This plan for Cannery Row represented a dramatic change from earlier forms of Monterey tourism. When the Pacific Improvement Company and the Del Monte Properties Company ran the Hotel Del Monte in the late nineteenth and early twentieth centuries, the canneries were their nemesis. Fish offal polluted the shoreline, while pungent odors from reduction plants purportedly wafted to the hotel and interfered with its genteel environment of manicured gardens, shady verandas, and ocean breezes. When visitors did venture beyond the hotel grounds, they typically wanted to see the coast in its "natural" form—rocky promontories, crashing waves, stunning sunsets—and did not include a visit to the industrial part of town. City planners now envisioned tourists walking along a beautiful shoreline punctuated by the physical evidence of the sardine industry's demise—decaying canneries, crumbling foundations, and rusting equipment.

To maintain Cannery Row's industrial ambience, the plan recommended that buildings retain the look of the former canneries. It urged developers to adopt one of two architectural forms: the large warehouse or the complex cannery collage, a hodgepodge of towers, skylights, smokestacks, and other "odd structures." Other building styles, such as Spanish, Victorian, Old English, or Colonial, would detract from the character of Cannery Row. The plan explained, "Sham architecture and garishness is out of place on Cannery Row because sham architecture and garishness destroy the quality of being unique. If the tendency towards sham architecture and garishness continues on Cannery Row, the tourist industry will be the second industry to destroy itself in the same location." To prevent this potential disaster, builders had to accurately reconstruct historic buildings with "proper" materials, such as corrugated sheet metal, horizontal wood siding, brick, and multi-lighted windows.[64] The crude, unrefined look of the canneries was now something to be reproduced and cultivated.

Cannery Row Square, which opened in 1972, was one example of how the former canneries could be both preserved and converted to commercial uses. This shopping mall development consisted of two former cannery warehouses enclosed by a walkway. The northern building was the former Custom House Cannery warehouse, while the southern building was once the warehouse of the Carmel Canning Company. The $1.5 million project was a joint venture by Shuler-Verga Diversified Developers of Monterey and Calpak Properties Inc., a subsidiary of the Del Monte Corporation, which had previously operated a Monterey cannery. Alfred Eames, chairman of the Del Monte board of directors, noted, "We'd like to think that the renovation of this building and its twin structure . . . represents the type of enterprise that can both preserve the flavor of Cannery Row and give it new life."[65] The Cannery Row Plan affirmed such ventures that stimulated visitor interest with commercial activities in the former canneries.[66]

Industrial architecture and shopping were only part of Cannery Row's allure, as the neighborhood offered many opportunities to enjoy the beauty of the coastline and ocean. Coastal vistas, rocky points, and tide pools dotted the waterfront, while three beaches provided entry points for scuba divers and "a desirable area of tranquility in an otherwise highly developed and active environment." The city wanted to show off this scenic coastline by creating public beaches and using a side-yard setback requirement of 30 percent to open up views and access to the bay. After all, the ocean was "only an asset to the Row if it can be seen." This strategy would require careful planning and negotiations, since most of the valuable oceanfront land was privately owned.[67]

By developing these plans for the built and natural environments along Cannery Row, the city implicitly proposed an entirely different social regime in the neighborhood. The class, racial, and ethnic diversity that defined Cannery Row during the sardine industry's heyday would be replaced by a more homogeneous group of middle- and upper-class tourists who would help to buoy the neighborhood's service economy. The former cannery buildings and relics might remind visitors of Cannery Row's industrial labor, but city planners really wanted them to provide ambience and visual novelty to the rocky coastline—to give people a reason to come to Monterey. The remaining fish plants did not explicitly memorialize the hundreds of cannery workers and fishermen who once worked along the coastline. Their history was seemingly erased in the city's plans for Cannery Row.

The Cannery Row Plan's efforts to blend Monterey's industrial past with the splendor of the coastline also neglected the major cause of this transformation: the collapse of the sardine fishery. Indeed, the former fish plants were more than just a testament of "American know-how and ingenuity," and the bay was more than just a scenic backdrop; they also represented the failings of sardine management and the perplexity of the ocean and its fisheries. The absence of any discussion of the sardine's demise was all the more curious, since ecological principles that accounted for human pressures on nature influenced the plan's development. To comply with the California Environmental Quality Act of 1970, which followed on the heels of the National Environmental Policy Act of 1969, the city prepared an environmental impact report that analyzed the possible effects of the Cannery Row Plan, such as damage to wildlife, vegetation, traffic, and air quality.[68] Even if the plan itself did not fully analyze the environmental complexities of Monterey Bay or past natural resource use, the state's expanding regulatory structure mandated that the city's new designs for the former industrial waterfront address any potentially deleterious impact on the natural world.

Although the Cannery Row Plan passed in November 1973 only as a guideline and not as an actual policy, it affirmed the continuing transformation of the waterfront area into a tourist destination. The closing of the Hovden cannery several months earlier in February made this development all the more imperative. For ten years, Hovden was the only plant trying to eke by on Cannery Row. Surrounded by half-burnt canneries, seafood restaurants, and art galleries, it could no longer keep going. As journalist Kevin Howe reported, "The last fish has been canned on Monterey's fabled Cannery Row."[69] Tourism had already eclipsed industrial activities for several years, but the closing of the Hovden cannery still held tremendous symbolic importance. Tourists, not cannery workers and sardines, would continue to fill the former fish plants. Cannery manager Anthony Souza concluded, "It's pitiful what Cannery Row's come to."[70]

The irony of Cannery Row's evolution did not escape building inspector John De Groot, the same person who had recorded the destruction that followed the industrial era. He argued that Steinbeck's novel had "created a romantic legend out of a bunch of stinking sweatshops" and that the name "Cannery Row" would "outlast every building as it has already outlived by a couple of decades the fish canning industry."[71] De Groot had no sentimental attachment to this once-bustling neighborhood and its fading industrial ambience; he did not fall for the city's nostalgic visions. City planners, on the other hand, wanted to transform Cannery Row into a tourist attraction that merged its natural setting with its industrial remains and spoke to Steinbeck's picturesque novel. Rather than starting over with a clean slate, they endeavored to make the name and legend of Cannery Row an enduring physical reality along the coastline. In the process, they affirmed Monterey's fishing identity in spite of the absence of sardines. Thus, even as Cannery Row's postwar tourism industry diverged sharply from the sardine's heyday, it intertwined with the recent industrial past.

By the mid- to late 1970s, environmental regulations began to further complicate tourism development on Cannery Row. The concentrated construction of fish processing plants during the first half of the twentieth century would never have been allowed under this new regime. In November 1972, California voters passed Proposition 20, the Coastal Initiative, establishing a coastal commission system made up of one statewide and six regional commissions. The California Coastal Act of 1976 later made the California Coastal Commission (CCC) the "permanent mechanism for coastal protection and management." The act required that the CCC approve all coastal projects and that local governments prepare a Local Coastal Program (LCP) for areas within the coastal zone, the region three miles from shore to the nearest coastal ridge.[72] Faulting the 1973 Cannery Row Plan for allowing too much development, the new commission asked the City of Monterey to address this issue in its Cannery Row LCP.[73]

In the meantime, the commission rejected a string of Cannery Row projects, generating considerable animosity from local merchants and would-be developers. Regional commissioner Robert Franco even received a threatening phone call after he voted against two Cannery Row hotels. To break the stalemate, the state commission assigned a senior staff member to work closely with the city to develop the LCP. After almost twenty public hearings, the commission and the city agreed on a plan in 1980. The Cannery Row LCP compromised between development and protection, allowing hotels and motels, providing public access to beaches, and requiring protection of marine habitats.[74] Many residents resented this strict government supervision. As Cannery Row property owner and merchant Frank Crispo noted, "Nobody should have the right to tell an owner that he can't do what he wants with his property."[75]

While some Montereyans saw this maze of regulations as a hindrance to Cannery Row's redevelopment, the policies reflected a concern for coastal protection and a desire for environmental amenities. These green ideals, along with growing public interest in the marine world, ultimately carried over to the tourism industry and brought another boom to Cannery Row. The natural diversity of Monterey Bay became an attraction that eclipsed the converted canneries and the persistent legend of *Cannery Row*. Knut Hovden's legacy was no longer reduced to an empty cannery on the edge of the sea, and Steinbeck's vision of doing "something new" on Cannery Row, "something that will add to the exciting beauty rather than cancel it out," came to fruition—though not in the form he likely anticipated.

7 THE FISH ARE BACK!

On October 20, 1984, the Monterey Bay Aquarium opened to great fanfare. Approximately thirty thousand people gathered on Cannery Row to attend the celebration, which included a boat parade in Monterey Harbor, music, food booths, and fireworks. Close to eleven thousand people also visited the aquarium, marveling at the intricate exhibits of Monterey Bay habitats.[1] As patron David Packard, cofounder of electronics company Hewlett-Packard, explained, the new facility created "a living replica of the environment that's just outside our windows."[2] With these beautiful displays of local marine life, the aquarium proudly proclaimed, "The Fish Are Back!"[3]

This slogan was a thinly veiled reference to the previous collapse of the sardine fishery. While the sardine's "departure" had forced the canneries to shut their doors at mid-century, the aquarium revived Cannery Row by re-creating Monterey Bay and enclosing it under acrylic panels. With the return of the fish, Monterey seemed to come nearly full circle. Over one hundred years after the opening of the Hotel Del Monte, the city again had a premiere tourist attraction that lured people from around the country. Much like the hotel, the aquarium used funding from San Francisco Bay area capitalists to become a vital local institution. And much like the hotel's opulent gardens and scenic drives, the aquarium manipulated nature to sell elite tourists a visually stimulating leisure experience, one that similarly blurred the boundaries between nature and artifice.[4]

But the aquarium also reflected visions for the coastline that were distinct from previous tourism enterprises. During the postwar period, many Americans grew concerned about the ecological health of the shoreline, particularly with the quickened pace of coastal development. The aquarium fed off this emergent environmentalism, developing exhibits that educated visitors about the complexities of marine ecosystems and the grave problems they faced worldwide. Whereas the Cannery Row Plans of 1961 and 1973 romanticized the sardine industry and glossed over its demise, the aquarium soon critiqued unchecked human pressures on the environment.

This environmental focus catered to a predominantly white, educated, and affluent audience. Much like earlier efforts to promote tourism on Cannery Row, the aquarium did not foster class, racial, and ethnic diversity and largely neglected the rich social history of the sardine industry. The homogeneity of the aquarium's clientele underscored environmentalism's appeal to well-heeled Americans who often expressed their green values through consumption.[5] It also spoke to the environmental movement's tendency to overlook *human* difference and highlight the intricacies of the *nonhuman* world. Indeed, at the aquarium, visitors learned all about the ecological diversity of Monterey Bay life—but not the diversity of the human communities that interacted with the coastline, past and present.

In advocating environmental stewardship, however, the aquarium did not completely reject the industrial past. Once again, the legacy of the fisheries was never far from the surface, and it helped to shape the new institution. Housed in the former Hovden cannery, the aquarium actually played off and integrated the history of the fish plant. Rather than razing the building and starting with a clean slate, as John Steinbeck had suggested, designers embraced the irony of the site. They decided to gut the defunct factory's interior while preserving its facade. The architecture served as a constant reminder of the building's former life, but there was no mistaking the aquarium for a cannery. It did not scare away visitors with foul odors. Labor and nature no longer intertwined visibly within its walls. Instead, this vestige of industry enclosed a place where mostly white visitors of comfortable means encountered nature and expressed their environmental values. The aquarium, then, promoted Monterey as a place close to nature, one that adopted an explicit environmental ethos. In this respect, it was indeed the "something new" that Steinbeck had advocated for Cannery Row.

The transformation of the Hovden cannery began at Stanford University's Hopkins Marine Station, where scientists grew concerned about development on neighboring Cannery Row. In 1961 Hopkins director Lawrence Blinks explained that purchasing the Hovden building would "protect us against further encroachment by industry."[6] More specifically, Professor Hubert Heffner feared that a small boat harbor might develop on Cannery Row, destroying nearby tide pools with oil refuse. In addition to providing a buffer from commercial expansion, the Hovden property could also be used for student and faculty housing.[7] Heeding these claims, Stanford bought the property in 1967 through a deal that contained a lease-back provision in which the Wilbur-Ellis Company of San Francisco ran the cannery as the Portola Packing Company. When Wilbur-Ellis moved to a nearby Moss Landing plant and closed Hovden's doors in 1973, Hopkins used the building as a warehouse.[8]

The Hovden plant continued to deteriorate until Steve Webster, Chuck Baxter, Robin Burnett, and Nancy Burnett came up with the idea of building an aquarium on the site. Baxter and Robin Burnett were faculty members at Hopkins, while Nancy Burnett did her graduate work at Moss Landing and Webster was a professor at San Jose State University. As an aquarium progress report noted in 1980, "This concept stemmed from an interest in Monterey Bay's rich marine life and the desire to share this with a broad range of the public, as well as a concern for preserving and revitalizing the historic Hovden Cannery."[9] Nancy Burnett approached her parents, Lucile and David Packard, and the Packard Foundation underwrote the cost of a feasibility study, conducted by the Stanford Research Institute.[10] When the results were favorable, the Packards established the Monterey Bay Aquarium Foundation in April 1978. This private, nonprofit corporation was to construct and operate an aquarium that would "expand the public interest in and enjoyment of the marine life and environment of Monterey Bay and the surrounding areas of ocean and shoreline."[11] David Packard agreed to fund construction, with the condition that the aquarium would be self-supporting once it opened.[12]

The aquarium planning group, which included the Burnetts, Webster, Baxter, and Julie Packard, another Packard daughter, wasted little time in getting the aquarium under way. The foundation bought the Hovden property from Stanford University for just under one million dollars.[13]

In the fall of 1978, it hired Linda Rhodes as project manager and the architectural firm of Esherick, Homsey, Dodge, and Davis (EHDD), which had designed the Long Marine Laboratory at the University of California, Santa Cruz.[14] To gather ideas for the exhibits, the Burnetts joined a two-week tour of fourteen Japanese aquariums.[15] The planning group initially envisioned a building of 40 to 50 thousand square feet that would cost five to seven million dollars to construct. By 1979 the plan had multiplied to 226,000 square feet of enclosed space with decks on three levels. Contractors Rudolph and Sletten estimated a period of thirty-one months to build the aquarium at a cost of thirty-one million dollars. The aquarium decided that it would make its own exhibits, bringing the total cost estimate to fifty million dollars. The rising costs did not pose major problems, as the Packards did not scrimp or rush the job.[16]

The aquarium project came on the heels of growing public interest in the marine environment. Rachel Carson's 1951 book *The Sea Around Us* climbed the best-seller lists and drew Americans' attention to the sea, while SCUBA, self-contained underwater breathing apparatus, literally opened up the oceans for human exploration. Television and film were also influential. The television show *Sea Hunt*, which aired from 1958 to 1961, the 1954 remake of *20,000 Leagues Under the Sea*, and MGM's 1963 film *Flipper* brought attention to the marine world.[17] Similarly, Jacques Cousteau displayed the depths of the ocean in his 1956 film *Le Monde du Silence* (Silent World) and his television show, *The Undersea World of Jacques Cousteau*, which began in 1968 and ran for almost nine years.[18]

The growing fascination with the marine world coincided with increasing concern about its ecological health. In particular, the Santa Barbara oil spill in 1969, which dumped 235,000 gallons of crude oil and polluted thirty miles of shore, focused national attention on the imperiled state of the coastline.[19] Congress responded by passing a wave of regulations in 1972: the Clean Water Act; the Marine Mammal Protection Act; the Marine Protection, Research, and Sanctuaries Act (MPRSA); and the Coastal Zone Management Act (CZMA). The MPRSA authorized the creation of national marine sanctuaries, which protected certain marine areas and sponsored comprehensive management. The CZMA provided funds to states that followed federal guidelines in developing coastal management plans.[20] California's Coastal Initiative also passed in 1972, subjecting the aquarium to Coastal Commission approval.

Although the aquarium advocated the appreciation and preservation of the marine environment, it could not escape stringent regulations at the city, county, state, and federal levels. Seventy percent of the aquarium fell within Monterey city limits and 30 percent rested in Pacific Grove, so both cities had to approve the Environmental Impact Report (EIR) and issue permits for demolition, parking, building, and design.[21] Because the aquarium both discharged into and took in water from the bay, the Central Coast Regional Water Quality Control Board and the United States Army Corps of Engineers, which kept navigable waters open, had to approve. The army corps also evaluated cultural resources and determined that the Hovden cannery was eligible for the National Register of Historic Places; to address "mitigation measures," the aquarium prepared a historical report on the cannery.[22] The United States Department of Agriculture's Animal and Plant Inspection oversaw the handling, care, treatment, and transportation of marine mammals, while the California Department of Fish and Game served as an advisory agency to limit negative impacts on fish and wildlife.[23]

The maze of government bureaucracies loomed large, but positive findings in the EIR facilitated the project's approval. First, the EIR determined that the aquarium would not significantly affect water quality, since it planned to dilute and release chemicals with the seawater or discharge them into the sanitary sewer. Any solids that the aquarium generated or took in would be filtered, settled, and disposed of on land or through the sewer. Its impact on local ecosystems was also deemed minimal. In the subtidal zone, where the aquarium would install its intake lines, construction could cause some animals to temporarily "shy away." In the intertidal zone along the shore, the dismantling of parts of the Hovden building and the construction of new foundations and pilings would cause a temporary decrease of organisms, but the new structures would provide substrate for creatures to colonize. At the same time, the aquarium would cover previously sun-exposed areas, favoring a growth of shade-tolerant species. The EIR also concluded that the aquarium's construction could stand up to its harsh natural locale.[24]

But the project did have the potential to cause other problems for the local community. The EIR identified parking as the most "significant impact." It estimated that the aquarium would require 140 spaces at its start and 197 spaces within ten years; the project proposed only 30 on-site parking spaces, primarily for employees. "Patron parking demand would have to be satisfied in off-site parking facilities of a public nature," the EIR noted. The EIR also projected a parking deficit on weekend evenings if aquarium and Cannery Row peak hours coincided. While parking in Pacific Grove could accommodate the aquarium's needs, there would still be an overflow of 196 cars from the rest of the Cannery Row area. The EIR explained that Cannery Row faced a weekend parking deficit even without the aquarium.[25]

Because the aquarium would be a major contribution to the community, aquarium planners asked Monterey and Pacific Grove to help with the parking situation. In March 1980, after extensive transit and parking studies, they reached a compromise in which the aquarium agreed to provide thirty-one on-site parking spaces, twenty off-site spaces, and three bus spaces, while Monterey absorbed the aquarium's parking assessment district fees and did not require additional public parking. Pacific Grove required a validation system to discount admission costs for visitors using the City of Monterey parking lot on Cannery Row and retained the option to demand mitigation measures in the future. Pacific Grove also asked the aquarium to restrict the restaurant and auditorium to aquarium patrons so as not to compete with other nearby businesses, hire an archaeologist for excavations, and pay for improvements and maintenance in the area within five years. In total, there were twenty-seven "conditions" on the Pacific Grove use permit and twenty-one on the Monterey permit.[26]

The aquarium needed two years to receive all of the necessary permits. As executive director Julie Packard remembered, "It was a nightmare."[27] By January 1980, Monterey, Pacific Grove, and the Regional Coastal Commission had granted permission to dismantle the cannery. This work began in March 1980. Construction started in March 1981 and continued for twenty-eight months.[28] This drawn-out process demonstrated that coastal development was far more complicated than in the days of the canneries or the Hotel Del Monte. Several groups, agencies, and interests now laid claim to the coastline and wanted to protect its resources. Nonetheless, the aquarium jumped through the requisite hoops to begin its transformation of the Hovden cannery.

"THE AQUARIUM FITS RIGHT IN"

Architects and planners put the new facility on paper. Because they were working with an existing building on a street of corroding industrial structures rather than an empty spot on the map, they faced a distinct challenge. How would the Hovden cannery—its architectural features and its history—shape the aquarium's design? How would the aquarium withstand the destructive natural conditions to which its neighbors had fallen victim? In the end, the aquarium restored and reinforced the Hovden building, reconciling its past life as a fish processing plant with its new life as a showcase for Monterey Bay.[29]

One major challenge was to integrate the aquarium into the aesthetics of Cannery Row. From day one, the designers wanted to retain the industrial feel of the Hovden cannery. As Linda Rhodes and Charles Davis of EHDD noted, "While many had grown up resenting the canneries because of their powerful odor, everyone favored reconstructing the building as a new aquarium rather than clearing the site altogether." The failure to preserve the original architecture "would be a big disservice to our visiting public and to the community," they concluded. The old cannery was "a special place . . . filled with history and metaphor that had to be imbedded in the building."[30] Thus, Davis did not want to "tamper needlessly" with the site, "whether natural or man-made." "When we do tamper, we tamper carefully, trying to weave the new into the fabric of the old, to graft perhaps rather than to make the 'surgical cuts' that until recently were the architect's stock-in-trade," he wrote.[31]

When Rhodes and EHDD arrived at the aquarium site, they found the Hovden cannery in severe disrepair. Initial investigations revealed that "an old conglomeration of dry-rotted wooden constructions could not possibly be salvaged and converted into a public-use building." But they also "fell in love" with the former plant, "savored its mixture of mill construction, white paint and sunlight pouring into the interior through skylights on the roof," and decided to reconstruct it. The first step was determining the footprint, or former outline of the building, part of which extended over the water. "We climbed over, under and all around the old Hovden Cannery, dissecting the mind of the fish processing engineer who put together the sardine canning systems. Like Hovden, we had to work from the inside out: plan the internal processing system and design the building around it," Rhodes and Davis explained.[32]

While the original cannery design provided guidance, the building's physical state determined what, if anything, could be salvaged. Designers managed to keep the major concrete elements in the water, the western section of the seawall, and a platform at the eastern end of the seawall.

With a new foundation and roof, the cannery warehouse became the aquarium's administrative offices.[33] The former cannery pump house, which had once carried sardines from the hoppers to the plant, now supplied seawater to the exhibits. As Rhodes and Davis proclaimed, "The heart of the old Hovden Cannery remains the heart of the Monterey Bay Aquarium today."[34]

The aquarium also preserved the cannery's boiler house, which had supplied steam for cooking fish, as an artifact of the sardine industry. Aquarium staff enlisted the assistance of former Hovden cannery boiler operators Al Campoy and Frank Bergara, who helped redraw room plans and identify the missing parts. After contacting boiler firms across the country, the staff discovered the vintage parts at the nearby Monterey Boiler Company. Construction crews put the boiler house back together and built the aquarium around it. For the finishing touches, they installed the original brass and bronze plaques, removed the walls to expose the pipes, valves, bells, pulleys, and gauges, and installed three fiberglass smokestacks, the tallest towering at 120 feet, back on their original pedestals. The restored boiler house did not actually work, but "it remains as a powerful reminder of the aquarium's first use as an industrial plant."[35] In October 1983, the aquarium held a small celebration with seven former cannery workers and executive director Julie Packard, who declared, "Let's call this a rebirth of the cannery."[36]

Of course, the restoration of the boiler house was merely a gesture to the past, not a true "rebirth." For one thing, Al Campoy and Frank Bergara could never return as real boiler operators. As an institution that contributed to Cannery Row's service economy, the aquarium attracted employees and visitors who would interact with nature in an entirely different manner from the cannery workers who preceded them. It would not employ people to engage in productive activities, like transforming sardines into tins of food or sacks of fertilizer. Instead, employees would help to enhance the visits of those in pursuit of stimulating leisure experiences. Together, aquarium employees and affluent white tourists would replace the immigrant Filipinos, Sicilians, Spaniards, Portuguese, and Japanese who once ran the canning lines, creating a much more socially homogenous environment. While the history of the Hovden cannery and the sardine industry as a whole provided a constant point of reference, designers preserved the form of the cannery, "not the substance."[37]

In addition to the boiler house, other aesthetic and structural features of the aquarium drew inspiration from the former cannery. The facade conformed to Cannery Row's industrial style, replicating the "hodge-podge of roofs" from the former plant. As Charles Davis explained, "we held on to the cannery's facade along Cannery Row as a means of welding the building to its past."[38] Inside, there were exposed pipes, ducts, and framing on the ceiling, just like in the cannery, and the aquarium windows were similar in design to the ones in the former plant. Designers also incorporated the cannery's wave-lip design, which turned back waves and provided structural protection during harsh storms.[39] Whether the building housed a cannery or an aquarium, it needed to account for exposure to severe conditions. The cannery's original design continued to perform this function with little modification.

The end result was a building that "looks and feels like the old canneries that Steinbeck haunted."[40] As another journalist proclaimed, "The aquarium fits right in because, with its plain cement walls and jumble of rooflines, it too looks like, well, a fish cannery."[41] Rhodes and Davis were aware of the "inherent irony" of turning a fish processing plant into a place for exhibiting marine flora and fauna, but they valued the building's history. As Davis elaborated, the aquarium "reflects the fact that our perceptions are somehow tied up in the history of the place, and that this legacy still pervades Cannery Row."[42] To recognize the aquarium's respect for the past, the California Historical Society presented the Monterey Bay Aquarium with an award of merit for historical preservation at its opening-day celebration.[43]

The aquarium design may have fit in with the former fish plants along Cannery Row, but designers also tried to highlight the beauty of the coastline. They opened up ocean vistas with twenty thousand square feet of decks that looked out into the bay and "a graceful plaza" and walkway above the shoreline. The goal was to create facilities that "interacted" with the shoreline and encouraged visitors to make some connections between the interior exhibits and "the ultimate exterior display—the bay itself."[44] Julie Packard elaborated, "Because we have this fabulous site, we wanted the whole aquarium to be a complete melding with the real world."[45] Just as the Cannery Row Plan of 1973 had recommended, these plans reconciled the industrial-style built environment with the beauty of the coastline. And because the design provided public access to the shore and encouraged respect for the marine environment, it also followed the guidelines of the California Coastal Act of 1976.[46]

Turning these plans into an actual, functioning aquarium was another story. The aquarium's enormous scale and harsh location made construction challenging. For instance, just after construction crews demolished the Hovden cannery in August 1980, they noticed that the old seawall had begun to crumble, taking with it fill material for the aquarium site. Because builders feared that a winter storm could wash away large amounts of soil and debris, damaging tide pools and destabilizing the boiler house, they began work on the new seawall immediately and completed it the following spring.[47] Laying the foundation, moreover, was also "full of surprises" because of the uneven topography of the coastline. By the fall of 1982, workers had completed the foundation and laid the concrete deck that extended over the water—a job that took fifteen days and required a 230-ton crane.[48]

Much like the workers who were called to the cannery whenever fishermen rolled into the harbor with their hauls, construction crews also had to conform to the irregular rhythms of nature. Because 40 percent of the aquarium extended over the shore into water up to 120 feet deep, workers had to install its forty-nine footings and support columns into a fluid mixture of land and water. The footings had to be embedded in at least six inches of solid granite, so construction crews had to work when the ground was exposed—typically during the low tide at night. As the tide receded, workers took sand and marine growth off rocks, jackhammered through granite, placed the rebar and footing formwork, and poured the concrete. At the top of each footing, workers created a depression to set the column form.[49] But the routine did not always go as planned. As Al Menchaca, Rudolph and Sletten's project manager, explained, "Some nights we were beaten by the tide, and sometimes we had to [dig] eight feet below the beach sand to hit granite. And there were times it [the granite] wasn't there and we lost the excavations."[50]

In the end, contractors overcame the physical realities of the coastline to build an aquarium that evoked its past life as a sardine factory and blended into the Cannery Row neighborhood. They made the aquarium compatible with what appeared to be an incompatible building and history. The new structure reflected the visions of designers, who valued both the natural beauty of the coast and historic preservation. But inside, the aquarium offered few reminders of its fish-processing past. Employees and visitors erased the social diversity that had once defined the sardine industry and adopted an entirely different vision of how people should interact with the marine world.

CULTIVATING NATURE AT THE AQUARIUM

In focusing on the complexity of local ecosystems, the aquarium represented a split from previous forms of tourism. Unlike Cannery Row of the 1960s and 1970s, industrial relics punctuated by scenic shoreline were not the major attraction. Unlike the Hotel Del Monte, nature was not a backdrop or potential nuisance. Nonetheless, the aquarium's active manipulation of nature showed continuity with the genteel resort that preceded it. And while aquarium visitors had a curiosity about the natural world that was distinct from that of many earlier tourists, they still sought an aesthetically pleasing experience. The aquarium did its part to fulfill those needs by creating and cultivating visually stimulating displays of Monterey Bay life.

First and foremost, the exhibits had to conform to the original goal of the aquarium—to create "a regional aquarium featuring just Monterey Bay and central California by a habitat approach: how things relate to each other, why they are where they are, how they make their living, and so forth," as director of education and aquarium founder Steve Webster explained. In other words, the aquarium's approach was "fairly intellectual"; it did not focus on charismatic mammals, decontextualize its specimens from their natural habitats, or make them perform tricks, as was the case in such places as SeaWorld or Marineland.[51] Instead, the aquarium showcased eighty-three exhibit tanks and twelve galleries, with three large tanks at its center. The Kelp Forest tank was sixty-six feet long and twenty-eight feet high. Representing deep reefs, shale reefs, the sandy seafloor, and the wharf, the Monterey Bay Habitats tank was figure eight–shaped and extended ninety feet. These two large tanks held over three hundred thousand gallons of water each. The third-largest tank, which held fifty-five thousand gallons, displayed rescued sea otters, the aquarium's only marine mammals. The aquarium also built sand dunes and marshes with an aviary for seabirds.[52] To encourage visitors to become "physically involved with the exhibits," a touch pool of intertidal creatures and a kelp lab provided hands-on activities.[53]

The "lifeblood" of the aquarium was the seawater system. Unlike many aquariums located near polluted urban harbors, the relative cleanliness of Monterey Bay allowed the aquarium to pump raw seawater directly from the bay and discharge it back to the ocean. The water was also cold enough that deadly protozoa could not reproduce, so the aquarium did not have to add copper sulfate, which eradicated other marine organisms in the process.[54] The resulting system consisted of two sixteen-inch-diameter polyethylene lines that snaked 980 feet into the bay at a depth of 55 feet and pumped in up to 2,050 gallons of water per minute.[55]

But raw seawater was not always healthy for the aquarium's marine organisms or conducive to a memorable visitor experience. As a result, the system had several modifications. In case of an oil spill or a red tide, harmful algal blooms that occurred seasonally in Monterey Bay, it went into a closed mode to protect the exhibits. To maintain water clarity during aquarium hours, the system also began to filter the water at 2 A.M. After the aquarium closed, the seawater system took in murkier, unfiltered water, rich with microscopic plankton that fed filter feeders and settled in the exhibits.[56] The aesthetic needs of the aquarium meant that the seawater system could provide the most nutrient-rich water only when visitors were absent.[57]

With the water system in place, the aquarium created the exhibit habitats or "scenery." To show a realistic slice of Monterey Bay, the tanks could not be filled solely with water and specimens. Since many local ecosystems abutted rockwork, on which marine life settled, the exhibits also had to include rocks. But this was not a simple matter of collecting rocks and dropping them into the tanks; the exhibits called for specific sizes with specific crevices. Because the aquarium's needs were so particular, planners decided to make artificial rocks. David Packard set up a "fabrication facility" in nearby Sand City and hired several engineers and craftsmen. To make the rocks, they placed fiberglass reinforced concrete (FRC), which was thin and light, on top of a framework. They then carved shapes and texture into the cement before it hardened and drilled thousands of tiny holes to create homes for small sea life.[58]

But exhibit designers did not want bare rocks installed in the tanks. To colonize the rocks, they placed a steel cage in an underwater area protected from storms, weighed it down with a half ton of concrete, fixed the rocks onto it, and left them for at least three years to give flora and fauna ample time to grow and multiply.[59] Given the fecund waters of Monterey Bay, the rocks soon teemed with life. Conversely, "Put something into New York harbor and you'd kill it immediately," Steve Webster noted.[60] After a period of growth, aquarium staff then gardened the rocks. If director of husbandry David Powell wanted an animal-dominated community, he mounted rocks on the sides of the cage where they would receive less sunlight and less plant growth. If he wanted a specific species, he would glue "starter" animals on the rocks with a nontoxic marine epoxy, giving them a head start on reproduction. He also made periodic dives to monitor progress and weeded out sea stars, which preyed on some choice species.[61] In the end, visitors did not discern the difference between "real" and "fake" rocks. "More important, neither do the fish," one journalist concluded.[62]

Aquarium designers took a similar approach in designing the tidal basin, an area just below the building decks. Construction crews anchored steel reinforcing bars into the rock and poured layers of concrete over the bars, the old cannery footings, and additional concrete blocks. They then sculpted the concrete to match surrounding rock and painted it to match the granite. The seawater system outfall dumped two thousand gallons of water per minute into the basin, keeping it permanently filled to eight feet. The aquarium hoped that the rocks would attract harbor seals and sea otters, which visitors could observe from the decks. As the aquarium newsletter proclaimed, "The results are amazingly convincing and leave visitors hard-pressed to tell where the artificial granite begins and ends in the rocky pools below the Aquarium."[63]

Ironically, the aquarium used the same techniques to re-create a human-constructed ecosystem: the wharf. For the small wharf habitat exhibit, aquarium staff members placed layers of fiberglass cloth with black polyester resin over a vinyl form to make six-foot-tall cylinders. They then bolted the fake pilings to actual wharf pilings in Monterey Harbor so that organisms could settle and grow. For the large Monterey Bay Habitats tank, the aquarium obtained real pilings from the Monterey Harbor Department. Staff chose those with the richest growth of marine life, cut them to fit in the tank, and reattached them to the wharf to await installation. The aquarium believed that the pilings "should provide a near-natural look at life under the wharf."[64]

The fake rocks and wharf pilings, overgrown with algae and invertebrates, illustrated how the aquarium cultivated nature. Monterey Bay's waters sustained the exhibits, but marine life often grew on and lived among items constructed with synthetic materials. Aquarium staff tried to control what grew on the rocks and pilings in order to create an attractive display. Just as the Hotel Del Monte constructed gardens, a lake, and a road with scenic coastal vistas, aquarium staff wanted to achieve effects that would be pleasing to tourists.

Monterey Peninsula Herald gardening columnist Bruce Cowan saw the aquarium as an artful re-creation of nature and not the "real thing"; it was an exercise in "nature-faking." When he observed the coastal stream exhibit, complete with trout and riparian vegetation, he noted, "With little imagination, you can immerse yourself into the stream and become one of those shimmering fish." The Sandy Shore aviary "suggest[ed] a real beach in miniature, except here you are practically right there as part of the flock, looking at them face to face." He concluded, "To be sure, all of the above are good examples of nature-faking. But isn't one of the purposes of landscaping to artificially re-create or bring nature closer to our unnatural human existence?"[65] Cowan recognized the human manipulation that went into the aquarium, but he still saw it as a place where people could come in close contact with the intricacies of the marine world. The "fakeness" did not necessarily detract from the aquarium's intrinsic value.

Cowan's critique overlooked the fact that the aquarium's specimens had specific environmental requirements to survive; it was not enough for the exhibits just to look good. Indeed, the aquarium went to great lengths to create exhibits that both "faked" nature well and allowed marine life to thrive. But in designing the Kelp Forest exhibit, planners stepped into uncharted terrain. Because no other aquarium had ever attempted to raise kelp in captivity, they consulted kelp scientists Wheeler North of the California Institute of Technology and Mike Neushal of the University of California, Santa Barbara. The aquarium learned that the tank had to constantly circulate fresh seawater so that kelp could extract needed nutrients. In response, David Packard designed a wave machine that moved a five-foot oval plunger up and down every six seconds to churn the exhibit water. To provide sunlight, the tank was opened to the sky. EHDD also rotated the tank so that the sun would hit the back wall, discouraging algae growth on the window and limiting shade on the surface of the water.[66]

The kelp tank's design proved to be a success. After anchoring twelve full-grown kelp plants to artificial rocks in June 1984, aquarium research biologist Jim Watanabe and phycologist Roger Phillips monitored the kelp's growth, comparing it to kelp near the Hopkins Marine Station. Not only did the aquarium kelp develop its own holdfasts and attach onto the rocks without assistance, but it also grew at rates similar to Monterey Bay kelp. Natural sunlight and seawater, moreover, ensured that aquarium kelp responded to the passing seasons; slow fall and winter growth was followed by a spurt in the spring and summer, when there were more light and nutrients in the water from coastal upwelling. While water motion and the size of the tank limited the kelp's growth, after eight years of careful study and observation, Watanabe concluded, "The aquarium's kelp does perfectly well compared with natural kelp—in fact, slightly better."[67]

In designing its other exhibits, the aquarium had a wide array of organisms at its fingertips in Monterey Bay. In some cases, Powell and his crew used conventional fishing equipment, such as hand-held nets, trawls, beach seines, and traps, to gather specimens. Some creatures required more specialized techniques. When collectors scuba dived to gather fish, they had to depressurize the fish bladder before the ascent, pushing a needle between two scales to remove air bubbles. One of the biggest challenges was catching king salmon, as nets broke its protective layer of mucus and opened up sites for infection or disease. To avoid contact with the fish, collectors used barbless hooks and put the salmon into tanks saturated with oxygen and anesthetic. Collectors then slipped them into plastic bags and transferred them to holding tanks.[68]

Sometimes nature did not cooperate with collecting expeditions. While the aquarium wanted visitors to see marine life found in Monterey Bay, specimens may have originated from distant places. Collectors often traveled far beyond Monterey to obtain certain species where they were more abundant.[69] When warm El Niño waters in 1992 caused jellyfish to disappear from Monterey Bay, moreover, the aquarium had to raise its own specimens before the opening of a special jelly exhibit. Colleagues in Japan sent moon jelly polyps, and senior aquarist Freya Sommer raised them to maturity. She concocted a formula of enriched brine shrimp and used a microscope and tweezers to feed it to the polyps.[70]

Other invertebrates also posed challenges for collectors. To expose anemones and clams, which clung to rocks or hid beneath the seafloor, they used a gas-driven pump and one hundred feet of garden hose.[71] Other stationary invertebrates, such as barnacles, sea squirts, and sponges, did not reattach in the aquarium tanks once broken from their substrate. Powell and Watanabe solved the problem by lowering the level of the exhibit and gluing the invertebrates in place with a special underwater epoxy, much as they did with the artificial rocks. In the large tanks, however, they could not drain the exhibits sufficiently to apply the glue and let it dry. Thus, they relied on the seawater system, which brought in spores and larvae that settled and attached on the rocks.[72]

The easiest and least invasive method for stocking the aquarium exhibits was natural reproduction. Many species thrived and procreated successfully in captivity. As supervising aquarist Mark Ferguson explained, "Many of our exhibits are as rich and complex as habitats in the wild. As a result there's a good deal of courtship and reproduction behavior going on." The reproductive activities of fish, in particular, increased as they matured. Ocean whitefish, halibut, lingcod, surfperch, cuttlefish, octopus, anemones, and several species of birds all produced offspring at the aquarium.[73] In its quarterly newsletter, the aquarium frequently reported when species were mating and when new creatures were born.[74]

But the particular needs and habits of its specimens also prevented aquarium staff from creating an exact replica of Monterey Bay. The precocious sea otters, for instance, required numerous adaptations to be kept in captivity.[75] If fed shellfish, they pounded them against the rocks and used the shell shards to scratch the acrylic panels. As a result, otters received shellfish only away from viewing windows or they ate crab.[76] Since the otters did not hunt for food, staff had to find ways to prevent boredom. They relied on a variety of toys, including stuffed footballs, plastic tubing, and large blocks of ice. These items, however, did not show otters' "natural behavior" or comprise their "natural" habitat. The aquarium renovated the tank in 1993, adding other fish and new rockwork covered with algae and invertebrates, in the hope of creating an exhibit more true to the otters' habitat.[77]

Simulating natural ecosystems was not always compatible with creating exhibits that visitors would enjoy. In the Kelp Forest and Monterey Bay Habitats tanks, staff overstocked species to exceed natural densities. As Jim Watanabe explained, "If we had a natural abundance of fish in there, the tank would look awfully empty." And an empty tank would be less eye-catching for aquarium visitors. The same considerations prompted aquarium staff to eliminate some predator-prey relationships. In the Kelp Forest, voracious kelp feeders like lingcod were kept out entirely, while sea urchins and red abalone were introduced only when the growth was particularly lush.[78] In other words, the aquarium eliminated species that the habitat would ordinarily attract. "The interaction between predators and prey may be part of the natural world, but it's not something we want in an aquarium. Apart from the loss of valuable specimens, we like to think that our charges will live a long life without the fear of ending up as lunch. As a result, compromises often have to be made in the design of the live exhibits," Powell noted.[79] While this concession meant that the exhibits were "not true to life," he explained, the alternative was to have "just one large fish in there."[80]

A devoted staff of aquarists and volunteers provided care for the exhibits' flora and fauna. Aquarists monitored the diets of all specimens, administered drugs if necessary, and studied their habits to keep them healthy and active. For instance, since the Sandy Shore aviary was enclosed and could not harbor as many insects as the wild, they hid flies to simulate a "natural feeding."[81] When an El Niño in 1997 pumped warm, nutrient-poor water into the aquarium and caused the kelp to look "stringy," aquarists sprayed it with ammonia-rich Miracle-Gro. As Joe Choromanski, husbandry curator, explained: "We're trying to display an ecosystem here, so we want the same thing that happens in nature to happen here. But El Niño is a different story. Fish don't like it."[82] Much like the predator-prey relationships, certain natural phenomena were not welcome in the aquarium.

Other natural processes caused more persistent maintenance issues. The seawater system brought in microorganisms that nourished filter feeders and colonized rocks, but this plankton also clogged intake lines. To clear the lines, aquarium staff projected a polyethylene foam torpedo—a "pig"—through the pipes once a month to clear out growing crab, shrimp, scallops, mussels, sponges, and sea stars. Water pressure forced the pig through the pipes in roughly three minutes, while backup lines fed water to the exhibits. If there was heavy buildup, staff used a "javelina" poly pig, which had a coating of steel brushes that scoured the pipe walls clean. Left unchecked, marine growth would make intake lines useless in six months and destroy the aquarium in short order.[83]

In effect, the aquarium's entertainment value meant that the specimens could not be left to their own devices. Exhibit planners envisioned realistic exhibits that showcased the intricacies of local habitats, but, paradoxically, creating such exhibits required them to lessen their realism. Some species could not prey on others, and most had to be fed by humans. El Niño—a naturally occurring phenomenon in Monterey Bay—had to be excluded because of its destructive properties. Thus, a stimulating and pleasurable nature—one that would inspire the oohs and aahs of visitors—had to be a mediated and modified nature. Of course, human efforts to maintain such spectacular exhibits were hidden from public view.[84]

The aquarium ultimately provided a healthful environment for a diverse array of marine wildlife. While some species, like blue sharks, did not fare well in captivity, many specimens flourished.[85] For instance, one study concluded that the Monterey Bay Habitats' seven-gill sharks grew at similar rates to seven-gill sharks in the wild.[86] The aquarium's first census in 1995 also spoke to its successful cultivation of Monterey Bay's marine life. There were 563 species and over 340,000 individual creatures in the Monterey Bay Aquarium, roughly three times as many as the aquarium had estimated. The strawberry anemone was the most abundant species, numbering just over 106,000. There were 7,767 fish, representing 146 species, and 719 plants, representing 160 species. According to Joe Choromanksi, "It's more documentation of the diversity of Monterey Bay. Personally, I find that very exciting."[87]

Even as the aquarium created habitats, it also allowed visitors to see the "real" Monterey Bay, though mediated by still more complex technology. In 1987 David Packard founded the Monterey Bay Aquarium Research Institute (MBARI) to study Monterey Bay's submarine canyon. In addition to a research facility in Moss Landing, MBARI had a research vessel and a remotely operated vehicle, or ROV, which explored the deep waters of the canyon. While MBARI was funded separately, Packard believed it would form a close relationship with the aquarium.[88] MBARI's research infiltrated the aquarium with the opening of the "Live from Monterey Canyon" program in 1989. Using a video camera mounted on its ROV, MBARI beamed live footage of the submarine canyon to an aquarium auditorium. A scientist or aquarium staff member led the presentation, describing MBARI's research, answering audience questions, and communicating with the scientists on the ship via radio.[89]

Live images of the submarine canyon, an area out of the scuba divers' reach and virtually impossible to re-create in an enclosed tank, was another example of how technology made nature accessible for aquarium visitors. The ROV footage demystified the ocean and allowed visitors to learn about a previously unseen and lesser-known landscape. While they saw only images and not real specimens, the program was still a testament to the diversity and beauty of Monterey Bay. Like other aquarium exhibits, it showed visitors the rich array of ocean life just beyond the aquarium's walls.

Efforts to educate visitors about Monterey Bay, however, also had the potential to turn nature into a show. At the Kelp Forest and Sea Otter exhibits, scheduled public feedings became crowd-pleasing events. Visitors became mesmerized by a scuba diver swimming through the kelp swarmed by hundreds of fish and answering audience questions through an underwater microphone.[90] They were even more entranced by the frolicking sea otters. Charismatic, furry, and cute, they became the aquarium's closest thing to a "celebrity" species. While the feedings were educational, they hinted at turning the aquarium animals into spectacles, in a manner not entirely unlike the choreographed marine mammal shows at theme parks like SeaWorld.[91]

More recently, the aquarium marketed a great white shark into a visitor sensation. The aquarium took in the year-old female shark in September 2004 after a halibut fisherman accidentally netted it off the Orange County coast. Many visitors subsequently made a beeline to see the shark. Ticket sales doubled, and the aquarium dedicated an entire gift store to selling shark merchandise. When the shark reached 100 days of residence, crushing the previous record of 16 days for holding this predator in captivity, the aquarium distributed souvenir bookmarks and "I saw her!" postcards. The aquarium released the shark in March 2005 after 198 days in captivity.[92]

The white shark's residence was a recent example of how aquarium staff members created entertaining exhibits. Much like the staff at the Hotel Del Monte, they turned nature into a spectacle for visitors to enjoy. They also blended nature and artifice to create particular constructions of the natural world, eliminating and circumventing natural processes that may have threatened their flora and fauna and made the exhibits less pleasing to the eye. When necessary, they made scenery and specimens. These modifications helped to create the aquarium's intricate, albeit incomplete, representations of Monterey Bay life and kept visitors coming in a steady stream.

The aquarium collected nature, altered it, and presented it to tourists, but it was also a local institution that shaped the surrounding community. As an influx of mostly white, affluent visitors descended on Cannery Row, the class, racial, and ethnic diversity that once characterized this neighborhood largely disappeared. These social changes attracted little attention among local residents, who were far more concerned about the aquarium's economic impact. Because it provided a tremendous lift to Monterey's tourism industry, the aquarium, after a short period of dissension, enjoyed widespread local support. Its popularity also suggested a greater appreciation of ecological thinking and the spread of environmentalism in American society as a whole.

From the day it opened its doors, the aquarium surpassed all original attendance estimates. The 1977 feasibility study predicted an attendance of 420,000 in 1985 and 510,000 in 1990.[93] Yet by March 1985, only six months after opening day and well before the busy summer months, the aquarium had its one millionth visitor. By October 1985, it became the sixth-most-popular paying attraction in California, trailing Disneyland, SeaWorld, and Knotts Berry Farm.[94] When compared to attendance records at other aquariums, the Monterey Bay Aquarium's record was equally impressive. In 1985, its first full year of operation, 2.2 million visitors came to the aquarium. By comparison, the National Aquarium in Baltimore had 1.4 million guests in its first year in 1981. In their first full years, the Seattle Aquarium and the New England Aquarium had 672,471 and 881,000 visitors, respectively.[95]

Some Cannery Row merchants initially did not see the aquarium's popularity as beneficial to the community. Skyrocketing attendance caused parking shortages and traffic jams, and they complained that these problems drove away their regular customers. The worst day of gridlock occurred on Thanksgiving in 1984. All Cannery Row parking lots were full by 10 A.M., and bumper-to-bumper traffic blocked the road from Cannery Row to the highway, a distance of about three miles. Facing outraged citizens, the aquarium began to sell advance tickets for weekends and holidays and limited maximum occupancy at any time to thirty-three hundred.[96]

Even though the aquarium attracted visitors, Cannery Row merchants also claimed that the new facility threatened to displace their businesses.

In particular, they noted that the aquarium bookstore vied with other Cannery Row stores, while the aquarium café served meals to evening visitors, reducing patronage at local restaurants. At a meeting with aquarium and city officials in May 1986, the merchants asked that the bookstore sell only educational materials and that the evening activities be limited to aquarium members. Bob Nix, the president of the Cannery Row Merchants Association, also asked that the city reexamine the aquarium's use permit.[97] Cannery Row resident and merchant Frank Crispo was one of the few dissenters. "I've seen the life, death and now the resurrection of Cannery Row. . . . I like the area a lot more during the resurrection than I did after that last sardine was canned," he explained.[98]

Crispo was in the minority among merchants, but his opinion was similar to those of other Monterey Peninsula residents. As the Monterey City Council considered changes in the use permit, letters in support of the aquarium poured into city hall. Pacific Grove resident Anita Hackett noted that the aquarium "has certainly put this place on the map all over the country and abroad" and explained that she had not experienced parking problems in the area. Ruth Carter of Carmel Valley called the controversy "irrational harassment of the Aquarium by a few of the Cannery Row merchant malcontents." Nancy Gullion of Salinas and L. L. Libby of Carmel drew attention to the shabby state of Cannery Row. Gullion noted, "Row merchants have done *nothing* to improve their tacky stores and businesses. . . . Cannery Row merchants should clean up their own act before dumping on the Aquarium." Libby added that his family went to Cannery Row only because of the aquarium: "If you will walk the Row, you know why tourists or residents don't go there. It's noisy, dirty, looks unsafe and is trashy."[99]

These Monterey Peninsula residents emanated a sense of class superiority. They implied that they had avoided Cannery Row in the past because it betrayed their social sensibilities. In their minds, the neighborhood was cheap and derelict. The juxtaposition of decaying canneries and rusted equipment with the rocky coastline was simply not a source of beauty, as the Cannery Row Plan of 1973 had argued. Nor did it arouse nostalgia for John Steinbeck's fiction. The aquarium, on the other hand, brought national acclaim to the former fish processing center and prevented Cannery Row from becoming a slum. This center of education and entertainment was worth defending and patronizing, they suggested, while the local merchants were not.

A study conducted by the Leadership Monterey Peninsula Project confirmed that many community members supported the aquarium and did not encounter parking difficulties in the Cannery Row area. Project participants interviewed 225 aquarium visitors in April 1985, which included 96 residents and 129 out-of-town visitors. Sixty-seven percent of the outside visitors claimed that finding parking was not a problem. It was only a problem for 19 percent of the residents. When asked how the aquarium affected mobility, only six responded "a great deal." The report concluded that aquarium visitors were not concerned about parking. "The bigger problem seems to be changes in traffic patterns for local residents who are not involved with the Aquarium most days," it noted.[100]

But the Monterey City Council finally caved in to pressure from disaffected local merchants. In the fall of 1986, it voted to require that the aquarium stock its bookstore with at least 90 percent "educational" or "scientific" merchandise and prohibited Friday- and Saturday-night special events.[101] Aquarium officials countered that these restrictions undermined the facility's ability to fund itself and maintained that the real problem was parking, for which the city also bore responsibility. They offered to restrict the bookstore to aquarium visitors and provide parking for nighttime events if the council rescinded its orders. But merchants insisted that the new rules were imperative. As Derek Cockshut noted, "Well, I was here before the Monterey Bay Aquarium, and I was doing very well—and so were many others. They are destroying a commercial infrastructure that has been here for 10 or 15 years."[102]

The following year, the merchants and the aquarium "buried the parking hatchet." The Monterey City Council restricted Friday and Saturday nighttime events to 362 people arriving by car and 1,500 by bus, and the aquarium agreed to provide 153 parking spaces. Plans for a 1,003-space Cannery Row parking garage were also under way.[103] The aquarium and the merchants subsequently established the Cannery Row Promotional District to develop projects for the benefit of the neighborhood as a whole. As merchant Ron Allen explained, "The Hatfields and McCoys are finally solving their differences. Merchants have realized that Cannery Row needs the aquarium and vice versa." By 1989 the completion of the parking garage alleviated parking problems, and most merchants agreed that the aquarium had improved business.[104]

As Cannery Row merchants' animosity faded away, the aquarium continued to gain community support and bolster the local economy. In August 1991, an independent firm polled three hundred Monterey residents and two hundred Pacific Grove residents to learn about their attitudes toward the aquarium. Ninety-four percent had a "favorable opinion"; 74 percent were "highly favorable." Ninety percent believed that the aquarium had a positive impact on the Monterey economy, while 70 percent stated that it was positive for Pacific Grove. When asked about the aquarium's negative impacts, 31 percent mentioned crowds, 17 percent noted parking, and 16 percent said traffic. Thirty-seven percent even noted that there was "nothing they don't like" about the aquarium.[105] At the same time, the aquarium continued to generate significant tourist dollars. A survey conducted in 1992 and 1993 indicated that 58 percent of aquarium visitors decided to come to Monterey expressly to see the aquarium; in short, it was the "big drawing card." More than half of these visitors stayed overnight in 1992, contributing $3.2 million in transient occupancy taxes to Monterey County. They also spent over $210 million while in town, which accounted for over 20 percent of the county's tourism revenues.[106]

With its incredible success, the aquarium built an expansion—the Outer Bay Wing—in the neighboring Sea Pride cannery, which the Packards had bought as a hedge against future commercial development. In its focus on the open ocean and deep sea, the Outer Bay Wing completed the aquarium's interpretation of Monterey Bay habitats and displayed "animals seldom seen and never before exhibited for the public."[107] After roughly seven years of planning and construction, the wing opened in March 1996 at a cost of $57 million. The centerpiece was the one-million-gallon, thirty-four-foot-deep Outer Bay exhibit tank, which was bigger than the Kelp Forest, Monterey Bay Habitats, and Sea Otter tanks combined.[108] The buzz surrounding the new wing caused a huge jump in attendance. In 1996 a record-breaking 2.4 million visitors came to the aquarium, compared to 1.6 million in 1995.[109]

A recent study affirmed the aquarium's continuing importance to the economic well-being of the community. Conducted by Stanford University business student Andrew Rourke, the study estimated that the aquarium pumped approximately $173 million into the Monterey County economy in 2003. Its direct economic contributions included $17.7 million in salaries and wages for its 433 employees and $3.5 million for 439 vendors in Monterey County. In addition, aquarium visitors accounted for 43 percent of all hotel taxes generated in Monterey in 2003—a total amounting to roughly $8.4 million.[110]

Visitors were undoubtedly attracted to the aquarium's polished displays and top-notch reputation, but its tremendous popularity also reflected the growth of the postwar environmental movement. As more middle- and upper-class Americans enjoyed greater prosperity and increased leisure time, they tried to improve their quality of life by seeking more environmental amenities, from clean air to wilderness areas. They also began to embrace popular ecological thinking that emphasized how human actions could imperil the natural environment. While Hal Rothman suggests that many people who embraced environmentalism "did little more than mouth these tenets," these changing values did contribute to the implementation of more environmental regulations and restrictions on development; indeed, the aquarium itself had to navigate the maze of rules that resulted. By the end of the 1980s, the environmental movement enjoyed widespread support nationwide.[111]

Many postwar Americans also "approached the natural world, like everything else, intuitively as consumers," as Jennifer Price explains. Experiencing nature through leisure—whether by skiing in the Rocky Mountains or sunbathing on a sandy beach—was another commodity that could be bought and sold. Consumption also provided an avenue for affirming environmental tenets. Buying biodegradable soap, organic produce, or admission to a national park, for instance, provided some consumers with the impression that they were doing their part to live lightly on the earth.[112]

A trip to the aquarium—an act of consumption in itself—also became an expression of visitors' environmental values.[113] The aquarium appealed to this "green" mind-set by creating such intricate exhibits that celebrated the diversity of marine life and suggested what could be lost without proper stewardship. It also developed programs that explicitly promoted its mission to "inspire conservation of the oceans." For instance, "Fishing for Solutions," a special exhibit in 1997, included hands-on activities, interactive displays, and videos on global fishery problems. In 1999 the aquarium began distributing "Seafood Watch," a consumers' guide to buying sustainable seafood, and it serves only acceptable species at its Portola Café.[114] These programs educated visitors about how they could exercise their power through environmentally friendly consumer choices.

While only 5 percent of aquarium visitors came from Monterey County in 1997, area residents were similarly concerned about environmental issues.[115] Michelle Ann Knight found voters in the Monterey Bay region to be very supportive of California environmental initiatives between 1972 and 1996. For twenty of the twenty-three measures, the Monterey vote in favor of environmental protection was higher than the state vote. Monterey Bay residents also participated in several local initiatives that protected the coastline, including the addition of 750 submerged acres to Point Lobos State Reserve in 1960 and the creation of the Pacific Grove Marine Gardens Fish Refuge in 1963, the Carmel Bay Ecological Reserve in 1975, and Elkhorn Slough in 1979. Citizen involvement culminated in 1992 with the creation of the Monterey Bay National Marine Sanctuary, an initiative that reflected considerable local participation and support.[116]

The aquarium became a major player in this environmentally conscious community. Recognizing the problem of drought, it began operating a desalination plant to flush toilets in 1992. In response to citizens' concerns about the health of nearby Point Pinos tide pools in 1999, the aquarium agreed to stop collecting specimens there until a two-year study, funded partly by the aquarium and the Packard Foundation, determined how scientific collection and foot traffic affected the area. As Julie Packard explained, "I'm gratified to see growing citizen involvement in coastal protection. . . . Once more complete information is in hand regarding the tide pools, the correct steps for their protection will be clear."[117] While some residents were not satisfied with this self-imposed moratorium, the aquarium nonetheless became part and parcel of Monterey's green reputation.

The ability to learn about environmental problems, past and present, and connect to nature as consumers was not available to everyone. Aquarium visitors were mostly white, well-educated, and affluent, supporting scholars' claims about the supporters of postwar environmentalism.[118] In 1995, 83 percent of aquarium visitors were white, 9 percent were Asian, 6 percent were Hispanic, and 2 percent were African American. Sixty-nine percent were college graduates; 30 percent of all visitors also held a postgraduate degree. Education corresponded with income. In 2000, 35 percent of aquarium visitors reported a household annual income of one hundred thousand dollars or more. Only 17 percent earned less than forty thousand dollars. Given the current price of admission—$24.95 for adults and $15.95 for children aged three to twelve—this demographic data is not entirely surprising.[119]

The aquarium seemed to recognize its skewed attendance figures and developed outreach programs for low-income, predominantly Hispanic residents in the Salinas Valley. Soon after the aquarium opened, the education staff began the "Aquaravan" program and traveled to migrant farm labor camps, where they presented skits on marine themes and brought live sea stars, sea urchins, and crabs. By 1988 the Aquaravan was on the road three to four times per week, bringing the marine environment to twenty-five thousand people each year. In 1992 the aquarium received two grants to buy 150 aquarium memberships for Salinas families and provide passes and a weekly summer bus service from the farm camps to the aquarium.[120]

These programs were well intentioned, but the aquarium still remained a place for mostly well-off white tourists. Its relative homogeneity stood in stark contrast to the diversity of marine life on display. It also highlighted just what a different place Cannery Row had become. Once a place where immigrants from all over the world labored in nature and engaged in a lucrative extractive industry, Cannery Row was now a place where millions of visitors consumed nature at the aquarium and sustained Monterey's service economy. The aquarium's success reflected a general shift in many Americans' attitudes toward the natural environment. In Monterey and elsewhere, an increasing number of people saw the natural world as something to be appreciated and protected. The Monterey Bay Aquarium reinforced and celebrated these popular ideals.

When the aquarium opened in 1984, Lucile Packard proclaimed, "In my long life, I've never been able to see what's down there. Now, at last, all of us can."[121] Indeed, the aquarium brought Monterey Bay ashore and placed it amid a faux industrial shell. Within these walls, technology both mediated and enhanced visitors' experiences with nature to a degree that earlier tourists had not witnessed. Tourists did not have to be satisfied to just see crashing waves or windswept cypress trees along a scenic drive. Now they could see several ecosystems at work, minus any natural processes that could have detracted from their beauty.

Preserving the look of the Hovden cannery was a vital part of the aquarium's conception; even after the sardine fishery collapsed, the industrial past continued to shape the tourist trade. Nonetheless, the institution represented an entirely different vision for human relations with the natural world than the former fish processing plant. Whereas the cannery processed sardines for a wide range of consumers, the aquarium transformed marine life in order to provide a stimulating educational experience for mostly white, well-heeled tourists intent on combining their leisure activities with their green values. Nature was a vital resource in both the cannery and the aquarium, but the aquarium packaged it in a different form, to different ends, and for different people. With a new mission and clientele, the aquarium helped to reinvent Monterey as a community that treasured its natural surroundings—a dramatic shift from the resource exploitation that had contributed to the sardine fishery's demise just a few decades earlier.[122]

CONCLUSION

Within a few years of its opening, the Monterey Bay Aquarium had become a world-renowned institution, the centerpiece of the local tourism industry, and the heart of Cannery Row. It would be easy to end the story here—with the successful revitalization of Cannery Row after the dramatic crash of the sardine fishery. Tourism, at least superficially, appeared to have triumphed. Of course, this ending would obscure the conflicts that continue to shape the Monterey coastline. Along Cannery Row, the role of the industrial past in guiding development has been particularly controversial. For some, Cannery Row is ripe for even more tourism amenities that capitalize on the success of the aquarium. Others see Cannery Row as a rare historic neighborhood whose ambience needs to be preserved and interpreted for posterity. Much like the battles that shaped the Monterey coastline in the past, these contemporary debates have social and environmental ramifications that reflect competing visions for the coastline.

Recent conflicts stemmed from the continuing deterioration of Cannery Row coupled with proposals to modify or destroy historic buildings to make way for high-end retail shops and housing.[1] To address the situation, the Monterey City Council ordered a historic resources survey of the Cannery Row district in May 1997.[2] When local historian Neal Hotelling believed that the city was dragging its heels on completing the survey, he took preemptive action and nominated Cannery Row to be included on the National Trust for Historic Preservation's tenth annual list of America's Most Endangered Historic Places. Much like endangered flora and fauna, the National Trust suggested that *places* could also be on the brink of extinction. In June 1998, Cannery Row became one of eleven historic sites nationwide to receive this dubious honor. The designation came with national publicity on The History Channel, which aired a documentary on the year's "winners." Richard Moe, president of the National Trust, explained that intensive development coupled with neglect had caused many of Cannery Row's historic buildings to be "lost" to demolition or alterations. Hotelling concluded, "It certainly seems that the city is putting the interests of commercial property owners ahead of the community's values."[3]

Not surprisingly, Mayor Dan Albert lambasted the designation as unfair and ticked off the city's measures to preserve Cannery Row. It bought San Carlos beach, which saved it from a hotel development. In one of many rails-to-trails programs nationwide, city planners helped to convert the Southern Pacific Railroad's former tracks into a recreational trail along the Monterey waterfront. And the city rehabilitated Ed Rickett's former laboratory and restored three cannery workers' shacks for a historic exhibit focusing on the experiences of Filipino, Japanese, and Spanish cannery workers and fishermen. Finally, Albert blamed fire, not greedy developers or insensitive city officials, for the destruction of some of the buildings. "I just don't think we're such bad guys as far as Cannery Row goes," he noted.[4]

While the "endangered" designation was symbolic and did not require any mitigation measures (unlike the Endangered Species Act), it suggested how the interplay between tourism and fisheries continued to shape the coastline. Even though the sardine fishery had been defunct for several decades, local citizens like Hotelling refused to allow tourism development to literally bulldoze Monterey's industrial past and its literary heritage. While not all Montereyans valued Cannery Row in the same way, as Hotelling assumed, the city did take additional responsibility for the neighborhood's preservation by establishing the Cannery Row Conservation District in 2004. When altering existing structures or constructing new ones within the district, developers had to adopt design principles consistent with the "traditional character" of Cannery Row. Recognizing the historic and literary significance of the area, the overarching goal of the conservation district was "to establish a framework for allowing Cannery Row to grow while retaining its ambiance and historical context."[5] Nonetheless, development continued to be a source of debate. Despite protests from residents, two large Cannery Row projects—the Monterey Peninsula Hotel and an IMAX theatre—received city approval.[6] Construction on the hotel began in August 2006 and is slated for completion in May 2008. In April and July 2006, the Planning Commission, the Architectural Review Committee, and the Historic Preservation Commission all gave the go-ahead on the IMAX theatre, which is scheduled to open in 2008.[7]

Perhaps the most controversial Cannery Row project was Ocean View Plaza, a retail-condominium complex conceived by Chris Treble, a Palo Alto real estate developer. Originally proposed and rejected in 1999 as the Cannery Row Marketplace, the project was reincarnated in 2000. Consisting of four buildings on a 3.5–acre stretch of Cannery Row, opponents claimed that its "suburban sprawl-style development" was inappropriate for the area. As Ann Swett, chairperson of the Monterey Historic Preservation Committee, explained, "If we start cluttering this up with strip malls, overloading it with cars, making it too difficult to get places, [tourists are] going to stop coming. They come to Monterey because of the historic flavor and we have to be careful not to lose that."[8]

However, city council member Theresa Canepa, the daughter of a fisherman and cannery worker and a former cannery worker herself, was impatient with overly sentimental ideas about Cannery Row. "Cannery Row was a working enterprise. . . . There was nothing glamorous or romantic about it," she noted. Preserving its industrial ambience at the expense of a project that would develop several derelict lots and contribute to the city's economic vitality would be foolish, she suggested: "Buildings are just things. Everything dies and gets replaced, that's part of life. I don't want to keep living in the past."[9] Even though Canepa's individual and family histories were deeply tied to the sardine industry, she held no nostalgic attachment to Cannery Row's remains. Yet many people with no connection to the sardine industry—individuals who had never stepped foot in a working cannery—now felt compelled to save it.

The city council approved the project by a narrow 3–2 margin in October 2002. Mayor Dan Albert, who cast the deciding vote, explained that the project would make Cannery Row "whole" again.[10] Visitors would be able to stroll from end to end and find a variety of amusements and amenities at every turn, from wine stores and art galleries to luxury hotels and seafood restaurants. Local activist groups Responsible Monterey

Planning and the Open Monterey Project disagreed and filed a lawsuit against the city, claiming that it had not adequately considered the project's impact on water, traffic, parking, growth, and historic preservation.[11] After three years of setbacks, the project received a major boost in December 2005 when Monterey County's Local Agency Formation Commission (LAFCO) approved the creation of a special district for a desalination plant that would supply water exclusively to the complex. The Save Our Waterfront Committee, a local group that advocated a "balanced approach to waterfront development and . . . innovative ways to protect and improve coastal access, views, and historical elements," responded by filing another lawsuit against the City of Monterey, the Monterey City Council, and LAFCO in February 2006. The committee charged that LAFCO based its decision on an outdated Environmental Impact Report, which did not include recent data on Monterey Bay contamination and local traffic patterns.[12] The suit is now pending in the state court of appeals, and the California Coastal Commission is supposed to review the project in 2008.[13]

Ironically, the conflicts over Cannery Row's past and future coincided with the comeback of the sardine fishery. Cannery Row may have been "endangered," but the sardine was no longer absent. In 1999 Doyle Hanan, a marine biologist with the California Department of Fish and Game, reported that the sardine population had increased by roughly 30 percent per year for the last twenty years. A combination of warmer water, natural fluctuations, and a ban on sardine fishing from 1967 to 1986 explained the rebound.[14] With a biomass estimate of over 1 million tons, Fish and Game declared that the sardine fishery was "rehabilitated" and set a statewide quota of 204,844 tons to be taken in 2000.[15] In 2005 commercial operators in the Monterey area brought in close to 9,000 tons of sardines, almost 25 percent of the state total. However, the vast majority of these sardines were landed in nearby Moss Landing; in fact, the port of Monterey did not report any sardine catch.[16] Without lucrative markets and fish processing plants, a sardine industry revival was nowhere in sight. Montereyans' visions for the coastline had also changed since the sardine's heyday. Some residents cherished the remnants of the sardine industry, but real fish canneries would be out of place on the tourist-oriented, environmentally friendly Cannery Row.

Instead, visitors continue to flock to the aquarium, where Cannery Row's history was also the subject of recent attention. Although the aquarium was housed in the former Hovden cannery, one of the largest plants during the sardine industry's peak, and exhibited live sardines, the building's storied past was lost on many visitors. Aquarium planners were meticulous in their efforts to replicate the look and feel of the cannery, but the history of the building was rarely anything more than an afterthought. Few visitors stopped to notice the former boiler house, a small display in honor of Ed Ricketts, and a modest exterior kiosk on Cannery Row's history. Some may not have realized that they were ambling through a former sardine plant as they made their way through re-created versions of Monterey Bay's depths.

This oversight was not surprising, given that these historic displays were not central to the aquarium's mission of highlighting the beauty and diversity of local ecosystems and inspiring conservation of the world's oceans. As a result, the history of the sardine industry figured only occasionally into the aquarium's educational programming. For instance, in 1997 it developed a living-history show in which staff members dressed up in professional women's attire from the 1940s and told stories about cutting and packing sardines on the processing lines. Visitors could also don the cannery worker's garb of boots, aprons, and gloves and try their hand at wrapping labels on sardine cans. The interactive show, however, provided visitors with only a nostalgic glimpse into Cannery Row's history, not a critical analysis of its meteoric rise during the first half of the twentieth century and its quick demise after World War II.[17]

This all changed in June 2004, a few months before the aquarium's twentieth anniversary. As part of a larger renovation that enclosed the old open-air entrance and created an indoor ticket lobby, the aquarium developed a historic exhibit on the sardine industry.[18] As Jenny Sayre Ramberg, senior exhibit developer/writer, explained, "There was both a desire to do a better job interpreting the historical boilers and a requirement from the City of Monterey as part of our building permit to interpret the history of our site." According to Ramberg, the boilers could serve as "a reminder of what we've learned about overfishing and the need for sustainable fisheries, for the ocean and people."[19] This historic relic, in other words, could be integrated into and used to reinforce the aquarium's conservation mission. Like the cannery building itself, Monterey's history could be reshaped into a usable past to teach lessons in the present.

Rather than making a beeline to the otters or the kelp forest after navigating the lines and paying for tickets, visitors are now funneled into the exhibit. Festooned with black-and-white historic photographs and cannery memorabilia, from sardine labels to canning machinery, they learn that they are entering the former Hovden cannery and stand before the former boilers. A sign proclaims: "These boilers were once the heart of a bustling sardine cannery. Today they stand at the heart of an aquarium committed to conserving our oceans." From there, visitors read displays about Cannery Row during the sardine industry's zenith, including the canning process and a day in the life of a cannery worker. They can even push a button and hear the sound of the whistles that once signaled the start of a shift. The exhibit also details the friendship between John Steinbeck and Ed Ricketts and their trip to the Sea of Cortez.

But the focus of the exhibit is the sardine's collapse. After detailing the science of the fishery, the exhibit proposes an explanation for its demise. While fishing was a major factor, it argues, sardines also declined in response to cool ocean temperatures in the 1940s. Thus, according to the exhibitors, "People and nature drove down the sardines."[20] Rather than placing blame on rapacious fishermen, powerless scientists, or an unpredictable natural world, exhibit planners and consultants provided a more nuanced interpretation that gestured at the multiple social and environmental factors behind the fishery's fall. This approach was necessary because many Montereyans had stakes in how the exhibit explained the collapse. According to Carol McKibben, a historical consultant to the exhibit and an expert on the Sicilian community, many fishermen were put on the defensive. Given the aquarium's "green" reputation, they feared that the exhibit would paint them as the bad guys, widening the divide between the aquarium's largely affluent clientele and its working-class past. They were proud of having built and sustained the sardine industry and did not want their many contributions to be overshadowed by an emphasis on overfishing.[21]

While the exhibit points to many factors to explain the sardine's demise and the end of Monterey's fishing era, it ultimately couches the sardine collapse as a cautionary tale: "Today, Cannery Row is back to life. Sardines are back in this building—and more important, they're back in the bay. . . . But now we know, and maybe we'll heed: there are limits to the stream of silver from the bay."[22] This take-away message presents Cannery Row's history as a transition from exploitation to conservation. It suggests that Montereyans had learned from the past and now cherished the natural beauty and ecological complexity of the coastline. And the aquarium stands as a symbol and embodiment of this modern environmental era.

This emphasis on the sardine collapse comes at the expense of humanizing the thousands of individuals who once worked in the fish plants. While the exhibit explains the arduous nature of their labor, it overlooks the diversity and divisions within the workforce. Visitors discover little about the workers as individuals or members of larger social groups. Quotations from former cannery workers do not provide names or backgrounds. There is mention of the women who labored in the canneries but no detailed discussion of the other immigrants and migrants who also found jobs in the canneries or at sea. As a result, the workers appear amorphous and anonymous. They are depicted as a class—not as a heterogeneous group. John Steinbeck and Ed Ricketts are the only figures who are fully fleshed characters in the story. In particular, the aquarium celebrates Ricketts as an enlightened scientist who was "an ecologist before his time" and continues to inspire marine biologists.

Because the mostly white, professional aquarium audience is distanced from the working-class world, the exhibit reinforces the divide between labor and leisure, fisheries and tourism. Even as they are surrounded by artifacts from the sardine cannery, tourists remain radically different from the cannery workers who once toiled inside the Hovden plant. Whereas the workers knew nature through labor, tourists came to know nature through leisure. Instead of processing sardines, they marvel at the exhibits. Along with the aquarium staff and scientists who are following in Ricketts's footsteps, many tourists also believe in the institution's conservation mission. The aquarium does indeed provide a more comprehensive historical interpretation of the boiler house and the Hovden cannery as a whole and does not shy away from its past life as a sardine plant. Yet the exhibit highlights the separate and apparently disparate paths of the fish factory and aquarium. Educated, well-to-do tourists have replaced working-class fish packers and boiler men; scientific research and conservation have replaced resource exploitation.

In reality, the fisheries and tourism have never been completely divorced from each other, and the interplay between the industries continues to shape the city's identity and its relationship to the natural world. While Monterey now lacks a thriving fishing industry, some tourists are still attracted to the city's long association with fishing. Sports fishing outfits on Fisherman's Wharf take adventurous visitors to fish for salmon, halibut, cod, and albacore tuna on the same waters once plied by Monterey's flotilla of purse seines. Moreover, the *history* of the sardine industry exerts a major influence over tourism-oriented development on Cannery Row. Multiple interpretations of the fishery's historic importance have generated debates about what to do with its remnants. Whereas the aquarium used the boiler house to affirm its conservation mission and the city's green reputation, the projects slated for and under construction on Cannery Row could have the opposite effect. To approve plans that could exacerbate traffic, eliminate public ocean vistas, and develop rare coastal parcels could be a sign that the city is abandoning its environmental laurels.[23] Others fear that the new projects could destroy the industrial character that inspired Steinbeck and marginalize Monterey's days as the sardine capital of the world.

These conflicts also come with social consequences. The new Cannery Row projects could displace long-term merchants. They also require an even larger number of service workers, including many Latin American immigrants, whose low wages preclude them from living in Monterey or most of its outlying communities, with their inflated real estate markets. In this sense, Monterey is similar to the scores of other high-priced resort towns dotting the American West from Jackson Hole to Palm Springs.[24] Recognizing the housing crunch, Monterey developer and former city council member Carl Outzen built an affordable housing complex in the Cannery Row neighborhood specifically for hospitality industry employees. With a loan from the city's redevelopment housing funds, the twenty-one-unit complex opened in July 2004 with monthly rents well below market rates.[25] While this project was noteworthy, it made only a symbolic dent in the housing problem. The growth of Monterey's tourism industry will undoubtedly continue to breed social inequalities and further separate well-heeled visitors and the workers who serve them.

For transient visitors who stay for only a few days, these social and environmental problems seem invisible. They come to Monterey to play in nature and to appreciate the beauty and diversity of the natural world. They paddle sea kayaks past the remains of Cannery Row and come ashore for a visit to the aquarium and a sunset stroll along the beach. Their activities seem distant from the working world, and their purchases—whether an admission ticket to the aquarium or a plate of local seafood—may even appear environmentally virtuous. They give the impression that they have forged a completely different relationship with nature from those who participated in the sardine industry. But leisure experiences, from the gleaming displays at the aquarium to the meals served at restaurants, are dependent on the labor of others—individuals whose work is often hidden from view, unlike the cannery workers and fishermen before them. Tourism also exacerbates environmental problems, like pollution, and overtaxes the infrastructure, from the water supply to the local roads. Of course, tourists usually leave town before they can witness the long-term consequences of their visits. And aside from hotel and sales taxes, they rarely have to pay for the remedies.

Thus, there was no clear separation between fisheries and tourism, labor and leisure, exploitation and conservation in Monterey's past, nor is there any in the present. At various points, the coastline's beauty, fecundity, literary fame, historical charm, and ecological diversity were all seen as valuable attributes that needed to be harnessed. As Montereyans tried to implement these divergent visions and battled for control over the coastline and its inhabitants, their activities often became entangled. Neither Hotel Del Monte guests nor Monterey Bay Aquarium visitors could exist in isolation from labor, whether at the Chinese squid-drying fields, the sardine canneries, or the ticket counter. Likewise, the postwar tourism industry could not escape the physical and cultural legacy of the fishing industry. It also transformed the natural world in ways that undermined the idea that it was a completely "green" business, in stark contrast to the extractive economy it replaced. While the fishing and tourism industries and their respective participants appeared distinct, they were, in fact, deeply connected to one another and not nearly as dissimilar as some believed.

It has become increasingly easy to reinforce the oversimplified dualities used to describe human interactions with the natural environment. In a world where distance does not pose a barrier to our desires, we can travel all over the globe to play in nature. We can buy foods that would never grow in our backyards. All the while, we never see the social and environmental impact of our consumption. But Monterey's history demonstrates that we simply cannot avoid these connections, however obvious or covert they may appear. Just because we do not see our links to labor or resource exploitation does not mean they are nonexistent. Adhering to these dualities allows us only to ignore our connections to people, places, and processes that appear unrelated and evade accountability for numerous social and environmental problems. To acknowledge the entanglements between extractive and service industries, work and play, and other seemingly opposing categories—not to mention our other ties to far-flung landscapes and activities—is to claim a collective responsibility for the nonhuman and human world.[26]

NOTES

INTRODUCTION: THE VOICE OF THE PACIFIC

1. Robert Louis Stevenson, "The Old Pacific Capital," in *Across the Plains with Other Memories and Essays* (New York: C. Scribner's Sons, 1892), 80. For Stevenson's stay in Monterey, see Anne Roller Issler, "Robert Louis Stevenson in Monterey," *Pacific Historical Review* 34, no. 3 (1965): 305–21.

2. Burton LeRoy Gordon, *Monterey Bay Area: Natural History and Cultural Imprints*, 3rd ed. (Pacific Grove, CA: Boxwood Press, 1996), 8–27.

3. Stevenson, "The Old Pacific Capital," 91, 94–101, 105.

4. Malcolm Margolin, *The Ohlone Way: Indian Life in the San Francisco–Monterey Bay Area* (Berkeley, CA: Heyday Books, 1978), 36–37, 52; John Walton, *Storied Land: Community and Memory in Monterey* (Berkeley and Los Angeles: University of California Press, 2001), 14–17; Gordon, *Monterey Bay Area*, 30–56.

5. Walton, *Storied Land*, 17–20; David J. Weber, *The Spanish Frontier in North America* (New Haven, CT: Yale University Press, 1992), 236–46, 259–60.

6. Walton, *Storied Land*, 60–61, 76–80; David J. Weber, *The Mexican Frontier, 1821–1846: The American Southwest Under Mexico* (Albuquerque: University of New Mexico Press, 1982), 136–39. Richard Henry Dana provides a vivid description of Monterey's hide and tallow trade in *Two Years Before the Mast* (New York: Harper and Brothers, 1840).

7. Stevenson, "The Old Pacific Capital," 91–92; Walton, *Storied Land*, 127.

8. J. D. Conway, *Monterey: Presidio, Pueblo, and Port* (Charleston, SC: Arcadia Publishing, 2003), 71–74; Work Projects Administration, *Monterey Peninsula: American Guide Series* (Berkeley, CA: Press of the Courier, 1941), 53.

9. For general histories of Monterey's fishing industry and Cannery Row, see Michael Kenneth Hemp, *Cannery Row: The History of John Steinbeck's Old*

Ocean View Avenue (Carmel, CA: The History Company, 2002); Tom Mangelsdorf, *A History of Steinbeck's Cannery Row* (Santa Cruz, CA: Western Tanager Press, 1986).

10. James O'Connor similarly calls for a history of Monterey Bay that "grasps the dialectics . . . and inner connections" of nature and culture. See James O'Connor, "Three Ways to Think About the Ecological History of Monterey Bay," *Capitalism, Nature, Socialism* 6, no. 2 (June 1995): 34, 39–41, 45–47.

11. William Cronon, "Modes of Prophecy and Production: Placing Nature in History," *Journal of American History* 76, no. 4 (March 1990): 1129.

12. Alan Taylor, "Unnatural Inequalities: Social and Environmental Histories," *Environmental History* 1, no. 4 (October 1996): 6–19.

13. Stephen Mosley, "Common Ground: Integrating Social and Environmental History," *Journal of Social History* 39, no. 3 (Spring 2006): 915–33. For studies that integrate social and environmental history, see Louis Warren, *The Hunter's Game: Poachers and Conservationists in Twentieth-Century America* (New Haven, CT: Yale University Press, 1997); Karl Jacoby, *Crimes Against Nature: Squatters, Poachers, Thieves, and the Hidden History of American Conservation* (Berkeley and Los Angeles: University of California Press, 2001); Richard White, *The Organic Machine: The Remaking of the Columbia River* (New York: Hill and Wang, 1995); Richard White, *The Roots of Dependency: Subsistence, Environment, and Social Change among the Choctaws, Pawnees, and Navajos* (Lincoln: University of Nebraska Press, 1983); Richard White, *Land Use, Environment, and Social Change: The Shaping of Island County, Washington* (Seattle: University of Washington Press, 1980); William Cronon, "Kennecott Journey: The Paths out of Town," in *Under an Open Sky: Rethinking America's Western Past*, ed. William Cronon, George Miles, and Jay Gitlin (New York: W. W. Norton, 1992), 28–51; Arthur F. McEvoy, *The Fisherman's Problem: Ecology and Law in the California Fisheries, 1850–1980* (New York: Cambridge University Press, 1986); Mart A. Stewart, *"What Nature Suffers to Groe": Life, Labor, and Landscape on the Georgia Coast* (Athens: University of Georgia Press, 1996). For an overview of African Americans, American Indians, and environmental history, see Carolyn Merchant, "Shades of Darkness: Race and Environmental History," *Environmental History* 8, no. 3 (July 2003): 380–94.

14. For the larger historical importance of the coastline, see John Stilgoe, *Alongshore* (New Haven, CT: Yale University Press, 1994); Lena Lenček and Gideon Bosker, *The Beach: The History of Paradise on Earth* (New York: Penguin Books, 1998); Alain Corbin, *The Lure of the Sea: The Discovery of the Seaside, 1750–1840*, trans. Jocelyn Phelps (New York: Penguin Books, 1995); W. Jeffrey Bolster, "Opportunities in Marine Environmental History," *Environmental History* 11, no. 3 (July 2006): 567–97.

15. The idea of competing visions of nature draws inspiration from Elliott

West's magisterial study *The Contested Plains: Indians, Goldseekers, and the Rush to Colorado* (Lawrence: University Press of Kansas, 1998).

16. For the historical scholarship on the American fisheries, see Joseph E. Taylor III, *Making Salmon: An Environmental History of the Northwest Fisheries Crisis* (Seattle: University of Washington Press, 1999); Margaret Beattie Bogue, *Fishing the Great Lakes: An Environmental History, 1783–1933* (Madison: University of Wisconsin Press, 2000); McEvoy, *The Fisherman's Problem*; Tim D. Smith, *Scaling Fisheries: The Science of Measuring the Effects of Fishing, 1855–1955* (New York: Cambridge University Press, 1994); Chris Friday, *Organizing Asian American Labor: The Pacific Coast Canned-Salmon Industry, 1870–1942* (Philadelphia: Temple University Press, 1994).

17. For the historical scholarship on American tourism, see Mansel Blackford, *Fragile Tourism: The Impact of Tourism on Maui, 1959–2000* (Lawrence: University Press of Kansas, 2001); Earl Pomeroy, *In Search of the Golden West: The Tourist in Western America* (New York: Knopf, 1957; repr., Lincoln: University of Nebraska Press, 1990); Marguerite S. Shaffer, *See America First: Tourism and National Identity, 1880–1940* (Washington, D.C.: Smithsonian Institution Press, 2001); Anne Farrar Hyde, *An American Vision: Far Western Landscapes and National Culture, 1820–1910* (New York: New York University Press, 1990); Dona Brown, *Inventing New England: Regional Tourism in the Nineteenth Century* (Washington, D.C.: Smithsonian Institution Press, 1995).

18. Bonnie Christensen, *Red Lodge and the Mythic West: From Coal Miners to Cowboys* (Lawrence: University Press of Kansas, 2002); Hal K. Rothman, *Devil's Bargains: Tourism in the Twentieth-Century American West* (Lawrence: University Press of Kansas, 1998); Blackford, *Fragile Tourism*; Annie Gilbert Coleman, *Ski Style: Sport and Culture in the Rockies* (Lawrence: University Press of Kansas, 2004).

19. For other scholars who explore this interplay between extractive and service industries, see Thomas Andrews, "'Made by Toile'?: Tourism, Labor, and the Construction of the Colorado Landscape, 1858–1917," *Journal of American History* 92, no. 3 (December 2005): 837–63, and Richard W. Judd, *Common Lands, Common People: The Origins of Conservation in Northern New England* (Cambridge, MA: Harvard University Press, 1997), 197–228.

20. Andrews, "'Made by Toile.'?"

1   CONTESTED SHORES

1. For unequal access to nature, see Jacoby, *Crimes Against Nature*; Mark Spence, *Dispossessing the Wilderness: Indian Removal and the Making of the National Parks* (New York: Oxford University Press, 1999); Warren, *The Hunter's Game*. For a spatial analysis of social divisions, see George Chauncey, *Gay New*

York: Gender, Urban Culture, and the Making of the Gay Male World, 1890–1940 (New York: Basic Books, 1994); Lisbeth Haas, *Conquests and Historical Identities in California, 1769–1936* (Berkeley and Los Angeles: University of California Press, 1995); and Andrew Hurley, *Environmental Inequalities: Class, Race, and Industrial Pollution in Gary, Indiana, 1945–1980* (Chapel Hill: University of North Carolina Press, 1995).

2. *Thirteenth Biennial Report of the State Board of Fish Commissioners of the State of California, 1893–94*, 87.

3. For California's immigrant fisheries, see McEvoy, *Fisherman's Problem*, 65–119.

4. Sandy Lydon, *Chinese Gold: The Chinese in the Monterey Bay Region* (Capitola, CA: Capitola Book Company, 1985), 30–32, 41, 152–58. See also *The Handbook to Monterey and Vicinity* (Monterey: Walton and Curtis, 1875), 49–50; L. Eve Armentrout-Ma, "Chinese in California's Fishing Industry, 1850–1914," *California History* 60, no. 2 (1981): 142–57.

5. *The Handbook to Monterey and Vicinity*, 50; George Brown Goode, "The Chinese Fishermen of the Pacific Coast, from Notes by David S. Jordan," in George Brown Goode, *The Fisheries and Fishery Industries of the United States*, 5 sections, 8 parts (Washington, D.C.: Government Printing Office, 1887), sec. 4: 38.

6. David Starr Jordan, "Coast of California," in Goode, *The Fisheries and Fishery Industries of the United States*, sec. 5, vol. 2: 57–58; Goode, "The Portuguese Fishermen on the Pacific Coast," in *The Fisheries and Fishery Industries of the United States*, sec. 4: 33–34; *Handbook to Monterey and Vicinity*, 44–48; Carol Card, "Shore Whaling in California," *What's Doing* 1, no. 12 (March 1947): 20–21.

7. McEvoy, *Fisherman's Problem*, 76–77; Lydon, *Chinese Gold*, 45–46; Walton, *Storied Land*, 143–44; George Brown Goode, "The Italian Fishermen on the Pacific Coast, from Notes by David S. Jordan," in Goode, *The Fisheries and Fishery Industries of the United States*, sec. 4: 30; Goode, "The Portuguese Fishermen on the Pacific Coast," 31–34; George Brown Goode, "The Fisheries of Monterey, Santa Cruz, Santa Clara, and San Mateo Counties," in Goode, *The Fisheries and Fishery Industries of the United States*, sec. 2: 604.

8. Carol M. Rose, "The Comedy of the Commons: Custom, Commerce, and Inherently Public Property," in *Property and Persuasion: Essays on the History, Theory, and Rhetoric of Ownership* (Boulder, CO: Westview Press, 1994), 105–10; McEvoy, *Fisherman's Problem*, 9–10.

9. Lydon, *Chinese Gold*, 47–48, 54; *Monterey Californian*, 27 March 1880.

10. For anti-Chinese activism in the West, see Alexander Saxton, *The Indispensable Enemy: Labor and the Anti-Chinese Movement in California* (Berkeley and Los Angeles: University of California Press, 1971). For Chinese miners, see Susan Lee Johnson, *Roaring Camp: The Social World of the California Gold Rush* (New York: W. W. Norton, 2000), 240–51.

11. J. W. Collins, "Report on the Fisheries of the Pacific Coast of the United States," in *Report of the Commissioner of Fish and Fisheries for 1888* (Washington, D.C., 1892), 59. For the Naturalization Act of 1790, see Ronald Takaki, *Strangers from a Different Shore: A History of Asian Americans*, updated and revised ed. (Boston: Back Bay Books, 1998), xiii, 113; Matthew Frye Jacobson, *Whiteness of a Different Color: European Immigrants and the Alchemy of Race* (Cambridge, MA: Harvard University Press, 1998), 7–8, 22–31.

12. Jacobson, *Whiteness of a Different Color*, 39–90, quotation on page 76; Thomas A. Guglielmo, "'No Color Barrier': Italians, Race, and Power in the United States," in *Are Italians White?: How Race Is Made in America*, ed. Jennifer Guglielmo and Salvatore Salerno (New York: Routledge, 2003), 29–43; Thomas Guglielmo, *White on Arrival: Italians, Race, Color, and Power in Chicago, 1890–1945* (New York: Oxford University Press, 2003). These studies join existing work on the Irish and whiteness. See Noel Ignatiev, *How the Irish Became White* (New York: Routledge, 1995), and David Roediger, *The Wages of Whiteness: Race and the Making of the American Working Class* (London and New York: Verso, 1995).

13. William A. Wilcox, "Notes on the Fisheries of the Pacific Coast in 1895," in *Report of the Commissioner of Fish and Fisheries* (Washington, D.C.: Government Printing Office, 1898), 643; Collins, "Report on the Fisheries of the Pacific Coast of the United States," 59.

14. The California Penal Code in the 1880s and 1890s prohibited the use of set or stationary nets. Trawl lines were not outlawed until 1913. See Penal Code, sections 636 and 636½ in *Statutes of California and Digest of Measures* (Sacramento: n.p., 1883, 1913).

15. McEvoy, *Fisherman's Problem*, 79, 86; Joseph E. Taylor III, "El Niño and Vanishing Salmon: Culture, Nature, History, and the Politics of Blame," *Western Historical Quarterly* 29, no. 4 (Winter 1998): 437–57, and *Making Salmon*, 105–7, 114–15.

16. McEvoy, *Fisherman's Problem*, 89, 95–100, 103, 112–19; Armentrout-Ma, "Chinese in California's Fishing Industry," 144.

17. David Starr Jordan, *The Days of Man, Being Memories of a Naturalist, Teacher and Minor Prophet of Democracy, Volume One, 1851–1899* (New York: World Book Company, 1922), 211; David Epel, "Stanford-By-The-Sea: A Brief History of Hopkins Marine Station," *Sandstone and Tile* 16, no. 4 (Fall 1992): 3–4. Agassiz's school led to the founding of Massachusetts's Woods Hole Marine Biological Station in 1888, the first marine station in America. When Jordan took the helm at Stanford in 1891, he wanted a similar center for the study of the Pacific Coast. Timothy Hopkins, a Stanford trustee, provided considerable funding. For David Starr Jordan, Stanford, and science, see Michael L. Smith, *Pacific Visions: California Scientists and the Environment, 1850–1915* (New Haven, CT: Yale University Press, 1987), 129–36.

18. O. P. Jenkins, "The Hopkins Seaside Laboratory" *Zoë* 4, no. 1 (April 1893): 58–63; Bashford Dean, "A Californian Marine Biological Station," *Natural Science* 11, no. 65 (July 1897): 28; Epel, "Stanford-By-The-Sea," 4.

19. Keith R. Benson, "From Museum Research to Laboratory Research: The Transformation of Natural History into Academic Biology," in *The American Development of Biology*, ed. Ronald Rainger, Keith R. Benson, Jane Maienschein (New Brunswick, NJ: Rutgers University Press, 1988), 49–83.

20. Dean, "A Californian Marine Biological Station," 32–33; F. M. McFarland, "The Hopkins Seaside Laboratory," *Journal of Applied Microscopy and Laboratory Methods* 5, no. 7 (July 1902): 1870.

21. For "knowing" nature through labor, see Richard White, "'Are You an Environmentalist or Do You Work for a Living?': Work and Nature," in *Uncommon Ground: Rethinking the Human Place in Nature*, ed. William Cronon (New York: W. W. Norton, 1996), 171–85, and *The Organic Machine*, 3–29.

22. Collins, "Report on the Fisheries of the Pacific Coast of the United States," 60–61; Wilcox, "Notes on the Fisheries of the Pacific Coast of the United States in 1895," 643; William A. Wilcox, "Fisheries of the Pacific Coast," in *Report of the Commissioner of Fish and Fisheries for the Year Ending June 30, 1893* (Washington, D.C., 1895), 195; Lydon, *Chinese Gold*, 54–58.

23. I am grateful to Ari Kelman for this insight. See also O'Connor, "Three Ways to Think About the Ecological History of Monterey Bay," 29.

24. J. R. Fitch, "A Glimpse of Monterey," in John Muir, ed., *Picturesque California and the Region West of the Rocky Mountains from Alaska to Mexico* (San Francisco: J. Dewing, 1888), 40; Wilcox, "Fisheries of the Pacific Coast," 160–66; Collins, "Report of the Fisheries of the Pacific Coast of the United States," 60; Lydon, *Chinese Gold*, 54–58.

25. For similar arguments, see Warren, *The Hunter's Game*; and Jacoby, *Crimes Against Nature*.

26. M. H. Field, "Mid-Winter Days at Monterey," *Overland Monthly*, December 1887, 620–21; Fitch, "A Glimpse of Monterey," 40.

27. Nancy F. Cott, *The Bonds of Womanhood* (New Haven, CT: Yale University Press, 1977); John D'Emilio and Estelle Freedman, *Intimate Matters: A History of Sexuality in America*, 2nd ed. (Chicago: University of Chicago Press, 1997), 172–73, 201; Kathy Peiss, *Cheap Amusements: Working Women and Leisure in Turn-of-the-Century New York* (Philadelphia: Temple University Press, 1986), 7.

28. Sandy Lydon, *The Japanese in the Monterey Bay Region: A Brief History* (Capitola, CA: Capitola Book Company, 1997), 32–37; David T. Yamada, *The Japanese of the Monterey Peninsula: Their History and Legacy, 1895–1995* (Monterey, CA: Monterey Japanese American Citizens League, 1995), 24–26.

29. *Pacific Grove Review*, 18 April 1903.

30. For anti-Japanese sentiment, see Takaki, *Strangers from a Different*

Shore, 180–85; Roger Daniels, *Asian America : Chinese and Japanese in the United States since 1850* (Seattle: University of Washington Press, 1988), 109–54.

31. Lydon, *The Japanese in the Monterey Bay Region*, 32.

32. McEvoy, *Fisherman's Problem*, 66.

33. Arthur Eugene Bestor, Jr., *David Jacks of Monterey, and Lee L. Jacks, His Daughter* (Stanford, CA: Stanford University Press, 1945), 6–7; *Biographical Material Relating to David Jacks: Monterey County*, n.d., Hubert Howe Bancroft Collection, The Bancroft Library, University of California, Berkeley.

34. In 1865 the City of Monterey declared the sale unauthorized and illegal, and the case went to the Supreme Court, which ruled in Jacks's favor in 1906. See Sondra L. Gould, "David Jacks: The Letter of the Law" (M.A. thesis, California State University, Fullerton, 1992), 53–86; Brian McGinty, "Monterey's Hated Benefactor," *Westways*, January 1967, 27–28; Walton, *Storied Land*, 114, 116, 131–34; August Fink, *Monterey County: The Dramatic Story of Its Past* (Santa Cruz, CA: Western Tanager Press, 1972), 122–25. The common council—consisting of seven to ten members, most of whom were merchants, and the mayor—was established in 1850. See Walton, *Storied Land*, 118.

35. "Point Pinos Rancho Containing Title to Pacific Grove Lots Not Conveyed to the PICo. owned by D. Jacks," 31 October 1900, Box B19, David Jacks Collection, The Huntington Library, San Marino, California (hereafter Jacks Collection); *Monterey Californian*, 1 April 1879.

36. Lease, David Jacks to China Man Hop Company, 8 December 1868, Business Papers, Box 14, Jacks Collection.

37. Daily Journal, 1874 and 1880, Business Papers (bound volumes), Jacks Collection. See entries for 21 February 1874, 1 May 1874, 7 January 1880, 24 February 1880, 29 March 1880, 2 August 1880.

38. Receipts from Sand Shipments and Statements of the San Francisco and Pacific Glassworks, Box B3, and Correspondence between David Jacks and David & Cowell and H. T. Holmes, Box C1, Jacks Collection. For shipments of Monterey pine and cypress, see, for example, George Bliss to David Jacks, 22 November 1870; J. M. Leutzarder to David Jacks, 17 November 1871; W. F. Miller to David Jacks, 15 January 1872; F. S. Fitch to David Jacks, 12 February 1872, Box C1, Jacks Collection.

39. For the Southern Pacific Railroad in California, see William Deverell, *Railroad Crossing: Californians and the Railroad, 1850–1910* (Berkeley and Los Angeles: University of California Press, 1994), 4; Richard Orsi, *Sunset Limited: The Southern Pacific Railroad and the Development of the American West, 1850–1930* (Berkeley and Los Angeles: University of California Press, 2005), 17–21.

40. *The Handbook to Monterey and Vicinity*, 60; Horace W. Fabing and Rick Hamman, *Steinbeck Country Narrow Gauge* (Boulder, CO: Pruett Publishing Co., 1985), 10; Walton, *Storied Land*, 140–41.

41. Walton, *Storied Land*, 144, 150; Fabing and Hamman, *Steinbeck Country Narrow Gauge*, 12–13, 19; *The Handbook to Monterey and Vicinity*, 60–62.

42. Orsi, *Sunset Limited*, 114–23; Stuart Daggett, *Chapters on the History of the Southern Pacific* (New York: The Ronald Press Company, 1922), 131–34; Articles of Incorporation, Pacific Improvement Company, 31 October 1878, Box B10, Jacks Collection.

43. Charles Crocker to Collis P. Huntington, 11 December 1879, Reel 18, Series 1, Collis P. Huntington Papers, Department of Special Collections, Syracuse University Library (hereafter Huntington Papers); Deed, David Jacks to Pacific Improvement Company, 22 January 1880, Box 19/2, Pacific Improvement Company Records, JL17, Special Collections, Stanford University Libraries (hereafter PICo. Records–JL17); Charles Crocker to Collis P. Huntington, 15 December 1879, Reel 18, Series 1, Huntington Papers; Deed, David Jacks to Pacific Improvement Company, 11 May 1880, Box 19/2, PICo. Records–JL17; Deed, David Jacks to Pacific Improvement Co. for Point Pinos and Pescadero Ranchos, 3 May 1880, Box B12, Jacks Collection.

44. For the connections between railroads and resorts, see Rothman, *Devil's Bargains*, 50–112; Brown, *Inventing New England*, 113, 127–28. For other seaside resorts, see John A. Jakle, *The Tourist: Travel in Twentieth-Century North America* (Lincoln: University of Nebraska Press, 1985), 53–63.

45. Many historians have discussed the creation of similar "hybrid" environments. See Mark Fiege, *Irrigated Eden: The Making of an Agricultural Landscape in the American West* (Seattle: University of Washington Press, 1999); White, *The Organic Machine*. For the nineteenth-century vacationing phenomenon, see Cindy S. Aron, *Working at Play: A History of Vacations in the United States* (New York: Oxford University Press, 1999).

46. N. C. Carnall and Co., *N. C. Carnall and Co.'s California Guide for Tourists and Settlers* (San Francisco: N. C. Carnall and Co, 1889), 33.

47. Charles Crocker to Collis P. Huntington, 15 December 1879, Reel 18, Series 1, Huntington Papers; Oscar Lewis, *The Big Four: The Story of Huntington, Stanford, Hopkins, and Crocker, and of the Building of the Central Pacific* (New York: Alfred A. Knopf, 1938), 121; Hyde, *An American Vision*, 164.

48. Hyde, *An American Vision*, 173. A disgruntled employee was charged with setting the fire and tampering with the water system but was later found innocent. For another theory about its origins, see Walton, *Storied Land*, 167–72.

49. Pomeroy, *In Search of the Golden West*, 19–20, 31–36.

50. *Monterey Californian*, 15 May 1880.

51. N. C. Carnall and Co., *N. C. Carnall and Co.'s California Guide for Tourists and Settlers*, 33; Raymond-Whitcomb, Inc., *Two Grand Winter Trips to California with Sojourns at the Hotel Del Monte, Monterey, and the Other Famous Health Resorts of Central and Southern California* (Boston: James S. Adams

Printer, 1883), 30; Raymond-Whitcomb, Inc., *A Winter Trip to California and a Sojourn of Five Months at the Hotel Del Monte, Monterey, California* (Boston: James S. Adams Printer, n.d.), 4.

52. *Hotel Del Monte, Monterey, California, U.S.A.* (Del Monte, CA: The Hotel, 1898).

53. W. C. Morrow, *Souvenir of the Hotel Del Monte, Monterey, California* (San Francisco: Press of H. S. Crocker, 1894), 16. For the Spanish fantasy heritage, see Carey McWilliams, *North from Mexico: The Spanish-Speaking People of the United States* (Philadelphia and New York: J. B. Lippincott Company, 1949), 35–47; Phoebe S. Kropp, *California Vieja: Culture and Memory in a Modern American Place* (Berkeley and Los Angeles: University of California Press, 2006).

54. *Hotel Del Monte: Monterey, California, U.S.A* (Monterey, CA: The Hotel, 1899).

55. Raymond-Whitcomb, Inc., *Two Grand Winter Trips to California*, 4, 32.

56. N. C. Carnall and Co., *N .C. Carnall and Co.'s California Guide for Tourists and Settlers*, 34.

57. Edward S. Harrison, *Souvenir Edition, Monterey County, Illustrated: Resources, History, Biography* (San Francisco: Pacific Press Publishing Company, 1890), 12. See also *Sunset*, December 1899.

58. For similar arguments, see Fiege, *Irrigated Eden*, 9; Anne Whiston Spirn, "Constructing Nature: The Legacy of Frederick Law Olmsted," in *Uncommon Ground: Rethinking the Human Place in Nature*, ed. William Cronon (New York: W. W. Norton, 1996), 91–113.

59. Pomeroy, *In Search of the Golden West*, 70.

60. David C. Streatfield, *California Gardens: Creating a New Eden* (New York: Abbeville Press, 1994), 45, 55, 63. See also David C. Streatfield, "Where Pine and Palm Meet: The California Garden as a Regional Expression," *Landscape Journal* 4, no. 2 (Fall 1985): 61–73.

61. Streatfield, *California Gardens*, 44–45, 262.

62. *Sunset*, January 1899; *Hotel Del Monte, California: George P. Snell, Manager* (San Francisco: Sunset Press, 1900); Susie Clark, *The Round Trip from the Hub to the Golden Gate* (Boston: Lee and Shepard, 1890), 116. See also letter from W. H. Dike of Minnesota in *Del Monte Wave*, June 1886; article by Clement Chase of the *Omaha Bee* in *Del Monte Wave*, October 1886; letter from D. T. McClelland of Gilroy, California, *Del Monte Wave* (February 1888).

63. *Monterey, California: The Most Charming Winter Resort in the World* (Monterey, CA: n.p., 1881), 8; *Sunset*, January 1899; *Hotel Del Monte: Monterey, California U.S.A.* (1899). For the use of biota from distant places to make new environments, see Ian Tyrrell, *True Gardens of the Gods: Californian-Australian Environmental Reform, 1860–1930* (Berkeley and Los Angeles: University of California Press, 1999), and Alfred Crosby, *Ecological Imperialism: The*

Biological Expansion of Europe, 900–1900 (New York: Cambridge University Press, 1986).

64. *Sunset,* December 1899; *Hotel Del Monte: Monterey, California, U.S.A.* (1899).

65. *Hotel Del Monte, Monterey, California, U.S.A.* (1898); *Hotel Del Monte: Monterey, California, U.S.A.* (1899).

66. For algae on Laguna Del Rey, see T. B. Hunter to A. D. Shepard, 25 March 1908, Box 63/1, Pacific Improvement Company Records, JL1, Special Collections, Stanford University Libraries (hereafter PICo. Records–JL1).

67. *Hotel Del Monte, Monterey, California, U.S.A.* (1898); *Hotel Del Monte: Monterey, California, U.S.A.* (1899); John S. Hittell, *Bancroft's Pacific Coast Guide Book* (San Francisco: A. L. Bancroft & Co., 1882), 117.

68. A. D. Shepard to Timothy Hopkins, 20 September 1909, Box 4/Folder 9, Stanford University Board of Trustees Records, Special Collections, Stanford University Libraries.

69. Clark, *The Round Trip from the Hub,* 115.

70. Quoted in Pomeroy, *In Search of the Golden West,* 71. Original citation: Charles S. Greene, "Where the Gray Squirrel Hides," *Overland Monthly,* July 1897, 61–62.

71. *Del Monte Wave,* October 1886. See also Rose Pender, *A Lady's Experiences in the Wild West in 1883* (Lincoln: University of Nebraska Press, 1978), 42–44. For tourism and labor, see Andrews, "'Made by Toile'?"

72. Streatfield, *California Gardens,* 55; *Del Monte Wave,* January 1886; *Monterey Cypress,* 5 January 1889; Lydon, *Chinese Gold,* 174–76.

73. Lydon, *The Japanese in the Monterey Bay Region,* 32.

74. *Del Monte Wave,* September 1888. For nature and the body, see Douglas Sackman, "'Nature's Workshop': The Work Environment and Workers' Bodies in California's Citrus Industry, 1900–1940," *Environmental History* 5, no. 1 (January 2000): 27–53, and Christopher Sellers, "Thoreau's Body: Towards an Embodied Environmental History," *Environmental History* 4, no. 4 (October 1999): 486–514.

75. Caroline H. Dall, *My First Holiday; Or, Letters Home from Colorado, Utah, and California* (Boston: Roberts Brothers, 1881), 326–30.

76. Lydon, *Chinese Gold,* 145.

77. Charles W. Hibbard, *The Sportsman at Del Monte, Illustrated* (San Francisco: Southern Pacific Company, Passenger Department, 1897), 6.

78. For masculinity and hunting, see Gail Bederman, *Manliness and Civilization: A Cultural History of Gender and Race in the United States, 1880–1917* (Chicago: University of Chicago Press, 1995), 170–215; Tina Loo, "Of Moose and Men: Hunting for Masculinities in British Columbia, 1880–1939," *Western Historical Quarterly* 32, no. 3 (2001): 296–319.

79. *Del Monte Wave*, January 1888; ibid., July 1888.

80. Ibid., October 1886.

81. For women's swimming activities, see ibid., August 1886; Stilgoe, *Alongshore*, 340–67. For aquarium building, see *Hotel Del Monte, Monterey, California, U.S.A.* (1898); Dall, *My First Holiday*, 328; Stilgoe, *Alongshore*, 306–8.

82. Aron, *Working at Play*, 69–100, quotations on pages 89 and 96.

83. *Monterey, California: The Most Charming Winter Resort in the World.*

84. P. C. Remondino, *Longevity and Climate: Relations of Climatic Conditions to Longevity, History, and Religion—Relations of Climate to National and Personal Habits—The Climate of California and Its Effects in Relation to Longevity* (San Francisco: Woodward and Co., 1890), 20–22.

85. Quoted in Stilgoe, *Alongshore*, 338–39. Original citation: John H. Packard, *Sea-Air and Sea-Bathing* (Philadelphia: Presley, 1880). Bushrod W. James, *American Resorts with Notes upon Their Climate* (Philadelphia: F. A. Davis, 1889), 155–69.

86. Mark Caldwell, *The Last Crusade: The War on Consumption, 1862–1954* (New York: Athenaeum, 1988), 69, 76–77; Rene and Jean Dubos, *The White Plague: Tuberculosis, Man and Society* (Boston: Little, Brown & Co., 1952), 25; Barbara Bates, *Bargaining for Life: A Social History of Tuberculosis, 1876–1938* (Philadelphia: University of Pennsylvania Press, 1992), 25–41. For landscape and disease, see Conevery Bolton Valenčius, *The Health of the Country: How American Settlers Understood Themselves and Their Land* (New York: Basic Books, 2002); Linda Nash, *Inescapable Ecologies: A History of Environment, Disease, and Knowledge* (Berkeley and Los Angeles: University of California Press, 2006); Gregg Mitman, "In Search of Health: Landscape and Disease in American Environmental History," *Environmental History* 10, no. 2 (April 2005): 184–210.

87. James, *American Resorts*, 17, 20–21.

88. A. M. Shew, *California as a Health Resort* (Boston: James S. Adams, 1885). Emphasis in the original.

89. Dall, *My First Holiday*, 4, 336.

90. Stevenson, *The Old Pacific Capital*, 23–24.

91. "General Notes," *Nautilus* 6, no. 4 (August 1892): 48.

92. Williard M. Wood, "On a Collecting Trip to Monterey Bay" *Nautilus* 7, no. 6 (October 1893): 70.

93. F. W. Hatch, "The Seaside Health Resorts of California," *Seventh Biennial Report of the California State Board of Health* (1882): 95–96. For urban pollution, see Martin Melosi, *The Sanitary City: Urban Infrastructure in America from Colonial Times to the Present* (Baltimore: Johns Hopkins University Press, 2000), 17–42, 73–99, 103–204.

94. Edward E. Eitel, *Picturesque Del Monte* (San Francisco: The Bancroft Company Printers, 1888).

95. *Monterey New Era*, 26 May 1892.

96. William P. Northup, "Diphtheria," in *Nothangel's Encyclopedia of Practical Medicine* (Philadelphia: W. B. Saunders, 1902), 20–21; George Chandler Whipple, *Typhoid Fever: Its Causation, Transmission and Prevention* (New York: John Wiley and Sons, 1908). For germ theory, see Nancy Tomes, *The Gospel of Germs: Men, Women, and the Microbe in American Life* (Cambridge, MA: Harvard University Press, 1998).

97. Valenčius, *The Health of the Country*, 114, 117–19.

98. Nayan Shah, *Contagious Divides: Epidemics and Race in San Francisco's Chinatown* (Berkeley and Los Angeles: University of California Press, 2001), 20–21, 28, 42. For the association of disease and pollutants with particular groups and neighborhoods, see also Melosi, *The Sanitary City*, 59–61; Adam Rome, "Coming to Terms with Pollution: The Language of Environmental Reform," *Environmental History* 1, no. 3 (July 1996): 9; Stanley K. Schultz, *Constructing Urban Culture: American Cities and City Planning, 1800–1930* (Philadelphia: Temple University Press, 1989), 111–28.

99. Work Projects Administration, Historical Survey of the Monterey Peninsula, Project No. 4080, File 40, June 15, 1937. Transcribed manuscript from the *Monterey New Era*, 14 May 1902, California History Room, Monterey Public Library.

100. For nineteenth-century nuisance law, see Schultz, *Constructing Urban Culture*, 42–47, 51–53.

101. WPA Manuscript from the *Monterey New Era*, 14 May 1902.

102. *Pacific Grove Review*, 24 May 1902.

103. *Monterey New Era*, 18 June 1902.

104. Ibid., 25 May 1904.

105. Lydon, *Chinese Gold*, 358; *Pacific Grove Review*, 16 February 1906; J. P. Pryor to A. D. Shepard, 5 May 1906; A. D. Shepard to J. P. Pryor, 7 May 1906; and J. P. Pryor to A D. Shepard, 8 May 1906, Box 60/53, PICo. Records–JL1.

106. Lydon, *Chinese Gold*, 362–66; *Pacific Grove Review*, 18 May 1906. For the arson theory, see John Woolfenden, "Once a Colorful Chinese Village Flourished along Monterey Bay," *The (Monterey Peninsula) Herald Magazine*, 16 November 1975.

107. *Pacific Grove Review*, 18 May 1906.

108. J. P. Pryor to A. D. Shepard, 15 June 1906; J. P. Pryor to A. D. Shepard, 16 June 1906; A .D. Shepard to R. H. Willey, 19 June 1906, Box 60/53, PICo. Records–JL1.

109. "Demand for Surrender of Real Property," 23 June 1906, Box 60/53, PICo. Records–JL1.

110. *Pacific Grove Review*, 25 May 1906; J. P. Pryor to A. D. Shepard, 17 May 1906, and J. P. Pryor to A. D. Shepard, 26 May 1906, Box 60/53, PICo.

Records–JL1; A. D. Shepard to John Penney, 21 May 1906, Box 60/55, PICo. Records–JL1.

111. J. P. Pryor to A. D. Shepard, 26 June 26 1906, Box 60/53, PICo. Records–JL1.

112. A. D. Shepard to J. P. Pryor, 5 November 1906; A. D. Shepard to Benjamin Wheeler, 6 November 1906, Box 61/53, PICo. Records–JL1; *Pacific Grove Review*. 9 November 1906.

113. J. P. Pryor to A. D. Shepard, 6 November 1906, Box 61/53, PICo. Records–JL1; *Pacific Grove Review*, 9 November 1906.

114. My analysis of the fire differs from the work of John Walton, who argues that the Chinese eventually participated in a "negotiated accommodation" that created a "multicultural community" in which "people learned to live together in distinctive ways." See Walton, *Storied Land*, 178–80.

115. Ordinance No. 140, June 27, 1907, and Ordinance No. 148, June 9, 1908, Ordinance Book 1, Monterey City Clerk's Office. See also "Trustees Get Busy," *Monterey Daily Cypress*, June 10, 1908. For ordinance violations, see Monterey Recorders and Police Court, July 11, 1907 (vol. 1), and June 11, 1908 (vol. 2), Monterey City Clerk's Office.

116. Lydon, *Chinese Gold*, 377, 380; *Directory of Monterey, New Monterey, Del Monte Grove, Seaside, Vista Del Rey, Del Monte Heights* (n.p.: Weybret-Lee Co., 1911).

117. Lydon, *Chinese Gold*, 59; *Feast of Lanterns, Pacific Grove, California* (n.p.: Pacific Grove, 1961). Copy in Local History Files, Pacific Grove Public Library; *Monterey County Locale*, Summer 1968. Pacific Grove held the festival annually until 1917 and sporadically until 1958. The city council has since held the festival annually.

118. J. P. Pryor to A. D. Shepard, 30 July 1906, Box 60/53, PICo. Records–JL1.

119. McWilliams, *North from Mexico*, 35–47; Kropp, *California Vieja*. For the decimation of the California Indians, see Albert L. Hurtado, *Indian Survival on the California Frontier* (New Haven, CT: Yale University Press, 1988).

2   THE DIVIDED COASTLINE

1. "Times Look Bright," *Monterey Daily Cypress*, 23 June 1907.

2. "Prospects Are Bright," *Monterey Daily Cypress*, 30 April 1907; "Great Growth of Monterey Peninsula," *Monterey Daily Cypress*, 10 May 1907.

3. "Development of Our Fisheries," *Monterey Daily Cypress*, 24 November 1907; "Now Is the Time to Plan for Next Summer," *Monterey Daily Cypress*, 5 October 1907; "Monterey Peninsula Should Be Advertised," *Monterey Daily Cypress*, 26 October 1907.

4. Pomeroy, *In Search of the Golden West*, 28–30.

5. For class and environmental history, see Karl Jacoby, "Class and Environmental History: Lessons from 'The War in the Adirondacks,'" *Environmental History* 2, no. 3 (July 1997): 324–42; Jacoby, *Crimes Against Nature*, 11–78; Benjamin Heber Johnson, "Conservation, Subsistence, and Class at the Birth of Superior National Forest," *Environmental History* 4, no. 1 (January 1999): 80–99.

6. "Monterey of the Future," *Monterey Daily Cypress*, 10 August 1907.

7. "Hotel Del Monte Expenses and Profits, 1903–1911," Box 55/29, PICo. Records–JL1; "Hotel Del Monte, 1899–1910," Box 35/24, PICo. Records–JL17; "Hotel Del Monte, Showing for Year 1912," Box 71/1, PICo. Records–JL1.

8. A. D. Shepard to William Woodhead (Sunset Magazine), 16 May 1911, Box 68/13, PICo. Records–JL1.

9. "Villas Planned," *Monterey Daily Cypress*, 30 March 1907; "Pebble Beach, Monterey," n.d., Box 69/50, PICo. Records–JL1.

10. "Villas Planned"; "Work to Commence," *Monterey Daily Cypress*, 14 June 1908; "Rustic Club House," *Monterey Daily Cypress*, 23 October 1908; A. D. Shepard, *Pebble Beach, Monterey County, California* (San Francisco: H. S. Crocker Co., 1909).

11. "Big Things Are Doing at Pebble Beach," *Monterey American*, 22 June 1915.

12. Shepard, *Pebble Beach*; for Louis Hill, see J. P. Pryor to A. D. Shepard, 20 March 1914, Box 76/50, PICo. Records–JL1; "Big Things Are Doing at Pebble Beach"; "Pebble Beach Sales Are Booming Right Along," *Monterey American*, 26 May 1916.

13. A. D. Shepard to William Woodhead, 16 May 1911, Box 68/13, PICo. Records–JL1.

14. Ben Conrad to Samuel Morse, 1 April 1918; C. S. Olmsted to Samuel Morse, 17 February 1919, Box 87/53, PICo. Records–JL1; "Del Monte Forest Camp: Pacific Grove by the Sea," n.d., Box 35/11, PICo. Records–JL17.

15. Shaffer, *See America First*, 133; Arthur Inkersley, "Touring in California," *Sunset*, December 1903, 116–27; Arthur Inkersley, "Automobiling at Del Monte," *Sunset*, January 1905, 284–87.

16. Pomeroy, *In Search of the Golden West*, 125–30, 146–50, quotation on pages 129–30; Shaffer, *See America First*, 130–37; Rothman, *Devil's Bargains*, 143–51; Jakle, *The Tourist*, 101–19.

17. Aron, *Working at Play*, 207–9, 228–32, quotation on page 229; Warren Belasco, *Americans on the Road: From Autocamp to Motel, 1910–1945* (Cambridge, MA: The MIT Press, 1979), 7–17, 41–69. Auto camps became more exclusionary in the mid-1920s.

18. Aron, *Working at Play*, 181–236, quotation on page 182.

19. A. D. Shepard to Thomas Hubbard, 2 January 1913, Box 72/50, PICo. Records–JL1; "Del Monte Forest Camp: Pacific Grove by the Sea."

20. "Interesting Points to Be Explained," Box 53/9, PICo. Records–JL17.

21. H. R. Warner to C. G White, 6 March 1909, Box 53/9, PICo. Records–JL17.

22. Samuel Morse to W. R. Scott, 12 January 1916, Box 82/1, PICo. Records–JL1.

23. "Fairyland of the Pacific," 1908, Box 64/46, PICo. Records–JL1; "Boost Grove in California," *Monterey Daily Cypress*, 19 March 1908; "Peninsula As It Is," *Monterey Daily Cypress*, 1 August 1908.

24. Yamada, *The Japanese of the Monterey Peninsula*, 55; Lydon, *The Japanese in the Monterey Bay Region*, 51, 55; J. P. Pryor to A D. Shepard, 17 August 1906, Box 60/53, PICo. Records–JL1. See also J. P. Pryor to A. D. Shepard, 7 January 1907, Box 62/53, PICo. Records–JL1; J. P. Pryor to A. D. Shepard, 3 February 1908, Box 63/53, PICo. Records–JL1. For Asian labor contractors, see Friday, *Organizing Asian American Labor*, 70–81, 88–97.

25. Takaki, *Strangers from a Different Shore*, 27, 46, 203–5.

26. Dorothee E. Kocks, *Dream a Little: Land and Social Justice in Modern America* (Berkeley and Los Angeles: University of California Press, 2000), 26–27.

27. *Pacific Grove Review*, 23 November 1906; Benjamin Wheeler to A. D. Shepard, 25 October 1907, 5 June 1908, Box 34/Folder 13; Benjamin Wheeler to A.D. Shepard, 1 May 1909, Box 50/Folder 47, University of California, Office of the President, Alphabetical Files, CU–5, Series 1, The Bancroft Library, University of California, Berkeley.

28. Samuel Morse to Pacific Improvement Company Board of Directors, 30 October 1916, Box 85/53, PICo. Records–JL1.

29. A. D. Shepard to T. H. Hubbard, 14 September 1908, Box 65/1, PICo. Records–JL1.

30. George A. Coleman, *Report upon Monterey Pine, Made for the Pacific Improvement Company, Based upon an Examination Made during 1904 and 1905 of the Pacific Improvement Company's 7000–Acre Property near Monterey and Pacific Grove* (Berkeley, CA: n.p., 1905), 22–31.

31. Coleman, *Report upon Monterey Pine*, 25–28, 32, 69–74; Duncan Dunning, "A Working Plan for the Del Monte Forest of the Pacific Improvement Company" (M.S. thesis, University of California, 1916), 37–38.

32. Gifford Pinchot, for instance, worked on the private Biltmore estate early in his career. See Char Miller, *Gifford Pinchot and the Making of Modern Environmentalism* (Washington, D.C.: Island Press/Shearwater Books, 2001), 102–19.

33. Samuel Hays, *Conservation and the Gospel of Efficiency: The Progressive Conservation Movement, 1890–1920* (Cambridge, MA: Harvard University Press, 1959), 1–2, 28–29, 35.

34. Dunning, "A Working Plan for the Del Monte Forest," 36–37.

35. Donald Bruce to Samuel Morse, 12 February 1916, Box 82/53, PICo. Records–JL1.

36. Dunning, "A Working Plan for the Del Monte Forest," 18–19, 40, 48, 50.

37. David T. Mason to Samuel Morse, 9 September 1916, Box 84/50, PICo. Records–JL1.

38. Samuel Morse to Colonel Allen Griffin, *Monterey Peninsula Herald*, 21 February 1969, Box 3/Folder 35, Samuel Finley Brown Morse Papers, JL16, Special Collections, Stanford University Libraries (hereafter Morse Papers).

39. Samuel Morse to Pacific Improvement Company Board of Directors, 12 July 1916, Box 84/1, PICo. Records–JL1; "Memoranda Regarding Monterey Peninsula Properties," n.d., Box 87/53, PICo. Records–JL1.

40. Morse to Griffin, 21 February 1969; "Detail of Real Estate—San Francisco Office, Special P.I. Co. Report, 31 October 1923, Box 164/9, PICo. Records–JL17; Samuel Morse to Pacific Improvement Company Board of Directors, 11 April 1919, Box 92B/53, PICo. Records–JL1; J. Beaumont to William H. Crocker, 25 April 1919, Box 92B/53, PICo. Records–JL1.

41. *Statutes of California and Digest of Measures, Seventeenth Session* (Sacramento, CA: n.p., 1868), 202; *Statutes of California and Digest of Measures, Thirty-fifth Session* (Sacramento, CA: n.p., 1903), 290; *Statutes of California and Digest of Measures, Forty-third Session* (Sacramento, CA: n.p., 1919), 1359.

42. Rose, "The Comedy of the Commons," 108–10; Bonnie McCay, *Oyster Wars and the Public Trust: Property, Law, and Ecology in New Jersey History* (Tucson: University of Arizona Press, 1998), xx–xxiii.

43. "To Utilize Products of Monterey Bay," *Monterey New Era*, 25 September 1901; Mangelsdorf, *Steinbeck's Cannery Row*, 7–8; Stephen Michael Payne, "Unheeded Warnings: A History of Monterey's Sardine Fishery" (Ph.D. diss., University of California, Santa Barbara, 1987), 42–43, 55–56.

44. "The Biggest Factor in Our Commercial Development," *Monterey American*, 13 May 1916.

45. *Monterey New Era*, 17 June 1896; McEvoy, *Fisherman's Problem*, 88, 126; Mangelsdorf, *Steinbeck's Cannery Row*, 7–9; Lydon, *The Japanese in the Monterey Bay Region*, 54; Earl Rosenberg, "A History of the Fishing and Canning Industries in Monterey, California" (M.A. thesis, University of Nevada, 1961), 59.

46. Payne, "Unheeded Warnings," 44–45; Mangelsdorf, *Steinbeck's Cannery Row*, 19.

47. In 1929 Carl Hubbs discovered that the Atlantic sardine (*Sardina pilchardus pilchardus*) and the Mediterranean sardine (*Sardina pilchardus sardine*) were distinct from the California sardines, which were renamed *Sardinops caerulea*. See Carl L. Hubbs, "The Generic Relationships and Nomenclatures of the California Sardine," *Proceedings of the California Academy of Sciences*, 4th ser., 18, no. 11 (April 5, 1929): 261–65.

48. Payne, "Unheeded Warnings," 41, 50–51.

49. Architectural Resources Group, *Cannery Row Historic Survey, September 1999* (San Francisco: Architectural Resources Group, 1999), 24; Payne, "Unheeded Warnings," 50.

50. Payne, "Unheeded Warnings," 45; Will F. Thompson, "Historical Review of California Sardine Industry," *California Fish and Game* 7, no. 4 (October 1921): 196.

51. Tom Mangelsdorf, "Knut Hovden—The Genius of Cannery Row," *The (Monterey Peninsula) Herald, Weekend Magazine*, 14 November 1982.

52. K. Hovden Company, *The History of Portola* (Monterey, CA: K. Hovden Co., n.d.), 3–4; Payne, "Unheeded Warnings," 46–49. For similar changes in the Pacific salmon industry, see Patrick W. O'Bannon, "Technological Change in the Pacific Coast Canned Salmon Industry, 1900–1925: A Case Study," *Agricultural History* 56 (1982): 151–66, and "Waves of Change: Mechanization in the Pacific Coast Canned-Salmon Industry, 1864–1914," *Technology and Culture* 28 (1987): 558–77.

53. K. Hovden Company, *The History of Portola*, 4.

54. Walton, *Storied Land*, 192, 194, 196–97.

55. Friday, *Organizing Asian American Labor*, 27–34; Walton, *Storied Land*, 192, 194, 196–97.

56. Richard White, *"It's Your Misfortune and None of My Own": A New History of the American West* (Norman: University of Oklahoma Press, 1991), 282–84; Friday, *Organizing Asian American Labor*, 16–17; Takaki, *Strangers from a Different Shore*, 140–41.

57. "A Larger Cannery," *Monterey Daily Cypress*, 19 December 1909; "Did the Right Thing," *Monterey Daily Cypress*, 2 February 1910. The board of trustees consisted of five elected members and held legislative and executive powers. This form of city government continued until July 1911, when a new charter provided for a mayor and four council members. See Works Progress Administration, *History of the City Government of Monterey* (Monterey, CA: n.p, 1937); *Charter of the City of Monterey, 1910* (Monterey, CA: n.p., 1910).

58. "Cannery a Modern One," *Monterey Daily Cypress*, 15 April 1910; "Enlarging the Booth Cannery," *Monterey Daily Cypress*, 26 March 1910.

59. Payne, "Unheeded Warnings," 58–59.

60. Ibid., 60; Thompson, "Historical Review of California Sardine Industry," 197; Donald H. Fry Jr., "The Ring Net, Half Ring Net, or Purse Lampara in the Fisheries of California," California Department of Natural Resources, Division of Fish and Game, *Fish Bulletin No. 27* (1931): 8.

61. Thompson, "Historical Review of the California Sardine Industry," 197; Fry, "The Ring Net," 8.

62. Payne, "Unheeded Warnings," 61–63.

63. Arthur Campbell, "The Conservation of the California Sardine" (M.A. thesis, Chico State College, 1952), 24–29; N. B. Scofield, "The Lampara Net," *California Fish and Game* 10, no. 2 (April 1924): 67; Payne, "Unheeded Warnings," 63; Fry, "The Ring Net," 9; Milton J. Lindner, "Luminescent Fishing," *California Fish and Game* 16, no. 3 (July 1930): 237–40.

64. Payne, "Unheeded Warnings," 65; McEvoy, *Fisherman's Problem*, 129; W. L. Scofield, "Sardine Fishing Methods at Monterey, California," California Department of Natural Resources, Division of Fish and Game, *Fish Bulletin No. 19* (1929): 19–20.

65. John Walton, "Cannery Row: Class, Community, and the Social Construction of History," in *Reworking Class*, ed. John R. Hall (Ithaca, NY: Cornell University Press, 1997), 252; Lydon, *The Japanese in the Monterey Bay Region*, 54–55.

66. Scofield, "The Lampara Net," 69.

67. "Price Fixed for Salmon," *Monterey Daily Cypress*, 20 April 1907.

68. "Fix Price of Salmon," *Monterey Daily Cypress*, 14 October 1908.

69. "Union Formed by Monterey Fishermen," *Monterey Daily Cypress*, 11 November 1914; "Compromise Is Scorned by Fishers," *Monterey Daily Cypress*, 17 April 1915.

70. Lydon, *The Japanese in the Monterey Bay Region*, 54–55; Yamada, *The Japanese of the Monterey Peninsula*, 50–55; *Directory of Monterey, New Monterey, Del Monte Grove, Seaside, Vista Del Rey, Del Monte Heights* (1911).

71. *A Directory of Monterey, Del Monte, Pacific Grove, Carmel-by-the-Sea, and Seaside, 1916–1917* (Monterey, CA: City Directory Co., 1917).

72. "Companies May Defy Local Fishermen," *Monterey Daily Cypress*, 16 April 1915; "Fishermen Say Booth Was Not Fair," *Monterey Daily Cypress*, 20 April 1915; "Japanese Join in Fish Rate Demand," *Monterey Daily Cypress*, 28 April 1915; "Fishermen to Validate Contract," *Monterey Daily Cypress*, 30 April 1915; Walton, *Storied Land*, 192, 205; Rosenberg, "A History of the Fishing and Canning Industries," 94.

73. "Along the Water Front," *Monterey Daily Cypress*, 27 March 1908.

74. "Fishermen Face Serious Charge," *Monterey Daily Cypress*, 11 August 1915; "Fate of Six Fishermen in Balance," *Monterey Daily Cypress*, 12 August 1915.

75. "Enlarging the Booth Cannery."

76. "Along the Shore," *Monterey Daily Cypress*, 17 February 1907; "Cleaning Fish on Wharf," *Monterey Daily Cypress*, 18 August 1907. For similar debates over fishing gear, see Taylor, *Making Salmon*, 133–65.

77. "Will Not Take Lease," *Monterey Daily Cypress*, 11 March 1910; "Enlarging the Booth Cannery."

78. "Along the Water Front," *Monterey Daily Cypress*, 6 August 1909.

79. "Things Waxing Warm Among Fishing Interests," *Monterey American*, 23 December 1912.

80. Ibid.; "Hurting Canneries," *Monterey Daily Cypress*, 24 December 1912.

81. "A Fisherman's Views on the Lompara Net," *Monterey American*, 26 December 1912.

82. Ibid.; "Hurting Canneries."

83. Scofield, "The Lampara Net," 66–70.

84. Ibid., 69–70.

85. The conflict over the lampara net resonates with debates on the Columbia River at the turn of the twentieth century. See Richard White, *The Organic Machine*, 40–47; Taylor, *Making Salmon*, 133–65.

86. A. D. Shepard to F. E. Booth, 13 November 1906, and A. D. Shepard to J. P. Pryor, 30 November 1906, Box 61/53, PICo. Records–JL1.

87. Ordinance No. 142, 3 September 1907, Ordinance Book No. 1, Monterey City Clerk's Office.

88. "Clean Up the Beach," *Monterey Daily Cypress*, 2 June 1911.

89. "California," *Pacific Fisherman*, September 1909, 22; "Cannery, Wharf," *Monterey Daily Cypress*, 8 August 1909.

90. "Affairs of the City," *Monterey Daily Cypress*, 22 December 1909.

91. "F. E. Booth's New Fish Meal Plant," *Pacific Fisherman*, June 1922, 50–52; "Centrifugal Separators Enhance Reduction Profits," *Pacific Fisherman*, December 1929, 23–24; W. L. Scofield, "Fertilizer, Stockfood and Oil from Sardine Offal," *California Fish and Game* 7, no. 4 (October 1921): 207–17; S. Ross Hatton and George R. Smalley, "Reduction Processes for Sardines in California," *California Fish and Game* 24, no. 4 (October 1938): 396–98.

92. Lydon, *Chinese Gold*, 387; Payne, "Unheeded Warnings," 56–57.

93. Thompson, "Historical Review of California Sardine Industry," 195.

94. *California Fish and Game* 2, no. 3 (July 1916): 154.

95. Fry, "The Ring Net," 10.

96. "New Fish Cannery at Monterey," *Pacific Fisherman*, November 1916, 17.

97. Work Projects Administration, *Monterey Peninsula*, 190.

3 REDUCE AND PROSPER

1. Payne, "Unheeded Warnings," 85, 288; Rich Lovejoy, "Interview with E. B. Gross," *Monterey Peninsula Herald*, 28 February 1952.

2. Sal Colletto, *The Sardine Fisherman* (Monterey, CA: the author, 1960), 9–10. J. B. Phillips Collection, The Maritime Museum of Monterey.

3. Ted Durein, "Sardine Plant Operations Mean Jingling Cash Registers Here," *Monterey Peninsula Herald*, 26 February 1937; Work Projects Administration, *Monterey Peninsula*, 69.

4. Payne, "Unheeded Warnings," 85–86.

5. McEvoy, *Fisherman's Problem*, 133–34, 139–40, 145, 148.

6. B. D. Marx Greene, "An Historical Review of the Legal Aspects of the Use of Food Fish for Reduction Purpose," *California Fish and Game* 13, no. 1 (January 1927): 9; Milner B. Schaefer, Oscar E. Sette, and John C. Marr, "Growth of the Pacific Coast Pilchard Fishery to 1942," United States Department of the Interior, Fish and Wildlife Service, *Research Report*, no. 29 (1951): 19–21; N. B. Scofield, "Report of the Department of Commercial Fisheries," *Twenty-ninth Biennial Report of the California Fish and Game Commission, 1924–1926*, 63–66.

7. N. B. Scofield, "Report of the Bureau of Commercial Fisheries," *Thirty-first Biennial Report of the California Fish and Game Commission, 1928–1930*, 113; "Sardine Law Approved," *Pacific Fisherman*, June 1930, 40; Payne, "Unheeded Warnings," 149–50. For an overview of sardine management, see Elbert H. Ahlstrom and John Radovich, "Management of the Pacific Sardine," in *A Century of Fisheries in North America*, Special Publication No. 7, ed. Norman G. Benson (Washington, D.C.: American Fisheries Society, 1970), 183–93.

8. F. J. Fay, "'Raw Packing' of Sardines Makes Notable Saving Possible," *Pacific Fisherman*, December 1929, 21–22; Richard S. Croker, "Sardine Canning Methods in California," *California Fish and Game* 21, no. 1 (January 1935): 10–21.

9. "New Equipment for C.P.C.," *Pacific Fisherman*, October 1929, 38; "High-Speed Closers at Monterey," *Pacific Fisherman*, March 1930, 43; "C.P.C. Develops Sardine Cutter," *Pacific Fisherman*, August 1931, 40–41; Croker, "Sardine Canning Methods," 18–19.

10. Payne, "Unheeded Warnings," 86–87, 97; "Interesting Solution of Reduction Problems by F. E. Booth Co.," *Pacific Fisherman*, June 1928, 21.

11. Scofield, "Sardine Fishing Methods at Monterey," 21–24, 28; J. B. Phillips, "Success of the Purse Seine Boat in the Sardine Fishery at Monterey, California, 1929–1930 Fishing Season," California Department of Natural Resources, Division of Fish and Game, *Fish Bulletin No. 23* (1930): 7.

12. Scofield, "Sardine Fishing Methods at Monterey," 25–26; Phillips, "Success of the Purse Seine Boat," 5, 13; W. L. Scofield, "Purse Seines for California Sardines," *California Fish and Game* 12, no. 1 (January 1926): 18.

13. Milton J. Lindner, "Fishing Localities at Monterey from November, 1919, to March, 1929, for the California Sardine (*Sardina caerulea*)," California Department of Natural Resources, Division of Fish and Game, *Fish Bulletin No. 25* (1930): 8–9, 16.

14. Phillips, "Success of the Purse Seine Boat," 7–8, 15, 20; Fry, "The Ring Net," 14.

15. Scofield, "Purse Seines for California Sardines," 16–19; Phillips, "Success of the Purse Seine Boat," 7–10; Fry, "The Ring Net," 12–14.

16. Phillips, "Success of the Purse Seine Boat," 13.

17. Payne, "Unheeded Warnings," 99; Paul Bonnot, "Report on the Relative Merits and Demerits of Purse Seines vs. Lampara Nets in the Taking of Sardines," *California Fish and Game* 16, no. 1 (January 1930): 125–30. J. B. Phillips came to a similar conclusion a few years later. See J. B. Phillips, "A Survey of the Destructiveness of the Sardine Nets Used in the Monterey Region," *California Fish and Game* 18, no. 3 (July 1932): 208–18. For a similar debate about fishing gear in the Maine fisheries, see Judd, *Common Lands, Common People*, 128–29.

18. Phillips, "Success of the Purse Seine Boat," 9, 27; Fry, "The Ring Net," 11–12, 17.

19. J. B. Phillips, "Changes in Sardine Fishing Gear in the Monterey Region, with a Note on Expansion of Fishing Grounds," *California Fish and Game* 20, no. 2 (April 1934): 135–36; J. B. Phillips, "Notes on Sardine Gear Changes at Monterey," *California Fish and Game* 23, no. 3 (July 1937): 221–23.

20. Colletto, *The Sardine Fisherman*, 127.

21. "Big Monterey Ring Craft Turning to Seines; F. Lucido Heads Group," *Pacific Fisherman*, July 1931, 41; "Northern Boats for Monterey," *Pacific Fisherman*, April 1930, 42; Phillips, "Changes in Sardine Fishing Gear," 135.

22. Phillips, "Success of the Purse Seine Boat," 15–17; N. B. Scofield, "Commercial Fishery Notes," *California Fish and Game* 15, no. 4 (October 1929): 355; "Monterey Unloads Fish with Pumps," *Pacific Fisherman*, December 1930, 24–25.

23. Phillips, "Success of the Purse Seine Boat," 15. The purse seine delivered forty-nine tons and the lampara twenty-five tons per haul during the 1929–30 season.

24. Scofield, "Sardine Fishing Methods at Monterey," 57.

25. Monterey Chamber of Commerce, *Monterey Harbor: What It Is and Has, and Why It Should be Improved* (Monterey, CA: Monterey Chamber of Commerce, 1909); R. M. Dorton, *Necessity of Extending the Breakwater at Monterey, California* (Monterey, CA: City Manager, 1932); John W. N. Schulz, *Report on the Question of Abandonment of Existing Project for Monterey Harbor, Calif.*, 18 December 1925, Box 17, United States Army Corps of Engineers Records, Record Group 77, National Archives and Records Administration, Pacific Region, San Bruno, California (hereafter RG77, NARA–PR); Fred H. Tibbetts, *Report to the City of Monterey, California on Municipal Harbor Improvement* (San Francisco: n.p., 1922), 20.

26. Tibbetts, *Report to the City of Monterey*, 20.

27. R. M. Dorton, *Report on the Economic Advantage of Breakwater at Monterey Harbor* (Monterey, CA: City of Monterey, 1927), 28–29, 46.

28. John W. N. Schulz, *Re-examination—Monterey Harbor, California*, 24 August 1927, Box 17, RG77, NARA–PR.

29. "Monterey Breakwater Work Progressing," *Pacific Fisherman*, January 1932, 29; Dorton, *Necessity of Extending the Breakwater*; Thomas M. Robins, "Review

of Reports on Monterey Harbor, California," 12 May 1932; Lieutenant Colonel H. A. Finch to Division Engineer, Pacific Division, 12 April 1934; Henry S. Pond to Chief of Engineers, U.S. Army, Washington, D.C., 23 August 1934, Box 17, RG77, NARA–PR. The army corps originally planned a 1,300-foot breakwater, but Dorton and other residents pushed for the larger project to deflect city sewage and provide jobs for unemployed residents. The army corps approved the extension.

30. *Pacific Fisherman Yearbook* (1941), 174, 297.

31. Arthur F. McEvoy and Harry N. Scheiber, "Scientists, Entrepreneurs, and the Policy Process: A Study of the Post-1945 California Sardine Depletion," *Journal of Economic History* 44, no. 2 (June 1984): 395; McCay, *Oyster Wars and the Public Trust*, xxi.

32. McEvoy, *Fisherman's Problem*, 157.

33. Schaefer et al., "Growth of Pacific Coast Pilchard Fishery to 1942," 17–19; N. B. Scofield, "Shall We Use Food Fish for Fertilizer?" *California Fish and Game* 7, no. 2 (April 1921): 124.

34. Phillips, "Success of the Purse Seine Boat," 13; Lindner, "Fishing Localities at Monterey," 9; W. L. Scofield, "Memo, Monterey Sardines," 10 July 1923, Box 12/Folder 11, William F. Thompson Papers, Special Collections, Manuscripts, and University Archives, University of Washington Libraries; *Twenty-seventh Biennial Report of the California Fish and Game Commission, 1920–1922*, 79.

35. B. Houssels, Van Camp Sea Food Co., Inc., to Major John L. Farley, Executive Officer, California Fish and Game Commission, 12 September 1929, Box 3735:770, Administration and Subject Files, Weights and Measures, 1925–1940, California Department of Natural Resources, Division of Fish and Game, Bureau of Marine Fisheries, California State Archives, Sacramento, California (hereafter CDNR–DFG–BMF).

36. Kendrick A. Clements, *Hoover, Conservation, and Consumerism: Engineering the Good Life* (Lawrence: University Press of Kansas, 2000), 59–77; Hal K. Rothman, *Saving the Planet: The American Response to the Environment in the Twentieth Century* (Chicago: Ivan R. Dee, 2000), 60–72; Clayton R. Koppes, "Efficiency/Equity/Esthetics: Towards a Reinterpretation of American Conservation," *Environmental Review* 11, no. 2 (Summer 1987): 133.

37. *Monterey Peninsula Herald*, 20 September 1929; J. S. Casey, George Brinan, and E. R. Lewis to Sardine Canners of Monterey and Other Ports of California, 15 June 1934, Box F3735:770, Administration and Subject Files, Weights and Measures, 1925–1940, CDNR–DFG–BMF; N. B. Scofield, "Report of the Bureau of Commercial Fisheries," *Thirty-second Biennial Report of the California Fish and Game Commission, 1930–1932*, 68; Colletto, *The Sardine Fisherman*, 194, 392.

38. *Monterey Peninsula Herald*, 13 March 1929. This ruling affected the Monterey Canning Company, the Carmel Canning Company, the San Carlos Canning Company, and the Sea Pride Packing Company.

39. "Sardine Packers Penalized," *Pacific Fisherman*, January 1930, 37. This order was against the E. B. Gross Canning Company, Del Mar Canning Corporation, and the Custom House Packing Corporation.

40. Hovden appealed to the California Supreme Court, which affirmed the decision. *The People v. K. Hovden Company*, 215 Cal. 54; 8P. 2d 481 (1932).

41. McEvoy, *Fisherman's Problem*, 145. Fish meal was 20 percent cheaper than processed meat scraps, farmers' next most inexpensive option.

42. "Sardine Association Plans Broader Scope," *Pacific Fisherman*, May 1930, 16–17.

43. "Sardine Legislation Storm Center," *Pacific Fisherman*, May 1931, 36–37; "California Legislature Fails to Pass New Sardine Measures," *Pacific Fisherman*, June 1931, 40.

44. N. B. Scofield, "Report of the Bureau of Commercial Fisheries," *Thirty-second Biennial Report of the California Fish and Game Commission, 1930–1932*, 70; Schaefer et al., "Growth of Pacific Coast Pilchard Fishery," 27–29. See also M. Kathryn Davis, "Factories on the Water: California's Floating Reduction Plants," *J. B. Phillips Historical Fisheries Report* 1, no. 1 (Spring 2000), and "Sardine Oil on Troubled Waters: The Boom and Bust of California's Sardine Industry, 1905–1955" (Ph.D. diss., University of California, Berkeley, 2002), 214–26.

45. N. B. Scofield, "Report on the Bureau of Commercial Fisheries," *Thirty-second Biennial Report, 1930–1932*, 69; Schaefer et al., "Growth of Pacific Coast Pilchard Fishery to 1942," 26.

46. "News Comments," *Monterey Peninsula Herald*, 26 July 1932.

47. "Sardine Reduction Attitude Liberalized," *Pacific Fisherman*, July 1932, 28; "Use of 110,000 Tons of Sardines for Edible Products Sanctioned," *Pacific Fisherman*, August 1932, 26–27; *Thirty-third Biennial Report of the California Fish and Game Commission, 1932–1934*, 49–50; Schaefer et al., "Growth of Pacific Coast Pilchard Fishery to 1942," 26–27.

48. Statement of Eugene D. Bennett, *Sardine Fisheries: Hearings Before the Committee on Merchant Marine and Fisheries. Seventy-fourth Congress, March 10 and 11, 1936* (Washington, D.C.: Government Printing Office, 1936), 4.

49. *Thirty-third Biennial Report of the California Fish and Game Commission, 1932–1934*, 50–51; "Additional Permits Send Sardine Plants into 1935 at Full Speed," *Pacific Fisherman*, January 1935, 47; N. B. Scofield, "Report of the Bureau of Commercial Fisheries," *Thirty-fourth Biennial Report of the California Fish and Game Commission, 1934–1936*, 41; Payne, "Unheeded Warnings," 188.

50. Quoted in McEvoy, *Fisherman's Problem*, 142.

51. N. B. Scofield, "Report of the Bureau of Commercial Fisheries," *Thirty-fourth Biennial Report of the California Fish and Game Commission, 1934–1936*,

43–44; N. B. Scofield, "Report of the Bureau of Marine Fisheries," *Thirty-fifth Biennial Report of the California Fish and Game Commission, 1936–1938*, 57. For the licensing of the floating plants, see William Denman and Lyman Henry, *A Review of the California Sardine Industry with Incidental Consideration of Its Racketeers, Its Politician Pseudo-Scientists, and Its Misguided Sportsmen Enemies* (San Francisco: n.p., 1936), 7.

52. Statement of Herbert Davis, *Sardine Fisheries*, 23, 26; statement of N. B. Scofield, *Sardine Fisheries*, 32–33.

53. Statement of Argyle Campbell, *Sardine Fisheries*, 35–36, 51–53.

54. Statement of Reginald H. Fiedler, *Sardine Fisheries*, 97; statement of Elmer Higgins, *Sardine Fisheries*, 101–6.

55. McEvoy, *Fisherman's Problem*, 158–66; McEvoy and Scheiber, "Scientists, Entrepreneurs," 396–97. See also John Radovich, "The Collapse of the California Sardine Fishery: What Have We Learned?" in *Resource Management and Environmental Uncertainty: Lessons from Coastal Upwelling Fisheries*, ed. Michael H. Glantz and J. Dana Thompson (New York: Wiley, 1981), 107–36.

56. Statement of Lyman Henry, *Sardine Fisheries*, 36–50, 125–29; statement of William Denman, *Sardine Fisheries*, 85–96; McEvoy, *Fisherman's Problem*, 163–64.

57. Denman and Henry, *A Review of the California Sardine Industry*, 2, 6, 15–16, 26–28.

58. *Twenty-fourth Biennial Report of the Fish and Game Commission, 1914–1916*, 49; McEvoy, *Fisherman's Problem*, 158–59.

59. Will F. Thompson and Elmer Higgins, "Notes from the State Fisheries Laboratory," *California Fish and Game* 6, no. 1 (January 1920): 32.

60. Will F. Thompson, "The Future of the Sardine," *California Fish and Game* 7, no. 1 (January 1921): 39–41; Will F. Thompson, "The Fisheries of California and Their Care," *California Fish and Game* 8, no. 3 (July 1922): 170–75; McEvoy, *Fisherman's Problem*, 159–60; Will F. Thompson, "The Proposed Investigation of the Sardine," *California Fish and Game* 6, no. 1 (January 1920): 10–12. For the impact of climatic events on fisheries, see Taylor, "El Niño and Vanishing Salmon," 437–57.

61. E. C. Scofield and M. J. Lindner, "Preliminary Report on the Early Life History of the California Sardine," *California Fish and Game* 16, no. 1 (January 1930): 120–24.

62. Frances N. Clark, "Dominant Size-Groups and Their Influence in the Fishery for the California Sardine (*Sardina caerulea*)," California Department of Natural Resources, Division of Fish and Game, *Fish Bulletin No. 31* (1931).

63. Eugene C. Scofield, "Early Life History of the California Sardine (*Sardina caerulea*), with Special Reference to Distribution of Eggs and Larvae," California Department of Natural Resources, Division of Fish and Game, *Fish*

Bulletin No. 41 (1934): 7–15, 19; Frances N. Clark, "Maturity of the California Sardine (*Sardina caerulea*), Determined by Ova Diameter Measurements," California Department of Natural Resources, Division of Fish and Game, *Fish Bulletin No. 42* (1934): 5, 41, 48; *Thirty-third Biennial Report of the California Fish and Game Commission, 1932–1934,* 52; J. B. Phillips, "Sizes of California Sardines Caught in Different Areas of the Monterey and San Pedro Regions," California Department of Natural Resources, Division of Fish and Game, *Fish Bulletin No. 50* (1937): 26, 29–30.

64. Frances N. Clark, "Interseasonal and Intraseasonal Changes in Size of the California Sardine (*Sardinops caerulea*)," California Department of Natural Resources, Division of Fish and Game, *Fish Bulletin No. 47* (1936): 27.

65. Frances N. Clark, "Measures of Abundance of the Sardine, *Sardinops caerulea,* in the California Waters," California Department of Natural Resources, Division of Fish and Game, *Fish Bulletin No. 53* (1939); Frances N. Clark, "Can the Supply of Sardines Be Maintained in California Waters?" *California Fish and Game* 25, no. 2 (April 1939): 172–76, quotation on p. 173.

66. W. L. Scofield, "Sardine Oil and Our Troubled Waters," *California Fish and Game* 24, no. 3 (July 1938): 210–23; W. L. Scofield, "Is the Purse Seine an Engine of Destruction?" *California Fish and Game* 25, no. 4 (October 1939): 329; McEvoy, *Fisherman's Problem,* 165.

67. Denman and Henry, *Review of the California Sardine Industry,* 1–4, 6–15, 17–24.

68. "E. S. Lucido—Veteran Monterey Sardine Fisherman," *Pacific Fisherman,* June 1938, 35. For gaining knowledge of nature through work, see White, "'Are You an Environmentalist?'" and *The Organic Machine,* 3–29.

69. *Thirty-third Biennial Report of the California Fish and Game Commission, 1932–1934,* 53; N. B. Scofield, "Report of the Bureau of Commercial Fisheries," *Thirty-fourth Biennial Report of the California Fish and Game Commission, 1934–1936,* 43–44; N. B. Scofield, "Report of the Bureau of Marine Fisheries," *Thirty-fifty Biennial Report of the California Fish and Game Commission, 1936–1938,* 57; McEvoy and Scheiber, "Scientists, Entrepreneurs," 396; Clark, "Can the Supply of Sardines Be Maintained in California Waters?" 172; "1938 Sardine Reduction Permits Reduced More Than 50 Percent," *Pacific Fisherman,* July 1938, 21.

70. "Attack Made on Floaters via Initiative," *Pacific Fisherman,* December 1936, 44; "Calif. Passes Anti-Floater Law," *Pacific Fisherman,* December 1938, 70; *Monterey Peninsula Herald, Sardine Edition No. 4,* 26 February 1939; McEvoy, *Fisherman's Problem,* 150.

71. McEvoy, *Fisherman's Problem,* 181–82; Radovich, "The Collapse of the California Sardine Fishery," 112–14.

72. Joseph E. Taylor III, "Burning the Candle at Both Ends: Historicizing

Overfishing in Oregon's Nineteenth-Century Salmon Fisheries," *Environmental History* 4, no. 1 (January 1999): 70; Taylor, *Making Salmon*, 66–67.

73. Payne, "Unheeded Warnings," 288–89.

74. Greene, "Historical Review," 1.

75. "Booth Warns of Depletion," *Pacific Fisherman*, February 1930, 41; F. E. Booth, "The Sardine Needs a Friend," *Pacific Fisherman*, March 1936, 25; McEvoy, *Fisherman's Problem*, 140. For the passenger pigeon, see Jennifer Price, *Flight Maps: Adventures with Nature in Modern America* (New York: Basic Books, 1999), 1–55.

4   LIFE, LABOR, AND ODORS ON CANNERY ROW

1. Most records and accounts use the term "Italian." Although evidence suggests that the most Italians in Monterey were Sicilian, I use "Sicilian" only when the distinction is clear.

2. Carol Lynn McKibben, *Beyond Cannery Row: Sicilian Women, Immigration, and Community in Monterey, California, 1915–99* (Urbana and Chicago: University of Illinois Press, 2006), 99–107; Robert Enea, "A Brief History of the Santa Rosalia Festival at Monterey," in *Festa Italia, September 6 and 7, 1997* (Monterey, CA: Festa Italia, 1997), 25–31 (copy in the California History Room, Monterey Public Library); "The Story of Santa Rosalia: The Patron Saint of the Mariner," *Game and Gossip*, September 14, 1951, 3, 22–23; Carol McKibben, "Festa Italia in Monterey: A Study of Italian Women Immigrants in Monterey," *Noticias del Puerto de Monterey* 69, no. 1 (October 1998): 2–14.

3. For the unifying effect of labor, see Lizabeth Cohen, *Making a New Deal: Industrial Workers in Chicago, 1919–1939* (New York: Cambridge University Press, 1990), 291–321.

4. "Fish Cutters Go Out on Strike," *Monterey Daily Cypress*, 26 July 1920. See also Walton, *Storied Land*, 206–7.

5. "Japs Stir Up Strife," *Monterey Daily Cypress*, 27 July 1920; "All Is Now Quiet on Cannery Row," *Monterey Daily Cypress*, 30 July 1920.

6. "Permanent Positions for Men and Women," *Monterey Daily Cypress*, 28 July 1920.

7. "Notice to Japanese Fish Cutters," *Monterey Daily Cypress*, 28 July 1920; "Japs Stir Up Strife," *Monterey Daily Cypress*, 27 July 1920.

8. "Workers Must Give In to Association or All Jap Help Will Be Discharged," *Monterey Daily Cypress*, 1 September 1920; "Statement of the Monterey Japanese Association," *Monterey Daily Cypress*, 2 September 1920.

9. "Canneries Closed," *Monterey Daily Cypress*, 2 September 1920; Walton, "Cannery Row," 267–68.

10. W. L. Scofield estimated that 86 percent of the fishermen who supplied

the canneries during the 1920–21 and 1921–22 seasons were Italian or of Italian parentage. Ten percent were Japanese, and 3 percent were Spanish. See Scofield, "Sardine Fishing Methods at Monterey," 17.

11. Ibid., 11, 17–18.

12. "Monterey Sardine Industries to Handle Catches of Boats," *Pacific Fisherman*, January 1932, 29; "Sardine Operations Start Slowly," *Pacific Fisherman*, September 1932, 28; Mangelsdorf, *Steinbeck's Cannery Row*, 24, 52–53, 89, 97–100, 114.

13. Walton, "Cannery Row," 272; Marvin T. Londahl, "Strikes Paralyze Fish Industry," *Monterey Peninsula Herald*, 18 January 1937; "Two Hurt, One Arrested in Inter-Union Squabble Here," *Monterey Peninsula Herald*, 8 June 1938.

14. Londahl, "Strikes Paralyze Fish Industry."

15. Marvin T. Londahl, "Fishermen Sign Contract with Boat Owners Ending Walk Out," *Monterey Peninsula Herald*, 20 January 1937; Marvin T. Londahl, "Sardine Strike May End Tonight," *Monterey Peninsula Herald*, 27 January 1937; Marvin T. Londahl, "Strike Over: Boats Go Out Tonight," *Monterey Peninsula Herald*, 28 January 1937.

16. "Text of Agreement That Settled Cannery Strike," *Monterey Peninsula Herald*, 28 January 1937.

17. "Contract between the Monterey Sardine Industries, Inc. and the AFL Seine and Line Union, 1940," J. B. Phillips Collection.

18. For conflicts between the AFL and CIO during the New Deal, see Melvyn Dubofksy, *The State and Labor in Modern America* (Chapel Hill: University of North Carolina Press, 1994), 107–67.

19. Work Projects Administration, *Monterey Peninsula*, 66–69. This analysis is also based on the 1930 census. See United States Bureau of the Census, *California, Monterey County, 1930 Population Schedule*, Microfilm Publication T626, Roll 179. For women cannery workers, see Carol McKibben, "Monterey's Cannery Women," *The Steinbeck Newsletter, Cannery Row Fiftieth Anniversary Edition* (Fall 1995): 26–28.

20. McKibben, *Beyond Cannery Row*, 42–45.

21. "Charter for New Cannery Union," *Monterey Peninsula Herald*, 17 July 1937; "Monterey Canners Sign Agreement with AFL Union," *Monterey Labor News*, 13 August 1937; "Ask NLRB for Election in Monterey Canneries," *Monterey Labor News*, 13 August 1937; Walton, *Storied Land*, 211.

22. "Central Council Drops Deep Sea Delegate," *Monterey Labor News*, 15 April 1938; "Seine Workers Promised Federation Local," *Monterey Labor News*, 6 May 1938; "AFL Charter for Fishermen Is Installed," *Monterey Labor News*, 20 May 1938.

23. "Two Hurt, One Arrested in Inter-Union Squabble Here"; "'Full House' On Hand for Enea Hearing," *Monterey Peninsula Herald*, 27 June 1938.

24. Walton, "Cannery Row," 272; "Information Collected by CIO Fish Cannery and Reduction Workers Union Local No. 73, Monterey (1937)" and "List of Names Unfair to AFL and Not to Be Employed by Canneries," Box 266/Folder 8, Norman Leonard Papers, Labor Archives and Research Center, San Francisco State University (hereafter Leonard Papers).

25. Jack Anderson to the National Labor Relations Board, 30 July 1937, Box 266/Folder 9, Leonard Papers.

26. Gladstein, Grossman & Margolis to Jack Anderson, 5 August 1937, Box 266/Folder 8, Leonard Papers; "Cannery Union Adds Hundreds to Its Roster," *Monterey Labor News*, 29 October 1937; "Unlimited Hours in Final Cannery Contract," *Monterey Labor News*, 27 August 1937.

27. "Cannery Workers Choose Bargaining Union in Election," *Monterey Labor News*, 10 February 1939; "Monterey Cannery Workers Vote AFL in NLRB Election," *Monterey Labor News*, 17 March 1939; "AFL Cannery Union Given Okeh at Last," *Monterey Labor News*, 13 October 1939; McKibben, *Beyond Cannery Row*, 44.

28. United States Bureau of the Census, *California, Monterey County, 1930 Population Schedule*.

29. Bonnot, "Report on the Relative Merits and Demerits of Purse Seines vs. Lampara Nets in the Taking of Sardines," 125–30.

30. "Fishermen's Union Now Big Factor in Industry," *Monterey Peninsula Herald*, 26 February 1937; Colletto, *The Sardine Fisherman*, 89, 102.

31. "AFL Fishermen Give Up Trip to Bristol Bay," *Monterey Labor News*, 2 June 1939.

32. Marvin T. Londahl, "Fishermen Picket Canneries, Wharf," *Monterey Peninsula Herald*, 30 August 1939.

33. *Del Mar Canning Company v. Joe Lopez "New Madrid," Francisco D'Agui "Cesare Augusta," United Fishermen's Union of the Pacific* (affiliate of the Congress of Industrial Organizations), Monterey Superior Court No. 19,639, filed 20 September 1939. "Cannery Union Strike Halts CIO Fish Haul," *Monterey Labor News*, 29 September 1939; "San Francisco Sardine Operations Held Up by Inter-Union Fight," *Pacific Fisherman*, October 1939, 32–33.

34. "Cannery Strike Moving Closer to End; Talk Wages and Hours," *Monterey Labor News*, 30 August 1940: "Cannery Men Vote on Bargain Agent," *Monterey Labor News*, 6 September 1940; "Settling of Strike Seen," *Monterey Labor News*, 13 September 1940.

35. "Sardine Catch Season Ending," *Monterey Labor News*, 7 February 1940.

36. McKibben, *Beyond Cannery Row*, 38, 41–42.

37. Juanita Lopez, Brian Rutherford, and Alberto Jaramillo, "The Hidden Past of Mexican American Cannery Workers in Monterey," *Sites and Citizens: Cannery Row—A Community Memory*, http://home.csumb.edu/o/olearycecilia/world/

cannery_row/student_reports/Mexican_Report_Group.htm#_ftn16 (accessed November 28, 2006).

38. *Fisherman's Almanac* (1937): 60–64; Colletto, *The Sardine Fisherman*, Addendum, 3.

39. *Polk's Salinas, Monterey, Pacific Grove, and Carmel City Directory, 1937* (San Francisco: R. L. Polk and Co., 1937), and *Polk's Salinas, Monterey, Pacific Grove, and Carmel City Directory, 1941* (San Francisco: R. L. Polk and Co., 1941). For other information on residential patterns, see Charles and Ray Nonella Oral History, 12 June 1983, Album 3, Tape 67, The Cannery Row Oral History Collection, The National Steinbeck Center, Salinas, California; Bonnie Gartshore, "'Papa Vince' Recalls Life in Shacks," *Monterey County Herald*, 6 June 1996; Architectural Resources Group, *Cannery Row Historic Survey*, 31. For ethnic and racial enclaves, see Sarah Deutsch, "Landscape of Enclaves: Race Relations in the West, 1865–1990," in *Under an Open Sky*, 110–31.

40. McKibben, *Beyond Cannery Row*, 65; Peter J. Cutino, *Monterey—A View from Garlic Hill* (Pacific Grove, CA: Boxwood Press, 1996), 5, 100–104.

41. McKibben, *Beyond Cannery Row*, 59–60, 64–67; Cutino, *View from Garlic Hill*, 48–49.

42. Carol McKibben, "Of All the Gifts You Gave Me the Most Important One Is That I Belong. The Sicilians: Chain Migration, Gender, and the Construction of Identity in Monterey, California, 1920–1999" (Ph.D. diss., University of California, Berkeley, 1999), 98–99, 105–6; McKibben, *Beyond Cannery Row*, 48–51, 53–56; Cutino, *View from Garlic Hill*, 110–11.

43. McKibben, "Festa Italia in Monterey," 6; McKibben, *Beyond Cannery Row*, 103, 105.

44. Jacobson, *Whiteness of a Different Color*, 91–98, 110.

45. McKibben, *Beyond Cannery Row*, 42–45.

46. Yamada, *The Japanese of the Monterey Peninsula*, 125–26; *Manaka v. Monterey Sardine Industries, Inc., et al.*, 41 F. Supp. 531 (N.D. Calif. 1941).

47. Frank Manaka Oral History, 23 September 1991, interview conducted by Heihachiro Takarabe, Tape II, Monterey Japanese Oral History Collection, The Bancroft Library, University of California at Berkeley (hereafter MJOHC).

48. Ibid.

49. Ibid.; Yamada, *The Japanese of the Monterey Peninsula*, 126.

50. Frank Manaka Oral History, Tapes I and II; Royal and Hiro Manaka Oral History, 2 September 1993, interview conducted by David Yamada, MJOHC.

51. "Workers Must Give In to Association or All Jap Help Will Be Discharged," *Monterey Daily Cypress*, 1 September 1920. It is safe to assume that Monterey's Filipino population was mostly male, as the total U.S. Filipino population in 1930 was only 6.5 percent female. See Takaki, *Strangers from a Different Shore*, 58.

52. "Chambers Talk Race Situation," *The Grove at High Tide*, 22 August 1930.

53. "Joint Chambers Decide on Action in Filipino Issue," *The Grove at High Tide*, no. 29 (August 1930); K. Hovden Company, *The History of Portola*, 18.

54. "Chambers Talk Race Situation"; "Joint Chambers Decide on Action in Filipino Issue."

55. "Local Sardine Plants Employ Few Filipinos," *Monterey Peninsula Herald*, 17 September 1930.

56. Ordinance No. 106 C.S., 2 January 1918, Ordinance Book 2, Monterey City Clerk's Office; H. D. Severance, "Control of Cannery Odors at Monterey," *Sewage Works Journal* 4, no. 1 (January 1932): 152–53.

57. Charles Gilman Hyde, "Outline of an Investigation of Various Factors Affecting the Interests of the Del Monte Property Company, October 1925," Box 3/Folder 28, Charles Gilman Hyde Papers, The Water Resources Center Archives, University of California, Berkeley.

58. Ibid., 3–9.

59. Ibid., 5.

60. "Morse Deplores Effect of Fish Odors on Realtors," *Monterey Daily Herald*, 7 October 1926; "Expert to Be Brought Here Immediately for Study of Odor Trouble," *Monterey Daily Herald*, 8 October 1926.

61. Marvin T. Londahl, "Issuance of Warrant for Firm Heads Is Probable," *Monterey Peninsula Daily Herald*, 25 October 1928.

62. "Fish Stench Drives Many Away, Think Hotel Heads," *Monterey Peninsula Herald*, 14 October 1929.

63. Ordinance No. 296 C.S., 22 October 1929, Ordinance Book 3; Ordinance No. 297 C.S., 19 November 1929, Ordinance Book 3, Monterey City Clerk's Office.

64. Ordinance No. 337, 7 July 1931, Ordinance Book 3, Monterey City Clerk's Office. The fine was a maximum of five hundred dollars, and the prison term was a maximum of six months.

65. Severance, "Control of Cannery Odors," 154–55; "Interesting Solution of Reduction Problems by F. E. Booth Co.," *Pacific Fisherman*, June 1928, 21–22.

66. *Del Monte Properties Co. v. F. E. Booth Company, Bay View Packing Company, California Packing Corporation, Carmel Canning Company, Custom House Packing Corporation, Del Mar Canning Corporation, E. B. Gross Canning Company, K. Hovden Company, Monterey Canning Company, San Carlos Canning Company, San Xavier Fish Packing Company, Sea Pride Packing Corporation, First Doe Corporation, Second Doe Corporation,* Monterey Superior Court, No. 14568, 6 February 1934.

67. Ibid.

68. Michael Berkowitz, "A 'New Deal' for Leisure: Making Mass Tourism during the Great Depression," in *Being Elsewhere: Tourism, Consumer Culture, and Identity in Modern Europe and North America*, ed. Shelley Baranowski and

Ellen Furlough (Ann Arbor: University of Michigan Press, 2001), 185–212. See also Aron, *Working at Play*, 237–57.

69. *Del Monte Properties Co. v. F. E. Booth et al.*

70. For population statistics, see Work Projects Administration, *Monterey Peninsula*, 190. I compiled the data on cannery workers and fishermen through an analysis of the United States Bureau of the Census, *California, Monterey County, 1930 Population Schedule*. I exclude Japanese abalone fishermen and market fishermen, and I include employees of the local can factory.

71. "Cannery Payroll Near Million," *Monterey Peninsula Herald Sardine Edition No. 2*, February 26, 1937.

72. *Del Monte Properties Co. v. F. E. Booth et al.*

73. Ibid.

74. For Booth, Hovden, and the San Carlos cannery, established by Pietro Ferrante, Angelo Lucido, and Orazio Enea in 1926, see Mangelsdorf, *Steinbeck's Cannery Row*, 24–26, 56. For the California Packing Corporation, see Dean Witter and Co., *California Packing Corporation: A Study of Impressive Progress* (San Francisco: Dean Witter and Co., 1950).

75. *Del Monte Properties Co. v. F. E. Booth et. al.*

76. Ibid.; "Odor Suit Ends in Compromise," *Monterey Peninsula Herald*, 6 February 1934.

77. For odor abatement, see "Believe Monterey Plant Odor Problem Solved by New Installations," *Pacific Fisherman*, October 1934, 63.

78. "News Comments," *Monterey Peninsula Herald*, 11 October 1934.

79. "Two Canneries Face Superior Court Hearing on Odor Decree Violation," *Monterey Peninsula Herald*, 21 November 1934; Mangelsdorf, *Steinbeck's Cannery Row*, 101.

80. "Canners Promise to Cooperate for Odor Elimination," *Monterey Peninsula Herald*, 5 January 1935.

81. "Cannery Payroll Poor Argument for Problems to City, Says Gilmer," *Pacific Grove Tribune*, 11 January 1935 (manuscript transcribed by WPA workers from original newspaper), in Work Projects Administration, Historical Survey of the Monterey Peninsula, File 28, 1937, California History Room, Monterey Public Library.

82. Ordinance No. 416 C.S., May 20, 1935, Ordinance Book 3, Monterey City Clerk's Office.

83. "Inspector Sees Real Progress in Odor Fight," *Monterey Peninsula Herald*, 26 February 1936.

84. "Attitude of Monterey Is Condemned," *Monterey Peninsula Herald*, 7 February 1936; "Resident Departs Because of Odor," *Pacific Grove Tide*, 16 October 1936.

85. "City May File Suit to Abate Cannery Odors as Plants Run at Capacity," *Pacific Grove Tide*, 25 September 1936; "Mayor Gilmer Instructs Attorney to Bring Suit to Abate Cannery Odors," *Pacific Grove Tide*, 20 November 1936; "Gilmer Orders Fish Odor Suit against Monterey," *Monterey Trader*, 20 November 1936; "'Drop Odor Suit,' Plea of Citizens," *Monterey Peninsula Herald*, 15 March 1937.

86. Contract between Monterey Canneries and the City of Monterey, December 15, 1937, Box F3735:707, Administrative and Subject Files, CDNR–DFG–BMF; "Anti-Pollution Program Features Preparation for Season at Monterey," *Pacific Fisherman*, August 1938, 24.

87. "Old Problem of Odor Now Solved, Hope," *Monterey Peninsula Herald*, 26 February 1937; "No More Fish Odor for P.G. Says Monterey," *Monterey Peninsula Herald*, 20 March 1938.

88. "Morse Protests Cannery Odors," *Monterey Peninsula Herald*, 29 November 1939.

89. "Renew Lease or We Quit, Booth Threat," *Monterey Peninsula Herald*, 6 March 1940; Marvin T. Londahl, "Booth Sardine Plant Must Be Removed," *Monterey Peninsula Herald*, 5 March 1941; Mangelsdorf, *Steinbeck's Cannery Row*, 136–37.

90. Quoted in Elmer Lagorio, "The Big Stink!" *The (Monterey) Herald Weekend Magazine*, 28 February 1988.

91. For the larger social and political implications of odors, see Alain Corbin, *The Foul and the Fragrant: Odor and the French Social Imagination* (Cambridge, MA: Harvard University Press, 1986); Andrew Hurley, "Busby's Stink Boat and the Regulation of Nuisance Trades, 1865–1918," in *Common Fields: An Environmental History of St. Louis*, ed. Andrew Hurley (St. Louis: Missouri Historical Society Press, 1997), 145–62; Christine Meisner Rosen, "Noisome, Noxious, and Offensive Vapors, Fumes and Stenches in American Towns and Cities, 1840–1865," *Historical Geography* 25 (1997): 49–82.

92. "May 'Fishermen's Luck' Mean Good Luck at Monterey," *Monterey Peninsula Herald*, 23 February 1940.

5   BOOM AND BUST IN WARTIME MONTEREY

1. For the impact of World War II on the American West and California, see Gerald D. Nash, *The American West Transformed: The Impact of the Second World War* (Lincoln: University of Nebraska Press, 1985), and Roger Lotchin, ed., *The Way We Really Were: The Golden State in the Second Great War* (Urbana and Chicago: University of Illinois Press, 2000).

2. Edgar C. Smith, "The Hotel Del Monte Goes to War," *Dogtown Territorial Quarterly* 49 (2002): 46–58.

3. Frances N. Clark, "Review of the California Sardine Fishery," *California Fish and Game* 38, no. 3 (July 1952): 370–71.

4. "Monterey Sardine Season Closes: Industry Faces Boat Problem," *Pacific Fisherman*, March 1942, 23; McEvoy, *Fisherman's Problem*, 150–53. For the Lend-Lease program, see Warren F. Kimball, *The Most Unsordid Act: Lend-Lease, 1939–1941* (Baltimore: The Johns Hopkins University Press, 1969).

5. Executive Order 9204, Coordination of Federal Activities Affecting the Fishery Industry, 21 July 1942, Box 6, United States Fish and Wildlife Service, Record Group 22, National Archives and Records Administration, Pacific Region, San Bruno, California (hereafter RG22, NARA–PR).

6. J. A. Folger to All Members of the Sardine Industry, 17 October 1942, Box 8, RG22, NARA–PR; Richard Van Cleve, "Sardine Allocation Problems," *Pacific Fisherman*, November 1942, 17; Richard Van Cleve, "Report of the Bureau of Marine Fisheries," *Thirty-eighth Biennial Report of the California Fish and Game Commission, 1942–1944*, 36; McEvoy, *Fisherman's Problem*, 174.

7. John M. Dennis, *Monterey's Cannery Row: A Brief Survey, June 4, 1945* (Stockton, CA: the author, 1945), 24–25, 40 (copy in the California History Room, Monterey Public Library); Colletto, *The Sardine Fisherman*, 206, 229; "The Sardine Problem from the Southern Viewpoint," *Pacific Fisherman*, February 1943, 16. For the allocation percentages for each Monterey plant, see "Fish Allocation Plan as Adopted by Monterey Fish Processors Association, October 13, 1942," Box 5, RG22, NARA–PR.

8. John Crivello to Harold Ickes, 7 December 1944 (copy of Western Union telegram), Box 14, RG22, NARA–PR.

9. "Historical Account of the Effect of World War II on the Fisheries of the Monterey Region," 6, Administration and Subject Files, War, 1941–42, Box F3735:766, CDNR–DFG–BMF.

10. Colletto, *The Sardine Fisherman*, 192, 204–5, 208, 239–44. See also "California Sardine Packers Seek Aid in Rebuilding Fleet," *Pacific Fisherman*, March 1942, 25.

11. Colletto, *The Sardine Fisherman*, 206, 229; Dennis, *Monterey's Cannery Row*, 24–25; "Fishing Resumed at Monterey," *Salinas Labor News*, 16 January 1942; "Historical Account of the Effect of World War II," 14–15.

12. "Sardine Pack Halted by War Boom Again," *Monterey Labor News*, 19 December 1941; "California Sardine Industry Adjusts Self to Wartime Restrictions," *Pacific Fisherman*, January 1942, 21.

13. Lydon, *The Japanese in the Monterey Bay Region*, 100–101; Mangelsdorf, *Steinbeck's Cannery Row*, 145; "Historical Account of the Effect of World War II," 3–6; Richard Van Cleve, "Report of the Bureau of Marine Fisheries," *Thirty-seventh Biennial Report of the California Fish and Game Commission, 1940–1942*, 47.

14. "Monterey Hook and Line Fishing Fleet Hard Hit by the War," *Monterey Peninsula Herald, Sardine Edition No. 7*, 27 February 1942.

15. United States Bureau of the Census, *Sixteenth Census of the United States, 1940, Population, Vol. 2, Characteristics of the Population* (Washington, D.C.: Government Printing Office, 1942–1943), 566, 568, 600.

16. "Historical Account of the Effect of World War II," 5, 13.

17. "Monterey Hook and Line Fishing Fleet Hard Hit by the War"; "Historical Account of the Effect of World War II," 5.

18. Quoted in Yamada, *The Japanese of the Monterey Peninsula*, 139; "Historical Account of the Effect of World War II," 10.

19. McKibben, *Beyond Cannery Row*, 75–97. See also Gary R. Mormino and George E. Pozzetta, "Ethnics at War: Italian Americans in California during World War II," in Lotchin, ed., *The Way We Really Were*, 143–63; Lawrence DiStasi, ed., *Una Storia Segreta: The Secret History of Italian American Evacuation and Internment During World War II* (Berkeley, CA: Heyday Books, 2001).

20. McKibben, *Beyond Cannery Row*, 87–94; Cutino, *View from Garlic Hill*, 17–18; "Monterey Fish Folks Buy Bonds," *Pacific Fisherman*, January 1943, 43. See also Guglielmo, *White on Arrival*, 172–76.

21. Yamada, *The Japanese of the Monterey Peninsula*, 138, 165. For the Japanese internment, see Roger Daniels, *Concentration Camps USA: Japanese Americans and World War II* (New York: Holt, Rinehart, and Winston, 1972).

22. Yamada, *The Japanese of the Monterey Peninsula*, 153, 115; Lydon, *The Japanese in the Monterey Bay Region*, 98–121.

23. "Fisheries School Advocated," *Monterey Peninsula Herald, Sardine Edition No. 7*, 27 February 1942.

24. "Sardine Labor Deferment Requested by Coordinator," *Pacific Fisherman*, January 1943, 14.

25. Memorandum for Area Coordinators, 26 May 1944, Box 2, RG22, NARA–PR.

26. Kenneth Mosher to State Director of Selective Services, 10 April 1944, Box 1, RG22, NARA–PR.

27. Horace Mercurio to K. H. Mosher, 14 April 1944, Box 2, RG22, NARA–PR.

28. Elmer Higgins to K. H. Mosher, 6 May 1944, Box 2, RG22, NARA–PR; Kenneth Mosher to State Director of Selective Services, 10 April 1944, Box 1, RG22, NARA–PR.

29. "AFL Fishermen's Union Seeks Essential Rating," *Monterey Peninsula Herald, Sardine Edition No. 8*, 26 February 1943.

30. "Historical Account of the Effect of World War II," 13; Dennis, *Monterey's Cannery Row*, 37.

31. Elmer Higgins to K. H. Mosher, 6 May 1944, Box 2, RG22, NARA–PR; Dennis, *Monterey's Cannery Row*, 27.

32. Dorothy Stephenson, "Labor Supply Will Be Major Problem for Sardine Plants," *Monterey Peninsula Herald, Sardine Edition No. 8,* 26 February 1943; "Along Cannery Row," *Monterey County Labor News,* 1 October 1943.

33. Dorothy Stephenson; "There's Poetry in Fish—If You Doubt It, Ask the Women," *Monterey Peninsula Herald, Sardine Edition No. 8,* 26 February 1943. For working women during World War II, see Karen Anderson, *Wartime Women: Sex Roles, Family Relations, and the Status of Women during World War II* (Westport, CT: Greenwood Press, 1981).

34. Dennis, *Monterey's Cannery Row,* 37.

35. Stephenson, "There's Poetry in Fish"; Dennis, *Monterey's Cannery Row,* 30.

36. "Work Permit System for Fish Canners Stirs Controversy," *Monterey County Labor News,* 10 December 1943.

37. "Monterey Sardine Season Closes; Industry Faces Boat Problem." See also Decision of William Denman, Arbiter, In the Matter of Arbitration Proceedings between Seine and Line Fishermen's Union of Monterey and International Fishermen and Allied Workers Union, 14 September 1942, Box 14, RG22, NARA–PR.

38. "AFL Fishermen Lose Dispute with CIO Group," *Monterey County Labor News,* 18 September 1942; "Sardine Industries Unique Group," *Monterey Peninsula Herald, Sardine Edition No. 8,* 26 February 1943.

39. "WLB Officials Says No to Fish Cannery Workers Wage Increase Requests," *Monterey County Labor News,* 3 December 1943.

40. "'Season Bonus' Plan Adopted in Canneries," *Pacific Fisherman,* September 1944, 27; "Bonus System," *Monterey County Labor News,* 11 August 1944; Dennis, *Monterey's Cannery Row,* 33–34.

41. "Fishing Resumed at Monterey," *Salinas Labor News,* 16 January 1942; "Monterey Is the Brightest Spot in California Sardine Picture," *Pacific Fisherman,* March 1944, 25.

42. Richard Van Cleve, "Report of the Bureau of Marine Fisheries," *Thirty-seventh Biennial Report of the California Fish and Game Commission, 1940–1942,* 48.

43. Dennis, *Monterey's Cannery Row,* 37.

44. "Monterey Sardine Season Closes; Industry Faces Boat Problem"; Clark, "Review of the California Sardine Fishery," 371.

45. "Sardine Output Lags," *Pacific Fisherman,* January 1943, 13–14; "Sardine Industry Wrestles with Production Problems to Attain War Requirement," *Pacific Fisherman,* December 1942, 15. For the 1942–43 season, see Confidential Report No. 2, "Recent Developments in the California Sardine Fishery," 10 November 1942, Box 5, RG22, NARA–PR.

46. "All Sardines Sent to Canning Plants," *Pacific Fisherman*, February 1943, 15; Richard Van Cleve, "Report of the Bureau of Marine Fisheries," *Thirty-eighth Biennial Report of the California Fish and Game Commission, 1942–1944*, 35–36.

47. Harold L. Ickes, "The Nation Turns to Its Fisheries," *Pacific Fisherman*, January 1943, 13.

48. Rothman, *Saving the Planet*, 82.

49. "Monterey Is the Brightest Spot in California Sardine Picture"; "Adding-Up the Score of 1943–44 California Sardine Season," *Pacific Fisherman*, April 1944, 25.

50. "Record Fishing: October Sardine Catches Greatest in History," *Pacific Fisherman*, November 1944, 33; "California Sardine Pack at Peak," *Pacific Fisherman*, December 1944, 33.

51. "More Sardines Needed," *Pacific Fisherman*, April 1945, 36; "Something to Shoot At," *Pacific Fisherman*, August 1945, 41.

52. Architectural Resources Group, *Cannery Row Historic Survey*; Mangelsdorf, *Steinbeck's Cannery Row*.

53. In 1938 the Bureau of Marine Fisheries replaced the Department/Bureau of Commercial Fisheries and continued to conduct fisheries research. See "Report of the Bureau of Marine Fisheries," *Thirty-ninth Biennial Report of the California Fish and Game Commission, 1944–1946*, 21.

54. Richard Van Cleve, "Report of the Bureau of Marine Fisheries," *Thirty-seventh Biennial Report of the California Fish and Game Commission, 1940–1942*, 53; "Report of the Bureau of Marine Fisheries," *Thirty-eighth Biennial Report of the California Fish and Game Commission, 1942–1944*, 36–37; McEvoy, *Fisherman's Problem*, 166.

55. Clark, "Review of the California Sardine Fishery," 371.

56. Takaki, *Strangers from a Different Shore*, 405.

57. "Organization to Discourage Return of Japanese to the Pacific Coast," *Monterey Peninsula Herald*, 23 April 1945; "The Democratic Way of Life for All," *Monterey Peninsula Herald*, 11 May 1945; "Letter Box," *Monterey Peninsula Herald*, 3 September 1945. See also "Monterey Rallies—and Intolerance Bows," *Christian Science Monitor*, 21 January 1946.

58. "Citizen-Japanese May Fish," *Pacific Fisherman*, February 1945, 48.

59. "State Alien Law Is Overruled," *Monterey Peninsula Herald*, 8 June 1948; Lydon, *The Japanese in the Monterey Bay Region*, 120–21.

60. "News Comments" and "Incident at Del Mar Is Ironed Out," *Monterey Peninsula Herald*, 11 September 1945.

61. "Leaders of Union Take Firm Stand," *Monterey Peninsula Herald*, 13 September 1945; "Fish Canners Hit Row on Discrimination," *Monterey County Labor News*, 21 September 1945.

62. "Sardine Fleet Abandons Northern Fishery," *Pacific Fisherman*, December 1946, 21; "What Caused Sardine Failure?" *Pacific Fisherman*, January 1947, 37; "Fishing Fleet Leaves; Season Is Poorest Yet," *Monterey County Labor News*, 22 November 1946; "Fish Canners Meet Feb. 17; Poor Season," *Monterey County Labor News*, 31 January 1947.

63. Clark, "Review of the California Sardine Fishery," 371.

64. Colletto, *The Sardine Fisherman*, 393.

65. W. L. Scofield, "Squid at Monterey," *California Fish and Game* 10, no. 4 (October 1924): 176–82; Ralph F. Classic, "Monterey Squid Fishery," *California Fish and Game* 15, no. 4 (October 1929): 317–20; W. Gordon Fields, "A Preliminary Report on the Fishery and on the Biology of the Squid, *Loligo Opalescens*," *California Fish and Game* 36, no. 4 (October 1950): 368–69. Wing Chong also owned a general merchandise store along Cannery Row and was the purported inspiration for the Lee Chong character in John Steinbeck's *Cannery Row*.

66. "Disastrous Season Fails to Dampen Optimism of Industry Here," *Monterey Peninsula Herald, Sardine Edition No. 12*, 7 March 1947; "Squid," *Pacific Fisherman*, April 1946, 79; "Report of the Bureau of Marine Fisheries," *Thirty-ninth Biennial Report of the California Fish and Game Commission, 1944–1946*, 22.

67. Fields, "A Preliminary Report on the Fishery and on the Biology of the Squid," 370.

68. McEvoy, *Fisherman's Problem*, 153–55.

69. Jimmy Costello, "Industry Weathers Crisis of Second Bad Year," *Monterey Peninsula Herald, Sardine Edition No. 13*, 3 April 1948; George Clemens, "Canners Went South for Fish," *Monterey Peninsula Herald, Sardine Edition No. 13*, 3 April 1948; "What Caused Sardine Failure?"; "Sardine Trucking," *Pacific Fisherman*, December 1947, 53, 55; "State Has New Sardine Control Law Up Its Sleeve," *Pacific Fisherman*, January 1948, 25. For air reconnaissance, see "Blimp Spots Fish," *Pacific Fisherman*, February 1944, 19.

70. "Approximately 2,500 Cannery Union Workers Signed Here," *Monterey Peninsula Herald, Sardine Edition No. 14*, 4 February 1949.

71. "Monterey Fishermen Averaged Only $800," *Monterey Peninsula Herald, Sardine Edition No. 12*, 7 March 1947.

72. "Fishermen's Benefits Set for Hearing," *Monterey Peninsula Herald*, 16 February 1949; "AFL Fishermen Seek Benefits," *Monterey County Labor News*, 22 February 1949.

73. Phyllis Rasmussen, "Summary on Monterey Office #027, July 12 through August 4, 1950," 14, Reports–Local Offices, Marysville–Napa, 1949–1950, Box 34/Folder 25, Department of Employment, Public Employment Office of Benefit Payments–Claims Review Unit, California State Archives, Sacramento, California.

74. "Monterey Fishermen Lose Out Before Unemployment Board," *Monterey Peninsula Herald*, 31 December 1953.

75. "Mayor of Monterey Has Plenty of Faith in Sardine Industry," *Monterey Peninsula Herald, Sardine Edition No. 12*, 7 March 1947.

76. Frank E. Raiter to Division of Fish and Game, 5 December 1947, Administrative and Subject Files, Sardine Advisory Committee, 1947–June 1948, Box F3735: 734, CDNR–DFG–BMF.

77. Colletto, *The Sardine Fisherman*, 394, 396.

78. "1946–47 Season Was One of Conjecture," *Monterey Peninsula Herald, Sardine Edition No. 12*, 7 March 1947.

79. "Custom House Packers Will Make $25,000 in Improvements," *Monterey Peninsula Herald, Sardine Edition No. 12*, 7 March 1947.

80. "Oxnard Canners Constructing New 10-Ton Reduction Plant," *Monterey Peninsula Herald, Sardine Edition No. 11*, 12 March 1946.

81. Knut Hovden to California Fish and Game Commission, 28 November 1947, Administrative and Subject Files, Sardine Advisory Committee, 1947–June 1948, Box F3735:734, CDNR–DFG–BMF.

82. Knut Hovden to Mr. Leard, 16 April 1948, Administrative and Subject Files, Sardine Advisory Committee, 1947–June 1948, Box F3735:734, CDNR–DFG–BMF.

83. "Pioneer Spirit Is Strong in K. Hovden," *Monterey Peninsula Herald, Sardine Edition No. 12*, 7 March 1947; Knut Hovden, "Hovden Links Ammunition Dumping with Sardine Disappearance," *Monterey Peninsula Herald, Sardine Edition No. 14*, 4 February 1949.

84. Knut Hovden to Mr. Leard, 16 April 1948; Clemens, "Canners Went South for Fish."

85. "How an 'Average Purse Seiner' Fared," *Monterey Peninsula Herald, Sardine Edition No. 13*, 3 April 1948. Southern California fishermen also rejected overfishing. See Paul G. Pinsky and Wayne Ball, *The California Sardine Fishery: Review and Analysis of the Biological, Statistical and Environmental Information about the California Sardine* (San Pedro: n.p., 1948).

86. For "knowing" nature through labor, see White, "'Are You an Environmentalist?'" and *The Organic Machine*, 3–29.

87. "What Caused Sardine Failure?"; "Sardine Failures Blamed upon Poor Spawnings, Heavy Fishing," *Pacific Fisherman*, October 1947, 65–67; "Report of the Bureau of Marine Fisheries," *Fortieth Biennial Report of the California Fish and Game Commission, 1946–1948*, 22–23; Clark, "Review of the California Sardine Fishery," 374.

88. John F. Janssen Jr., "First Report of Sardine Tagging in California," *California Fish and Game 23*, no. 3 (July 1937), 190–204.

89. Frances N. Clark and John F. Janssen Jr., "Movements and Abundance

of the Sardine as Measured by Tag Returns," California Department of Natural Resources, Division of Fish and Game, *Fish Bulletin No. 61* (1945).

90. "Sardine Failures Blamed upon Poor Spawnings, Heavy Fishing."

91. "150,000-Ton Quota," *Pacific Fisherman*, December 1947, 17.

92. "100,000-Ton Sardine Quota Set; Industry Offers 6-Point Program," *Pacific Fisherman*, June 1948, 26; "Report of the Bureau of Marine Fisheries," *Fortieth Biennial Report of the California Fish and Game Commission, 1946–1948*, 23–24.

93. "Specialty Sardine Season Abolished by New Law," *Pacific Fisherman*, July 1949, 31.

94. Richard Astro, *John Steinbeck and Edward F. Ricketts: The Shaping of a Novelist* (Minneapolis: University of Minnesota Press, 1973), 3–25; Joel W. Hedgpeth, "Ed Ricketts (1897–1948) Marine Biologist," *The Steinbeck Newsletter, Cannery Row Fiftieth Anniversary Edition* 9, no. 1 (Fall 1995): 17–18. For descriptions of the friendship, see Jackson J. Benson, *The True Adventures of John Steinbeck, Writer* (New York: Viking Press, 1984), 183–99; Jay Parini, *John Steinbeck: A Biography* (London: Heinemann, 1994), 130–41; John Steinbeck, "About Ed Ricketts," in *The Log from the Sea of Cortez* (New York: Viking Press, 1951; repr., New York: Penguin Books, 1995), 225–74.

95. Susan Shillinglaw, introduction to *Cannery Row*, by John Steinbeck (New York: Viking Press, 1945; repr., New York: Penguin Books, 1994), x–xi.

96. For Warder Clyde Allee, see Warder Clyde Allee, *Animal Aggregations: A Study in General Sociology* (Chicago: University of Chicago Press, 1931); *Animal Life and Social Growth* (Baltimore: The Williams and Wilkins Company and Associates in cooperation with the Century of Progress Exposition, 1932); *The Social Life of Animals* (New York: W. W. Norton and Company, 1938). For Allee and the cooperative model for the animal world, see Gregg Mitman, *The State of Nature: Ecology, Community, and American Social Thought, 1900–1950* (Chicago: University of Chicago Press, 1992).

97. John E. McCosker, "Ed Ricketts: A Role Model for Marine Biologists," *The Steinbeck Newsletter, Cannery Row Fiftieth Anniversary Edition*, Fall 1995, 12–14; Joel W. Hedgpeth, "Philosophy on Cannery Row," in *Steinbeck: The Man and His Work*, ed. Richard Astro and Testumaro Hayashi (Corvallis: Oregon State University Press, 1971), 89–129; Astro, *John Steinbeck and Edward F. Ricketts*, 7–12; Edward F. Ricketts and Jack Calvin, *Between Pacific Tides: An Account of the Habits and Habitats of Some Five Hundred of the Common, Conspicuous Seashore Invertebrates of the Pacific Coast between Sitka, Alaska and Northern Mexico* (Stanford: Stanford University Press, 1939).

98. John Steinbeck and Edward F. Ricketts, *Sea of Cortez: A Leisurely Journal of Travel and Research* (New York: Viking Press, 1941). For a description of the journey, see Astro, *John Steinbeck and Edward F. Ricketts*, 12–19; Ben-

son, *True Adventures of John Steinbeck*, 435–47, 477–83; Parini, *John Steinbeck*, 291–97.

99. Edward F. Ricketts, "Scientists Report on Sardine Supply," *Monterey Peninsula Herald, Sardine Edition No. 13*, 3 April 1948.

100. Ed Ricketts to Ritch Lovejoy, 22 October 1946, Box 9/Folder 36, and Ed Ricketts to Joseph Campbell, 25 October 1946, Box 9/Folder 17, Edward F. Ricketts Papers, Special Collections, Stanford University Libraries (hereafter Ricketts Papers).

101. Ricketts, "Scientists Report on Sardine Supply."

102. Manuscript editorial for the *Monterey Peninsula Herald*, 4 December 1946, Box 10/Folder 5, Ricketts Papers.

103. Edward F. Ricketts, "Science Studies the Sardine," *Monterey Peninsula Herald, Sardine Edition No. 12*, 7 March 1947.

104. Astro, *True Adventures of John Steinbeck*, 24–30; McCosker, "Ed Ricketts: A Role Model," 14.

105. Clark, "Review of the California Sardine Fishery," 371.

106. Rothman, *Saving the Planet*, 90–92, 95.

107. McEvoy and Scheiber, "Scientists, Entrepreneurs," 394–99; McEvoy, *Fisherman's Problem*, 191. The decimation of the bison and the Dust Bowl spawned similar debates about their root causes. See Andrew Isenberg, *The Destruction of the Bison: An Environmental History, 1750–1920* (New York: Cambridge University Press, 2000), and Donald Worster, *Dust Bowl: The Southern Plains in the 1930s* (New York: Oxford University Press, 1979).

108. McEvoy and Scheiber, "Scientists, Entrepreneurs," 400–401; McEvoy, *Fisherman's Problem*, 1, 193–94. See also "Report of Bureau of Marine Fisheries," *Fortieth Biennial Report of the California Fish and Game Commission, 1946–1948*, 23; California Cooperative Oceanic Fisheries Investigations (hereafter CalCOFI), *Progress Report, 1 July 1952 to 30 June 1953* (Sacramento: State of California, Department of Fish and Game, Marine Research Committee, 1953), 7.

109. McEvoy, *Fisherman's Problem*, 194, 199–200; California Cooperative Sardine Research Program, *Progress Report 1950* (Sacramento: State of California, Department of Natural Resources, Marine Research Committee, 1950), 7–8; CalCOFI, *Progress Report, 1 July 1953 to 31 March 1955* (Sacramento: State of California, Department of Fish and Game, Marine Research Committee, 1955), 7–8.

110. California Cooperative Sardine Research Program, *Progress Report 1950*, 7; McEvoy, *Fisherman's Problem*, 194, 199–200.

111. "Monterey Fights," *Pacific Fisherman*, November 1951, 19.

112. Wilbert Chapman to Vern O. Knudsen, 22 October 1947, Box 11, Wilbert McLeod Chapman Papers, Special Collections, Manuscripts, and University Archives, University of Washington Libraries (hereafter Chapman Papers).

113. Radovich, "The Collapse of the California Sardine Fishery," 118. The other members of the MRC were the chairman of the California Fish and Game Commission, the executive officer of the California Division of Fish and Game, another person from the division, and the director of the California Academy of Sciences.

114. "What to Do about Sardines?" *Pacific Fisherman*, January 1952, 11–12.

115. California Cooperative Sardine Research Program, *Progress Report, 1 January 1951 to 30 June 1952* (Sacramento: State of California, Department of Fish and Game, Marine Research Committee, 1952), 5, 9, 45.

116. CalCOFI, *Progress Report, 1 July 1952 to 30 June 1953*, 5, 7; CalCOFI, *Progress Report, 1 July 1953 to 31 March 1955*, 7.

117. Clark, "Review of the California Sardine Fishery," 374, 378–79; "Sardine Outlook Cloudy, with No Silver Shining Through," *Pacific Fisherman*, October 1953, 15–16; Richard S. Croker, "Loss of California's Sardine Fishery May Become Permanent," *Outdoor California* 15, no. 1 (January 1954): 1, 6, 8.

118. "Sardine Outlook Cloudy"; McEvoy, *Fisherman's Problem*, 201.

119. Frances N. Clark and John C. Marr, "Population Dynamics of the Pacific Sardine," in CalCOFI, *Progress Report, 1 July 1953 to 31 March 1955*, 23–25, 31, 38; McEvoy, *The Fisherman's Problem*, 201.

120. Wilbert Chapman to Carl L. Hubbs, 30 April 1948, Box 11, Chapman Papers.

121. CalCOFI, *Reports, 1 July 1959 to 30 June 1960* (Sacramento: State of California, Department of Fish and Game, Marine Research Committee, 1961), 6–7.

122. Garth I. Murphy, "Oceanography and Variation in the Pacific Sardine Population," in CalCOFI, *Reports, 1 July 1959 to 30 June 1960*, 57–59; California Cooperative Sardine Research Program, *Progress Report 1950*, 23–25, 39–40.

123. CalCOFI, *Reports, 1 July 1959 to 30 June 1960*, 6; CalCOFI, *Reports, 1 July 1960 to 30 June 1962* (Sacramento: State of California, Department of Fish and Game, Marine Research Committee, 1963), 5–6; Radovich, "The Collapse of the Sardine Fishery," 124–30.

124. CalCOFI, *Reports, Volume XI, 1 July 1963 and 30 June 1966* (Sacramento: State of California, Department of Fish and Game, Marine Research Committee, 1967), 5–9.

125. McEvoy and Scheiber, "Scientists, Entrepreneurs," 402–6; McEvoy, *Fisherman's Problem*, 200–203; Wesley Marx, "Dr. Frances Clark: A California Pioneer in Marine Conservation," *J. B. Phillips Historical Fisheries Report* 2, no. 1 (Spring 2001): 30–33.

126. CalCOFI, *Report, Volume XIII, 1 July 1967 to 30 June 1968* (Sacramento: State of California, Department of Fish and Game, Marine Research Com-

mittee, 1969), 11; McEvoy, *Fisherman's Problem*, 226–29. For the rise of post-war environmentalism, see Samuel P. Hays, *Beauty, Health, and Permanence: Environmental Politics in the United States, 1955–1985* (New York: Cambridge University Press, 1987); Theodore Steinberg, *Down to Earth: Nature's Role in American History* (New York: Oxford University Press, 2002), 239–61.

127. CalCOFI, *Reports, Volume XVIII, 1 July 1973 to 30 June 1975* (Sacramento: State of California, Department of Fish and Game, Marine Research Committee, 1976), 20–21; CalCOFI, *Volume XII, 1 July 1966 to 30 June 1967* (Sacramento: State of California, Department of Fish and Game, Marine Research Committee, 1968), 5–7, 22; CalCOFI, *Reports, Volume XV, 1 July 1969 to 30 June 1970* (Sacramento: State of California, Department of Fish and Game, Marine Research Committee, 1971), 5, 13.

128. Radovich, "The Collapse of the Sardine Fishery," 131–32; McEvoy and Scheiber, "Scientists, Entrepreneurs," 402–3; McEvoy, *Fisherman's Problem*, 203, 229, 241–47, quotation on page 203.

129. *Monterey Peninsula Herald, Sardine Edition No. 5*, 23 February 1940.

130. Clark, "Review of the California Sardine Fishery," 371.

131. Steinbeck and Ricketts, *Sea of Cortez*, 7.

6   REMAKING CANNERY ROW

1. John Steinbeck, *Sweet Thursday* (New York: Viking Press, 1954), 1.

2. Ed B. Larsh, *Doc's Lab: Myth and Legends from Cannery Row* (Monterey, CA: PBL Press, 1995), 12.

3. Rothman, *Devil's Bargains*, 1–9, 187–201, 205–29; Christensen, *Red Lodge and the Mythic West*; Patricia Nelson Limerick, "Seeing and Being Seen: Tourism in the American West," in *Over the Edge: Remapping the American West,* ed. Valerie J. Matsumoto and Blake Allmendinger (Berkeley and Los Angeles: University of California Press, 1999), 15–31. For a non-western locale, see M. Christine Boyer, "Cities for Sale: Merchandising History at South Street Seaport," in *Variations on a Theme Park: The New American City and the End of Public Space,* ed. Michael Sorkin (New York: Hill and Wang, 1992), 181–204. For an overview of Cannery Row's transformation, see James R. Curtis, "The Boutiquing of Cannery Row," *Landscape* 25, no. 1 (1981): 44–48.

4. Martha K. Norkunas, *The Politics of Public Memory: Tourism, History, and Ethnicity in Monterey, California* (Albany: State University of New York Press, 1993), 49–67, 71, 95. See also Walton, *Storied Land*, 272–76; Hal K. Rothman, "Stumbling toward the Millennium: Tourism, the Postindustrial World, and the Transformation of the American West," *California History* 77, no. 3 (Fall 1998): 143.

5. Norkunas, *Politics of Public Memory*, 50–51, 59. While Norkunas makes

similar points, her analysis focuses more on the exclusion of Cannery Row's working class and ethnic history than on its environmental history.

6. "Monterey, Great Sardine Port, Idled by Dearth of Fish," *Pacific Fisherman*, December 1950, 25.

7. Ray A. March, *A Guide to Cannery Row* (Monterey, CA: the author, 1962); Mary Porter, "Thomas J. Logan," *Sites and Citizens: Cannery Row—A Community Memory*, http://home.csumb.edu/o/olearycecilia/world/cannery_row/oral_histories/tomlogan.htm (accessed November 28, 2006); "Monterey Loses More of Its Oldtime Savor," *Monterey Peninsula Herald*, 20 April 1962.

8. "Monterey Cannery Converted," *Monterey Peninsula Herald*, 1 July 1958.

9. "5 Tuna Plants at Monterey," *Pacific Fisherman*, June 1951, 41; "Diversified Canning Operation Sustains Monterey's Economy," *Pacific Fisherman*, February 1952, 21–23; "Up-Swinging Sardines Hit 100,000-Ton Catch Total," *Pacific Fisherman*, January 1959, 4; "Returning Sardines Bring Problems with Them," *Pacific Fisherman*, February 1959, 9; Larry Spence, "Cannery Row Revival?" *Monterey Peninsula Herald*, 26 April 1962; Fred Sorri, "Sen. Farr and the Anchovies," *Monterey Peninsula Herald*, 23 October 1963; Don Mitchell, "Half a Century on Fishing . . . ," *Game and Gossip*, 30 October 1959, 13, 27–28.

10. Mangelsdorf, *Steinbeck's Cannery Row*, 185; Spence, "Cannery Row Revival?"

11. Richard Person, *The History of Cannery Row* (Monterey, CA: City Planning Commission, 1972), 14; "Company Buying Up Cannery Row," *Monterey Peninsula Herald*, 26 February 1957; "Cannery Row Plant En Route to Peru," *Monterey Peninsula Herald*, 1 July 1960; Ray March, "Cannery Row Moves to Peru," *Monterey Peninsula Herald*, 11 December 1962; Ray March, "Fishing Industry Booms in Peru," *Monterey Peninsula Herald*, 12 December 1962.

12. Sal Colletto, "Growing Up in a Monterey Fishing Family," *J. B. Phillips Historical Fisheries Report* 1, no. 1 (Spring 2000); McKibben, *Beyond Cannery Row*, 113–14; Mike Thomas, "Habit, Stubbornnness and Hope," *Monterey Peninsula Herald*, 20 April 1959.

13. Monterey County Industrial Development, Inc., *Information About Monterey County* (Salinas, CA: n.p., 195–); Harold Kermit Parker, "Population, Employment, and Post High School Education in the Monterey Peninsula" (Ph.D. diss., Stanford University, 1952), 95.

14. Mary Porter, "Hope Gradis," *Sites and Citizens: Cannery Row—A Community Memory*, http://home.csumb.edu/o/olearycecilia/world/cannery_row/oral_histories/hopegradis.htm (accessed November 28, 2006).

15. State of California, Department of Employment, "Community Labor Market Survey—Monterey, 1952," 69–132, Box 14/Folder 18, Department of Employment, Administration—Research and Statistics, California State Archives, Sacramento, California.

16. John Woolfenden, "A Colorful Life Remembered," *The (Monterey Peninsula) Herald Weekend Magazine*, 28 August 1977, 10, 12–14.

17. McKibben, *Beyond Cannery Row*, 115.

18. Ibid., 6, 114.

19. Ibid., 54–56, 114–16.

20. Smith, "The Hotel Del Monte Goes to War," 57; *Monterey Peninsula Herald*, 21 May 1946, 30 March 1948, 16 June 1948, 21 June 1950.

21. Parker, "Population, Employment," 95, 120–27, 135, 138, 145.

22. State of California, Department of Employment, "Community Labor Market Survey—Monterey, 1952"; Porter, "Hope Gradis."

23. Elaine D. Johnson, *A Sociological Study of the Monterey Area* (Monterey, CA: City Planning Commission, 1968), 61–62; Neal Hotelling, *Pebble Beach Golf Links: The Official History* (Chelsea, MI: Sleeping Bear Press, 1999), 116.

24. Richard Raymond Associates, *An Economic Analysis of the Monterey Area* (Monterey, CA: City Planning Commission, 1969), 10–11. For the postwar West military buildup, see Roger Lotchin, *Fortress California, 1910–1961: From Warfare to Welfare* (Berkeley and Los Angeles: University of California Press, 1992).

25. State of California, Department of Employment, "Community Labor Market Survey—Monterey, 1952."

26. Rothman, *Devil's Bargains*, 202–4; Jakle, *The Tourist*, 185–98; *The Peninsula Tomorrow: Preliminary Area Plan* (California: Hall and Goodhue—Eisner Stewart and Associates, 1963), 52.

27. Benson, *True Adventures of John Steinbeck*, 196–97, 225; Hedgpeth, "Philosophy on Cannery Row," 94–95; Parini, *John Steinbeck*, 130–34.

28. Parini, *John Steinbeck*, 133–34.

29. Benson, *True Adventures of John Steinbeck*, 553–60; Roy Simmonds, *John Steinbeck: The War Years, 1939–1945* (Lewisburg, PA: Bucknell University Press, 1996), 214; Parini, *John Steinbeck*, 356–57.

30. Orville Prescott, "Books of the Times," *New York Times*, 2 January 1945; Parini, *John Steinbeck*, 347; Benson, *True Adventures of John Steinbeck*, 561–62; Simmonds, *War Years*, 253, 279.

31. Steinbeck, *Cannery Row*, 5–6.

32. Robert M. Benton, "The Ecological Nature of *Cannery Row*," in Richard Astro and Tetsumaro Hayashi, eds., *Steinbeck: The Man and His Work* (Corvallis: Oregon State University Press, 1971), 133–35.

33. James C. Kelley, "Ed Ricketts, Ecologist," *The Steinbeck Newsletter, Cannery Row Fiftieth Anniversary Edition* 9, no. 1 (Fall 1995): 15–16.

34. Margaret Hensel, "Cannery Row," *Game and Gossip*, July 1952, 12, 34; Norkunas, *Politics of Public Memory*, 49–67. See also Walton, *Storied Land*, 273–75.

35. For the discrepancies between the real and the fictional Cannery Row, see Walton, *Storied Land*, 234, and Norkunas, *Politics of Public Memory*, 62–63.

36. Steinbeck, *Cannery Row*, 9; Peggy Rink, "Pilgrimage to Wing Chong's," *What's Doing on the Monterey Peninsula* 6, no. 7 (9 May 1953): 32–33; Mangelsdorf, *Steinbeck's Cannery Row*, 185.

37. Rink, "Pilgrimage to Wing Chong's," 32.

38. John Steinbeck, "John Steinbeck States His Views on Cannery Row," *Monterey Peninsula Herald*, 8 March 1957.

39. Mike Thomas, "What Will Emerge from the Cannery Row Cocoon?" *Monterey Peninsula Herald*, 21 April 1959; John Steinbeck to Toby Street, 9 December 1957, Box 3/Folder 28, John Steinbeck Papers, Special Collections, Stanford University Libraries.

40. Paul Carter and David Malouf, "Spatial History," *Textual Practice* 3 (1989): 173; Paul Carter, *The Road to Botany Bay: An Essay in Spatial History* (Boston: Faber and Faber, 1987), 1–33; Norkunas, *Politics of Public Memory*, 51, 56–59, 63, 95.

41. Dudley Towe, "This Is Cannery Row," *Game and Gossip*, 3 March 1958, 2–5, 14; Lorraine McNulty, "Old New Cannery Row," *Game and Gossip*, 30 October 1959, 2–7; March, *A Guide to Cannery Row*; *Polk's Monterey Peninsula (Monterey County, Calif.) Directory: Including Monterey, Carmel, Del Rey Oaks, Pacific Grove, Sand City and Seaside* (South El Monte, CA: R. L. Polk and Co., 1957, 1962).

42. Pacific Planning and Research, *Monterey, California: General Plan for Future Development* (Palo Alto, CA: Pacific Planning and Research 1959), 3–4, 11, 20, 25.

43. John Steinbeck, *Travels with Charley: In Search of America* (New York: Viking Press, 1962), 182–83.

44. "Cannery Row Plan Unveiled," *Monterey Peninsula Herald*, 29 August 1961; Sydney Williams, *Cannery Row Plan* (Monterey, CA: City Planning Commission, 1961), 1–2, 5, 7, 11.

45. Williams, *Cannery Row Plan*, 1–2, 11–14.

46. "Something New Urged for 'Row,'" *Monterey Peninsula Herald*, 25 January 1962; "Urban Renewal Plan Proposed for Cannery Row," 5 May 1962; Williams, *Cannery Row Plan*, 17.

47. "Urban Renewal Plan Proposed for Cannery Row"; "Cannery Row Master Plan Wins Endorsement," *Monterey Peninsula Herald*, 4 January 1962; Sydney Williams, *A Plan for the Cannery Row Area of the City of Monterey*, 3rd printing (Monterey, CA: the author, 1967).

48. Anne Poindexter, "More Nostalgia Than Noise Now, and Only the Faintest of Stinks," *Game and Gossip*, 1 July 1969, 3–8, 27.

49. Norkunas, *Politics of Public Memory*, 49–73, 95–96.

50. "Cannery Row Fire Damage Now Set above $2,000,000," *Monterey Peninsula Herald*, 28 November 1956; "Fire Guts Monterey Cannery," *Monterey Peninsula Herald*, 10 October 1967; "Arson Probe in Cannery Fire," *Monterey Peninsula Herald*, 26 December 1967; "Man Says He Set Three Fires," *Monterey Peninsula Herald*, 14 August 1972; "Vacant Cannery Row Warehouse Hit by Fire," *Monterey Peninsula Herald*, 11 July 1977; Everett Messick, "$2 Million Fire Guts 15 Cannery Row Businesses," *Monterey Peninsula Herald*, 24 February 1978; Everett Messick, "Last Week's Cannery Row Fire Just One of Many Mysterious Blazes Laid to Arson over Past Year," *Monterey Peninsula Herald*, 3 March 1978; Mangelsdorf, *Steinbeck's Cannery Row*, 184–85.

51. "Vacant Cannery Row Warehouse Hit by Fire."

52. Mark Hazard Osmun, "Finding Steinbeck along Monterey's Cannery Row," *San Francisco Examiner*, 14 June 1987. For decay and relics, see David Lowenthal, *The Past Is a Foreign Country* (New York: Cambridge University Press, 1985), 127–81, 240–49.

53. Towe, "This Is Cannery Row," 2–5, 14; McNulty, "Old New Cannery Row," 2–7.

54. John De Groot, "Structural Conditions," in Monterey Planning Department, *Cannery Row Plan Revision: Existing Physical Conditions Working Paper, July 1972* (Monterey, CA: The Commission, 1972).

55. Ibid.

56. Norkunas makes a similar point about a later period in *Politics of Public Memory*, 71.

57. De Groot, "Structural Conditions."

58. Monterey Department of City Planning, *Cannery Row Plan: An Element of the General Plan* (Monterey, CA: Department of City Planning, 1973), 35; Mangelsdorf, *Steinbeck's Cannery Row*, 195; Poindexter, "More Nostalgia," 3–8, 27.

59. *Monterey Peninsula Herald*, 14 April 1960 and 25 August 1970; Monterey Department of City Planning, *Cannery Row Plan*, 29–30.

60. *Peninsula Tomorrow*, 2, 52–54; Monterey Department of City Planning, *Cannery Row Plan*, 31, 35; Walton, *Storied Land*, 240–49.

61. Monterey Department of City Planning, *Cannery Row Plan*, 23, 26–28, 31, 35, 37.

62. Ibid., 23–26, 62, 68–69.

63. Ibid., 25–26; Lowenthal, *The Past Is a Foreign Country*, 175.

64. Monterey Department of City Planning, *Cannery Row Plan*, 67, 74, 76–77, 79; Brown and Takigawa, *Cannery Row Plan Revision: Existing Visual and Design Qualities* (Monterey, CA: Monterey Planning Commission, 1972).

65. "Cannery Row Square Now Officially Opens," *Monterey Peninsula Herald*, 5 August 1972; Person, *History of Cannery Row*, 18. For historic preser-

vation efforts nationwide, see Charles B. Hosmer Jr., *Presence of the Past: A History of the Preservation Movement in the United States Before Williamsburg* (New York: G. P. Putnam's Sons, 1965) and *Preservation Comes of Age: From Williamsburg to the National Trust, 1926–1949*, 2 vols. (Charlottesville: University Press of Virginia, 1981). See also Lowenthal, *The Past Is a Foreign Country*, 263–362.

66. Monterey Department of City Planning, *Cannery Row Plan*, 67.

67. Ibid., 22–23, 62, 72, 86.

68. Monterey Planning Department, *Environmental Impact Report: Cannery Row Plan* (Monterey, CA: Monterey Planning Department, 1973). For postwar environmentalism, see Hays, *Beauty, Health, and Permanence*, 26–29, 32–33, passim; Hal K. Rothman, *The Greening of a Nation?: Environmentalism in the United States Since 1945* (Fort Worth, TX: Harcourt Brace and Company, 1998), 1–5, 84–94, passim.

69. Kevin Howe, "Cannery Row Plan Updated, Approved," *Monterey Peninsula Herald*, 27 November 1973; Kevin Howe, "Closing of Last Cannery Ends Monterey's 78-Year Industry," *Monterey Peninsula Herald*, 9 February 1973.

70. Mike W. Edwards, "California's Land Apart—The Monterey Peninsula," *National Geographic* 142, no. 5 (November 1972): 699.

71. DeGroot, "Structural Conditions."

72. For the Coastal Initiative and the Coastal Commission, see Michelle Ann Knight, "A Political Culture of Conservation: Citizen Action and Marine Conservation in Monterey Bay" (Ph.D. diss., University of California, Santa Cruz, 1997), 83–87; Walton, *Storied Land*, 250–52.

73. Paul Denison, "Cannery Row Turmoil Simmers over Long Planning Stalemate," *Monterey Peninsula Herald*, 19 March 1978.

74. Tom Mikkelson, "Aquarium at the End of Cannery Row," *California Waterfront Age* 1, no. 2 (Spring 1985): 30–32; Walton, *Storied Land*, 251–52; City of Monterey Planning Commission, *Cannery Row Local Coastal Program: Land Use Plan* (Monterey, CA: City Planning Commission, 1981). For local debates about the LCP, see Denison, "Cannery Row Turmoil Simmers over Long Planning Stalemate"; Larry Parsons, "Cannery Row Survived 5-Year Freeze," *Monterey County Herald*, 1 September 1997.

75. Abby Ray, "Frank Crispo," *The Coast Gazette*, 23 April 1981.

7 THE FISH ARE BACK!

1. Fred Hernandez, "Aquarium Readies for Opening," *Monterey Peninsula Herald*, 20 October 1984; Ken Peterson, "Aquarium Opening Packed," *Monterey Peninsula Herald*, 21 October 1984; Gail Allison Baxter, "Monterey Bay Aquarium" (M. Arch. thesis, University of California, Berkeley, 1986), 70.

2. David Perlman, "Monterey's Aquarium Will Look Inside the Sea," *San Francisco Chronicle*, 3 September 1984.

3. "The Fish Are Back!" *Monterey Bay Aquarium Shorelines* 1, no. 1 (Winter 1985). For general overviews of the aquarium, see John Boykin, "Monterey Bay Aquarium," *The Stanford Magazine* 12, no. 4 (Winter 1984): 18–27; Marquis Childs, "A Novel Aquarium Depicts the Story of Monterey Bay," *Smithsonian*, June 1985, 94–100; Jane C. Desmond, *Staging Tourism: Bodies on Display from Waikiki to Sea World* (Chicago: University of Chicago Press, 1999), 177–86; Monterey Bay Aquarium, *Monterey Bay Aquarium* (Monterey, CA: Monterey Bay Aquarium Foundation, 1992).

4. For a similar argument pertaining to zoos and theme parks, see Gregg Mitman, *Reel Nature: America's Romance with Wildlife on Film* (Cambridge, MA: Harvard University Press, 1999), 3.

5. For environmentalism and consumption, see Susan G. Davis, *Spectacular Nature: Corporate Culture and the Sea World Experience* (Berkeley and Los Angeles: University of California Press, 1997), 28–39; Price, *Flight Maps*, 195–206; Matthew Klingle, "Spaces of Consumption in Environmental History" (Theme Issue on Environment and History), *History and Theory* 42, no. 4 (December 2003): 94–110.

6. L. R. Blinks to Dean Albert H. Bowker, Stanford Graduate Division, 10 March 1961, Box 1/Folder 14, Stanford University, Department of Biology, Division of Systemic Biology Records, Special Collections, Stanford University Libraries (hereafter Stanford Biology Records).

7. Hubert Heffner to Kenneth M. Cuthbertson, 5 April 1965, Box 2/Folder 1, Stanford Biology Papers; John H. Phillips, "Hovden Acquisition—Status Report," 11 July 1967, Box 1/Folder 10, Stanford Biology Records.

8. Donald Fitzgerald, *The History and Significance of the Hovden Cannery, Cannery Row, Monterey, California, 1914–1973*, submitted by Carroll W. Pursell Jr., principal investigator to the Monterey Bay Aquarium Foundation, 15 November 1979, 13; Baxter, "Monterey Bay Aquarium," 2.

9. Monterey Bay Aquarium, *Monterey Bay Aquarium, Project Status, January 1980* (Monterey, CA: n.p., 1980). Copy in Local History Files, Pacific Grove Public Library. "Aquarium Timeline," *Monterey Bay Aquarium*, http://www.mbayaq.org/aa/timelineBrowser.asp?tf=1 (accessed January 29, 2008).

10. Linda Rhodes and Charles Davis, "Preserving the Form, Reversing the Function: From Fish Cannery to Aquarium," *California Historical Society*, September 1984, 6–7; Baxter, "Monterey Bay Aquarium," 3–4.

11. *Monterey Bay Aquarium, Project Status, January 1980*; Ken Peterson, "Monterey's Age of Aquarium Begins Saturday," *Monterey Peninsula Herald*, 14 October 1984.

12. Carleton Knight III, "Purposeful Chaos on Cannery Row," *Architecture*, June 1985, 53; Boykin, "Monterey Bay Aquarium," 18–21.

13. Calvin Demmon, "Monterey's Age of the Aquarium Begins Saturday," *Monterey Peninsula Herald*, 14 October 1984.

14. Knight, "Purposeful Chaos," 53; Baxter, "Monterey Bay Aquarium," 9; Joseph Esherick, "An Architectural Practice in the San Francisco Bay Area, 1938–1996: Oral History Transcript," interviewed by Suzanne B. Riess (Berkeley: Regional Oral History Office, The Bancroft Library, University of California, Berkeley, 1996), 314–16; Baxter, "Monterey Bay Aquarium," 9–10.

15. *Monterey Bay Aquarium Newsletter* 1, no. 1 (October 1979).

16. Baxter, "Monterey Bay Aquarium," 4, 33–34, 41–46; The Planning Collaborative, *Environmental Impact Report, Monterey Bay Aquarium, Monterey, California* (San Francisco: The Planning Collaborative, 1979), 22 (hereafter abbreviated EIR–MBA); "Proposed Cannery Row Aquarium Costs Jump," *Monterey Peninsula Herald*, 25 January 1979.

17. Rachel Carson, *The Sea Around Us* (New York: Oxford University Press, 1951). For the influence of Carson and SCUBA, see Helen M. Rozwadowski, "Engineering, Imagination, and Industry: Scripps Island and Dreams for Ocean Science in the 1960s," in *The Machine in Neptune's Garden: Historical Perspectives on Technology and the Marine Environment*, ed. Helen M. Rozwadowski and David van Keuren (Sagamore Beach, MA: Science History Publications/USA, 2004), 321, 344–45. For television and film, see Mitman, *Reel Nature*, 157–79, and Rozwadowski, "Engineering, Imagination," 321–22.

18. Richard Munson, *Cousteau: The Captain and His World* (New York: Paragon House, 1989).

19. Rothman, *Greening of a Nation*, 101–5.

20. Knight, "A Political Culture of Conservation," 83–84, 181–82; Cornelia Dean, *Against the Tide: The Battle for America's Beaches* (New York: Columbia University Press, 1999), 188–89; Hays, *Beauty, Health, and Permanence*, 167–70.

21. EIR–MBA, 28–30; Baxter, "Monterey Bay Aquarium," 48–49.

22. Abby Ray, "The Creation of Monterey Bay Aquarium," *The Coast Gazette*, 28 May 1981; EIR–MBA, 33–35; *Monterey Bay Aquarium Newsletter* 1, no. 1 (October 1979). The resulting report, *The History and Significance of the Hovden Cannery*, was finished in November 1979. For the National Historic Preservation Act of 1966, see Hosmer, *Preservation Comes of Age*, 1065–74; Michael Kammen, *Mystic Chords of Memory: The Transformation of Tradition in American Culture* (New York: Alfred A. Knopf, 1991), 558–70.

23. EIR–MBA, 36–40; Baxter, "Monterey Bay Aquarium," 50; "Aquarium Plan Backed before Coastal Board," *Monterey Peninsula Herald*, 5 August 1980.

24. EIR–MBA, 109–14, 116–23, 129–30.

25. Ibid., 1–2, 89–95.

26. "Proposed Cannery Row Aquarium Costs Jump"; *Monterey Bay Aquarium Newsletter* 1, no. 1 (October 1979); Baxter, "Monterey Bay Aquarium," 54–61; "Proposed Monterey Bay Aquarium Wins Pacific Grove Approval after Compromise on Parking," *Monterey Peninsula Herald*, 8 May 1980; Ken Peterson, "Pacific Grove Keeping Wary Eye on Impact of Aquarium Parking," *Monterey Peninsula Herald*, 15 October 1984; EIR–MBA, 89–92; Ray, "The Creation of Monterey Bay Aquarium."

27. Ray, "The Creation of Monterey Bay Aquarium."

28. *Monterey Bay Aquarium, Project Status, January 1980*; *Monterey Bay Aquarium Annual Report* (1985).

29. Rhodes and Davis, "Preserving the Form," 7. For the conversion of industrial buildings, see Randolph Langenbach, *A Future from the Past: The Case for Conservation and Reuse of Old Buildings in Industrial Communities* (Washington, D.C.: U.S. Department of Housing and Urban Development, 1978); Hosmer, *Presence of the Past*, 273–87; Lowenthal, *The Past Is a Foreign Country*, 263–324.

30. Rhodes and Davis, "Preserving the Form," 7; Knight, "Purposeful Chaos," 53.

31. Charles M. Davis, "Aquarium Architecture: Some Notes on Monterey Bay Aquarium," *Monterey Bay Aquarium Newsletter* 3 (Spring 1981): 4–5.

32. Rhodes and Davis, "Preserving the Form," 6; Davis, "Aquarium Architecture," 4.

33. Davis, "Aquarium Architecture," 4–5; Knight, "Purposeful Chaos," 56.

34. Rhodes and Davis, "Preserving the Form," 6; Baxter, "Monterey Bay Aquarium," 29.

35. Rhodes and Davis, "Preserving the Form," 6–7. On preserving historical artifacts and relics, see Lowenthal, *The Past Is a Foreign Country*, 238–49.

36. Kathleen McGuire, "Ex-Workers Toast Aquarium Project's Cannery Restoration," *Monterey Peninsula Herald*, 4 October 1983.

37. Lowenthal, *The Past Is a Foreign Country*, 385.

38. Davis, "Aquarium Architecture," 4–5.

39. Knight, "Purposeful Chaos," 56; Joe Graziano, "Heart of Hovden Cannery Survives at Aquarium" *Monterey Peninsula Herald*, 14 October 1984; Rhodes and Davis, "Preserving the Form," 7.

40. Knight, "Purposeful Chaos," 53.

41. Boykin, "Monterey Bay Aquarium," 27.

42. Rhodes and Davis, "Preserving the Form," 6; Davis, "Aquarium Architecture."

43. Rhodes and Davis, "Preserving the Form," 7.

44. Knight, "Purposeful Chaos," 55; Mikkelson, "Aquarium at the End of Cannery Row," 33–34, 37.

45. Boykin, "Monterey Bay Aquarium," 27.

46. Mikkelson, "Aquarium at the End of Cannery Row," 37.

47. *Monterey Bay Aquarium Newsletter* 2 (Fall 1980); *Monterey Bay Aquarium Newsletter* 3 (Spring 1981); *Monterey Bay Aquarium Newsletter* 3 (Fall 1981).

48. *Monterey Bay Aquarium Newsletter* 4 (Spring 1982); *Monterey Bay Aquarium Newsletter* 4 (Fall 1982).

49. "Monterey Bay Aquarium Construction Uses Innovative Materials and Methods," *California Builder and Engineer*, January 21, 1985, 20.

50. Baxter, "Monterey Bay Aquarium," 66.

51. Boykin, "Monterey Bay Aquarium," 27, 21. For Shamu, see Davis, *Spectacular Nature*, 152–232. For dolphin shows, see Mitman, *Reel Nature*, 157–79.

52. Knight, "Purposeful Chaos," 56; Boykin, "Monterey Bay Aquarium," 26; Childs, "A Novel Aquarium," 99; Judy Rand and Hank Armstrong, *Monterey Bay Aquarium* (Monterey, CA: Blake Printing and Publishing and Monterey Bay Aquarium, 1985).

53. Ken Schultz, "Aquariums Now Let You Get Your Hand In," *Monterey Peninsula Herald*, 14 October 1984; Monterey Bay Aquarium, *Monterey Bay Aquarium*, 14.

54. Monterey Bay Aquarium, *Monterey Bay Aquarium*, 11; David C. Powell, *A Fascination for Fish: Adventures of an Underwater Pioneer* (Berkeley and Los Angeles: University of California Press, 2001), 189.

55. "Designers Overcome Multiple Challenges to Build a Handsome New Aquarium," *Specifying Engineer*, June 1984; Childs, "A Novel Aquarium," 96–97.

56. "Designers Overcome Multiple Challenges"; Childs, "A Novel Aquarium," 96–97; Boykin, "Monterey Bay Aquarium," 26; Powell, *Fascination for Fish*, 204; *Monterey Bay Aquarium Shorelines* 2, no. 2 (Spring 1986).

57. For a similar argument, see Desmond, *Staging Tourism*, 178.

58. Boykin, "Monterey Bay Aquarium," 22–23; Powell, *Fascination for Fish*, 199–200; Baxter, "Monterey Bay Aquarium," 17; Calvin Demmon, "Monterey Bay Aquarium Gets the Finishing Touches," *Monterey Peninsula Herald*, 15 March 1984; Jacqueline Frost, "They Make the Fakes Look Real," *Monterey Peninsula Herald*, 14 October 1984, 75–76.

59. Debra Van Dusen, "The Nation's Newest Aquarium," *BioScience* 35, no. 10 (November 1985): 616; Powell, *Fascination for Fish*, 198, 200.

60. Boykin, "Monterey Bay Aquarium," 22.

61. Van Dusen, "Nation's Newest Aquarium," 615–16; Powell, *Fascination for Fish*, 201.

62. Boykin, "Monterey Bay Aquarium," 23.

63. "More Rocks?!" *Monterey Bay Aquarium Newsletter* 5 (Spring 1983): 3.

64. Powell, *Fascination for Fish*, 201–3; "Stockpilings," *Monterey Bay Aquarium Newsletter* 5 (Spring 1983): 6.

65. Bruce Cowan, "Aquarium Success at 'Nature-Faking,'" *Monterey Peninsula Herald*, 29 December 1984.

66. Powell, *Fascination for Fish*, 192–93.

67. "Kelp Forest Report," *Monterey Bay Aquarium Shorelines* 2, no. 1 (Winter 1986); Powell, *Fascination for Fish*, 213; Baxter, "Monterey Bay Aquarium," 18, 66–67; Steve Hank, "Expert 'Amazed' at Success of Aquarium's Kelp Forest," *Monterey Peninsula Herald*, 18 October 1985; "A Harvest of Knowledge," *Monterey Bay Aquarium Shorelines* 8, no. 3 (Summer 1992): 4.

68. Judie Telfer, "Collectors Take a Dive, Looking for Specimens," *Monterey Peninsula Herald*, 18 October 1985; Powell, *Fascination for Fish*, 208; Van Dusen, "Nation's Newest Aquarium," 616–17.

69. Powell, *Fascination for Fish*, 225.

70. "Learning to Care for Jellies," *Monterey Bay Aquarium Shorelines* 8, no. 3 (Summer 1992).

71. *Monterey Bay Aquarium Shorelines* 1, no. 3 (Summer 1985).

72. Van Dusen, "Nation's Newest Aquarium," 615–16.

73. *Monterey Bay Aquarium Shorelines* 10, no. 3 (Summer 1994).

74. For example, see the "Current Affairs" section of *Monterey Bay Aquarium Shorelines* 6, no. 4 (Fall 1990); vol. 7, no. 4 (Fall 1991); vol. 8, no. 2 (Spring 1992).

75. The otters had participated in the Sea Otter Research and Conservation Program but lacked skills needed to return to the wild. The program was transferred to the Marine Mammal Center in Sausalito, California, in 1996. See Ken Schultz, "Monterey Bay Aquarium Ends Sea Otter Rescue Program," *Monterey County Herald*, 9 February 1996.

76. Childs, "A Novel Aquarium," 99; Boykin, "Monterey Bay Aquarium," 22–24.

77. "Play with a Purpose," *Monterey Bay Aquarium Shorelines* 8, no. 2 (Summer 1992): 6; *Monterey Bay Aquarium Shorelines* 9, no. 2 (Winter 1993).

78. Van Dusen, "Nation's Newest Aquarium," 615.

79. Powell, *Fascination for Fish*, 184, 187.

80. Van Dusen, "Nation's Newest Aquarium," 614.

81. Powell, *Fascination for Fish*, 212–13; "Spring Cleaning at the Aquarium," *Monterey County Herald*, 27 February 1998.

82. Thom Akeman, "Miracle-Gro vs. El Niño," *Monterey County Herald*, 6 September 1997.

83. Childs, "A Novel Aquarium," 97; *Monterey Bay Aquarium Shorelines* 2, no. 2 (Spring 1986); *Monterey Bay Aquarium Shorelines* 9, no. 1 (Winter 1993).

84. For a similar discussion, see Mitman, *Reel Nature*, 163–64.

85. Powell, *Fascination for Fish*, 220–21; "Shark Euthanized after Developing Infection," *Monterey County Herald*, 22 February 1996; Lori Oshita, "Monterey Bay Aquarium Is One Year Old," *Salinas Californian*, 12 October 1985.

86. Gilbert Van Dykhuizen and Henry F. Mollet, "Growth, Age Estimation and Feeding of Captive Sevengill Sharks, *Notorynchus cepedianus*, at the Monterey Bay Aquarium," *Australian Journal of Marine Freshwater Research*, no. 43 (1992): 297.

87. "Counting Noses," *Monterey Bay Aquarium Shorelines* 11, no. 3 (Fall/Winter, 1995): 6–7; Kevin Howe, "Aquarium's First Census Shows Surprisingly Large Population," *Monterey Herald*, 20 October 1995.

88. Powell, *Fascination for Fish*, 251.

89. Paul Rogers, "Showplace of the Sea," *San Jose Mercury News*, 19 October 1994; Monterey Bay Aquarium, *Monterey Bay Aquarium*, 42; Monterey Bay Aquarium Research Institute, *MBARI's First Decade: A Retrospective* (Moss Landing, CA: Monterey Bay Aquarium Research Institute, 1997), 56–57. For "Live from Monterey Canyon," see Judith L. Connor, "Promoting Deeper Interest in Science," *Curator* 34, no. 4 (December 1991): 245–60. For the connections between scientific research and marine parks, see Mitman, *Reel Nature*, 161–79.

90. Monterey Bay Aquarium, *Monterey Bay Aquarium Visitor Map* (Monterey, CA: Monterey Bay Aquarium, 2000); Childs, "A Novel Aquarium," 98–99.

91. Davis, *Spectacular Nature*, 152–232; Desmond, *Staging Tourism*, 217–50. In addition, the Monterey Bay Aquarium has installed Web cameras at various exhibits so online visitors can watch live footage. See "Live Web Cams," *Monterey Bay Aquarium*, http://www.mbayaq.org/efc/cam_menu.asp (accessed November 28, 2006).

92. Steve Rubenstein, "Shark Hits 100th day at Grateful Aquarium," *San Francisco Chronicle*, 23 December 2004; "White Shark Goes On Display," *Monterey Bay Aquarium*, http://www.mbayaq.org/aa/timelineBrowser.asp?tf=100 (accessed November 28, 2006).

93. EIR–MBA, 25.

94. *Monterey Bay Aquarium Annual Report* (1985); *Monterey Peninsula Herald*, 18 October 1985.

95. Ken Peterson, "Aquarium Looks to the Future," *Monterey Herald*, 3 June 1985.

96. Calvin Demmon, "Traffic Clogged by Shoppers, Tourists," *Monterey Peninsula Herald*, 24 November 1984; Calvin Demmon, "Aquarium Crowds Causing Traffic, Business Problems," *Monterey Peninsula Herald*, 30 October 1984; "Aquarium Plans to Sell Advance Tickets to Ease Traffic Woes," *Monterey Peninsula Herald*, 9 January 1985; "Aquarium Will Limit Admissions on May 1," *Monterey Peninsula Herald*, 27 March 1985.

97. "Cannery Row Merchants Trying to Curb Aquarium Operations," *Monterey Herald*, 19 May 1986.

98. Miles Corwin, "Aquarium's Tourist Appeal Puts Strain on Cannery Row," *Los Angeles Times*, 13 May 1985.

99. Letters to Monterey City Hall, July 1986, in "Monterey Bay Aquarium,"

Local History Files, California History Room, Monterey Public Library. Emphasis in original.

100. Leadership Monterey Peninsula, Monterey Bay Aquarium Scrapbook, 1984–1985, California History Room, Monterey Public Library.

101. "Council's Interference," *Monterey Herald*, 8 September 1986.

102. Mark A. Stein, "Aquarium—Angry Wave Sweeps over Cannery Row," *Los Angeles Times*, 6 October 1986; *Monterey Bay Aquarium Shorelines* 2, no. 4 (Fall 1986).

103. "Monterey Approves Aquarium Restrictions," *Monterey Herald*, 18 March 1987; Judy Hammond, "Aquarium, Row Group Bury Parking Hatchet," *Monterey Herald*, 24 June 1987.

104. Judy Hammond, "Merchants, Aquarium Join Forces," *Monterey Herald*, 16 November 1987; Jennifer McNulty, "Monterey Bay Aquarium Gives Visitors a Thrill," *Los Angeles Times*, 30 April 1989.

105. "Director's Note," *Monterey Bay Aquarium Shorelines* 7, no. 1 (Winter 1991); Thom Akeman, "Aquarium Poll Shows Residents' Support," *Monterey Herald*, 4 February 1991.

106. "The Aquarium Is a Major Player," *Monterey County Herald*, 29 March 1994.

107. Powell, *Fascination for Fish*, 250–51; Judy Hammond, "Aquarium Unveils $25 Million Expansion Plan," *Monterey Herald*, 1 November 1989; *Monterey Bay Aquarium Shorelines* 6, no. 3 (Summer 1990).

108. "Aquarium's 'Awesome' New Wing Cheered," *Monterey County Herald*, 3 March 1996; "The New Look," *Monterey Bay Aquarium Shorelines* 6, no. 3 (Summer 1990); Powell, *Fascination for Fish*, 277–79.

109. Monterey Bay Aquarium, *2000 Visitor Highlights* (Monterey, CA: Monterey Bay Aquarium, 2001); "Aquarium's Busy Year Aids Community," *Tourism Report, Monterey County Herald*, 2 November 1997.

110. Victoria Manley, "Aquarium's Impact: $250 Million," *Monterey Herald*, 14 December 2004.

111. Rothman, *Greening of a Nation*, 192; Hays, *Beauty, Health, and Permanence*, 21–39; Samuel P. Hays, "The New Environmental West" and "A Historical Perspective on Contemporary Environmentalism," in *Explorations in Environmental History: Essays by Samuel P. Hays* (Pittsburgh: University of Pittsburgh Press, 1998), 156–71, 379–99; Adam Rome, "'Give Earth a Chance': The Environmental Movement and the Sixties," *Journal of American History* 90, no. 2 (September 2003): 525–54.

112. Price, *Flight Maps*, 195–206; James Morton Turner, "From Woodcraft to 'Leave No Trace': Wilderness, Consumerism, and Environmentalism in Twentieth-Century America," *Environmental History* 7, no. 3 (July 2002): 462–84.

113. For similar ideas, see Walton, *Storied Land*, 253.

114. "Fishing for Solutions," *Monterey Bay Aquarium Shorelines* 13, no. 3 (Summer 1997): 6–7; William J. Broad, "Conservationists Write a Seafood Menu to Save Fish," *New York Times*, 9 November 1999.

115. "Aquarium's Busy Year Aids Community."

116. Knight, "Political Culture of Conservation," 93–102, 112–39, 226–89. For the sanctuary, see Monterey Bay Aquarium, *A Natural History of the Monterey Bay National Marine Sanctuary* (Monterey, CA: Monterey Bay Aquarium Foundation, 1997), 1–9.

117. "Desalination: A Fresh Solution," *Monterey Bay Aquarium Shorelines* 8, no. 1 (Winter 1992): 2; Melissa Heckscher, "Tide Pools Get a Break," *Monterey County Herald*, 15 October 1999; "Letters to the Editor," *Monterey County Herald*, 10 August 1999.

118. Hays, "A Historical Perspective," 380; Rothman, *Greening of a Nation*, 7–31.

119. Monterey Bay Aquarium, *1995 Visitor Highlights* (Monterey, CA: Monterey Bay Aquarium 1996); Monterey Bay Aquarium, *2000 Visitor Highlights*. For admission prices, see "Aquarium Ticket Prices and Ordering Information," *Monterey Bay Aquarium*, http://www.mbayaq.org/vi/tickets.asp (accessed January 22, 2008). I am grateful to Dr. Steve Yalowitz, Monterey Bay Aquarium audience research specialist, for providing me with these reports and explaining the polling process. Since 1993, the aquarium has conducted exit surveys on two days each month, one weekday and one weekend day. They poll one hundred visitors each day, for a total of twenty-four hundred per year. Personal communication with Dr. Steve Yalowitz, 8 January 2002.

120. Susan Ferriss, "Aquarium Takes Bilingual Show to Migrant Camps," *Monterey Herald*, 16 July 1991; *Monterey Bay Aquarium Shorelines* 5, no. 3 (Summer 1989); "A Bridge to the Salinas Valley," *Monterey Bay Aquarium Shorelines* 8, no. 1 (Winter 1992): 4; "Sea Life on the Farm," *Monterey Bay Aquarium Shorelines* 8, no. 3 (Summer 1992): 2.

121. *Monterey Bay Aquarium Shoreline* 1, no. 1 (Winter 1985).

122. For communities reinventing their identities to focus on nature, see Christensen, *Red Lodge and the Mythic West*, 168–211.

CONCLUSION

1. Alex Hulanicki, "Cannery Row: Times Change," *Monterey Herald*, 19 February 1996; Rothman, "Stumbling toward the Millennium," 143.

2. Neal B. Hotelling, "History Is Future," *Monterey County Herald*, 11 January 1998.

3. Calvin Demmon, "Cannery Row Considered Endangered," *Monterey County Herald*, 15 June 1998; Tom Gorman, "Monterey Defends Efforts on Can-

nery Row," *Los Angeles Times*, 17 June 1998; "Monterey Defends Historic Support," *Monterey County Herald*, 17 June 1998. For the National Trust for Historic Preservation's Eleven Most Endangered Places and lists of past "winners," see "America's 11 Most Endangered Historic Places," *National Trust for Historic Preservation*, http://www.nthp.org/11most/index.html (accessed November 28, 2006).

4. Bonnie Gartshore, "Windows to Our Past: Historic Cannery Row Shacks to Be on View at New Park," *Alta Vista Magazine, Monterey County Herald*, 16 February 1996; Demmon, "Cannery Row Considered Endangered." For the Monterey Peninsula Recreational Trail, see Calvin Demmon, "Monterey Council Oks Design for Hiking-Biking Trail," *Monterey Peninsula Herald*, 22 January 1986; Ted Castle, "A Walk on the Quiet Side," *The (Monterey) Herald Weekend Magazine*, 9 April 1989.

5. Winter & Company, *Cannery Row Conservation District, Monterey, California* (Boulder, CO: Winter & Company, 2004), 1.

6. Victoria Manley, "Cannery Row Hotel Wins OK," *Monterey County Herald*, 8 June 2000; Calvin Demmon, "Monterey Approves IMAX," *Monterey County Herald*, 6 October 1999.

7. Marie Vasari, "IMAX Fan Won't Give Up on Dream Theater," *Monterey County Herald*, 1 December 2005; Andre Briscoe, "Monterey IMAX Permit Sought," *Monterey County Herald*, 25 April 2006; Dania Akkad, "Construction Blues," *Monterey County Herald*, 19 December 2006; "Major Development Projects," *City of Monterey, Community Development Department*, http://www.monterey.org/commdevelop/proj_status.html (accessed January 22, 2008); Julia Reynolds, "Worker Injured at Future IMAX Site," *Monterey County Herald*, 13 September 2007.

8. Dan Laidman, "Romancing the Zone," *Monterey County Herald*, 13 October 2002.

9. Ibid.

10. Dan Laidman, "Narrow Win for Ocean View Plaza," *Monterey County Herald*, 16 October 2002.

11. Dan Laidman, "Lawsuit Challenges Ocean View Plaza," *Monterey County Herald*, 16 November 2002.

12. Julia Reynolds, "Council Doubles as Water Board," *Monterey County Herald*, 16 November 2005; Julia Reynolds, "Monterey Delays Ocean View Action," *Monterey County Herald*, 2 November 2005; Julia Reynolds, "Groups Suit Seeks to Block Cannery Row Desal Plant," *Monterey County Herald*, 17 February 2006; "Save Our Waterfront Committee History," *Save Our Waterfront Committee*, http://www.evansmonterey.com/history.html (accessed February 3, 2007).

13. Kevin Howe, "Coastal Panel May Hear Ocean View Plans," *Monterey*

County Herald, 24 December 2007; Jessica Lyons, "Monterey City Council Approves Letter of Support," *Monterey County Weekly*, 3 January 2008.

14. "Sardines Making Comeback in West," *Buffalo News*, 24 January 1999; John Balzar, "The Big Net," *Los Angeles Times*, 29 May 1999.

15. Robert Leos, "Pacific Sardine: A Little Silver Fish That is a Silver Lining," *The J.B. Phillips Historical Fisheries Report* 1, no. 1 (Spring 2000).

16. "Final California Commercial Landings for 2005," *California Department of Fish and Game*, http://www.dfg.ca.gov/mrd/landings05.html (accessed January 27, 2007).

17. "Programs and People," *Monterey Bay Aquarium Shorelines* 13, no. 4 (Fall 1997).

18. Sukhjit Purewal, "Whale of a Remodel: Aquarium Unveils Its New Look," *Monterey County Herald*, 29 May 2004.

19. Jenny Sayre Ramberg, e-mail communication with author, 29 March 2006.

20. Text of Monterey Bay Aquarium exhibit, personal observation, June 2004.

21. Carol McKibben, personal conversation with author, August 2005.

22. Text of Monterey Bay Aquarium exhibit, personal observation, June 2004.

23. For opposition to the Cannery Row projects, see "Waterfront Challenges," *Save Our Waterfront Committee*, http://www.evansmonterey.com/challenges.html (accessed February 3, 2007). For the environmental problems associated with tourism, see Limerick, "Seeing and Being Seen," 28.

24. In September 2006 the median home price in Monterey County was $680,000. See Marie Vasari, "Home Sales Slow, but Local Prices Holding," *Monterey County Herald*, 27 October 2006. For the problem of affordable housing in Western resort towns, see Allen Best, "How a Resort Town Loses Its Soul," *High Country News*, 23 August 2004; Ray Ring, "The New West's Servant Economy," *High Country News*, 17 April 1995.

25. Victoria Manley, "Low-Cost Rents for Row Workers," *Monterey County Herald*, 12 April 2001; Victoria Manley, "Affordable Apartment OK'd," *Monterey County Herald*, 3 May 2001; Larry Parsons, "Clean, Roomy, below Market Rate," *Monterey County Herald*, 21 June 2004.

26. For an excellent discussion of these issues in California, see Tom Knudson, "State of Denial: A Special Report on the Environment," *Sacramento Bee*, 27 April 2003. Also available online: http://www.sacbee.com/static/live/news/projects/denial/pro_1.html (accessed December 30, 2006).

SELECTED BIBLIOGRAPHY

MANUSCRIPT SOURCES

California State Archives, Sacramento, California
    Department of Employment
    Department of Natural Resources
Cannery Row Foundation Oral Histories, National Steinbeck Center,
    Salinas, California
Huntington, Collis P. Papers (microform). Syracuse University Libraries,
    Special Collections
Hyde, Charles Gilman Hyde. Papers. The Water Resources Center Archives,
    the University of California, Berkeley.
Jacks, David. Collection. The Huntington Library, San Marino, California.
Leonard, Norman. Papers. Labor Archives and Research Center, San Francisco
    State University.
Monterey City Clerk's Office
    City Council Minutes
    City Ordinances
    City Resolutions
    City Recorders Court
Monterey Public Library, California History Room
    Leadership Monterey Peninsula, Monterey Bay Aquarium Scrapbook,
        1984–1985
    Local History Files
National Archives and Records Administration—Pacific Region, San Bruno,
    California
    Record Group 22. United States Fish and Wildlife Service.
    Record Group 77. United States Army Corps of Engineers.
Pacific Grove Public Library, Local History Files
Phillips, J. B. Collection. The Maritime Museum of Monterey.

Stanford University Libraries, Special Collections
  Morse, Samuel Finley Brown. Papers.
  Pacific Improvement Company Records (JL1 and JL17)
  Ricketts, Edward F. Papers.
  Stanford University, Board of Trustees
  Stanford University, Department of Biology, Division of Systemic Biology
  Steinbeck, John. Papers.
University of California, Berkeley, The Bancroft Library
  Monterey Japanese Oral History Collection
  University of California, Office of the President
University of Washington Libraries, Special Collections, Manuscripts, and
  University Archives, Seattle, Washington
  Chapman, Wilbert McLeod. Papers.
  Thompson, William F. Papers.

BOOKS, ARTICLES, PAMPHLETS, THESES, GOVERNMENT DOCUMENTS

Ahlstrom, Elbert H., and John Radovich. "Management of the Pacific Sardine." In *A Century of Fisheries in North America*, Special Publication No. 7, edited by Norman G. Benson, 183–93. Washington, D.C.: American Fisheries Society, 1970.

Andrews, Thomas G. "'Made By Toile'?: Tourism, Labor, and the Construction of the Colorado Landscape, 1858–1917." *Journal of American History* 92, no. 3 (December 2005): 837–63.

Architectural Resources Group. *Cannery Row Historic Survey, September 1999.* San Francisco: Architectural Resources Group, 1999.

Armentrout-Ma, L. Eve. "Chinese in California's Fishing Industry, 1850–1941." *California History* 60, no. 2 (1981): 142–57.

Aron, Cindy S. *Working at Play: A History of Vacations in the United States.* New York: Oxford University Press, 1999.

Astro, Richard. *John Steinbeck and Edward F. Ricketts: The Shaping of a Novelist.* Minneapolis: University of Minnesota Press, 1973.

Astro, Richard, and Tetsumaro Hayashi, eds. *Steinbeck: The Man and His Work.* Corvallis: Oregon State University Press, 1971.

Baxter, Gail Allison. "Monterey Bay Aquarium." M.Arch. thesis, University of California, Berkeley, 1986.

Belasco, Warren James. *Americans on the Road: From Autocamp to Motel, 1910–1945.* Cambridge, MA: The MIT Press, 1979.

Benson, Jackson J. *The True Adventures of John Steinbeck, Writer.* New York: Viking Press, 1984.

Berkowitz, Michael. "A 'New Deal' for Leisure: Making Mass Tourism during the Great Depression." In *Being Elsewhere: Tourism, Consumer Culture, and Identity in Modern Europe and North America*, edited by Shelley Baranowski and Ellen Furlough, 185–212. Ann Arbor: University of Michigan Press, 2001.

Blackford, Mansel. *Fragile Tourism: The Impact of Tourism on Maui, 1959–2000*. Lawrence: University Press of Kansas, 2001.

Bonnot, Paul. "Report on the Relative Merits and Demerits of Purse Seines vs. Lampara Nets in the Taking of Sardines." *California Fish and Game* 16, no. 1 (January 1930): 125–30.

Booth, F. E. "The Sardine Needs a Friend." *Pacific Fisherman*, March 1936, 25.

Boyer, M. Christine. "Cities for Sale: Merchandising History at South Street Seaport." In *Variations on a Theme Park: The New American City and the End to Public Space*, edited by Michael Sorkin, 183–204. New York: Hill and Wang, 1992.

Boykin, John. "Monterey Bay Aquarium." *The Stanford Magazine* 12, no. 4 (Winter 1984): 18–27.

Brown, Dona. *Inventing New England: Regional Tourism in the Nineteenth Century*. Washington, D.C.: Smithsonian Institution Press, 1995.

Brown and Takigawa. *Cannery Row Plan Revision: Existing Visual and Design Qualities*. Monterey, CA: Monterey Planning Commission, 1972.

Campbell, Arthur. "The Conservation of the California Sardine." M.A. thesis, Chico State College, 1952.

Carson, Rachel L. *The Sea Around Us*. New York: Oxford University Press, 1951.

Carter, Paul, and David Malouf. "Spatial History." *Textual Practice* 3 (1989): 173–83.

Childs, Marquis. "A Novel Aquarium Depicts the Story of Monterey Bay." *Smithsonian*, June 1985, 94–100.

Christensen, Bonnie. *Red Lodge and the Mythic West: From Coal Miners to Cowboys*. Lawrence: University Press of Kansas, 2002.

City of Monterey Planning Commission. *Cannery Row Local Coastal Program: Land Use Plan*. Monterey, CA: City Planning Commission, 1981.

Clark, Frances N. "Dominant Size-Groups and Their Influence in the Fishery of the California Sardine (*Sardina caerulea*)." California Department of Natural Resources, Division of Fish and Game. *Fish Bulletin No. 31* (1931).

———. "Maturity of the California Sardine (*Sardina caerulea*), Determined by Ova Diameter Measurements." California Department of Natural Resources, Division of Fish and Game. *Fish Bulletin No. 42* (1934).

———. "Interseasonal and Intraseasonal Changes in Size of the California Sardine (*Sardinops caerulea*)." California Department of Natural Resources, Division of Fish and Game. *Fish Bulletin No. 47* (1936).

———. "Measures of Abundance of the Sardine, *Sardinops caerulea*, in the California Waters." California Department of Natural Resources, Division of Fish and Game. *Fish Bulletin No. 53* (1939).

———. "Can the Supply of Sardines Be Maintained in California Waters?" *California Fish and Game* 25, no. 2 (April 1939): 172–76.

———. "Review of the California Sardine Fishery." *California Fish and Game* 38, no. 3 (July 1952): 367–80.

Clark, Frances N., and John F. Janssen Jr. "Movements and Abundance of the Sardine as Measured by Tag Returns." California Department of Natural Resources, Division of Fish and Game. *Fish Bulletin No. 61* (1945).

Clark, Frances N., and John C. Marr. "Population Dynamics of the Pacific Sardine." In California Cooperative Fisheries Investigations, *Progress Report, 1 July 1953 to 31 March 1955*. Sacramento: State of California, Department of Fish and Game, Marine Research Committee, 1955.

Classic, Ralph F. "Monterey Squid Fishery." *California Fish and Game* 15, no. 4 (October 1929): 317–20.

Clements, Kendrick A. *Hoover, Conservation, and Consumerism: Engineering the Good Life*. Lawrence: University Press of Kansas, 2000.

Coleman, Annie Gilbert. *Ski Style: Sport and Culture in the Rockies*. Lawrence: University Press of Kansas, 2004.

Coleman, George A. *Report upon Monterey Pine, Made for the Pacific Improvement Company, Based upon an Examination Made during 1904 and 1905 of the Pacific Improvement Company's 7000 Acre Property near Monterey and Pacific Grove*. Berkeley, CA: n.p., 1905.

Colletto, Sal. *The Sardine Fisherman*. Monterey, CA: the author, 1960.

Collins, J. W. "Report on the Fisheries of the Pacific Coast of the United States." In *Report of the Commissioner of Fish and Fisheries for 1888*. Washington, D.C.: Government Printing Office, 1892.

Connor, Judith L. "Promoting Deeper Interest in Science." *Curator* 34, no. 4 (December 1991): 245–60.

Conway, J. D. *Monterey: Presidio, Pueblo, and Port*. Charleston, SC: Arcadia Publishing, 2003.

Corbin, Alain. *The Foul and the Fragrant: Odor and the French Social Imagination*. Cambridge, MA: Harvard University Press, 1986.

———. *The Lure of the Sea: The Discovery of the Seaside in the Western World, 1750–1840*. Translated by Jocelyn Phelps. New York: Penguin Books, 1995.

Croker, Richard S. "Sardine Canning Methods in California." *California Fish and Game* 21, no. 1 (January 1935): 10–21.

———. "Loss of California's Sardine Fishery May Become Permanent." *Outdoor California* 15, no. 1 (January 1954): 1, 6–8.

Cronon, William. "Modes of Prophecy and Production: Placing Nature in History." *Journal of American History* 76, no. 4 (March 1990): 1122–31.

————. "Kennecott Journey: The Paths out of Town." In *Under an Open Sky: Rethinking America's Western Past*, edited by William Cronon, George Miles, and Jay Gitlin, 28–51. New York: W. W. Norton, 1992.

————. *Uncommon Ground: Rethinking the Human Place in Nature*. New York: W. W. Norton, 1996.

Crosby, Alfred. *Ecological Imperialism: The Biological Expansion of Europe, 900–1900*. New York: Cambridge University Press, 1986.

Curtis, James R. "The Boutiquing of Cannery Row." *Landscape* 25, no. 1 (1981): 44–48.

Cutino, Peter J. *Monterey—A View from Garlic Hill*. Pacific Grove, CA: Boxwood Press, 1995.

Dall, Caroline H. *My First Holiday; Or, Letters Home from Colorado, Utah, and California*. Boston: Roberts Brothers, 1881.

Dana, Richard Henry. *Two Years Before the Mast*. New York: Harper and Brothers, 1840.

Daniels, Roger. *Asian America: Chinese and Japanese in the United States since 1850*. Seattle: University of Washington Press, 1988.

Davis, Charles M. "Aquarium Architecture: Some Notes on Monterey Bay Aquarium." *Monterey Bay Aquarium Newsletter* 3 (Spring 1985).

Davis, M. Kathryn. "Sardine Oil on Troubled Waters: The Boom and Bust of California's Sardine Industry, 1905–1955." Ph.D. dissertation, University of California, Berkeley, 2002.

Davis, Susan G. *Spectacular Nature: Corporate Culture and the Sea World Experience*. Berkeley and Los Angeles: University of California Press, 1997.

Dean, Bashford. "A Californian Marine Biological Station." *Natural Science* 11, no. 65 (July 1897): 28–35.

Del Mar Canning Company v. Joe Lopez "New Madrid," Francisco D'Agui "Cesare Augusta," United Fishermen's Union of the Pacific. Monterey Superior Court No. 19639, 29 September 1939.

Del Monte Properties Co. v. F. E. Booth, Bay View Packing Company, California Packing Corporation, Carmel Canning Company, Custom House Packing Corporation, Del Mar Canning Corporation, E. B. Gross Canning Company, K. Hovden Company, Monterey Canning Company, San Carlos Canning Company, San Xavier Fish Packing Company, Sea Pride Packing Corporation, First Doe Corporation, Second Doe Corporation. Monterey Superior Court No. 14,568, 6 February 1934.

Denman, William, and Lyman Henry. *A Review of the California Sardine Industry with Incidental Consideration of Its Racketeers, Its Politician Pseudo-Scientists, and Its Misguided Sportsmen Enemies*. San Francisco: n.p., 1936.

Dennis, John M. *Monterey's Cannery Row: A Brief Survey, June 4, 1945*. Stockton, CA: the author, 1945.

"Designers Overcome Multiple Challenges to Build a Handsome New Aquarium." *Specifying Engineer*, June 1984.

Deutsch, Sarah. "Landscape of Enclaves: Race Relations in the West, 1865–1990." In *Under an Open Sky: Rethinking America's Western Past*, edited by William Cronon, George Miles, and Jay Gitlin, 110–31. New York: W. W. Norton, 1992.

Deverell, William. *Railroad Crossing: Californians and the Railroad, 1850–1910*. Berkeley and Los Angeles: University of California Press, 1994.

DiStasi, Lawrence, ed. *Una Storia Segreta: The Secret History of Italian American Evacuation and Internment during World War II*. Berkeley, CA: Heyday Books, 2001.

Dorton, R. M. *Report on the Economic Advantages of Breakwater at Monterey Harbor*. Monterey, CA: City of Monterey, 1927.

———. *Necessity of Extending the Breakwater at Monterey, California*. Monterey, CA: City Manager, 1932.

Dunning, Duncan. "A Working Plan for the Del Monte Forest of the Pacific Improvement Company." M.S. thesis, University of California, 1916.

Eitel, Edward E. *Picturesque Del Monte*. San Francisco: The Bancroft Company Printers, 1888.

Epel, David. "Stanford-by-the-Sea: A Brief History of Hopkins Marine Station." *Sandstone and Tile* 16, no. 4 (Fall 1992): 3–9.

Esherick, Joseph. "An Architectural Practice in the San Francisco Bay Area, 1938–1996: Oral History Transcript." Interviewed by Suzanne B. Riess. Berkeley: Regional Oral History, The Bancroft Library, University of California, Berkeley, 1996.

Fay, F. J. "'Raw Packing' of Sardines Makes Notable Saving Possible." *Pacific Fisherman*, December 1929, 21–22.

Fiege, Mark. *Irrigated Eden: The Making of an Agricultural Landscape in the American West*. Seattle: University of Washington Press, 1999.

Field, M. H. "Mid-Winter Days at Monterey." *Overland Monthly* 10, no. 60 (December 1887): 612–22.

Fields, W. Gordon. "A Preliminary Report on the Fishery and on the Biology of the Squid, *Loligo opalescens*." *California Fish and Game* 36, no. 4 (October 1950): 366–77.

Fitch, J. R. "A Glimpse of Monterey." In *Picturesque California and the Region West of the Rocky Mountains from Alaska to Mexico*, edited by John Muir, 39–48. San Francisco: J. Dewing, 1888.

Fitzgerald, Donald. *The History and Significance of the Hovden Cannery, Cannery Row, Monterey, California, 1914–1973*. Submitted by Carroll W. Pursell Jr., principal investigator to Monterey Bay Aquarium Foundation, 15 November 1979.

Friday, Chris. *Organizing Asian American Labor: The Pacific Coast Canned-Salmon Industry, 1870–1942*. Philadelphia: Temple University Press, 1994.

Fry, Donald H., Jr. "The Ring Net, Half Ring Net, or Purse Lampara in the Fisheries of California." California Department of Natural Resources, Division of Fish and Game. *Fish Bulletin No. 27* (1931).

Goode, George Brown. *The Fisheries and Fishery Industries of the United States*. 5 sections, 8 parts. Washington, D.C.: Government Printing Office, 1887.

Gordon, Burton LeRoy. *Monterey Bay Area: Natural History and Cultural Imprints*. 3rd ed. Pacific Grove, CA: Boxwood Press, 1996.

Gould, Sondra L. "David Jacks: The Letter of the Law." M.A. thesis, California State University, Fullerton, 1992.

Greene, B. D. Marx. "An Historical Review of the Legal Aspects of the Use of Food Fish for Reduction Purposes." *California Fish and Game* 13, no. 1 (January 1927): 1–17.

———. "An Historical Review of the Legal Aspects of the Use of Food Fish for Reduction Purposes." *California Fish and Game* 14, no. 1 (January 1928): 42–44.

Guglielmo, Thomas A. "'No Color Barrier': Italians, Race, and Power in the United States." In *Are Italians White? How Race is Made in America*, edited by Jennifer Guglielmo and Salvatore Salerno, 29–43. New York: Routledge, 2003.

———. *White on Arrival: Italians, Race, Color, and Power in Chicago, 1890–1945*. New York: Oxford University Press, 2003.

Haas, Lisbeth. *Conquests and Historical Identities in California, 1769–1936*. Berkeley and Los Angeles: University of California Press, 1995.

The Handbook to Monterey and Vicinity. Monterey: Walton and Curtis, 1875.

Hatch, F. W. "The Seaside Health Resort of California." *Seventh Biennial Report of the California Board of Health* (1882): 85–103.

Hatton, S. Ross, and George R. Smalley. "Reduction Processes for Sardines in California." *California Fish and Game* 24, no. 4 (October 1938): 391–414.

Hays, Samuel P. *Conservation and the Gospel of Efficiency: The Progressive Conservation Movement, 1890–1920*. Cambridge, MA: Harvard University Press, 1959.

———. *Beauty, Health, and Permanence: Environmental Politics in the United States, 1955–1985*. New York: Cambridge University Press, 1987.

———. *Explorations in Environmental History: Essays by Samuel P. Hays*. Pittsburgh: University of Pittsburgh Press, 1998.

Hemp, Michael Kenneth. *Cannery Row: The History of John Steinbeck's Old Ocean View Avenue*. Carmel, CA: The History Company, 2002.

Hensel, Margaret. "Cannery Row." *Game and Gossip*, July 1952, 12, 34.

Hibbard, Charles W. *The Sportsman at Del Monte, Illustrated*. San Francisco: Southern Pacific Company, Passenger Department, 1897.

Hosmer, Charles B., Jr. *Presence of the Past: A History of the Preservation Movement in the United States Before Williamsburg.* New York: G. P. Putnam's Sons, 1965.

———. *Preservation Comes of Age: From Williamsburg to the National Trust, 1926–1949.* 2 vols. Charlottesville: University Press of Virginia, 1981.

Hotel Del Monte, California: George P. Snell, Manager. San Francisco: Sunset Press, 1900.

Hotel Del Monte, Monterey, California, U.S.A. Del Monte, CA: The Hotel, 1898.

Hotel Del Monte: Monterey, California, U.S.A. Monterey, CA: The Hotel, 1899.

Hurley, Andrew. *Environmental Inequalities: Class, Race, and Industrial Pollution in Gary, Indiana, 1945–1980.* Chapel Hill: University of North Carolina Press, 1995.

———. "Busby's Stink Boat and the Regulation of Nuisance Trades, 1865–1918." In *Common Fields: An Environmental History of St. Louis,* edited by Andrew Hurley, 145–62. St. Louis: Missouri Historical Society Press, 1997.

Hyde, Anne Farrar. *An American Vision: Far Western Landscapes and National Culture, 1820–1910.* New York: New York University Press, 1990.

Isenberg, Andrew. *The Destruction of the Bison: An Environmental History, 1750–1920.* New York: Cambridge University Press, 2000.

Issler, Anne Roller. "Robert Louis Stevenson in Monterey." *Pacific Historical Review* 34, no. 3 (1965): 305–21.

Jacobson, Matthew Frye. *Whiteness of a Different Color: European Immigrants and the Alchemy of Race.* Cambridge, MA: Harvard University Press, 1998.

Jacoby, Karl. "Class and Environmental History: Lessons from 'The War in the Adirondacks.'" *Environmental History* 2, no. 3 (July 1997): 324–42.

———. *Crimes against Nature: Squatters, Poachers, Thieves, and the Hidden History of American Conservation.* Berkeley and Los Angeles: University of California Press, 2001.

Jakle, John A. *The Tourist: Travel in Twentieth Century North America.* Lincoln: University of Nebraska Press, 1985.

James, Bushrod. *American Resorts with Notes upon Their Climate.* Philadelphia: F. A. Davis, 1889.

Janssen, John F., Jr. "First Report of Sardine Tagging in California." *California Fish and Game* 23, no. 3 (July 1937): 190–204.

Jenkins, O. P. "The Hopkins Seaside Laboratory." *Zoë* 4, no. 1 (April 1893): 58–63.

Johnson, Benjamin Heber. "Conservation, Subsistence, and Class at the Birth of Superior National Forest." *Environmental History* 4, no. 1 (January 1999): 80–99.

Johnson, Elaine D. *A Sociological Study of the Monterey Area.* Monterey, CA: City Planning Commission, 1968.

Jordan, David Starr. "Coast of California." In George Brown Goode, *The Fisheries and Fishery Industries of the United States*. Section 5, Volume 2. Washington, D.C.: Government Printing Office, 1887.

———. *The Days of Man, Being Memories of a Naturalist, Teacher and Minor Prophet of Democracy, Volume One, 1851–1899*. New York: World Book Company, 1922.

Judd, Richard W. *Common Lands, Common People: The Origins of Conservation in Northern New England*. Cambridge, MA: Harvard University Press, 1997.

K. Hovden Company. *The History of Portola*. Monterey, CA: K. Hovden Co., n.d.

Klingle, Matthew. "Spaces for Consumption in Environmental History" (Theme Issue on Environment and History). *History and Theory* 42, no. 4 (December 2003): 94–110.

Knight, Carleton, III. "Purposeful Chaos on Cannery Row." *Architecture*, June 1985, 52–59.

Knight, Michelle Ann. "A Political Culture of Conservation: Citizen Action and Marine Conservation in Monterey Bay." Ph.D. dissertation, University of California, Santa Cruz, 1997.

Kocks, Dorothee E. *Dream a Little: Land and Social Justice in Modern America*. Berkeley and Los Angeles: University of California Press, 2000.

Koppes, Clayton R. "Efficiency/Equity/Esthetics: Towards a Reinterpretation of American Conservation." *Environmental Review* 11, no. 2 (Summer 1987): 127–46.

Kropp, Phoebe S. *California Vieja: Culture and Memory in a Modern American Place*. Berkeley and Los Angeles: University of California Press, 2006.

Langenbach, Randolph. *A Future from the Past: The Case for Conservation and Reuse of Old Buildings in Industrial Communities*. Washington, D.C.: U.S. Department of Housing and Urban Development, 1978.

Larsh, Ed. *Doc's Lab: Myth and Legends from Cannery Row*. Monterey, CA: PBL Press, 1995.

Lenček, Lena, and Gideon Bosker. *The Beach: The History of Paradise on Earth*. New York: Penguin Books, 1998.

Leos, Robert. "Pacific Sardine: A Little Silver Fish That Is a Silver Lining." *The J.B. Phillips Historical Fisheries Report* 1, no. 1 (Spring 2000).

Limerick, Patricia Nelson. "Seeing and Being Seen: Tourism in the American West." In *Over the Edge: Remapping the American West*, edited by Valerie J. Matsumoto and Blake Allmendinger, 15–31. Berkeley and Los Angeles: University of California Press, 1999.

Lindner, Milton J. "Luminescent Fishing." *California Fish and Game* 16, no. 3 (July 1930): 237–40.

———. "Fishing Localities at Monterey from November, 1919 to March, 1929, for the California Sardine (*Sardina caerulea*)." California Department of Natural Resources, Division of Fish and Game. *Fish Bulletin No. 25* (1930).

Lotchin, Roger W. *Fortress California, 1910–1961: From Warfare to Welfare.* Berkeley and Los Angeles: University of California Press, 1992.

———. *The Way We Really Were: The Golden State in the Second Great War.* Urbana and Chicago: University of Illinois Press, 2000.

Lowenthal, David. *The Past Is a Foreign Country.* New York: Cambridge University Press, 1985.

Lydon, Sandy. *Chinese Gold: The Chinese in the Monterey Bay Region.* Capitola, CA: Capitola Book Company, 1985.

———. *The Japanese in the Monterey Bay Region: A Brief History.* Capitola, CA: Capitola Book Company, 1997.

Manaka v. Monterey Sardine Industries, Inc., et al. 41 F. Supp. 531 (N.D. Calif. 1941).

Mangelsdorf, Tom. *A History of Steinbeck's Cannery Row.* Santa Cruz, CA: Western Tanager Press, 1986.

March, Ray A. *A Guide to Cannery Row.* Monterey, CA: the author, 1962.

Margolin, Malcolm. *The Ohlone Way: Indian Life in the San Francisco–Monterey Bay Area.* Berkeley, CA: Heyday Books, 1978.

McCay, Bonnie J. *Oyster Wars and the Public Trust: Property, Law, and Ecology in New Jersey History.* Tucson: University of Arizona Press, 1998.

McCosker, John E. "Ed Ricketts: A Role Model for Marine Biologists." *The Steinbeck Newsletter, Cannery Row Fiftieth Anniversary Edition,* Fall 1995, 12–14.

McEvoy, Arthur F. *The Fisherman's Problem: Ecology and Law in the California Fisheries, 1850–1980.* New York: Cambridge University Press, 1986.

McEvoy, Arthur F., and Harry N. Scheiber. "Scientists, Entrepreneurs, and the Policy Process: A Study of the Post-1945 California Sardine Depletion." *Journal of Economic History* 44, no. 2 (June 1984): 393–406.

McFarland, F. M. "The Hopkins Seaside Laboratory." *Journal of Applied Microscopy and Laboratory Methods* 5, no. 7 (July 1902): 1869–75.

McKibben, Carol. "Festa Italia in Monterey: A Study of Italian Women Immigrants in Monterey." *Noticias del Puerto de Monterey* 69, no. 1 (October 1998): 2–14.

———. "Of All the Gifts You Gave Me the Most Important One Is That I Belong. The Sicilians: Chain Migration, Gender, and the Construction of Identity in Monterey, California, 1920–1999." Ph.D. dissertation, University of California, Berkeley, 1999.

———. *Beyond Cannery Row: Sicilian Women, Immigration, and Community in Monterey, California, 1915–99.* Urbana and Chicago: University of Illinois Press, 2006.

McNulty, Lorraine. "Old New Cannery Row." *Game and Gossip*, 30 October 1959, 2–7.

McWilliams, Carey. *North from Mexico: The Spanish-Speaking People of the United States*. Philadelphia and New York: J. B. Lippincott Company, 1949.

Merchant, Carolyn. "Shades of Darkness: Race and Environmental History." *Environmental History* 8, no. 3 (July 2003): 380–94.

Mikkelson, Tom. "The Aquarium at the End of Cannery Row." *California Waterfront Age* 1, no. 2 (Spring 1985): 26–41.

Mitman, Gregg. *The State of Nature: Ecology, Community, and American Social Thought, 1900–1950*. Chicago: University of Chicago Press, 1992.

———. *Reel Nature: America's Romance with Wildlife on Film*. Cambridge, MA: Harvard University Press, 1999.

———. "In Search of Health: Landscape and Disease in American Environmental History." *Environmental History* 10, no. 2 (April 2005): 184–210.

Monterey Bay Aquarium. *Monterey Bay Aquarium*. Monterey, CA: Monterey Bay Aquarium Foundation, 1992.

———. *1995 Visitor Highlights*. Monterey, CA: Monterey Bay Aquarium, 1996.

———. *A Natural History of the Monterey Bay National Marine Sanctuary*. Monterey, CA: Monterey Bay Aquarium Foundation, 1997.

———. *2000 Visitor Highlights*. Monterey, CA: Monterey Bay Aquarium, 2001.

"Monterey Bay Aquarium Construction Uses Innovative Materials and Methods." *California Builder and Engineer*, January 21, 1985, 20–21.

Monterey Bay Aquarium Research Institute. *MBARI's First Decade: A Retrospective*. Moss Landing, CA: Monterey Bay Aquarium Research Institute, 1997.

Monterey, California: The Most Charming Winter Resort in the World. Monterey, CA: n.p., 1881.

Monterey Chamber of Commerce. *Monterey Harbor, What It Is and Has, and Why It Should Be Improved*. Monterey, CA: Monterey Chamber of Commerce, 1909.

Monterey Department of City Planning. *Cannery Row Plan: An Element of the General Plan*. Monterey, CA: Department of City Planning, 1973.

Monterey Planning Department. *Cannery Row Plan Revision: Existing Physical Conditions, Working Paper, July 1972*. Monterey, CA: The Commission, 1972.

———. *Environmental Impact Report: Cannery Row Plan*. Monterey, CA: Monterey Planning Department, 1973.

Morrow, W. C. *Souvenir of the Hotel Del Monte, Monterey, California*. San Francisco: Press of H. S. Crocker, 1894.

Mosley, Stephen. "Common Ground: Integrating Social and Environmental History." *Journal of Social History* 39, no. 3 (Spring 2006): 915–33.

Murphy, Garth I. "Oceanography and Variation in the Pacific Sardine Population." In California Cooperative Oceanic Fisheries Investigations. *Reports, 1*

July 1959 to 30 June 1960. Sacramento: State of California, Department of Fish and Game, Marine Research Committee, 1961.

N. C. Carnall and Co. *N. C. Carnall and Co.'s California Guide for Tourists and Settlers*. San Francisco: N. C. Carnall and Co., 1889.

Nash, Gerald D. *The American West Transformed: The Impact of the Second World War*. Lincoln: University of Nebraska Press, 1985.

Nash, Linda. *Inescapable Ecologies: A History of Environment, Disease, and Knowledge*. Berkeley and Los Angeles: University of California Press, 2006.

Norkunas, Martha K. *The Politics of Public Memory: Tourism, History, and Ethnicity in Monterey, California*. Albany: State University of New York Press, 1993.

O'Connor, James. "Three Ways to Think About the Ecological History of Monterey Bay." *Capitalism, Nature, Socialism* 6, no. 2 (June 1995): 21–47.

Orsi, Richard. *Sunset Limited: The Southern Pacific Railroad and the Development of the American West, 1850–1930*. Berkeley and Los Angeles: University of California Press, 2005.

Pacific Planning and Research. *Monterey, California: General Plan for Future Development*. Palo Alto, CA: Pacific Planning and Research, 1959.

Parini, Jay. *John Steinbeck: A Biography*. London: Heinemann, 1994.

Parker, Harold Kermit. "Population, Employment, and Post High School Education in the Monterey Peninsula." Ph.D. dissertation, Stanford University, 1952.

Payne, Stephen Michael. "Unheeded Warnings: A History of Monterey's Sardine Fishery." Ph.D. dissertation, University of California, Santa Barbara, 1987.

The Peninsula Tomorrow: Preliminary Area Plan. California: Hall and Goodhue—Eisner Stewart and Associates, 1963.

The People v. K. Hovden Company. 215 Cal. 54, 8 P.2d 481 (1932).

Person, Richard. *The History of Cannery Row*. Monterey, CA: City Planning Commission, 1972.

Phillips, J. B. "Success of the Purse Seine Boat in the Sardine Fishery at Monterey, California, 1929–1930 Fishing Season." California Department of Natural Resources, Division of Fish and Game. *Fish Bulletin No. 23* (1930).

———. "A Survey of the Destructiveness of the Sardine Nets Used in the Monterey Region." *California Fish and Game* 18, no. 3 (July 1932): 208–18.

———. "Changes in Sardine Fishing Gear in the Monterey Region, with a Note on Expansion of Fishing Grounds." *California Fish and Game* 20, no. 2 (April 1934): 134–39

———. "Notes on Sardine Gear Changes at Monterey." *California Fish and Game* 23, no. 3 (July 1937): 221–23.

———. "Sizes of California Sardines Caught in Different Areas of the Monterey and San Pedro Regions." California Department of Natural Resources, Division of Fish and Game. *Fish Bulletin No. 50* (1937).

Pinsky, Paul G., and Wayne Ball. *The California Sardine Fishery: Review and*

Analysis of the Biological, Statistical and Environmental Information about the California Sardine. San Pedro, CA: n.p., 1948.

The Planning Collaborative. *Environmental Impact Report, Monterey Bay Aquarium, Monterey, California.* San Francisco: The Planning Collaborative, 1979.

Poindexter, Anne. "More Nostalgia Than Noise Now, and Only the Faintest of Stinks." *Game and Gossip,* 1 July 1969, 3–8, 27–28.

Pomeroy, Earl. *In Search of the Golden West: The Tourist in Western America.* Lincoln: University of Nebraska Press, 1990. First published 1957 by Knopf.

Powell, David C. *A Fascination for Fish: Adventures of an Underwater Pioneer.* Berkeley and Los Angeles: University of California Press, 2001.

Price, Jennifer. *Flight Maps: Adventures with Nature in Modern America.* New York: Basic Books, 1999.

Radovich, John. "The Collapse of the California Sardine Fishery: What Have We Learned?" In *Resource Management and Environmental Uncertainty: Lessons from Coastal Upwelling Fisheries,* edited by Michael H. Glantz and J. Dana Thompson, 107–36. New York: Wiley, 1981.

Rand, Judy, and Hank Armstrong. *Monterey Bay Aquarium.* Monterey, CA: Blake Printing and Publishing and Monterey Bay Aquarium, 1985.

Raymond-Whitcomb, Inc. *Two Grand Winter Trips to California with Sojourns at the Hotel Del Monte, Monterey, and the Other Famous Health Resorts of Central and Southern California.* Boston: James S. Adams Printer, 1883.

———. *A Winter Trip to California and a Sojourn of Five Months at the Hotel Del Monte, Monterey, California.* Boston: James S. Adams Printer, n.d.

Remondino, P. C. *Longevity and Climate: Relations of Climatic Conditions to Longevity, History, and Religion—Relations of Climate to National and Personal Habits—The Climate of California and Its Effects in Relation to Longevity.* San Francisco: Woodward and Co., 1890.

Rhodes, Linda, and Charles Davis. "Preserving the Form, Reversing the Function: From Fish Cannery to Aquarium." *California Historical Society,* September 1984, 6–7.

Richard Raymond Associates. *An Economic Analysis of the Monterey Area.* Monterey, CA: City Planning Commission, 1969.

Ricketts, Edward F., and Jack Calvin. *Between Pacific Tides: An Account of the Habits and Habitats of Some Five Hundred of the Common, Conspicuous Seashore Invertebrates of the Pacific Coast between Sitka, Alaska and Northern Mexico.* Stanford: Stanford University Press, 1939.

Rink, Peggy. "Pilgrimage to Wing Chong's." *What's Doing on the Monterey Peninsula,* 9 March 1953, 11, 32–33.

Rome, Adam. "Coming to Terms with Pollution: The Language of Environmental Reform." *Environmental History* 1, no. 3 (July 1996): 6–28.

————. "'Give Earth a Chance': The Environmental Movement and the Sixties." *Journal of American History* 90, no. 2 (September 2003): 525–54.

Rose, Carol M. *Property and Persuasion: Essays on the History, Theory, and Rhetoric of Ownership*. Boulder, CO: Westview Press, 1994.

Rosen, Christine Meisner. "Noisome, Noxious, and Offensive Vapors, Fumes and Stenches in American Towns and Cities, 1840–1865." *Historical Geography* 25 (1997): 49–82.

Rosenberg, Earl H. "A History of the Fishing and Canning Industries in Monterey, California." M.A. thesis, University of Nevada, 1961.

Rothman, Hal K. *Devil's Bargains: Tourism in the Twentieth-Century American West*. Lawrence: University Press of Kansas, 1998.

————. *The Greening of a Nation?: Environmentalism in the United States Since 1945*. Fort Worth, TX: Harcourt Brace and Company, 1998.

————. "Stumbling toward the Millennium: Tourism, the Postindustrial World, and the Transformation of the American West." *California History* 77, no. 3 (Fall 1998): 140–57.

————. *Saving the Planet: The American Response to the Environment in the Twentieth Century*. Chicago: Ivan R. Dee, 2000.

Sardine Fisheries: Hearings Before the Committee on Merchant Marine and Fisheries. Seventy-fourth Congress, March 10 and 11, 1936. Washington, D.C.: Government Printing Office, 1936.

Saxton, Alexander. *The Indispensable Enemy: Labor and the Anti-Chinese Movement in California*. Berkeley and Los Angeles: University of California Press, 1971.

Schaefer, Milner B., Oscar E. Sette, and John C. Marr. "Growth of the Pacific Coast Pilchard Fishery to 1942." United States Department of the Interior, Fish and Wildlife Service. *Research Report*, no. 29 (1951): 1–31.

Schultz, Stanley K. *Constructing Urban Culture: American Cities and City Planning, 1800–1930*. Philadelphia: Temple University Press, 1989.

Scofield, E. C., and M. J. Lindner. "Preliminary Report on the Early Life History of the California Sardine." *California Fish and Game* 16, no. 1 (January 1930): 120–24.

Scofield, Eugene C. "Early Life History of the California Sardine (*Sardina caerulea*), with Special Reference to the Distribution of Eggs and Larvae." California Department of Natural Resources, Division of Fish and Game. *Fish Bulletin No. 41* (1934).

Scofield, N. B. "Shall We Use Food Fish for Fertilizer?" *California Fish and Game* 7, no. 2 (April 1921): 124.

————. "The Lampara Net." *California Fish and Game* 10, no. 2 (April 1924): 66–70.

————. "Commercial Fishery Notes." *California Fish and Game* 15, no. 4 (October 1929): 353–55.

Scofield, W. L. "Fertilizer, Stockfood and Oil from Sardine Offal." *California Fish and Game* 4, no. 4 (October 1921): 207–17.

———. "Squid at Monterey." *California Fish and Game* 10, no. 4 (October 1924): 176–82.

———. "Purse Seines for California Sardines." *California Fish and Game* 12, no. 1 (January 1926): 16–19.

———. "Sardine Fishing Methods at Monterey." California Department of Natural Resources, Division of Fish and Game. *Fish Bulletin No. 19* (1929).

———. "Sardine Oil and Our Troubled Waters." *California Fish and Game* 24, no. 3 (July 1938): 210–23.

———. "Is the Purse Seine an Engine of Destruction?" *California Fish and Game* 25, no. 4 (October 1939): 325–29.

Severance, H. D. "Control of Cannery Odors at Monterey." *Sewage Works Journal* 4, no. 1 (January 1932): 152–55.

Shah, Nayan. *Contagious Divides: Epidemics and Race in San Francisco's Chinatown.* Berkeley and Los Angeles: University of California Press, 2001.

Shepard, A. D. *Pebble Beach, Monterey County, California.* San Francisco: H. S. Crocker Co., 1909.

Shew, A. M. *California as a Health Resort.* Boston: James S. Adams, 1885.

Simmonds, Roy. *John Steinbeck: The War Years, 1939–1945.* Lewisburg, PA: Bucknell University Press, 1996.

Smith, Edgar C. "The Hotel Del Monte Goes to War." *Dogtown Territorial Quarterly* 49 (2002): 46–58.

Smith, Tim D. *Scaling Fisheries: The Science of Measuring the Effects of Fishing, 1855–1955.* New York: Cambridge University Press, 1994.

Spence, Mark. *Dispossessing the Wilderness: Indian Removal and the Making of the National Parks.* New York: Oxford University Press, 1999.

Steinbeck, John. *Cannery Row.* New York: Viking Press, 1945.

———. *The Log from the Sea of Cortez.* New York: Viking Press, 1951.

———. *Sweet Thursday.* New York: Viking Press, 1954.

———. *Travels with Charley: In Search of America.* New York: Viking Press, 1962.

Steinbeck, John, and Edward F. Ricketts. *Sea of Cortez: A Leisurely Journey of Travel and Research.* New York: Viking Press, 1941.

Steinberg, Theodore. *Down to Earth: Nature's Role in American History.* New York: Oxford University Press, 2002.

Stevenson, Robert Louis. *Across the Plains with Other Memories and Essays.* New York: C. Scribner's Sons, 1892.

Stewart, Mart. *"What Nature Suffers to Groe": Life, Labor, and Landscape on the Georgia Coast, 1680–1920.* Athens: University of Georgia Press, 1996.

Stilgoe, John. *Alongshore.* New Haven, CT: Yale University Press, 1994.

Streatfield, David C. "Where Pine and Palm Meet: The California Garden as a Regional Expression." *Landscape Journal* 4, no. 2 (Fall 1985): 61–73.

———. *California Gardens: Creating a New Eden.* New York: Abbeville Press, 1994.

Takaki, Ronald. *Strangers from a Different Shore: A History of Asian Americans.* Updated and revised edition. Boston: Back Bay Books, 1998.

Taylor, Alan. "Unnatural Inequalities: Social and Environmental Histories." *Environmental History* 1, no. 4 (October 1996): 6–19.

Taylor, Joseph E. III. "El Niño and Vanishing Salmon: Culture, Nature, History, and the Politics of Blame." *Western Historical Quarterly* 29, no. 4 (Winter 1998): 437–57.

———. "Burning the Candles at Both Ends: Historicizing Overfishing in Oregon's Nineteenth-Century Salmon Fisheries." *Environmental History* 4, no. 1 (January 1999): 54–79.

———. *Making Salmon: An Environmental History of the Northwest Fisheries Crisis.* Seattle: University of Washington Press, 1999.

Thompson, Will F. "The Proposed Investigation of the Sardine." *California Fish and Game* 6, no. 1 (January 1920): 10–12.

———. "The Future of the Sardine." *California Fish and Game* 7, no. 1 (January 1921): 38–41.

———. "Historical Review of the California Sardine Industry." *California Fish and Game* 7, no. 4 (October 1921): 195–206.

———. "The Fisheries of California and Their Care." *California Fish and Game* 8, no. 3 (July 1922): 165–77.

Thompson, Will F., and Elmer Higgins. "Notes from the State Fisheries Laboratory." *California Fish and Game* 6, no. 1 (January 1920): 32–33.

Tibbetts, Fred H. *Report to the City of Monterey, California on Municipal Harbor Improvement.* San Francisco: n.p., 1922.

Towe, Dudley. "This Is Cannery Row." *Game and Gossip,* 3 March 1958, 2–5, 14.

Turner, James Morton. "From Woodcraft to 'Leave No Trace': Wilderness, Consumerism, and Environmentalism in Twentieth-Century America." *Environmental History* 7, no. 3 (July 2002): 462–84.

Tyrrell, Ian. *True Gardens of the Gods: Californian-Australian Environmental Reform, 1860–1930.* Berkeley and Los Angeles: University of California Press, 1999.

United States Bureau of the Census. *California, Monterey County, 1930 Population Schedule.* Microfilm Publication T626, Roll 179.

———. *Sixteenth Census of the United States, 1940, Population, Vol. 2, Characteristics of the Population.* Washington, D.C.: Government Printing Office, 1942–43.

Valenčius, Conevery Bolton. *The Health of the Country: How American Settlers Understood Themselves and Their Land*. New York: Basic Books, 2002.

Van Dusen, Debra. "The Nation's Newest Aquarium." *BioScience* 65, no. 10 (November 1985): 614–17.

Walton, John. "Cannery Row: Class, Community, and the Social Construction of History." In *Reworking Class*, edited by John R. Hall, 243–83. Ithaca, NY: Cornell University Press, 1997.

———. *Storied Land: Community and Memory in Monterey*. Berkeley and Los Angeles: University of California Press, 2001.

Warren, Louis S. *The Hunter's Game: Poachers and Conservationists in Twentieth-Century America*. New Haven, CT: Yale University Press, 1997.

Weber, David J. *The Mexican Frontier, 1821–1846: The American Southwest Under Mexico*. Albuquerque: University of New Mexico Press, 1982.

———. *The Spanish Frontier in North America*. New Haven, CT: Yale University Press, 1992.

West, Elliott. *The Contested Plains: Indians, Goldseekers, and the Rush to Colorado*. Lawrence: University Press of Kansas, 1998.

White, Richard. *Land Use, Environment, and Social Change: The Shaping of Island County, Washington*. Seattle: University of Washington Press, 1980.

———. *The Roots of Dependency: Subsistence, Environment, and Social Change among the Choctaws, Pawnees, and Navajos*. Lincoln: University of Nebraska Press, 1983.

———. *"It's Your Misfortune and None of My Own": A New History of the American West*. Norman: University of Oklahoma Press, 1991.

———. *The Organic Machine: The Remaking of the Columbia River*. New York: Hill and Wang, 1995.

———. "'Are You an Environmentalist or Do You Work for a Living?': Work and Nature." In *Uncommon Ground: Rethinking the Human Place in Nature*, edited by William Cronon, 171–85. New York: W. W. Norton, 1996.

Wilcox, William A. "Fisheries of the Pacific Coast." In *Report of the Commissioner of Fish and Fisheries for the Year Ending June 30, 1893*. Washington, D.C.: Government Printing Office, 1895.

———. "Notes on the Fisheries of the Pacific Coast in 1895." In *Report of the Commissioner of Fish and Fisheries*. Washington, D.C.: Government Printing Office, 1898.

Williams, Sydney. *Cannery Row Plan*. Monterey, CA: City Planning Commission, 1961.

———. *A Plan for the Cannery Row Area of the City of Monterey*. Third printing. Monterey, CA: the author, 1967.

Wood, Williard M. "On a Collecting Trip to Monterey Bay." *Nautilus* 7, no. 6 (October 1893): 70–72.

Works Progress Administration. *History of the City Government of Monterey.* Monterey, CA: n.p., 1937.

Work Projects Administration. *Monterey Peninsula: American Guide Series.* Berkeley, CA: Press of the Courier, 1941.

Worster, Donald. *Dust Bowl: The Southern Plains in the 1930s.* New York: Oxford University Press, 1979.

Yamada, David. *The Japanese of the Monterey Peninsula: Their History and Legacy.* Monterey, CA: Monterey Peninsula Japanese American Citizens League, 1995.

INDEX

abalone: as aquarium displays, 171; cannery processing of, 48; fisheries, 13, 18; World War II restrictions on Japanese fishermen, 107

Abbott, Carlisle, 20

Aeneas Sardine Products Company, 133

affordable housing issues, 189

Agassiz, Louis, 16, 197n17

Agudo, Luis, 91

Alaska Fishermen's Union (CIO), 85

Albert, Dan, 183–84

Allan, Alexander M., 18

Allee, Warder Clyde, 124

Allen, Ron, 176

Allen, W. F., 57

Alliotti, Tom, 114

American Federation of Labor (AFL), 82–86, 104, 112, 120

America's Most Endangered Historic Places list, 182–83

anchovies, 129–30, 134–35

Anderson, Jack, 84

Aquaravan, 180

Aron, Cindy, 27

arson, 33, 146

Ashley, Delos, 19

Asian imports of fish, 16, 49

Asians. See Chinese community; Filipino workers; Japanese community

auto camping, 41

Balbo, Giovanna, 79

Batinovich, Matt, 82

Baxter, Chuck, 157

beaches, public, 152

Beaumont, Jack, 92

Benson, Jackson, 139

Benton, Robert M., 140

Bergara, Frank, 162

Bernays, D. E., 42–43

Best, Neely S., 110

Between Pacific Tides (Ricketts), 124

Biological Board of Canada, 123

Blinks, Lawrence, 157

Bonnot, Paul, 63, 85

Boone, Jane, 112

Booth, Alfred, 49

Booth, Frank E.: closing of cannery, 100; fish canning technology, 62; fish odors and tourism, 96–97; fishermen employed by, 51–53; opening and expansion of canneries, 48–50; reduction, 58, 62, 77

269

Bottoms, William F., 134
Bowen, Mildred, 84
brailing, 51
breakwaters, 67, 213n29
Brown, Arthur, 22
Bruce, Donald, 45
Bruno Fish Market, 136
Bryan, Jesse W., 32
Burnett, Nancy, 157–58
Burnett, Robin, 157–58

Cafferty, Dave, 145
California, State of: anti-Asian legislation, 16; granting of shoreline ownership to Monterey, 47; Health Board on sewage problems, 30; lampara net-banning proposals, 54–55; taking of young fish prohibited by, 15; Unemployment Insurance Appeals Board, 120. *See also* Fish and Game Commission (California)
California Academy of Sciences, 127
California Coastal Commission (CCC), 153–54, 158, 185
California Coastal Initiative, 153, 158
California Cooperative Oceanic Fisheries Investigation (CalCOFI), 128–30
California Cooperative Sardine Research Program, 127–28
California Current, 126–27
California Historical Society, 163
California Marine Research Committee, 126–30
California Packing Corporation (Cal-Pack), 62, 96, 110, 112, 133
California Sardine Fishermen's Association, 72
California State Fisheries Laboratory, 126, 130

California State Real Estate Convention, Monterey, *1926*, 93–94
Californios, 5
Calpak Properties, Inc., 151
Campbell, Argyle, 72
Campbell, Dwight, 118
Campbell, James, 145
Campoy, Al, 162
Canepa, Theresa, 88, 184
canneries: as abstract visual composition, 150; adaptation to purse-seine boats, 65; after collapse of sardine fishery, 132–35; automating of, 49, 61–62; Cannery Row map (ca. *1946*), 116; city inspectors at, 94; closing of last plant, 153, 157; closures by restraining order, 69–70; demographics of workers in, 49–50; deterioration of, 146–48; establishment of, 47; evasion of laws limiting reduction, 68–69; failure to adopt conservation measures, 124–25; fires in, 100, 146–147; growth of, 48, 50; labor struggles with, 79–86; measurement of fish quantities by, 68–69; migrant workers, 86, 106; as objects of nostalgia, 141–54; odors from, 91–101; plans for redevelopment of, 144–45; preservation of, 182–83; union agreements with, 83; vandalism of, 147–48; women as workers in, 49–50, 86–87, 110, 111*fig*, 112; working hours in, 83; World War II's impact on, 102; yearly cycle in, 60–61. *See also* reduction; sardine industry
Cannery Row Conservation District, 183
Cannery Row Local Coastal Program, 154
Cannery Row Plan (*1961*), 144–45

Cannery Row Plan (*1973*), 149, 151–
  54, 163, 175
Cannery Row Promotional District,
  176
Cannery Row Properties Company,
  135, 144, 148
Cannery Row Square, 151
Cannery Row (Steinbeck), 10, 124,
  132–33, 138–41, 153
Cannery Workers Union Local
  No. *20305* (AFL), 82, 84
Cannery Workers Union Local
  No. *20986* (AFL), 84
Carmel, 4, 99, 175
Carmel Bay Ecological Reserve, 179
Carmel Canning Company, 62, 111*fig*,
  120, 146
Carmel Valley, 4, 26–27, 175
Carnegie, Andrew, 22
Carson, Rachel, 158
Carter, Ruth, 175
Catania, Salvatore, 53
Caveny, Les, 135
Central Coast Regional Water Quality
  Control Board, 159
Cesare Augusta, 86, 90
Chambers of Commerce, Monterey
  and Pacific Grove, 91
Chapman, Wilbert McLeod, 126–27,
  129
China Man Hop Company, 19
chinchola nets, 50
Chinese community: autonomy in
  pre-cannery era fishing, 52; can-
  nery strikes by, 80–81; decline of
  fishing in, 35–36; formation of, 13;
  hotel workers, 25–26, 29; McAbee
  Beach settlement, 34; Point Alones
  fire, 12–13, 33; Portuguese conflict
  with, 14; processing of fish offal
  by, 57–58; rental of land from
  David Jacks, 19–20; squid fishing,

17, 31–36; as supplier to Hopkins
  Seaside Laboratory, 16; as tourist
  attraction, 26, 35; white attitudes
  toward, 14
Chinese Fishing Company, 20
Chong, Wing, 119, 141, 150
Choromanski, Joe, 171–72
Clark, Frances, 74–75, 128, 130–31
Clark, Susie, 25
class: in aquarium vs. merchants
  controversy, 175; competition
  for resources and, 7; diversity in
  tourist accommodations and, 41–
  42; as factor in industrial growth,
  39; geography of, 87–88; land
  ownership and, 46, 59; as rhetoric
  used in defense of pollution, 95–
  97; and tourism, 152, 156, 174,
  179, 188; in the work environment, 80, 88; and World War II,
  108, 112
Clemens, George, 110, 119, 121
climate of Monterey, 28, 44
Coast Guard, U.S., 106
coastline, 6–7
Cockshut, Derek, 176
Coleman, George A., 44
collapse of sardine fishery: canneries
  after, 132–35; conservation advocacy, 120–21; diversified catch in
  response to, 119–20; as imminent,
  71–73; Italian community after,
  136–37; Monterey's identity as
  fishing town and, 10; popular
  theories for, 121–22; reduced
  income from, 120; scientists' conclusions regarding, 122–26; sudden
  loss of fish stocks, 103, 117–18;
  tourism after, 132–33
Colletto, Sal, 65, 87, 104, 106, 119,
  121
Collins, J. W., 14

Colton, David, 21
Conger, Gwyndolyn, 139
Congress of Industrial Organizations (CIO), 83–86, 112
conservation: aquarium's approach to, 187–88; canneries' failure to practice, 124–25, 152; and Cannery Row projects, 154; as popular value, 178–81; post-collapse advocacy of, 120–21; in the post–World War II era, 126; pro-business slant in 1920s toward, 69; World War II approach to, 113
consumption, 178, 190–91
Contract and Finance Company, 21
Corps of Engineers, U.S. Army, 67, 159
Cousteau, Jacques, 158
Cowan, Bruce, 168
Crispo, Frank, 154, 175
Crivello, John, 104
Crocker, Charles, 20–22
Croker, Richard, 122–23
Cronon, William, 6
Custom House Packing Corporation, 110, 151

D'Agui, Francisco, 86
Dall, Caroline, 28
Dall, W. H., 30
Dante Alighieri, 104
Davis, Charles, 161–63
Davis, Herbert, 72
De Groot, John, 147–48, 153
Dean, Bashford, 16–17
Deep Sea and Purse Seine Fishermen's Union (AFL), 82–83
Defense Language Institute, 137
Del Mar Cannery, 86, 89–90, 98, 118
Del Monte Corporation, 151
Del Monte Forest, 40, 44–46, 59

Del Monte Forest Camp, 41–42
Del Monte Properties Company: Filipino workers seen as threat by, 91–92; fish industry conflict with, 80; fish odors, 91–95, 97–100, 150; formation of, 46
Del Vista Packing Company, 114
Denman, William, 73, 75, 112
desalination, 179, 185
Dillon, Mamie, 84
diversity: among workers, 49–50; awareness of nonhuman over human, 156; Cannery Row's lack of, 141; and residential patterns, 87; Stevenson's view of, 4; tourism and erasure of, 133, 152, 156, 165–66, 179–80. See also ethnicity; race
Dodge, Wesley, 135
Dollar, George, 110
Dollar, Robert, 48
Dorton, R. M., 67, 93
Doughery, Jack, 145
dual labor system, 50
Duarte, Emanual, 27
Dubrasich, Donald, 144–45
Dunning, Duncan, 45

Eames, Alfred, 151
Eardley, B. A., 32
earthquakes, 44
El Niño, 169, 171–72
Elkhorn Slough, 179
Employment, California State Department of, 136–37
Enea, Domenica, 79
Enea, Horace, 84
Enterprise Packers, 114
Environmental Impact Reports (EIRs), 159–60
environmental movement, 178–80. See also conservation

Esherick, Homsey, Dodge, and Davis (EHDD), 158, 161, 168
ethnicity: and conflict over development, 7; and fishing gear used, 15; and focus of fishing harvest, 13–14; lacking as factor in *Cannery Row* (novel), 141; lacking as factor in Cannery Row projects, 152, 156, 174; race and, 15; of tourists, 179. *See also* diversity
extractive industries, 8, 191. *See also* canneries; fishing industry; reduction; sardine industry

Fahrion, Margaret, 110
Farley, Maj. John L., 69
Feast of Lanterns, 35–36
Fee, James Alger, 90
Ferrante, Giachino, 53
Ferrante, Pietro, 51–52
Ferrante, Rosa, 79
Ferrante, Rosalie, 88
Ferrante, Sal, 121, 135
Ferrante, Vincente, 53
fertilizer from fish. *See* reduction
fiberglass reinforced concrete (FRC), 166
Fiedler, Reginald, 72
Fields, W. Gordon, 119
Filipino workers, 83, 91–92, 183
fires, 12–13, 33, 44, 146–47
Fish and Game Commission (California): collapse of sardine fishery, 122–23; expansion of sardine industry, 61; fisheries research, 73–76, 114, 117; General Order No. 12, 69; net types studied by, 55–56, 63, 66*fig*; post–World War II research by, 127, 130; Proposition No. 5, 76; regulation of by-product production, 67–72; *Takahashi v. Commission*, 118;

union disagreements, 86; World War II allocation program, 104. *See also* California, State of
Fish and Wildlife Service, U.S., 104, 126
fish by-products. *See* reduction
Fish Cannery and Reduction Workers Union Local No. 73 (CIO), 84
Fisheries, U.S. Bureau of, 72–73
Fisherman's Wharf, Monterey, 47, 49, 53, 93, 122, 150, 189
fishing boats: lateen sailboats, 50; lighters, 51, 62–63; motorized, 51–52, 62; purse seine boats, 63, 64*fig*; for sports fishing, 189
fishing industry: emergence of, 6, 13–14; ethnic differences in equipment used, 15; local vs. migrant workers in, 85–86; as part of extractive economy, 8; post-war diversification of catch, 119–20; technological advances in, 51, 62–63; tourism's relationship with, 7, 10–13, 39, 80, 134–35, 182, 188–90; World War II restrictions on, 103–4, 106–7, 112–13. *See also* sardine industry
fishing settlements: McAbee Beach, 34; Point Alones fire, 12–13, 33; rental of land for, 19–20; seen as unhealthy, 29–32
Fitch, J. R., 17
fixed total tonnages, 128
Fleishhacker, Herbert, 46
floating reduction plants, 70–73
forestry, 44–45
Fort Ord, 106, 134, 137
Foster, Reginald, 99
Franco, Robert, 154

Galigher, A. E., 123
Garlic Hill, 88

Gentlemen's Agreement (1907), 43
Giamona, Francesca, 79
gill netting, 15, 50, 54–56
Gilmer, Sheldon, 98–99
gold rush, California, 5
Gould, W. J., 92
Gradis, Hope, 135–36
Great Depression, 70–71, 75–77, 91, 95, 99
great white sharks, 173
Gross, E. B., 58, 60, 98
Guglielmo, Thomas, 15
Gullion, Nancy, 175

Hackett, Anita, 175
Harper, George, 98
Harrison, Benjamin, 22
Heffner, Hubert, 157
Henry, Lyman, 73, 75
Hensel, Margaret, 141
Higashi, Unosuke, 53
Higgins, Elmer, 72–73, 109
Hill, Louis, 40
Hopkins, Mark, 21
Hopkins, Timothy, 197n17
Hopkins Marine Station, 43, 73, 127, 157, 169
Hopkins Seaside Laboratory, 16, 30, 43
Hotel Del Monte: artificial lake, 24; bathhouse, 24–25, 93; canneries as nemesis of, 150; Chinese laborers, 25–26, 29; construction of, 21–22; decline in profits of, 39; destruction and rebuilding of, 22; gardens of, 23–24, 173; as health resort, 27–28; maintenance costs, 25; as Naval Postgraduate School, 137; odors from canneries, 92, 95, 101, 150; promotion of, 22–23; R.L. Stevenson's view of, 28–29; sale by Pacific Improvement Company of,

46; sewage outflow into bay from, 30; struggle for shoreline by, 9; waterworks, 25–26; women's social activities at, 27; as World War II flight school, 102. See also Pacific Improvement Company; tourism; tourist accommodations
Hotelling, Neal, 182–83
House Committee on Commerce's Fisheries Subcommittee, 71–72
House Committee on Merchant Marine and Fisheries, 71
Houssels, B., 69
Hovden, Knut: arrival in Monterey of, 49; on immigrant labor, 54; legacy of, 154; opening of Hovden Cannery by, 58; retirement and death of, 134; sardine depletion, 121–22, 131; World War II labor shortages, 108, 110
Hovden Cannery: after the collapse of sardine fishery, 134–35; closure of, 153, 157; conversion to aquarium of, 156–57, 159–64, 180, 186–88; employment of white workers, 92; fire in, 146; government regulation, 128; as object of nostalgia, 150; opening of, 58; ownership of, 96
Howe, Kevin, 153
Hubbs, Carl, 208n47
Hudson, W. G., 93
Huntington, Collis P., 21
Hyde, Charles Gilman, 93

Ickes, Harold, 104, 106, 108, 113
Interior, U.S. Department of, 106
International Seamen's Union (AFL), 84
Italian community: after collapse of sardine fishery, 136–37; attainment of whiteness, 15, 89;

class divisions in, 88; conflict with Chinese fishermen, 13–14; domination of canneries by, 86–87, 89–90; domination of sardine fishing by, 52; interaction with Japanese fishermen, 53; lampara net controversy, 54–56; provision of services to fishermen, 53; Santa Rosalia *festa*, 79–80, 88–89; Sicilian dominance of, 89; World War II restrictions on, 102, 106–7

Jacks, David, 19–21
Jacobson, Matthew Frye, 15, 89
James, Bushrod, 28
Japanese community: cannery strikes by, 80–82; construction workers, 43, 59; hotel workers, 26; interaction with Italian fishermen, 53; post–World War II return of, 117–18; provision of services to fishermen, 53; salmon fishermen, 43, 52, 53; sardine fishermen, 52; Sicilian conflict with, 89–90; white attitudes toward, 18, 43; World War II restrictions and internment of, 102, 107–8
Japanese Fishermen's Association, 52–53
jellyfish, 169
Jenkins, Oliver Peebles, 16
Johnson, Elaine, 137
Johnson, Robert F., 32
Johnson, S. B., 118
Jordan, David Starr, 16, 197n17
Juillard, Jean, 94

kelp, 168–69, 173
Knight, Michelle Ann, 179
Kocks, Dorothee, 43
Kodani, Gennosuke, 18

labor unions. *See* unions
Laguna Del Rey, 24
Lake Miraflores, 70
lampara nets, 51, 54–56, 62–63, 65, 66fig
Landers, Maj. W. H., 99
Lang, Otto, 113
Lansing, 70
Larsh, Ed, 132
Laurelles Ranch, 27
Leadership Monterey Peninsula Project, 176
Leard, Frank J., 110
legislation and ordinances: against Chinese shrimp industry, 16; alien fishing prohibition, 16; alien land law (*1913*), 43; anti-squid drying ordinance, 34; California Coastal Act of *1976*, 153–54, 164; Clean Water Act of *1972*, 158; Coastal Zone Management Act (CZMA) of *1972*, 158; Environmental Quality Act of *1970* (California), 152; Fish Conservation Act of *1919*, 62, 68; Fishery Conservation and Management Act of *1976*, 130; Immigration Act of *1924*, 89; Land Act of *1851*, 19; Marine Mammal Protection Act of *1972*, 158; Marine Protection, Research, and Sanctuaries Act (MPRSA) of *1972*, 158; Murphy-Youngman Bill (*1929*), 62, 68; National Environmental Policy Act of *1969*, 152; odor mitigation ordinances, 98–99; permits required for fertilizer plants, 94; Proposition *20* (California Coastal Initiative), 153, 158; Sanborn Young bill (*1931*), 70; sardine tax, 127
Lend-Lease program, 103
Leutzinger, George, 135

Libby, L. L., 175
Local Agency Formation Commission, Monterey County, 185
Local Coastal Program (LCP), 154
Lopez, Joe, 86
Lovejoy, Ritchie, 139
Lovejoy, Tal, 139
Lowenthal, David, 150
Lucido, Angelo, 119
Lucido, E. S., 76
Lucido, Ray, 114
Lucido, Slats, 136
Lunde, William O., 128, 134

Madison, James, 48
Maiorana, Mike, 88
Malpas, Henry, 48
Manaka, Frank, 89–91
Manaka, Royal, 90
Mangelsdorf, Tom, 148
maps, 2, 29, 116
March, Ray, 143
Marr, John C., 128–29
Mason, David T., 45
Mathers, Wallace, 53
McAbee Beach, 34–35, 57
McCafferty, Dave, 145
McEvoy, Arthur, 18, 68, 76, 127, 130
McFarland, F. M., 16
McKibben, Carol, 89, 107, 137, 187
Menchaca, Al, 164
Mercurio, Horace, 109
Mexican community, 81, 83–84, 87
Mexican era in Monterey, 5
miasma, 31
migrant workers, 85–86, 91–92, 106, 180
military role in Monterey, 137–38
Miracle-Gro, 171
Moe, Richard, 183
Monterey American, 40

Monterey and Salinas Valley Railroad Company, 20
Monterey Bay Aquarium: architectural designing of, 160–63; boiler house preserved at, 162; conflicts with merchants, 174–75; construction of, 164; economic impact of, 177–78; EIR for, 159–60; environmental focus of, 156, 173–74, 178; exhibits at, 165–69, 177; exit surveys, 247n119; maintenance problems, 171–72; making artificial rocks for, 166–67; marine life in, 169–72; opening of, 155; parking at, 159–60, 174, 176; planning of, 157–58; popularity of, 174, 177; predation in exhibits at, 171–72; sardine industry history exhibits at, 186–87; seawater system at, 165–67; as source of tourist renewal, 10; staff of, 171; wave machines at, 168. *See also* tourism
Monterey Bay Aquarium Foundation, 157
Monterey Bay Aquarium Research Institute, 172
Monterey Bay Council on Japanese Relations, 117–18
Monterey Bay Sardine and Squid Union, 52
Monterey Boiler Company, 162
Monterey Californian, 14
Monterey Canning Company, 62, 98, 115fig, 146
Monterey Canyon, 172–73
Monterey city government, 209n57
Monterey clipper, 51
Monterey County Labor News, 110
Monterey Daily Cypress, 38, 40, 50, 53, 81
Monterey Fish Processors Association, 110, 118

Monterey Fishermen's Association, 52–53

Monterey Fishermen's Protective Union, 82

Monterey Fishing and Canning Company, 48

Monterey Japanese American Citizens League, 118

Monterey Packing Company, 48

Monterey Peninsula Herald: canneries vs. tourism, 97, 100–101; collapse of sardine fishery, 120, 125; Monterey Bay Aquarium, 168; post–World War II return of Japanese, 117–18; reduction, 70–71; Steinbeck's cannery row proposals, 142; World War II, 105*fig*, 107, 110, 111*fig*, 114

Monterey Peninsula Hotel, 184

Monterey Sardine Industries (MSI), Inc., 72, 79, 82–83, 89–90, 109

Monterey Whaling Company, 14

Morse, Samuel, 42–43, 46, 93, 98–99

Mosher, Kenneth, 109

Mosley, Stephen, 6

Moss Landing, 157, 172, 185

Murphy, Garth, 129

National Labor Relations Board (NLRB), 84, 86

National Marine Fisheries Service, 130

National Register of Historic Places, 159

National Trust for Historic Preservation, 182–83

nativism, 15, 54, 56

Naval Postgraduate School, U.S., 137

Navy, U.S., 102, 104, 121

Neushal, Mike, 168

New Madrid, 86, 90

Nichols, Joseph R., 48

Nix, Bob, 175

Nobusada, Kiyoshi, 118

Noda, Otosaburo, 48

Norkunas, Martha, 141, 234*n*5, 238*n*56

North, Wheeler, 168

Ocean Gift, 89

Ocean View Hotel, 135

Ocean View Plaza, 184

O'Donnell, W. M., 110

odors, 30–35, 91–101, 150

Office of Fishery Coordination, 104

Ohio III, 89

Ohlone Indians, 4

oil spill, Santa Barbara *(1969)*, 158

Okie community, 83–84, 87

Olson, Culbert, 113–14

Ono, Rokumatsu, 53

Open Monterey Project, 185

Osbourne, Fanny, 3

Osmun, Mark Hazard, 147

Outzen, Carl, 189

Oxnard Canners, 121, 135

Pacific Biological Laboratory, 123

Pacific Fish Company, 48, 53, 58

Pacific Fisherman, 58, 113–14, 127, 133

Pacific Grove: fish odors, 98–99; parking issues for aquarium, 160; restaurants in, 136; Steinbeck as resident of, 124

Pacific Grove Hotel, 41

Pacific Grove Marine Gardens Fish Reserve, 179

Pacific Grove Review, 31, 33, 34

Pacific Improvement Company: advertising campaigns, 42–43; ban on squid-drying, 32–33; Chinese workers hired by, 25–26;

Pacific Improvement Company
development of alternate tourist
accommodations, 40–41; development of peninsula holdings, 38–
40, 138; expulsion of Chinese by,
33–35, 37; Feast of Lanterns, 35;
forest improvement objectives, 44–
46, 59; formation of, 21; liquida-
tion of properties of, 46; on sewage
discharge, 57, 150; struggle for
shoreline by, 9; transformation of
coastline by, 28. *See also* Hotel Del
Monte
Packard, David, 155, 157, 166, 168,
172
Packard, John H., 28
Packard, Julie, 157, 160, 162–63,
179
Packard, Lucile, 157, 180
Packard Foundation, 157, 179
Palma, Christopher, 114
Parini, Jay, 138
Parker, Harold, 137
Passanessi, Guiseppe, 53
Pearl Harbor attacks, 90, 107
Pebble Beach, 26, 39–40, 42, 45–46,
101
Peninsula Health and Welfare League,
98
Peralta, 70
Perry, J. R., 120
Phillips, J. B., 122
Phillips, Roger, 168
Phister, Montgomery, 126
pigs (for cleaning aquarium intake
lines), 171
Pinchot, Gifford, 44, 207n32
Pizzimento, Natale, 53
plankton, 122, 125, 129, 166, 171
Platt, Horace, 33
Poindexter, Anne, 148
Point Alones: destruction of Chinese

settlement, 12–13, 33; Hopkins
Marine Station moved to, 43;
resettlement of Chinese from,
34; seen as unhealthy, 29–32
Point Lobos Canning Company, 18
Point Lobos State Reserve, 179
pollution: air, 91–101; by the tourist
industry, 190; water, 30, 56–57, 93
Pomeroy, Earl, 23
population growth, 58–59
Portola Cafe, 178
Portola Packing Company, 157
Portuguese community, 14–15, 52,
83–84, 86–87
Powell, David, 167, 169–71
Prescott, Orville, 139
Presidio of Monterey, 137
Price, Jennifer, 178
Progressive era principles, 44, 56,
69, 72
Proposition 20 (California Coastal
Initiative), 153, 158
Pryor, J. P., 33–35, 57, 98
pueblo lands, Monterey, 19, 21
Pulitzer, Joseph, 22
purse seines, 17, 51, 63, 64*fig*, 65,
66*fig*, 85

race: ethnicity and, 15; government
enforcement of discrimination by,
18–19; of visitors to aquarium,
179; in the work environment, 80,
83, 92. *See also* diversity
racial attitudes: about Asian non-
support of white businesses, 53–
54; toward Asian fishing techniques, 53; about Chinese, 14, 58;
toward squid-drying by Chinese,
31–36
Radovich, John, 127
rails-to-trails programs, 183
Raiter, Frank, 120

Ramberg, Jenny Sayre, 186
Rancho El Pescadero, 19, 21
Rancho Punta de Pinos, 19, 21
Reagan, Ronald, 130
reduction: anchovies used in, 134–35; Chinese processing of offal for, 57–58; fertilizer, 47, 57–58; fishing community disagreements over, 77–78; floating plants for, 70–73; as improper use of fish, 68, 77; odors from, 92, 94–95, 97; profit margins with, 61–62, 76; World War II's effect on, 102, 113–14. See also canneries
Regional Coastal Commission, California, 160
Remondino, P. C., 28
remotely operated vehicles (ROVs), 172–73
Responsible Monterey Planning, 184–85
Review of the California Sardine Industry with Incidental Consideration of Its Racketeers, Its Politician Psuedo-Scientists, and Its Misguided Sportsmen Enthusiasts (Denman and Henry), 73
Rhodes, Linda, 158, 161–63
Richmond Transfer and Storage Company, 134
Ricketts, Edward F., 123–25, 135, 138–40, 150, 186, 187–88
Rink, Peggy, 141
Robbins, H. R., 47–48
Roosevelt, Franklin D., 103–4, 107
Rosales, Rudy, 87
Rothman, Hal, 178
Rourke, Andrew, 177
Rudolph and Sletten, 158, 164
Rumsen tribelet, 4, 13
Russo, John, 122
Russo, Salvatore, 53

Salinas, 20, 107, 108, 110, 119
Salinas Valley, 19–20, 47, 180
salmon, 47–48, 52, 59, 169, 189
Sam, C. M., 141
San Carlos Canning Company, 96, 119, 146–47
San Francisco earthquake and fire (1906), 44
San Francisco Sardine Fisheries, Inc., 72
San Xavier Cannery, 120, 146
Sand City, 166
Santa Rosalia (Rosalia Sinibaldi), 79
Santa Rosalia festa, 79–80, 88–89
Sardine Advisory Committee, 123
Sardine Canners' Association of California, 70
sardine industry: collapse of, 10, 103, 117–20; development of canneries, 48; government intervention in, 103–4, 106, 112–13; overfishing, 75; partial renewal of, 185; in the post–World War I era, 9, 60; struggle within, 61; World War II production increases, 101–4, 105fig, 108–15. See also canneries; collapse of sardine fishery; fishing industry
sardines: collection of data on, 73–74; depletion of stock of, 75; differing view toward stock of, 55; as exhibit in aquarium, 186; harvest levels, 77; moratorium on catching of, 130; recovery of population, 185; research into disappearance of, 126–31; sizes of, 74–75; spawning ground of, 74; tagging of, 123; varieties of, 208n47
Save Our Waterfront Committee, 185
Saxby, D. T., 133
Scales, Herb, 146
Scher, Philip, 79

Schoeninger, Mrs. Joseph, 118
Schulz, Maj. John W. N., 67
Scofield, Norman Bishop, 55–56,
    72–73
Scofield, W. L., 65, 75
Scripps Institution of Oceanography
    (SIO), 126
SCUBA apparatus, 158
sea anemones, 169, 172
Sea Beach Packing Company, 114
*Sea of Cortez: A Leisurely Journal
    of Travel and Research* (Steinbeck
    and Ricketts), 124
sea otters, 4, 165, 167, 170, 173,
    244*n*75
Sea Pride Cannery, 177
seasonal bag limits, 128
Seine and Line Fishermen's Union
    (AFL), 86, 104, 112, 120
Senderman, Benjamin, 48, 53
Sette, Oscar E., 73, 104, 114
seven-gill sharks, 172
Seventeen Mile Drive, 26, 42
Severance, H. D., 92
sewage, 30, 56–57, 93, 150
Shah, Nayan, 31
Shea, Ag, 147
Shepard, A. D., 25–26, 33–34, 39–
    42, 57
Shew, A. M., 28
shrimp industry, 16
Shuler-Verga Diversified Developers,
    151
Sicilians. *See* Italian community
Simmonds, Roy, 139
Sinibaldi, Rosalia (Santa Rosalia), 79
Slat's Fish Grotto, 136
Sollecito, Buster, 114
Sommer, Freya, 169
Soto, Mary, 86
South Pacific Fishery Investigation,
    128

Southern Pacific Railroad, 19–20,
    183
Souza, Anthony, 153
Spadaro, Pat, 136
Spadaro, Vito, 136
Spaghetti Hill, 88
Spanish community, 50, 52, 84, 87,
    136, 183
Spanish era in Monterey, 4–5
Spanish fantasy heritage, 23, 35
sports fishing, 27, 73, 189
squid fishery, 17, 31–36, 119–20
Stanford, Leland, 21
Stanford University, 157. *See also*
    Hopkins Marine Station; Hopkins
    Seaside Laboratory
Stanley, Carl, 94
Star of Monterey, 122
Steele, James King, 43
Steinbeck, Carol, 129
Steinbeck, John: call for "something
    new" on Cannery Row, 138–44,
    156; *Cannery Row* legend, 10,
    153–54; death of fishing industry,
    132; on fishermen, 131; friendship
    with Ricketts, 123–24, 187–88
Steinbeck, Thom, 139
Stevenson, Robert Louis, 3–5, 28–29
Streatfield, David C., 23
Superior Court, Monterey County,
    69–70, 86, 94–98
Supreme Court, U.S., 118
Sweet Thursday (Steinbeck), 132, 139
Swett, Ann, 184
Swig, Ben, 148

Tabata, Jim, 107
Takigawa, Ikutaro, 53
Taylor, Alan, 6
Taylor, Joseph E., 76
Teaby, Walter L., 98
Thompson, John Milton, 95–97

Thompson, Will F., 73–74
Tibbetts, Fred H., 67
tide pools, 157, 164, 179
Toomes Tract, 21–22
Tortilla Flat (Steinbeck), 139
tourism: Cannery Row as attraction
    for, 141–54; dependence on labor
    for, 190; emergence of, 6; environ-
    mental impact of, 190; environ-
    mentally-focused, 155–56, 190–
    91; erasure of diversity from, 133,
    152, 156, 165; and extractive
    industries, 191; fish odors as inter-
    fering with, 30–35, 91–101; fish-
    eries' relationship with, 7, 10–13,
    39, 80, 134–35, 182, 188–90;
    following collapse of sardine fishery,
    132–33; IMAX theatre, 184; lack
    of unionization of workers in, 85;
    World War II's effect on, 102. *See
    also* Hotel Del Monte; Monterey
    Bay Aquarium
tourist accommodations, 40–41,
    177–78. *See also* Hotel Del Monte
Travels with Charley (Steinbeck), 143
trawl lines, 15, 197n14
Treaty of Guadalupe Hidalgo, 19

Uchida, Onojiro, 43, 53
Ulrich, Rudolf, 24
unions: AFL/CIO conflicts, 83–86,
    112; Alaska Fishermen's Union
    (CIO), 85; Cannery Workers Union
    Local No. 20305 (AFL), 82, 84;
    Cannery Workers Union Local
    No. 20986 (AFL), 84; Deep Sea
    and Purse Seine Fishermen's Union
    (AFL), 82–83; early activity in
    Monterey, 80; Fish and Game
    Commission disagreements with,
    86; Fish Cannery and Reduction
    Workers Union Local No. 73 (CIO),
    84; fish cutters strike, 80–82, 91;
    fishermen's, 52; International Sea-
    men's Union (AFL), 84; local vs.
    migrant workers, 85–86; Monterey
    Fishermen's Protective Union, 82;
    Seine and Line Fishermen's Union
    (AFL), 86, 104, 112, 120; Sicilian
    attitudes toward, 83–84; under-
    payment of crews and, 68; United
    Fishermen's Union (CIO), 84;
    women's unwillingness to join,
    110
United Fishermen's Union (CIO),
    84
University of California, 43, 130

Valenčius, Conevery Bolton, 31
Van Camp Sea Food Company, 69,
    126
Vandeleur, Edward, 84

Walton, John, 205n114
War Food Administration, 114
War Labor Board, 112
War Manpower Commission, 108
War Production Board, 104, 113
War Relocation Authority, 118
Warner, H. R., 42
Warren, Earl, 113, 126
Watanabe, Jim, 168–70
Watkins, Harlan, 145
Watsonville, 110
Webster, G., 18
Webster, Steve, 157, 165, 167
Western Development Company,
    20–21
Western Flyer, 124
Westgate-Sun Harbor Cannery, 134
Whaler's Cove, 19
whaling, 14
Wheeler, Benjamin, 43
Wilbur-Ellis Company, 157

Williams, Sydney, 144, 148
women: as cannery supervisors, 87;
as cannery workers, 49–50, 86–87,
110, 111*fig*, 112; Chinese, 17–18;
class difference among, 88; separate recreational activities of, 27;
unionization and, 110; as World
War II workers, 110, 111*fig*, 112
Woman's Civic Club, 110
Woods Hole Marine Biological
Station, 197*n17*
World War I, 58–60
World War II: canneries as affected
by, 102; class issues in, 108, 112;
conservation approach during,
113; government intervention in
sardine industry, 103–4, 106–7,
112–13; Italian relocation, 102,
107–8; Japanese relocation, 102,
107–8; labor shortages, 108–10;
local focus on fish during, 101,
105*fig*; military deferments, 108–
9; production levels during, 101–
4, 105*fig*, 108–15; reduction as
affected by, 102, 113–14; tourism
during, 102; women as cannery
workers during, 110, 111*fig*, 112;
workers as soldiers, 115*fig*

Yee, Frances, 141
Yee, Won, 141
Yee, Yock 141
Young, Sanborn, 70
Yuen, Tom, 33

WEYERHAEUSER ENVIRONMENTAL BOOKS

The Natural History of Puget Sound Country
by Arthur R. Kruckeberg

*Forest Dreams, Forest Nightmares: The Paradox of Old Growth
in the Inland West* by Nancy Langston

Landscapes of Promise: The Oregon Story, 1800–1940
by William G. Robbins

*The Dawn of Conservation Diplomacy: U.S.-Canadian Wildlife
Protection Treaties in the Progressive Era* by Kurkpatrick Dorsey

*Irrigated Eden: The Making of an Agricultural Landscape
in the American West* by Mark Fiege

*Making Salmon: An Environmental History of the Northwest
Fisheries Crisis* by Joseph E. Taylor III

George Perkins Marsh, Prophet of Conservation by David Lowenthal

*Driven Wild: How the Fight against Automobiles Launched the Modern
Wilderness Movement* by Paul S. Sutter

The Rhine: An Eco-Biography, 1815–2000 by Mark Cioc

Where Land and Water Meet: A Western Landscape Transformed
by Nancy Langston

*The Nature of Gold: An Environmental History
of the Alaska/Yukon Gold Rush* by Kathryn Morse

Faith in Nature: Environmentalism as Religious Quest
by Thomas R. Dunlap

Landscapes of Conflict: The Oregon Story, 1940–2000
by William G. Robbins

The Lost Wolves of Japan by Brett L. Walker

Wilderness Forever: Howard Zahniser and the Path to the Wilderness Act
by Mark Harvey

On the Road Again: Montana's Changing Landscape
by William Wyckoff

Public Power, Private Dams: The Hells Canyon High Dam Controversy
by Karl Boyd Brooks

*Windshield Wilderness: Cars, Roads, and Nature
in Washington's National Parks* by David Louter

Native Seattle: Histories from the Crossing-Over Place
by Coll Thrush

The Country in the City: The Greening of the San Francisco Bay Area
by Richard A. Walker

*Drawing Lines in the Forest: Creating Wilderness Areas
in the Pacific Northwest* by Kevin R. Marsh

Plowed Under: Agriculture and Environment in the Palouse
by Andrew P. Duffin

Making Mountains: New York City and the Catskills
by David Stradling

The Fisherman's Frontier: People and Salmon in Southeastern Alaska
by David F. Arnold

Shaping the Shoreline: Fisheries and Tourism on the Monterey Coast
by Connie Y. Chiang

WEYERHAEUSER ENVIRONMENTAL CLASSICS

The Great Columbia Plain: A Historical Geography, 1805–1910
by D. W. Meinig

*Mountain Gloom and Mountain Glory: The Development
of the Aesthetics of the Infinite* by Marjorie Hope Nicolson

Tutira: The Story of a New Zealand Sheep Station
by Herbert Guthrie-Smith

*A Symbol of Wilderness: Echo Park and the American Conservation
Movement* by Mark Harvey

Man and Nature: Or, Physical Geography as Modified by Human Action
by George Perkins Marsh, edited and annotated by David Lowenthal

Conservation in the Progressive Era: Classic Texts
edited by David Stradling

DDT, Silent Spring, *and the Rise of Environmentalism: Classic Texts*
edited by Thomas R. Dunlap

CYCLE OF FIRE BY STEPHEN J. PYNE

Fire: A Brief History

World Fire: The Culture of Fire on Earth

Vestal Fire: An Environmental History, Told through Fire,
of Europe and Europe's Encounter with the World

Fire in America: A Cultural History of Wildland and Rural Fire

Burning Bush: A Fire History of Australia

The Ice: A Journey to Antarctica

CPSIA information can be obtained
at www.ICGtesting.com
Printed in the USA
FFOW03n1638080115
10170FF